P9-CAH-924

Reference Library of

BLACK AMERICA

Reference Library of

BLACK AMERICA

VOLUME IV

Edited by
Jessie Carney Smith
Joseph M. Palmisano

Distributed exclusively by:

African American Publications

Staff

Jessie Carney Smith and Joseph M. Palmisano, *Editors*
Patrick J. Politano, *Assistant Editor*
William Harmer, Ashyia N. Henderson, Brian J. Koski, Gloria Lam, Jeffrey Lehman, Allison McClintic Marion, Mark F. Mikula, David G. Oblender, Rebecca Parks, Shirelle Phelps, Kathleen Romig, *Contributing Staff*
Linda S. Hubbard, *Managing Editor, Multicultural Team*

Maria Franklin, *Permissions Manager*
Margaret Chamberlain, *Permissions Specialist*
Keasha Jack-Lyles and Shalice Shah-Caldwell, *Permissions Associates*

Justine H. Carson, *Manager, Vocabulary Development and Indexer*
Rebecca Abbott Forgette, *Indexing Specialist*

Mary Beth Trimper, *Production Director*
Wendy Blurton, *Senior Buyer*
Cynthia Baldwin, *Product Design Manager*
Gary Popiela, *Graphic Artist*
Barbara J. Yarrow, *Imaging/Multimedia Manager*
Randy Bassett, *Image Database Supervisor*
Pamela A. Reed, *Imaging Coordinator*
Robert Duncan, *Imaging Specialist*
Christine O'Bryan, *Desktop Publisher*

Victoria B. Cariappa, *Research Manager*
Barbara McNeil, *Research Specialists*
Patricia Tsune Ballard, *Research Associate*

Printed in 2001
Gale Group, Inc.
27500 Drake Road
Farmington Hills, MI 48331-3535

ISBN 0-7876-4363-7 (set)
ISBN 0-7876-4364-5 (volume 1)
ISBN 0-7876-4365-3 (volume 2)
ISBN 0-7876-4366-1 (volume 3)
ISBN 0-7876-4367-X (volume 4)
ISBN 0-7876-4368-8 (volume 5)

Printed in the United States of America

10 9 8 7 6 5 4 3 2

Advisory Board

Contributors

Donald F. Amerman, Jr.
Editorial Consultant, A & M Editorial Services

Stephen W. Angell
Associate Professor of Religion, Florida A & M University

Calvert Bean
Associate Editor, *International Dictionary of Black Composers*

Lean'tin Laverne Bracks
Editorial Consultant

Rose M. Brewer
Morse Alumni Distinguished Teaching Professor of Afro-American and African Studies, University of Minnesota-Minneapolis

Christopher A. Brooks
Professor of African American Studies, Virginia Commonwealth University

Paulette Coleman
General Officer, African Methodist Episcopal Church

DeWitt S. Dykes, Jr.
Professor of History, Oakland University

James Gallert
Vice President, Jazz Alliance of Michigan

Joseph Guy
Jazz and Touring Coordinator, Southern Arts Federation

Tracey Desirnaí Hicks
Membership and Volunteer Services Coordinator,
Charles H. Wright Museum of African American History

Phyllis J. Jackson
Assistant Professor of Art and Art History, Pomona College

Kristine Krapp
Editor, *Notable Black American Scientists* and *Black Firsts in Science and Technology*

Kevin C. Kretschmer
Reference Librarian, Blazer Library, Kentucky State University

Bernadette Meier
Editorial Consultant

Hollis F. Price, Jr.
Professor of Economics, Tennessee State University

Guthrie P. Ramsey Jr.
Assistant Professor of Music, University of Pennsylvania

Houston B. Roberson
Assistant Professor of History, University of the South

Gil L. Robertson IV
Founder, The Robertson Treatment

Audrey Y. Williams
Professor of Management, Zicklin School of Business, Baruch College, City University of New York

Raymond A. Winbush
Director, Race Relations Institute, Fisk University
Benjamin Hooks Professor of Social Justice, Fisk University

Michael D. Woodard
President, Woodard & Associates

Linda T. Wynn
Assistant Director of State Programs, Tennessee Historical Commission
Adjunct Professor, Department of History, Fisk University

Contents

◆ VOLUME 3

Introduction

The *Reference Library of Black America* is based on the eighth edition of *The African American Alamanac*, first published in 1967 as *The Negro Almanac* and subsequently cited by *Library Journal*, in conjunction with the American Library Association, as "Outstanding Reference Source." It offers a comprehensive and accurate survey of black culture in the United States and around the world.

New Features in This Edition

All material was extensively reviewed by the editors and a board of prominent advisors and, where appropriate, updated and/or expanded; in many instances completely new topics were added to the existing essays. As a result, most chapters have been rewritten and focus on issues facing African Americans as we enter a new millenium.

African American women and their significant contributions have been given greater emphasis in the reference work than ever before. Examples of this expanded coverage include: speeches and writings of Sojourner Truth, Ida B. Wells-Barnett, Mary McLeod Bethune, and Barbara Jordan (Chapter 3); genetic evidence of a link between Sally Hemings and Thomas Jefferson (Chapter 6); biographical profiles of historic female activists of the black nationalist and civil rights movements (Chapters 8 and 9); female leadership in African American churches (Chapter 17); prominent women artists in the musical fields of gospel, blues, and jazz (Chapters 23, 24, and 25); and the increasing presence of female athletes in professional sports (Chapter 28).

The tremendous impact of the Internet is also reflected in the content of the *Reference Library of Black America*. Many entry listings in such sections as "National Organizations" (Chapter 9); "Historically and Predominantly African American Colleges and Universities" and "Research Institutions" (Chapter 16); "African American Media in Cyberspace" and "Magazines and Journals" (Chapter 19); "Museums and Galleries Exhibiting African American Art" (Chapter 26); and "Popular African American Internet Sites" (Chapter 27) now include website addresses. In addition, the promising effects of information technology on the African American community are discussed in "Entrepreneurship" (Chapter 14), "Media" (Chapter 19), and "Science and Technology" (Chapter 27).

Important African American towns and settlements are described for the first time in "African American Landmarks" (Chapter 4) and "Population" (Chapter 12). Included are listings of such historic sites as Nicodemus, Kansas; Boley, Oklahoma; the Sea Islands in South Carolina and Georgia; and Eatonville, Florida. In addition, expanded, up-to-date profiles of African and Western Hemisphere nations are offered in "Africa and the Black Diaspora" (Chapter 5).

Two new chapters have been added that significantly enhance the broad coverage of the *Reference Library of Black America:*

- "Film and Television" (Chapter 20) offers an overview of African Americans in the film and television industries, a selected filmography of more than two hundred films and documentaries depicting African American themes and issues, and biographical profiles of actors, filmmakers, and industry executives both current and historical.
- "Sacred Music Traditions" (Chapter 23) provides an essay that thoroughly describes the important periods

and styles of African American sacred music, as well as concise biographical profiles of notable sacred music composers, musicians, and singers.

Approximately thirty new statistical charts compiled by the Bureau of the Census for the *Statistical Abstract of the United States* appear in pertinent chapters. Finally, a completely revised name and keyword index provides improved access to the contents of the *Reference Library of Black America.*

Content and Arrangement

Information in this edition of the *Reference Library of Black America* appears in 29 subject chapters. Many chapters open with an essay focusing on historical developments or the contributions of African Americans to the subject area, followed by concise biographical profiles of selected individuals. Although the listees featured here represent only a small portion of the African American community, they embody excellence and diversity in their respective fields of endeavor. Where an individual has made a significant contribution in more than one area, his or her biographical profile appears in the subject area for which he or she is best known.

Nearly seven hundred photographs, illustrations, maps, and statistical charts aid the reader in understanding the topics and people covered in the reference work. An expanded appendix contains the names and contributions of African American recipients of selected awards and honors.

Media

◆ Book Publishers ◆ Newspaper and Magazine Publishers ◆ Broadcasting
◆ African American Media in Cyberspace ◆ Publishing, Radio, and Television Professionals
◆ Print and Broadcast Media

by Tracey Desirnaí Hicks

◆ BOOK PUBLISHERS

Since African American book publishing began in the United States in 1817, three types of publishers have emerged in this sector of the industry: religious publishers, institutional publishers, and trade book publishers.

Religious Publishers

African American religious denominations established religious publishing enterprises in order to publish books and other literature to assist clergy and laity in recording denominational history and provide religious instruction. Some religious publishers also published books on secular subjects that celebrated some aspect of African American culture or documented African American history.

Prior to the Civil War, two African American religious publishing enterprises existed. The African Methodist Episcopal Church organized the A.M.E. Book Concern in Philadelphia in 1817—the first African American-owned book publishing enterprise in the United States. Publishing its first book in that same year, *The Book of Discipline*, the A.M.E. Book Concern published a host of classic religious and secular books until its operations were suspended in 1952 by the General Conference of the African Methodist Episcopal Church. In 1841 the African Methodist Episcopal Zion Church formed the A.M.E. Zion Book Concern in New York City. This firm, which only published religious works, was moved to its present location in Charlotte, North Carolina, in 1894, where it continues to be an active book publisher.

In Jackson, Tennessee, the Colored Methodist Episcopal Church (CME), presently known as the Christian Methodist Episcopal Church, started the CME Publishing House in 1870. The CME Publishing House, which only publishes books on religious subjects, is currently located in Memphis, Tennessee. Another book publishing enterprise owned by African American Methodists is the A.M.E. Sunday School Union and Publishing House, established in Bloomington, Illinois, in 1882, but later moving to Nashville, Tennessee, in 1886. Publishing secular and religious books, the A.M.E. Sunday School Union and Publishing House remains today as the oldest publishing unit owned by the African Methodist Episcopal Church.

One of the most successful African American religious publishers to come into existence during the nineteenth century was the National Baptist Publishing Board. Under the leadership of Dr. Richard Henry Boyd and the auspices of the National Baptist Convention, USA, the National Baptist Publishing Board was organized in Nashville in 1896. By 1913, this well-managed firm, publishing religious and secular books, grew to become one of the largest African American-owned businesses in the United States. In 1915, however, a dispute arose between the National Baptist Convention, USA and Dr. Richard Henry Boyd over the ownership of the National Baptist Publishing Board. In a court suit, the Tennessee Supreme Court decided in favor of Dr. Boyd; today the National Publishing Board, owned by the Boyd family, is a thriving religious publishing enterprise.

In 1907 the Church of God in Christ established the Church of God in Christ Publishing House in Memphis. Restricting its publications to religious books and pamphlets, this publisher continues today to meet the ever-expanding need for religious literature for one of the fastest-growing African American religious denominations in the United States.

Faced with the loss of the National Baptist Publishing Board, the National Baptist Convention, USA, Inc. established in 1916 the Sunday School Publishing Board of the National Baptist Convention, USA, Inc., in Nashville. Over the years, this firm developed into one of the largest African American-owned publishing enterprises in the United States, publishing religious and secular books and pamphlets.

Similar to the Sunday School Publishing Board of the National Baptist Convention, USA, Inc., Muhammad's Temple No. 2, Publications Department, which was founded in 1956 by the Nation of Islam, published religious as well as secular books. Between 1956 and 1974, this firm issued several books. However, since 1974, Muhammad's Temple No. 2 Publications Department has become inactive.

Institutional Publishers

During the last decades of the nineteenth century and the early decades of the twentieth century, educational, cultural, social, and political institutions were established to meet the specific needs of African Americans. Many of these institutions developed publishing programs.

Colleges and Universities

Hampton Institute became the first African American educational institution to publish books when the Hampton Institute Press was established in 1871. An active publisher until 1940, the Hampton Institute Press published travel books, poetry, textbooks, songbooks, conference proceedings, and *The Southern Workman*, one of the leading national African American periodicals published between 1871 and its demise in 1939.

In 1896 the Atlanta University Press entered the book publishing market with the release of *Atlanta University Publication Series*, which consisted of monographs reporting on the findings of studies conducted by the university's department of sociology under the direction of Dr. W. E. B. Du Bois. These works represented some of the earliest studies in urban sociology conducted in the South. The Atlanta University Press remained in operation until 1936.

Industrial Work of Tuskegee Graduates and Former Students During the Year 1910, compiled by Monroe N. Work (1911), was the first book released by the Tuskegee Institute Press. With the publication of this book and other works by the press, Booker T. Washington sought to publicize the success of Tuskegee's program to white philanthropists in the North. The Tuskegee Institute Press, which was active until 1958, published several other important works including John Kenny's *The Negroes in Medicine* (1912) and *Lynching by States, 1882–1958* (1958) by Jessie Parkhurst Guzman.

In 1910, another book publishing enterprise was launched on the campus of Tuskegee Institute—the Negro Yearbook Publishing Company. A partnership consisting of Robert E. Park, the famed white sociologist, Emmett J. Scott, secretary to Booker T. Washington, and Monroe N. Work, a sociology professor, this firm published the first edition of *The Negro Yearbook* in 1912. The most comprehensive reference book to appear to date on African Americans, *The Negro Yearbook* was highly regarded as the definitive work on statistics and facts on blacks worldwide. However, the Negro Yearbook Publishing Company fell into financial trouble in 1929, and the Tuskegee Institute financed its operation until 1952. Between 1912 and 1952, *The Negro Yearbook* remained a classic model for most general reference works on blacks.

John W. Work's *The Negro and His Song* (1915) was the first book issued under the Fisk University Press imprint. During the 1930s and 1940s, when Charles Spurgeon Johnson chaired the university's department of sociology, Fisk University Press issued several important studies including E. Franklin Frazier's *The Free Negro Family* (1932); *The Economic Status of the Negro* by Charles Spurgeon Johnson (1933); and *People versus Property* by Herman Long and Charles Spurgeon Johnson (1947). The last publication released by the Fisk University Press was *Build a Future: Addresses Marking the Inauguration of Charles Spurgeon Johnson* (1949).

Although the board of trustees of Howard University approved the establishment of a university press on February 17, 1919, no university press existed at the university until 1974. Nonetheless, between 1919 and 1974, several books bearing the "Howard University Press" imprint were published, including *The Founding of the School of Medicine of Howard University, 1868–1873* by Walter Dyson (1929); and *The Housing of Negroes in Washington, DC: A Study in Human Ecology* by William H. Jones (1929). On April 8, 1974, the Howard University Press officially organized as a separate administrative unit within the university with a staff of 12 professionals experienced in book publishing. The Howard University Press's inaugural list of 13 books included such titles as *A Poetic Equation: Conversations Between Nikki Giovanni and Margaret Walker* (1974) and *Saw the House in Half, a Novel* by Oliver Jackman (1974). The Howard University Press continues to flourish as one of the most viable university presses in the country.

Cultural and Professional Organizations and Institutions

African American cultural and professional organizations and institutions have also developed publishing programs that include book publishing. The books published by these organizations document areas of African American history and depict various aspects of African American culture.

Founded in 1897 by the Reverend Alexander Crummell, nineteenth century African American scholar, clergyman, and missionary, the American Negro Academy quickly organized a publishing program that embraced book publishing. The Academy, whose membership included many of the foremost African American intellectuals of the day, released 21 occasional papers as pamphlets and monographs. The American Negro Academy ceased to exist in 1928.

The Association for the Study of Negro Life and History (now the Association for the Study of Afro-American History and Literature) began its book publishing program in 1918. By 1940, the association had published 28 books. After that year, the book publishing activities of the association declined until 1950, when its founder Carter G. Woodson died and provided in his will for the transfer of the Associated Publishers, Inc. to the association.

The Associates of Negro Folk Education, organized in Washington, DC by Howard University philosophy professor Alain Locke with a grant from the American Adult Education Association, published a series of seven books known as the Bronze Booklets from 1935 to 1940. Written by black scholars on various aspects of African American life and edited by Locke, some of these titles included: *A World View of Race* by Ralph J. Bunche (1936); *The Negro and Economic Reconstruction* by T. Arnold Hill (1937); and *Negro Poetry and Drama* by Sterling Brown (1937).

Civil Rights, Social Welfare, and Political Organizations

In 1913, five years after its founding, the National Association for the Advancement of Colored People (NAACP) launched its publishing program with the publication of three books: *A Child's Story of Dunbar* by Julia L. Henderson (1919); *Norris Wright Cuney* by Maude Cuney Hare (1913); and *Hazel* by Mary White Ovington (1913). In 1914 George Williamson Crawford's *Prince Hall and His Followers* appeared and *Thirty Years of Lynching in the United States, 1889–1918* was released in 1919. After 1919 the NAACP published few books, with the organization limiting its publishing to *Crisis* magazine, pamphlets, and its annual reports.

In contrast, the National Urban League has been a very active book publisher. The League first embarked on book publishing in 1927 when it published *Ebony and Topaz*, an anthology of Harlem Renaissance writers, poets, and artists edited by Charles Spurgeon Johnson. Through the years numerous sociological and economic studies on the plight of African Americans have been published by the Urban League including *Negro Membership in Labor Unions* (1930), *Race, Fear and Housing in a Typical American Community* (1946), and *Power of the Ballot: A Handbook for Black Political Participation* (1973). In addition to these monograph studies, the organization began publishing *The State of Black America* in 1976.

Although the publishing program of the Universal Negro Improvement Association and African Communities League focused on the publication of its newspaper *The Negro World*, this political organization also published books. Two volumes of *The Philosophy and Opinions of Marcus Garvey*, compiled and edited by Amy Jacques-Garvey, were published under the imprint of the press of the Universal Negro Improvement Association.

Commercial Publishers

Until the 1960s, most African American commercial publishers engaged in book publishing enterprises were short-lived. However, in 1967 Haki Madhubuti founded Third World Press in Chicago. Third World Press is now the oldest continually-operating African American commercial book publisher in the United States.

Over the years, African American publishers have come to find that a sizable African American readership exists; since 1970 several major African American publishers have emerged. In 1978, Black Classic Press was founded by librarian Paul Coates to publish obscure, but significant, works by and about people of African descent. In 1978, Dempsey Travis founded Urban Research Press. Open Hand Publishing Inc. was founded in 1981 by Anna Johnson.

In 1983 Kassahun Checole founded Africa World Press to publish material on the economic, political, and social development of Africa. Checole, a former African studies instructor at Rutgers University, found it difficult to attain books needed for his courses. Now African World Press publishes nearly sixty titles a year and its sister company, Red Sea Press, is now one of the largest distributors of material by and about Africans.

Just Us Books, Inc., founded by writer Wade Hudson and graphic artist Cheryl Willis Hudson, publishes books and educational material for children that focus on the African American experience. The idea to start the company first came to Cheryl in 1976, when she was unable to find African American images to decorate her daughter's nursery. Just Us Books published its first book in 1988—an alphabet book featuring African American children posed to create the letters. The company currently has sales of over $800,000.

Independent African American-owned book stores have recently benefitted from a resurgence of African American authors and an abundance of titles, but major bookstore chains, which are white-owned, make competition stiff. Although books purchased by African Americans grew from $181 million in 1990 to $296 million in 1995, with the decline in hardcover sales, publishers are more cautious about placing books with specialty stores for fear that a book will lose mainstream appeal.

Comic Book Publishers

In the 1990s, African American comics have peaked in popularity. Once relegated to a form of children's entertainment, comic books have found an audience with young adults in their twenties to thirties. In fact, in 1990, Cable News Network noted that sales of multiracial comics had jumped nine percent, thus accounting for ten percent of all comic book sales. Once reason for the growth among the African American adult readership is collectibility—since most African American series are short-lived, each issue has the potential to become a rarity. Another reason is the fact that nowadays, African American comics better represent African Americans by addressing their cultural and artistic concerns.

African American characters of yore, often grotesquely drawn by whites, were either sidekicks or afterthoughts—never the stars. For example, Ebony, an African American character, paraded around with white superhero, The Spirit, in the 1940s. Meanwhile, Captain America had his own version of the Lone Ranger's Native American sidekick Tonto in Falcon. Other African American characters were portrayed as ignorant, uneducated, and inept at worst. Blatantly stereotypical, most were created and drawn by white males who did not know much about the reality of African Americans. Over the years, the status of African American comic book characters evolved in the same negative ways that whites's perceptions of blacks did. By the 1960s and 1970s, African Americans were depicted either as drug addicts or Uncle Toms.

True change did not occur until a few enterprising African Americans took matters into their own hands. By 1992, Africa Rising Comics, Afrocentric Books, Dark Zulu Lies, Omega 7 Comics, and UP Comics had created ANIA (the Swahili word for "serve and protect") Comics under the leadership of Eric Griffin. Though the group disbanded within a short time, their existence highlighted the growing line of African American and other culturally diverse superheroes. Their titles included *Heru*, *Zwanna*, *Purge*, and *Ebony Warrior*.

In the mid-1990s, Big City Comics was producing *Brotherman*, revolving around a public defender who also fights crime as an alter-persona know as the "dictator of discipline." Omega 7 Inc., founded by Alonzo Washington, a former member of ANIA, is based in Kansas City, Kansas. To date, it is the largest independent African American comic book publisher. Omega 7 Inc. has introduced fans to *The Original Man*, a champion of morality and supporter and protector of African American women; *The Mighty Ace*, with an anti-drug, anti-gang, anti-violence message; and *Darkforce*, a revolutionary African American hero. Other characters include *Omega Man*, *Original Boy*, *Original Woman*, and *The Omega 7*. Washington develops each comic and writes the storylines.

UP Comics offered *Purge*, which detailed the trials and tribulations of a man whose sole goal was to rid his city of evil. Prophesy Comics's *Lionheart* also emphasized morality lessons. In a unique twist, Castel Publications came up with *The Grammar Patrol*, multi-ethnic heros with a penchant for good grammar. Geared towards children, that comic showed that the medium can be used for more than entertainment purposes.

Most of these companies were African American-owned and operated, with everyone from the artists to the storywriters to the marketers being African American. Mainstream publishers entered the fray when industry giant DC Comics began distributing Milestone Comics in 1991 as part of their new imprint Milestone Media, formerly a African American-owned, independent publisher run by Derek T. Dingle. With a broad, full-process color system at hand, the company made history as the first major publisher to back African American creators. Among their titles have been *Hardware*, *Blood Syndicate*, *Icon*, *Kobalt*, *Shadow Cabinet*, *Xombi*, and *Static*, the latter featuring a teen hero.

Although the desire to read comic books with African American characters and the number of new African American comic books continues to increase, approximately 25 to 30 percent of comic book buyers are minorities. Since the demise of ANIA and many other African American independently owned publishers, it has become difficult for African Americans to produce their own publications. The two major comic book publishers, DC Comics and Marvel Comics, have both created several or more African American comic book characters and are not usually open to purchasing outside characters unless they can own them outright. In addition, some of the more popular African American comic book characters have been created by whites: For example, *Spawn*, *Luke Cage*, *The Black Panther*, *The Falcon*, and *Blade*. Therefore, aspiring African Ameri-

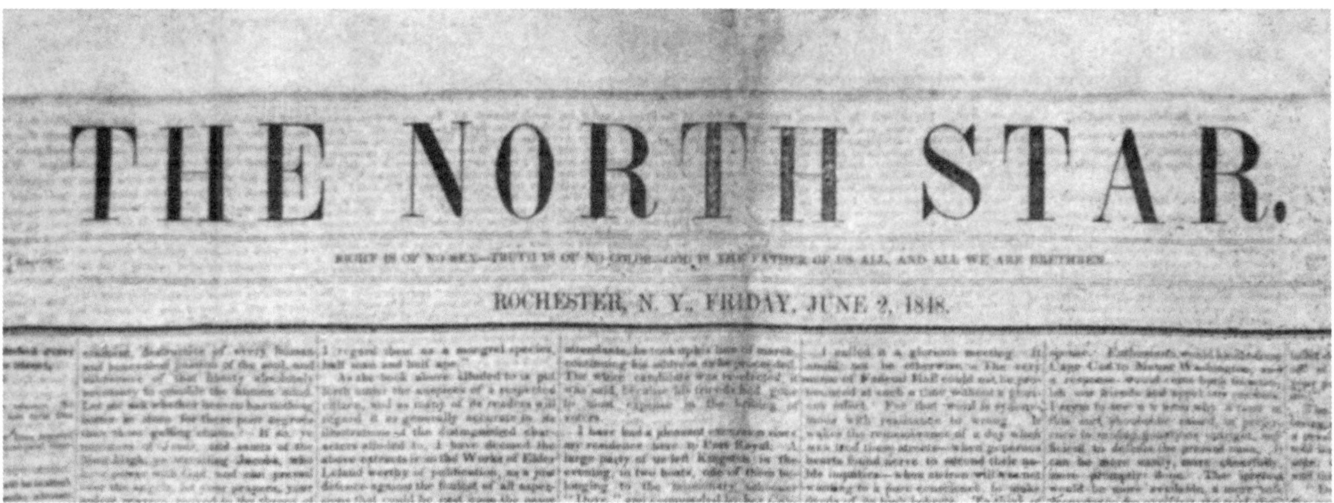

THE NORTH STAR.

ROCHESTER, N. Y., FRIDAY, JUNE 2, 1848.

The North Star newspaper was founded by Frederick Douglass in 1847 (The Library of Congress).

can comic book artists have two options. They can find an independent publisher or self-publish. Since both are usually difficult, many artists opt to work on more established characters (Superman, Spiderman, Batman, etc.) to ensure their financial stability with the goal of eventually saving enough money to publish their own characters. Two notable exceptions are Alex Simmons, creator of *Blackjack* and P. Skylar Owens, creator of *Knightmare*, *Team Sexecutioner*, and *CyJax*.

◆ NEWSPAPER AND MAGAZINE PUBLISHERS

Newspapers

The African American press in the United States is heir to a great, largely-unheralded tradition. It began with the first African American newspaper *Freedom's Journal*, edited and published by Samuel Cornish and John B. Russwurm on March 16, 1827. *The North Star*, the newspaper of abolitionist Frederick Douglass, first appeared on December 3, 1847.

In the 1880s, African Americans's ability to establish a substantial cultural environment in many cities of the North led to the creation of a new wave of publications including the *Washington Bee*, the *Indianapolis World*, the *Philadelphia Tribune*, the *Cleveland Gazette*, *Baltimore Afro-American*, and the *New York Age*. By 1900, daily papers appeared in Norfolk, Kansas City, and Washington, DC.

Among famous African American newspaper editors were William Monroe Trotter, editor of the *Boston Guardian*, a self-styled "radical" paper that showed no sympathy for the conciliatory stance of Booker T. Washington; Robert S. Abbott, whose *Chicago Defender* pioneered the use of headlines; and T. Thomas Fortune of the *New York Age*, who championed free public schools in an age when many opposed the idea.

In 1940, there were over two hundred African American newspapers, mostly weeklies with local readerships, and about 120 African American magazines in the country. The *Pittsburgh Courier*, a weekly, had the largest circulation—about 140,000 per issue.

African Americans are also gaining influence as columnists, editorial page editors, assistant managing editors, and reporters on key beats. But although progress has been made in the newsroom—the executive editors at the *Detroit Free Press* and *The Courier-Journal* in Louisville are African American, as are the managing editors at *Newsweek*, *The Boston Globe*, *The Miami Herald*, *The News Journal* in Wilmington and the *Seattle Post-Intelligencer*—the prospect of African Americans assuming positions in a managerial capacity is still at an all-time low. Recent gains do not negate the 1998 report by the American Society of Newspaper Editors that stated that the representation of African Americans on news staffs has stagnated at a rate of just below six percent.

The lack of minority representation in the newsrooms of mainstream publications has not hindered the rise of the ethnic press, which is steadily building circulation and advertising revenue. Traditionally, the survival of the ethnic press depended on classified advertising and advertisements from local auto repair stores, grocers, and travel agents. Some of the more established African American newspapers have always attracted some mainstream advertising. However, many of the larger billings are now going to publications that serve smaller and diverse communities. Among the largest advertisers are

Headquarters of the *Baltimore Afro-American* newspaper.

telecommunications companies, airlines, financial services companies, and health care corporations.

The National Negro Newspaper Publishers Association

The National Negro Newspaper Publishers Association was founded in 1940 to represent African American newspaper publishers. The organization scheduled workshops and trips abroad to acquaint editors and reporters with important news centers and news sources. A result was a trend to more progressive and interpretive reporting. In 1956 the association changed its name to the National Newspaper Publishers Association. As of 1999, it represented 148 publishers.

The Amsterdam News

Founded in 1909 by James H. Anderson, the *Amsterdam News* has become one of the most well-known African American newspapers in the nation. It was first published on December 4, 1909, in Anderson's home on 132 W. 65th Street in New York City. At that time one of only fifty African American "news sheets" in the country, the *Amsterdam News* had a staff of ten, consisted of six printed pages, and sold for two cents a copy. In 1935 the paper was sold to two African American physicians, Clilan B. Powell and P.M.H. Savory. In 1971 the paper was again sold to a group of investors, headed by Clarence B. Jones and Percy E. Sutton.

African American Newspapers in the 1990s

A number of newspapers that began publishing in the 1960s, 1970s, and 1980s have gone out of business, mainly due to their inability to attract advertising, both locally and nationally, and because of general economic decline. Today there are a reported 214 African American newspapers in the United States. Of these, the papers with the largest paid circulations include New York's *Black American*, the *Hartford Inquirer*, and the *Atlanta Voice*.

Magazines

As early as the 1830s, African American magazines were published in the United States. However, it was not until the 1900s that the first truly successful magazines appeared. In 1910 the NAACP began publishing *Crisis*. In November of 1942, John H. Johnson launched the *Negro Digest*, and in 1945 he published the first issue of

Ebony. The idea for the new magazine came from two *Digest* writers, and Johnson's wife, Eunice, contributed the magazine's name. Its first print run of 25,000 copies sold out immediately. The success of *Ebony* led to the demise of the *Negro Digest*, and in 1951 the magazine ceased publication. *Ebony* now has a circulation rate of almost two million.

In 1950, Johnson launched the magazine *Tan*, and in 1951 *Jet* magazine. Similar to *Ebony*, *Jet* was an instant success, selling over 300,000 copies in its first year. *Tan*, a woman's magazine, later became a show business and personality monthly called *Black Stars*.

Since the founding of *Ebony*, several new and specialized African American magazines have appeared. In 1967 *Black American Literature Review*, a journal presenting essays, interviews, poems, and book reviews, was founded. Also in 1967, Project Magazines, Inc. began publishing *Black Careers*. In 1969 the Black World Foundation published the first edition of *The Black Scholar*.

In 1970, Earl G. Graves, a young businessman, embarked on a concept to publish a monthly digest of news, commentary, and informative articles for African Americans interested in business. Within a few short years his magazine *Black Enterprise* was accepted as the authority on African Americans in business and as an important advocate for an active, socially-responsive, African American middle class. Today *Black Enterprise* has a subscription rate of over 251,000. A second magazine directed at black women, *Essence* has steadily gained in circulation since its inception in 1970. Featuring health and beauty, fashion, and contemporary living sections, *Essence* is considered one of the top women's magazines. Since 1981 Susan Taylor has been the magazine's editor-in-chief.

In 1980, *Black Family*, a magazine promoting positive lifestyles for African Americans, was founded. In 1986, *American Visions: The Magazine of Afro-American Culture*, the official magazine of the African American Museums Association, was first published.

While African American-owned magazines continue to flourish (*Heart & Soul*, *American Legacy*, *BET Weekend*, *Emerge*, *Black Child*), securing high-end advertising remains a problem. Even though African American magazines have made significant progress in attracting automotive, tobacco, and liquor advertisements, whole categories such as fashion, travel, and technology are almost completely absent from their pages. With the increase of the African American middle class, advertising agencies believe that they can reach African Americans through mainstream advertising, in particular through television.

◆ BROADCASTING

Radio

African American radio can be divided into three general periods of historical development: blackface radio (1920–1941), black-appeal radio (1942–1969) and black-controlled radio (1970 to the present). White performers who imitated black humor and music for a predominantly white listening audience was the trademark of blackface radio. During this period, African Americans were essentially outside of the commercial loop, both as radio entertainers and consumers. In the era of black-appeal radio, African Americans entered the industry as entertainers and consumers. However, the ownership and management of the African American-oriented stations remained mostly in the hands of white businessmen. This situation impelled the development of independent African American radio stations. With the onset of the black-controlled radio era, African Americans began to own and operate their own radio stations, both commercial and public. Nevertheless, the percentage of African American-owned stations still lags far behind the percentage of African American listeners.

While early radio shows featured African American singing groups, they featured no African Americans talking. To Jack L. Cooper, this "was like taxation without representation," and so, on Sunday, November 3, 1929, at 5 P.M., Chicago's white-owned WSBC premiered "The All-Negro Hour" starring Cooper and friends. Born was the concept of African American radio, and Cooper went on to become the nation's first African American radio station executive, the first African American newscaster, the first African American sportscaster, and the first to use radio as a service medium.

Cooper wore many hats. He played second base for a semi-pro baseball team; he had been a singer, a buck-and-wing dancer, and an end man in a minstrel show. He fought 160 amateur boxing bouts and he managed theaters. Between about 1910 and 1924, he worked as a journalist, writing for a number of African American newspapers including the *Freeman*, *Ledger*, and *Recorder* in Indianapolis; and the *Bluff City News* and *Western World Reporter* in Memphis. In 1924, he became the assistant theatrical editor of the *Chicago Defender*.

"The All-Negro Hour" was similar to a vaudeville revue on the air, featuring music, comedy, and serials. When it ended its run in 1935, Cooper continued with WSBC, pioneering the African American-radio format by producing several African American-oriented shows. Crucial to that format was local news and public affairs of interest to African Americans.

The first example of public service programming aired December 9, 1938, when Cooper launched the "Search for Missing Persons" show. Aimed at reuniting people who had lost contact with friends and relatives over time, it reportedly had reunited 20,000 people by 1950. According to *Ebony* magazine, Cooper also remodeled a van into a mobile unit to relay on-the-spot news events directly to four radio stations in the Chicago and suburban area including news flashes from the *Pittsburgh Courier* and interviews with famous personalities who came to town, such as boxer Joe Louis. Cooper also did play-by-play sportscasts of African American baseball games from the van.

"Listen Chicago," a news discussion show that ran from 1946 to 1952, provided African Americans with their first opportunity to use radio as a public forum. Following Cooper's lead, between 1946 and 1955 the number of African American-oriented stations jumped from 24 to 600. News was a part of the explosion. "We have learned to do newscasts that answer the question, 'How is this news going to affect me as a Negro?,'" Leonard Walk of WHOD Pittsburgh said in 1954. "We have learned that church and social news deserve a unique place of importance in our daily Negro programming." Yet by and large, these broadcasters were not trained journalists. African American stations did not begin to broadcast news as we know it today until the 1960s.

In 1972, the Mutual Black Network was formed for news and sports syndication under the auspices of the Mutual Broadcasting Network. By the end of the 1970s, the Mutual Black Network had just over one hundred affiliates and 6.2 million listeners. The Sheridan Broadcasting Corporation, an African American-owned broadcasting chain based in Pittsburgh, purchased the Mutual Black Network in the late 1970s, renaming it the Sheridan Broadcasting Network. A second African American radio network, the National Black Network, was formed in 1973. In the 1980s, it averaged close to one hundred affiliates and four million listeners. Among its regular features was commentary by journalist Roy Wood, which he named "One Black Man's Opinion," and Bob Law's "Night Talk." In January of 1992, the American Urban Radio Network was formed, and the National Black Network has since gone out of business.

The networks were a mixed blessing. They provided their affiliates with broadcast-quality programs produced from an African American perspective. But this relatively inexpensive access to news, sports, and public affairs features discouraged the local stations that subscribed from producing their own shows. News and public affairs staffs at the African American-oriented stations remained minimal. There were some notable exceptions. New York's WLIB-AM had an African American format that included a highly acclaimed news and public affairs department. A series of shows produced by the station on disadvantaged youth in the city won two Peabody Awards in 1970.

In Washington, DC, *The Washington Post* donated its commercial FM radio license to Howard University in 1971. The new station, WHUR-FM, inaugurated "The Daily Drum," a full hour-long evening newscast that featured special coverage of the local African American community, as well as news from Africa and the black diaspora.

Two major formats have dominated African American-owned commercial radio since the 1970s: "talk" and "urban contemporary." Talk radio formats emerged on African American AM stations in the early 1970s and featured news, public affairs, and live listener call-in shows. By this time, FM stations dominated the broadcasting of recorded music due to their superior reproduction of high fidelity and stereo signals. In 1972, Inner City Broadcasting initiated the move toward talk radio when it purchased WLIB-AM and the station became "Your Total Black News and Information Station," offering more news and public affairs programming than any other African American-formatted radio outlet in the country.

A pioneer in both "talk" and "urban contemporary" formats, Cathy Hughes, the founder and owner of Radio One, Inc., owns the largest African American-owned and operated broadcast company in the United States. Radio One's 14 broadcast properties include stations in Philadelphia, Pennsylvania, Washington, DC, Baltimore, Maryland, Atlanta, Georgia, and Detroit, Michigan. Radio One stations are recognized continually for their active community involvement, which is Hughes's trademark.

In 1971, Hughes became a lecturer at Howard University's School of Communication under the direction of Tony Brown. She was instrumental in creating a curriculum that would be accredited by academic associations around the world. In 1973, she began her transition into radio as general sales manager at WHUR-FM, eventually becoming vice president and general manager. Her skills in sales and marketing strategies turned the station into the university's first profit venue in its one hundred-year history, increasing the station's revenue from $250,000 to $3,000,000 in her first year. In 1975, she developed the now widely-imitated format known as the "Quiet Storm." She purchased her first station, WOL-AM, in Washington, DC, in 1980.

Since the 1970s, the number of African Americans who have entered the public broadcasting arena has increased. In 1990, there were 32 public FM stations owned and operated by African American colleges around the country and another 12 owned by African American community boards of directors. These stations are not subject to the pervasive ratings pressures of commercial radio, thus giving them more latitude in programming news, public affairs, talk, and unusual cultural features. As a result, the growth of African American public radio has expanded the variety and diversity of African American programming now found on the airways, while also increasing the numbers of African Americans working in radio.

Television

Until the late 1960s, most serious African American journalists were in print journalism rather than in broadcasting. An exception was Lionel Monagas who worked in the early 1950s as a director of CBS-TV network programs, such as "Person to Person" and "Face the Nation." He had started out as a traffic typist with the CBS affiliate in Washington, DC. In 1956, Monagas became the first African American professional at public station Channel 35 in Philadelphia, later known as WHYY-TV. At WHYY-TV, he produced several children's programs including a ten-part series on "The History of the Negro," narrated by Ossie Davis.

Mal Goode became the first African American network TV reporter in 1962 at ABC-TV. Baseball great Jackie Robinson complained to James Hagerty, an ABC vice president hired to set up a competitive news department, that the only two Negroes he had seen at ABC were "a lady with a white uniform in the lobby dusting and a Negro doorman. [Hagerty's] face got red, and he said we intend to do something about that," Goode said. Goode was a reporter at *The Pittsburgh Courier* at the time, but in 1949 Pittsburgh's KQV Radio had given the newspaper two 15-minute slots to fill on Tuesday and Wednesday nights. Goode read the news on the program. According to Goode, ABC chose him for the job after spending half a year interviewing 38 African American male candidates. One reason he was chosen, he said, was because he was dark enough to appeal to an African American audience, but light enough so that whites would not feel threatened. Goode went on to work for ABC for 11 years. He was its United Nations correspondent and covered the Cuban missile crisis, the aftermath of Martin Luther King, Jr.'s assassination, and the Poor People's March on Washington.

Jobs similar to Goode's were hard to find. In his memoir *Black Is the Color of My TV Tube*, Emmy-winner Gil Noble of New York's WABC-TV recalls being at WLIB-AM radio during this era. "We would sit in the newsroom and fantasize about earning $300 a week, but few of our number worked at that level. Pat Connell, a former disc jockey at Newark's WNJR, known as 'Pat the Cat,' was anchoring the CBS morning newscast. Mal Goode was reporting for ABC-TV news, as well as for the local station WABC. NBC didn't have any blacks at that time, as far as I can recall, and in the mid-1960s, WNEW-TV had none, nor did WPIX-TV or WOR-TV have any." When Noble went downtown to audition for a major radio station job, he recalled, he would intone in the ultimate radio voice-"a [Walter] Cronkite delivery that outdid the original"-only to get the familiar brushoff, "Thanks very much. You're fine, but we already have a Negro on staff."

Mal Goode (ABC)

"Inside Bedford-Stuyvesant" was an innovative show in New York City. Albeit short-lived—on the air from 1968–1970—it was the city's first program written, produced, and presented by African Americans at a time when African Americans were largely unseen on television, except for news footage about protests, riots, or crime. "Inside Bedford-Stuyvesant" was unique because it offered a look into an ignored African American neighborhood, and, to a degree, African America. In 52 half-hour programs, it was filmed throughout the Bedford-Stuyvesant neighborhood, often outdoors. Attracting such major celebrities as Harry Belafonte and musician Max Roach, the show mostly revolved around the ordinary people in the neighborhood.

Film scholars and social historians consider "Inside Bedford-Stuyvesant" a rare video time capsule, perhaps the only one of its kind, documenting an African American community. Its creator, Charles Hobson, announced the debut of the show two months after the federal government's Kerner Commission issued a report on race relations, criticizing the media for failing to adequately cover African American communities.

However, a few African Americans made it onto the white-controlled airwaves. William C. Matney, Jr., who had been managing editor of the *Michigan Chronicle*, an African American community paper, and a reporter for the *Detroit News* in 1963, became a TV and radio reporter for WMAQ-TV, the NBC-owned station in Chicago. He joined NBC-TV news in 1966. Veteran Norma Quarles, now at CNN, was hired as a trainee at NBC News in 1966, moving a year later to the NBC station in Cleveland as a reporter and anchor. Lem Tucker, who died in March of 1991, joined NBC News as a copy boy in 1965 and moved up to assistant bureau chief in Vietnam.

In 1967, a self-described "teacher moonlighting as a jazz disc jockey" who also called play-by-play for basketball games and read the news applied for a job at soon-to-be all-news WCBS radio in New York. Ed Bradley, who would later co-host CBS-TV's most successful news show "60 Minutes" impressed a news director by refusing to write copy and record it because, he explained, "You won't learn enough about me that way." Instead, he borrowed a tape recorder, went out on the street, did an update of a story about an anti-poverty program, and got the job. But in Portsmouth, Virginia, an audacious 25-year-old newscaster named Max Robinson was fired from a UHF station after he broke the rules by showing his face on camera. It was 1964, and only the word "News" was to appear on the screen. White viewers were enraged to see one of "those people" working in the studio. According to his news director, James Snyder, in 1971 Robinson became the first African American anchor in a major market, at WTOP-TV in Washington, DC. Robinson later became ABC-TV's first African American regular co-anchor.

It took the riots of the 1960s and a stern warning from a federal commission for the broadcast industry to undertake any concentrated hiring of African Americans. When American cities began to burn, African Americans held about 3.6 percent of TV news jobs. White news directors had to scramble to find African American journalists to cover the riots. In 1968, the National Advisory Commission on Civil Disorders, also known as the Kerner Commission, concluded that "the world that television and newspapers offer to their black audience is almost totally white, in both appearance and attitude." "Within a year," wrote Noble, "many of us found ourselves working downtown at major radio and TV stations."

Max Robinson (AP/Wide World Photos, Inc.)

In June of 1969, the Federal Communications Commission adopted rules prohibiting discrimination in broadcast industry employment and required stations to file annual reports showing the racial makeup of their workforce by job category. African American public affairs shows, such as Noble's "Like It Is," "Black Journal" hosted by Tony Brown, and Philadelphia's "Black Perspectives on the News," aired in nearly every city with a substantial African American population. Still, by the time Mal Goode retired in 1973, there were only seven African American reporters at the three networks.

In the 1990s, African Americans began breaking into broadcast management and ownership, yet numbers were and still are small. TV general managers included Charlotte Moore English of KSHB-TV, Kansas City; Marcellus Alexander of WJZ-TV in Baltimore; Eugene Lothery of WCAU-TV in Philadelphia; Clarence McKee, CEO and chairman of WTVT-TV in Tampa, Florida; and Dorothy Brunson, owner of a small UHF station, WGTW-TV, in Philadelphia.

Ronald Townsend, president of the Gannett Television Group, comprising ten stations, chaired the National Association of Broadcasters's TV board. Jonathan Rodgers became president of the CBS Television Stations Division in August of 1990, making him network television's highest-ranking African American news executive. Bryant Gumbel, co-host of the NBC-TV "Today" show, CBS News correspondent Ed Bradley, and talk show host Oprah Winfrey became three of the highest-paid and most recognized faces on television. ABC-TV's Carole Simpson became a substitute and weekend network TV anchor. African Americans anchored local newscasts in markets around the country.

Still, African Americans, while 12 percent of the population in the 1990 census, represented only 9.8 percent of the television news workforce and 5 percent of the radio workforce. They were four percent of the news directors at commercial TV stations and about five percent at commercial radio stations. Those heading news operations included Gary Wordlaw at WJLA-TV Washington, DC, and Will Wright at WWOR-TV New York. According to an annual survey by the Center for Media and Public Affairs, most of the news on nightly network television shows continued to be presented by white males. African Americans accounted for only five percent of all field reports and anchor stories combined, its 1991 survey found. The most visible African American correspondent was George Strait, ABC-TV health reporter, who tied for fifty-seventh in the number of stories filed. Simpson was in sixth place, based on the number of brief news reports read.

The number of African American television and radio owners has decreased because of the consolidation frenzy in the broadcasting industry compounded by the elimination of a federal tax credit that favored minority groups. According to a 1995 survey, of the 1,221 television stations, members of minority groups own 37 and of the 10,191 radio stations, 293 were minority owned. Although this is a small number, it is a significant increase over the number of licenses that minorities held in 1978. That same year, the Federal Communications Commission agreed to grant tax credits to radio and television station owners who sold their properties to minority buyers. The objective of the tax credits benefit was to broaden broadcast ownership and promote more diverse viewpoints. The result effectively lowered the acquisition costs of a television or radio station for a minority.

One benefactor of the tax credit was Ragan A. Henry, an African American lawyer and founder of U.S. Radio. He used the tax break to assemble what had been the largest African American-owned radio group in the nation by 1996 with 25 stations. In 1996, Henry sold U.S. Radio for $140 million to Clear Channel Communications, Inc. of San Antonio. His financial backers were unwilling to put up more money to buy increasingly expensive stations. It is expected that minority owners will continue to sell their broadcast holdings as station prices escalate. Ross Love, founder of Blue Chip Broadcasting Ltd. in 1995, may be the exception to the liquidation of broadcasting entities by minority owners because of lack of capital. His company, based in Cincinnati, Ohio, continues to expand and currently has four urban-formatted stations.

The tax credit was eliminated in 1995 when Congress swept aside affirmative action policies. The program came under attack because of its use by Viacom, Inc. to escape $600 million in taxes in a proposed sale of its cable television properties. Viacom had arranged to sell its cable systems to an African American entrepreneur whose company received financial backing from Tele-Communications, Inc., the nation's largest cable operator. Since the elimination of the tax credit, the number of minority-owned stations has declined slightly to three hundred.

Although no longer required to adhere to the affirmative action guidelines established by the Federal Communications Commission (FCC), the four major networks and several of the largest owners of radio stations have agreed to continue to follow them in their outreach and recruitment efforts. The demise of the affirmative action guidelines came about when it was declared unconstitutional—naysayers believed it would lead to quotas—by a federal court in the spring of 1998.

The list of companies that agreed to continue following the affirmative action guidelines set by the FCC include ABC, CBS, NBC, the Fox network, Time Warner Inc., which includes CNN, the Tribune Company, and Clear Channel Communications, Inc., the owner of 183 radio stations and 18 television stations. Cox Communications, the Cablevision Systems Corporation, the TCI Group, and Comcast Corporation—all cable outlets—have also agreed. According to BIA, a company that monitors revenues in broadcasting, all of these companies earn roughly one-third of the annual advertising revenue in the broadcast industry.

Radio and Television Advertising

A study conducted earlier this year by the U.S. broadcast regulators found that advertisers discriminate against minority-owned radio and television stations or stations that target African American audiences. Furthermore, a recent FCC-sponsored report determined that minority stations earn an estimated 63 percent less in advertising revenue per listener than similar non-minority stations. Many advertisers believe that they can reach African American listeners who are most likely to buy their products by sticking to mainstream radio.

It is a general belief that the lack of advertising dollars allocated to African American-formatted stations is due to the lack of minority representation at advertising firms. To remedy this situation, many advertising firms have stepped up their recruitment of minorities. In 1998, minority professionals comprised 11 percent of employees at the nation's 25 leading advertising agencies, up from 7.6 percent in 1995.

Public Television

For most of its short history, public television, begun in the early 1950s, failed to realize the hopes of many African Americans. Tony Brown's "Black Journal," later "Tony Brown's Journal," was well-received by African American viewers as the only national African American public affairs series on television. It was constantly threatened with cancellation, however, after conservatives complained about its anti-administration attitude. The show stayed on the air after it secured underwriting from Pepsi Cola.

In 1975, the only African American FCC commissioner, Benjamin Hooks, joined the critics, accusing public broadcasters of "arrogance" and of concentrating their efforts on the cultured, white cosmopolitans. A 1975 review of public broadcasting stations's top three job categories (officials, managers, and professionals) showed that 59 percent (or 108) of the 184 public radio licensees and 33 percent (52) of the 160 public television licensees had no minority staff at these levels.

In the early 1990s, the highest-ranking African Americans in public television were: Jennifer Lawson, who joined PBS in November of 1989 as its first executive vice president for national programming and promotion services; Donald L. Marbury, director of the Television Program Fund of the Corporation for Public Broadcasting; and George L. Miles, Jr., executive vice president and chief operating officer of WNET-TV New York. Lawson obtained and commissioned the programs that PBS provides to its member stations as well as the promotion of those programs. Marbury managed the $45 million television program fund, which provides funding support for major series in public television, such as "Frontline."

The most visible African American journalist on public television has been "MacNeil-Lehrer News Hour" correspondent Charlayne Hunter-Gault, a former *New York Times* reporter noted for her in-depth reporting. Other African American journalists with the show include Kwame Holman, a Washington correspondent, and producer Jackie Farmer. The most acclaimed piece of African American journalism on PBS was "Eyes on the Prize," a history of the civil rights movement produced by Henry Hampton, which aired in 1987, with a sequel in 1990. The network's most controversial was a one-hour film on African American homosexual men, "Tongues Untied," by filmmaker Marlon Riggs in 1991.

Tony Brown (Courtesy of Tony Brown)

In 1980, Howard University launched WHMM-TV, becoming the first licensee of a public TV station on an African American campus and the only African American-owned public television station in the nation. On August 31, 1991, San Francisco's Minority Television Project went on the air with KMTP-TV, which became the nation's second African American-owned public television station. One of the principals was Adam Clayton Powell III, son of the late Harlem congressman, Adam Clayton Powell, Jr.

Public Radio

Before 1967, there were only two African American educational outlets in the country; by 1990 there were forty African American public radio stations. Many of them were community radio stations, owned and operated by nonprofit foundations, controlled by a local board of directors, and dependent on listener donations. Others were on college campuses. One of the most successful was WPFW-FM, a 50,000-watt outlet controlled by African Americans, launched in 1977 by the Pacifica Foundation.

Stations such as WCLK-FM at Clark College in Atlanta, WBVA-FM in Harrodsburg, Kentucky, and WVAS-FM at Alabama State University in Montgomery, tailored news and public affairs programming to their local African American audiences. WVAS was used as a broadcast journalism lab by students majoring in the field. On National Public Radio, African American journalists Phyllis Crockett, Vertamae Grosvenor, Cheryl Duvall, and Brenda Wilson have won awards for reports on South Africa and issues involving African Americans.

Cable Television

The 1980s saw the explosion of cable television and the decline of television networks. Black Entertainment Television (BET), founded by former congressional aide Robert L. Johnson, made its debut in 1980 and established a news division by the end of the decade. That division produced a weekly news show "BET News" and "Lead Story," a talk show featuring African American pundits.

The biggest development in cable journalism, however, was the spectacular growth of Ted Turner's Cable News Network (CNN), which went on air in June of 1980. By the 1991 Persian Gulf war, CNN had established itself as the station to watch in a crisis. Transmitted across the globe, it became a medium for world leaders to communicate with one another.

Veteran journalist Bernard Shaw, principal Washington anchor, was one of three CNN reporters who captivated the world's audiences with their continuous coverage of the first night of bombing on Baghdad during Operation Desert Storm on January 16, 1991. Other African Americans at CNN include Jay Suber, vice president and executive producer, news features, CNN Newsroom; Graylian Young, Southeast bureau chief; CNN anchors Andrea Arceneaux, Leon Harris, and Joe Oliver; Cassandra Henderson, anchor for CNN Newsroom; Lyn Vaughn and Gordon Graham, Headline News anchors; sports anchor Fred Hickman; and correspondent Norma Quarles.

◆ AFRICAN AMERICAN MEDIA IN CYBERSPACE

African Americans were cruising the information superhighway—a vast electronic communications network comprised of telephones, computers, and televisions—in growing numbers during the late 1990s. An increasing number of African Americans—5.6 million, according to a 1999 Nielsen-CommerceNet study—are using the Internet at home, work, school, and at libraries. This represents an increase of more than fifty percent from just one year ago. Therefore, it was little surprise that an African American was one of the key spokespeople for cyberspace-related equity issues.

Robert Johnson (BET)

Branded "The Net's Conscience," Larry Irving was director of the National Telecommunications and Information Administration. But far from being the only person of color with clout on the net, Irving was one of many experts working in the burgeoning industry that links millions of people across the globe, providing access to a wide array of information for educational, business, and entertainment purposes. Other high-ranking African Americans included Andrew C. Barrett, the only black commissioner of the Federal Communications Commission (FCC); Ray Winbush, director of the Bishop Joseph Johnson Black Cultural Center at Vanderbilt University—a network linking black colleges, students, and professors; Jimmy Davies, who partnered with Apple Computer, Inc. to establish a national electronic bulletin board service for blacks called the African American Information Network; and Eugene and Phyllis Tucker Vinson Jackson, founders of the World African Network, a 24-hour, pay cable television network for blacks; and Cleo Manago, founder of the Black Men's Xchange (BMX), an Africentric national communications clearinghouse.

The World Wide Web comprises a major component of the "highway." Many African American news-oriented web sites that have developed are mentioned below, as well as in the newspaper, magazine, and journal listings in this chapter. In addition, some of the most popular African American web sites offering information on the various subjects covered in this reference work can be found in the Science and Technology chapter.

Afro-Americ@: The Afro-American Newspapers Home Page
www.afroam.org

AFRONET.com
www.afronet.com

Black on Black Communications
www.bobc.com

An electronic newsletter covering issues of interest to African Americans via news stories and positive dialogue. Available only by subscription.

Black Talk
www.blacktalk.com

Online discussion of numerous topics open to all people.

Black Voices
www.blackvoices.com

A wide assortment of African American-related topics, from business and career center to headlines and entertainment.

The Black World Today
www.tbwt.com

Online news web site containing a wide variety of topics ranging from news and business to games and weather.

The Drum
FAQ@drum.ncat.edu

Includes information regarding such diverse topics as African American universities, federal government internship opportunities, a speeches page, chat rooms, and a kids page.

Gravity Discussion Zones
www.newsavanna.com

Discussion pages geared towards African Americans.

MelaNet: The UnCut Black Experience
www.melanet.com

Provides a presence for African American businesses via an online marketplace, a year-round Kwanzaa Bazaar, an African Wedding Guide, the Ida Wells-Barnett Media Center, and the UnCut Chat Series.

Minority Affairs Forum
ftp://heather.cs.ucdavis.edu/pub/README.html

Contains articles on minority related topics including immigration, affirmative action, bilingual education, and race relations.

MSBET
www.msbet.com

News and information of interest to African Americans.

NetNoir Online: The Black Network
www.netnoir.com

A gateway to everything Afrocentric including cultures, lifestyles, music, sports, business, and education.

◆ PUBLISHING, RADIO, AND TELEVISION PROFESSIONALS

(To locate biographical profiles more readily, please consult the index at the back of the book.)

Robert S. Abbott (1870–1940)
Newspaper Publisher

A native of St. Simon Island, Georgia, Abbott studied at Beach Institute in Savannah, and later completed his undergraduate work at Claflin College in Orangeburg, South Carolina. Migrating to Chicago, he attended Kent Law School and took a job in a printing house until he completed his law studies in 1899.

Abbott returned to Chicago and published the first edition of the *Defender* on May 5, 1905, which he initially sold on a door-to-door basis. After Abbott's death, the *Defender* was handed over to his nephew, John H. Sengstacke, who introduced a daily edition of the paper in 1956.

William Banks (1903–1985)
Broadcasting Executive, Attorney, Minister

Born in Geneva, Kentucky, in 1903, William Banks relocated to Detroit as a young man and, after earning a law degree, became a Baptist minister during his forties. Long active in numerous African American community organizations in the city, Banks founded the International Free and Accepted Masons and Eastern Star in 1950 and, under his guidance, the growing group soon became a financially-sound and charity-driven fraternal organization. He continued to work as an attorney in private practice until well past the age of retirement.

In 1964, the Black Masons made their first venture into media ownership with a Detroit FM radio outlet that mixed R&B music and religious broadcasting. Banks's business savvy helped make the station a financial success in the same way that the Masons's other ventures—such as vocational training schools—also caused the organization to thrive. His ties to the Republican community eventually brought him to U.S. President Richard Nixon's White House as a guest in the early 1970s, and the chief executive helped him obtain the first television station license granted to an African American in the United States by the Federal Communications Commission.

The UHF television outlet that Banks and the Masons went on the Detroit airwaves with in 1975 was called WGPR, or "Where God's Presence Radiates." Its first years in operation were shaky, since many members of Banks's team—employees that included his wife, Ivy Bird, and daughter Tenicia Gregory—had little media experience. Within a few years, however, the station gained ratings and financial health. More importantly, WGPR-TV served as a training ground for a legion of African American on-air and behind-the-scenes technical personnel, a group of young people who would eventually go on to figure prominently in Detroit media. Banks died in 1985 at the age of 82. The Black Mason organization that Banks founded owned the station until 1994, when it was purchased by CBS as a local affiliate.

Donald H. Barden (1943–)

Communications Executive

Born on December 20, 1943, Donald Barden struggled in a number of low-wage jobs as an adult, dreaming of one day working for himself in some sort of entrepreneurial venture. A nest egg of $500 helped him to open a record store, then launch a record label, then a public relations firm in Lorain, Ohio. The capital Barden accumulated through these ventures was later parlayed into real estate deals. By the early 1970s, the executive had become a dynamic member of Lorain's business community, owning a newspaper, holding a seat on the city council, and hosting a talk show on Cleveland's NBC affiliate.

Barden's interest in and familiarity with cutting-edge media evolved into his most lucrative undertaking. Foreseeing the rise of the cable industry—and the lack of African American representation within it—Barden invested in Lorain's new cable television provider and used the remunerative rewards to begin his own cable company, Barden Cablevision. He researched and found that African American communities were entertaining franchise offers from giants in the industry and offered them a socially-conscious alternative. One of the first cities to award Barden's company a contract was Inkster, Michigan, a suburb of Detroit. His success in wiring the city for cable service and the obvious financial soundness of his company paid off when the city of Detroit awarded Barden Cablevision its much-coveted contract.

Don Barden (AP/Wide World Photos, Inc.)

Barden launched cable television in Detroit with the help of Canadian financing and began wiring the city in 1986. Always looking into what was on the forefront of the communications industry, Barden's next venture was in the realm of personal communications services, a new messaging technology that would allow small devices to transmit faxes, voice messages, and computer data. He planned to bid on several of the licenses when they were auctioned off for the first time by the Federal Communications Commission in 1994. That same year, he sold his interest in Barden Cablevision for a reported $100 million, reaping a dramatic profit from the company he had started with only a few thousand dollars. In early 1995, it was announced that Indiana authorities had granted Barden a riverboat casino operating license, one of two to be established in the city of Gary.

With the success of his riverboat casino in Indiana, Barden expressed an interest in obtaining a license for one of the three casinos earmarked for Detroit. When Mayor Archer rejected his bid, Barden recruited celebrity Michael Jackson to help him campaign for a contract in the hopes that Detroit voters would overturn Archer's decision. His billion dollar casino proposal was to be called the "Majestic Kingdom" and included plans for an 800-room hotel, botanical gardens, nightclubs, restaurants, and the Michael Jackson Thriller Theme Park, which would have incorporated advanced technology enabling it to operate regardless of the weather. Despite Barden's vigorous campaigning, Detroit voters rejected his proposal on August 8, 1998.

Barden recently entered into a contract with General Motors to establish an automotive plant in Namibia and South Africa. He, along with his business partner Michael Jackson, took several trips in 1998 to central and southern Africa to investigate other business opportunities in Namibia, Angola, and South Africa. In May 1999, it was announced that Barden has reached a deal to invest in Sengstacke Enterprises, Inc., owner of several African American newspapers in Chicago, Detroit, Pittsburgh, and Memphis.

Edward R. Bradley (1941–)
Television News Correspondent

Born on January 22, 1941, in Philadelphia, Pennsylvania, Edward R. Bradley received a bachelor of science degree in education from Cheyney State College in 1964. From 1963 to 1967, Bradley worked as a jazz host and news reporter for WDAS radio in Philadelphia. He then spent four years at WCBS radio in New York. His first television assignment was in September of 1971, when he joined CBS as a stringer in the Paris bureau. Within a few months he moved to the Saigon bureau, where he remained until he was assigned to the Washington bureau in June of 1974. From 1974 until 1978, Bradley served as White House correspondent for CBS.

Bradley worked as an anchor for "CBS Sunday Night News" from 1976 until 1981 and as principal correspondent for "CBS Reports." In 1981, he replaced Dan Rather as a correspondent for the weekly news program "60 Minutes." In 1992, Bradley became host of the CBS news program "Street Stories." An avid jazz and blues aficionado, Bradley also is the host of "Jazz from Lincoln Center." He has hosted the show since 1991.

Due to his outstanding coverage of issues both nationally and internationally, Bradley has received eleven Emmy Awards, two Alfred I. duPont-Columbia University Awards for broadcast journalism, a George Foster Peabody Broadcasting Award, a George Polk Award, and an NCAA Anniversary Award. In 1992, he won an Emmy for his "60 Minutes" segment "Made in China."

Ed Bradley (Archive Photos, Inc.)

The National Press Foundation presented Bradley with the Sol Taischoff Award in 1993.

In October of 1995, Bradley filed a report called "The Other America" on "60 Minutes." In that piece, he examined shantytown homes—known as "colonias"—in the Texas desert along the U.S.-Mexico border. The colonias were designed for low-income, mainly Hispanic families. The woman who built the shanties claimed that Bradley's report wrecked her reputation and falsely accused her and other members of her family of unethical business and political practices. She sued for defamation. However, in late 1997, a Texas jury cleared Bradley of libel in the investigation.

James Brown (1951–)
Sports Anchor

James Brown was born on February 25, 1951, in Washington, DC. Having completed his third season as co-host of "Fox NFL Sunday," America's most watched and Emmy Award-winning pregame show, Brown also serves as co-host of "NHL on Fox" studio segments. Brown joined Fox Sports in June of 1994 and is widely recognized as one of the most versatile and multi-talented on-air personalities in television.

Prior to entering the communications field, Brown received a bachelor of arts degree in American government from Harvard University in 1973 and then was drafted in the fourth-round by the NBA's Atlanta Hawks. He officially began his broadcasting career in 1984 with WJLA-TV in Washington, DC, and WUSA-TV (1984–1990). He also served as an analyst for the NBA's Washington Bullets local television broadcasts (1978–1983) and co-hosted two weekly Washington area sports programs. At one time, he even hosted a midday program on all-sports radio WTEM in the nation's capital.

In 1984, he joined CBS Sports as a college basketball analyst and co-host of the NCAA basketball championship (1984–1994). Other host roles for CBS included the weekday program during the 1992 Winter Olympics, the Heisman Trophy Award show "CBS Sports Saturday/Sunday" anthology series, and the Emmy Award-winning special "Let Me Be Brave: A Special Climb of Mt. Kilimanjaro."

Not one to limit himself, in addition to college basketball and NFL play-by-play, Brown has served as a reporter for CBS Sports's coverage of the NBA Finals and Pan American Games. He also delved into other sports areas. He served as commentator of freestyle skiing for CBS at the 1994 Lillehammer Winter Olympics and hosted four "Fox Saturday Night Fight" programs, as well as several pay-per-view boxing events.

Brown is a contributor to the sports magazine program "Real Sports with Bryant Gumbel," which premiered on HBO in April of 1995 and served as a moderator for a roundtable discussion of the documentary "Hoop Dreams: A Reunion" on PBS. Brown's hard work over the years paid off last fall when he received the prestigious Sportcaster of the Year Award from the Quarterback Club of Washington for his "outstanding contribution to the world of sports."

Les Brown (1945–)

Motivational Speaker, Talk Show Host, Author

As a renowned motivational speaker, author, and television personality, Les Brown—born Leslie Calvin Brown along with his twin brother Wesley on February 17, 1945—rose to national prominence by delivering a highly-charged message that instructs people on how to shake off mediocrity and live up to their potential.

Brown and his twin brother were born in low-income Liberty City, Florida. They were adopted at six weeks of age by Mamie Brown, a single woman with a heart of gold but little education or money. As a child, Brown lacked concentration, especially in reading. His restlessness and inattentiveness, coupled with his teachers's failure to recognize his real potential, resulted in him being labeled as a slow learner. Although this label damaged his self-esteem and stayed with him for many years, he was finally able to overcome it through perseverance and the realization that he was responsible for his destiny. His mother's unyielding belief in his greatness, along with support from a speech and drama teacher in high school, aided him in this journey of discovery.

Brown received no formal education past high school. However, through sheer will, initiative, and persistence, he prides himself on being self-educated. This fact has distinguished him as an authority on human virtue. Brown's insatiable thirst for knowledge and hunger to succeed allowed him to rise from a hip-talking radio announcer to a broadcast manager; from a community activist to a community leader; from a political commentator to three-term legislator; and from a banquet and nightclub emcee to a prominent motivational speaker.

In 1986, Brown entered the public speaking arena on a full-time basis and formed his own company, Les Brown Unlimited, Inc. The company provides motivational tapes and materials, as well as workshops and personal/professional development programs aimed at individuals, companies, and organizations. He is also the author of *Live Your Dreams* and *It's Not Over Until You Win.* The former host of "The Les Brown Show," a nationally syndicated daily television talk show that focused on solutions rather than problems, Brown continues to mesmerize audiences with his customized presentations that teach and inspire.

In 1989, Brown was the recipient of the National Speakers Association's highest honor: The Council of Peers Award of Excellence (CPAE). In 1990, he recorded his first in a series of speech presentations entitled *You Deserve*, which was awarded a Chicago-area Emmy. This program eventually became the leading fund-raising program of its kind for pledges to PBS stations nationwide. In addition, in 1992, he was selected as one of the World's Top Five Speakers by Toastmasters International and the recipient of the Golden Gavel Award.

Tony Brown (1933–)

Talk Show Host, Producer, Columnist, Author, Film Director

William Anthony Brown, born in Charleston, West Virginia, in 1933, is probably best known as the producer and host of the longest-running minority affairs program in history "Tony Brown's Journal." The show was selected in the *New York Daily Times* as one of the top ten television shows of all time that presents positive African American images. In 1991, the show was also nominated for the NAACP Image Award for outstanding news, talk or information series/special.

Brown received his bachelor of arts degree in sociology in 1959 and his master's of social work in 1961 from Wayne State University in Detroit. Brown took a job with the *Detroit Courier* as drama critic. During this time he began to be active in the Civil Rights movement, helping to organize the 1963 "March to Freedom" with Dr. Martin Luther King, Jr. in Detroit. After leaving the paper, where he had been promoted to the position of city editor, Brown landed a job with the local PBS station, WTVS, where he became involved in television programming and production. At WTVS, he produced the station's first series aimed at a black audience, "C.P.T." (Colored People's Time). He joined the New York staff of the PBS program "Black Journal" in 1970 as the show's executive producer and host; in 1977 the show's name was changed to "Tony Brown's Journal" and can still be seen on PBS.

In 1971, Brown founded and became the first dean of Howard University's School of Communications. He continued in that post until 1974. While in this position, he initiated an annual careers conference that is still in place today because of his concern for the lack of African American representation in the communications industry.

Brown has been an advocate of community and self-help programs. In 1980 he organized a "Black College Day," designed to emphasize the importance of historically African American colleges and universities. In 1985 Brown organized the Council for the Economic Development of Black Americans and launched the "Buy Freedom" campaign (now known as the "Buy Freedom Network"), which encourages African American consumers nationwide to patronize African American-owned businesses.

Brown wrote two powerful books *Black Lies, White Lies: The Truth According to Tony Brown* in 1995 and *Empower the People: A 7-Step Plan to Overthrow the Conspiracy That Is Stealing Your Money and Freedom* in 1998. Although both books address problems that cannot be ignored, they also focus on the future and on solutions. Offering innovative plans for making America more competitive through Brown's Team America Concept, the books strive to solve the country's race problem through cultural diversity.

Brown has written, produced, and directed a film *The White Girl*, appeared as a commentator for National Public Radio, and is a syndicated newspaper columnist. He is also host of a radio talk show "Tony Brown" on WLIB in New York, which will soon be syndicated nationally. He is a member of the National Association of Black Television and Film Producers, the National Association of Black Media Producers, the National Communications Council, and the National Black United Fund. Brown is the recipient of a Black Emmy Award, an NAACP Image Award, the Educator of the Year Award, and the Communicator of the Year Award from the Academy's national board of trustees. He is currently president of Tony Brown Productions, Inc. in New York. In addition to producing movies and television programs, the company also offers a videotape duplication service and markets videotapes from a collection called *The Library of Black History*.

Ron Buckmire (1968–)
Mathematician, Internet Directory Founder

Born on May 21, 1968, Ron Buckmire is the creator of the oldest and largest Internet online resource of information about gay, lesbian, bisexual, and transgendered people, The Queer Resources Directory (QRD). Currently, he serves as its executive director and is responsible for its quality control and auditing of user services.

Buckmire spent nearly ten years of his youth in Barbados. In 1986, he relocated to Troy, New York, earning a bachelor of science degree in mathematics (1989), a master of arts degree (1992) and a Ph.D. in applied mathematics (1994), all from Rensselaer Polytechnic Institute. Though the Queer Resources Directory (QRD) was initially started as an electronic archive for the radical group Queer Nation, Buckmire transformed the repository into a broader-based electronic library, featuring news clippings, political contact information, essays, images, and hyperlinks—all dedicated to sexual minorities that have traditionally born the brunt of discrimination.

In addition to his QRD duties, Buckmire is currently an assistant professor in the mathematics department at Occidental College, where he teaches mathematical modeling and complex analysis. Most of his work has been in theoretical aerodynamics and computational fluid dynamics. Buckmire's other activities include participation on the board of directors of the International Gay and Lesbian Human Rights Commission and of Overnight Productions, which is responsible for the international gay and lesbian radio news magazine "This Way Out."

In 1996, *Out Magazine* listed him among the Top 100 Gay and Lesbian Activists of the Year. In 1997, for its thirtieth anniversary issue, *The Advocate* named him as a member of "Generation Q," thirty activists under age thirty who have made a difference.

Edward J. Castleberry (1928–)
Broadcast Journalist

Born July 28, 1928, in Birmingham, Alabama, Castleberry spent two years at Miles College. His career in radio broadcasting includes many stations in the United States. He started as a disc jockey at WEDR and

WJLD in Birmingham, Alabama (1950–1955), and has worked in the various capacities of program host, program director, and news personality at WMBM in Miami, Florida (1955–1958), WCIN in Cincinnati, Ohio (1958–1961), WABQ in Cleveland, Ohio (1961–1964), WVKO in Columbus, Ohio (1964–1967), WHAT in Philadelphia, Pennsylvania (1967–1968) and WEBB in Baltimore, Maryland. He then became an anchorman and entertainment editor at the Mutual and National Black Networks.

Castleberry was named Newsman of the Year in 1980 by both the Coalition of Black Media Women and Jack the Rapper Family Affair and received the Outstanding Citizen Award from the Alabama House of Representatives in 1983. In 1985 he was honored by the Smithsonian Institute in Washington, DC. Later, Castleberry was awarded the World War II Victory Medal for his service in the United States Navy.

Spencer Christian (1947–)

Television Weatherperson

Born in Newport News, Virginia, in 1947 and a veteran of the U.S. Army Reserves, Spencer Christian received his bachelor of arts degree in English from Hampton University in 1970. Upon graduation, he taught English at the Stony Brook School in Long Island, New York before launching his television career.

In 1971, Christian went to work for WWBT-TV in Richmond as a news reporter; from 1972 to 1975 he served as the station's weatherperson. In 1975, he moved to WBAL-TV in Baltimore, where he hosted "Spencer's World," a weekly, half-hour talk show. He also produced and narrated the Emmy Award-winning, five-part report on declining verbal skills entitled "Does Anyone Here Speak English?" In 1977, he moved to New York's WABC-TV. Christian joined the "Good Morning America" team on ABC in 1986 as weather forecaster. He left the show in 1999 to join a local television station in San Francisco.

During 1988, he was the ABC Television's official on-air spokesperson for the "Readasaurus" campaign, which was part of the company's overall Project Literacy U.S., promoting interest in reading among young children. In 1993, Christian hosted the "Triple Threat" game show on Black Entertainment Television and was inducted into the Virginia Communications Hall of Fame. Later in the same year, he was named Virginian of the Year by the Virginia Press Association. He published *Spencer Christian's Weather Book*, *Spencer Christian's Geography Book*, and, most recently, *Electing Our Government*, a light and lively refresher course on how the United States electoral procedure works. He also co-hosted an experimental, late night series on ABC called "Day's End," which aired in 27 markets across the country from March through June of 1989.

Spencer Christian (AP/Wide World Photos, Inc.)

In 1996, Christian worked on a public education campaign, in conjunction with Everready, that focused on weather emergency preparedness. In addition, he wrote a brochure that contains helpful weather emergency tips. It is available through Energizer and endorsed by the National Weather Service.

Christian worked with a variety of charities in New York and New Jersey. They include Up With People, The March of Dimes, the Huntington's Disease Society of America, Special Olympics, Big Brothers, Make-a-Wish Foundation, and many others. His affiliation with the March of Dimes dates back to 1979 when he served as honorary chair of the North New Jersey chapter.

Xernona Clayton (1930–)

Broadcast Executive

Clayton was born Xernona Brewster on August 30, 1930, in Muskogee, Oklahoma. She received a bachelor of science degree from Tennessee Agricultural and Industrial State University (now Tennessee State University) in 1952 and later pursued graduate studies at the University of Chicago. She also attended the Ru-Jac School of Modeling in Chicago.

Clayton was the first African American woman to have her own television show in the South when she became host of the "Xernona Clayton Show" at WAGA-TV in Atlanta. She has also been a newspaper columnist for the *Atlanta Voice*, taught public school in Chicago and Los Angeles, and dabbled in photography and fashion modeling.

Clayton was active in the Civil Rights movement. Her first husband, now deceased, was the public relations director for Dr. Martin Luther King, Jr. Clayton came to the attention of Atlanta officials and was appointed to the position of community relations director of the Model Cities Program. She has also raised funds for sickle cell anemia research and the Dr. Martin Luther King, Jr. Birthplace Memorial Restoration Committee.

In 1968, Clayton won the Outstanding Leadership award given by the National Association of Market Developers and a year later the Bronze Woman of the Year in Human Relations award given by Phi Delta Kappa sorority. She is also the recipient of the Georgia Associated Press award for Superior Television Programming 1969–1971. In 1987, Clayton won an Emmy Award for a documentary on juvenile justice. She was named Media Woman of the Year in 1989.

Clayton is the founder of the Atlanta chapter of the National Association of Media Women and a member of the National Academy of Television Arts and Sciences and the National Association of Press Women. She is also a member of the Urban League's board of directors. She co-starred in a major motion picture *House on Skull Mountain*. Clayton married Paul L. Brady, a federal administrative judge, after the death of her first husband, and is currently the corporate vice president for urban affairs at the Turner Broadcasting System in Atlanta, Georgia.

Don Cornelius (1936–)
Broadcasting Executive

Don Cornelius, the creative mind behind the hit African American dance show "Soul Train" was born in Chicago on September 27, 1936, and grew up on the city's predominantly African American South side. At the age of thirty, he fulfilled his dream of becoming a radio announcer when he landed a part-time job as an announcer with WVON in Chicago. Acting as an all-around substitute became too exhausting, however, and he moved to the small UHF television station, WCIU-TV with the seed for "Soul Train" already in mind. Although he initially had trouble convincing sponsors to take a chance on an "ethnic" show, Cornelius was able to get the financial backing he needed, and the first show of "Soul Train" aired in Chicago on August 17, 1970. The show was essentially a dance party that featured African American performers and dancers and aired once a week.

Samuel E. Cornish (The Granger Collection Ltd.)

The inexpensive program, hosted and produced by Cornelius, went national a little over a year later. Cornelius attributed the speed of "Soul Train"'s success to the overall absence of entertainment television programs for African American audiences. The show spawned a record label, Soul Train Records, in 1975, although the label folded after three years. The "Soul Train Music Awards" proved to be a more enduring spin-off; created in 1986, the awards program was the first to be dedicated exclusively to African American musicians. By 1992 "Soul Train" had become the longest-running music program in the history of syndication.

Samuel E. Cornish (1795–1858)
Newspaper Publisher

Samuel Cornish was born in Sussex County, Delaware, in 1795. Ordained as an evangelist by the Presbyterian Church, Cornish acted as an advocate for African Americans through the mouthpiece of the newspaper he co-founded with John Russwurm, *Freedom's Journal.* The paper, which began printing in March of 1827, countered racist propaganda and served as a means of communication for African Americans. He changed the paper's name to *Rights of All* in May of 1829, and the newspaper ceased publication later that year.

Cornish continued editing after the demise of the publication, serving as editor of the *Weekly Advocate* (later changed to *Colored American*) from 1837 to 1838. He was also involved with the African Free Schools, the Negro Convention movement, the American Anti-Slavery Society, and the American Missionary Society. Cornish died on November 6, 1858, in Brooklyn, New York.

David E. Driver (1955–)
Book Publisher, Writer, Social Activist, Investor

David E. Driver was born on October 17, 1955, and grew up on Chicago's West side. Because of his excellent grades, he attended Lindblom High School, an exceptional public trade school. From there, he earned a bachelor's of arts from Bradley University in Peoria, Illinois, and after he passed the CPA exam, he joined Arthur Young & Company as a staff accountant. In 1978, Driver took a job at the International Hospital Supply Corporation. Until 1980, Driver worked as a finance manager, specializing in foreign currency markets. He moved on to Merrill Lynch Capital Markets where he was promoted to vice president in 1982. While working in stock and bond futures, he received his MBA from the University of Chicago in 1984.

In 1988 with $250,000 and one book that he had written himself—*The Good Heart Book: A Guide to Volunteering*—he founded the Noble Press. Within three years, he had a staff of five, a renovated loft for office space, and books receiving critical attention. The book that earned the Noble Press its reputation was the 1993 release *Volunteer Slavery: My Authentic Negro Experience* by Janet Nelson, that sold 40,000 hardcover copies. Driver sold the paperback rights to Penguin for whom it became a national best-seller and earned an American Book Award in 1994.

By 1993, Noble's annual sales reached the million mark and its distribution outlets grew to number 6,000. Driver founded the Black Literary Society, a book club that posts reading lists on the Internet. Driver also started Young Chicago Authors, a workshop program for aspiring teenage authors. In addition, Driver wrote *Defending the Left: An Individual's Guide to Fighting for Social Justice, Individual Rights and the Environment*, published in 1992. He has served as secretary of the Society of Illinois Book Publishers and is a founding member of the National Association of Black Book Publishers.

Timothy Thomas Fortune (1856–1928)
Newspaper Publisher

Born on October 3, 1856, in Marianna, Florida, Timothy Thomas Fortune was one of the most prominent African American journalists involved in the flourishing African American press of the post-Civil War era. The son of a Reconstruction politician, Fortune was particularly productive before his thirtieth year, completing such works as *Black and White: Land, Labor and Politics in the South* and *The Negro in Politics* while in his twenties.

Fortune attended Howard University for two years, leaving to marry Carrie Smiley of Jacksonville, Florida. The couple went to New York in 1878, with Fortune taking a job as a printer for the *New York Sun*. In time, Fortune caught the attention of *Sun* editor Charles A. Dana, who eventually promoted him to the editorial staff of the paper.

Fortune also edited *The Globe*, an African American daily, and was later chief editorial writer for *The Negro World*. In 1900 Fortune joined Booker T. Washington in helping to organize the successful National Negro Business League. His later activity with Washington gained him more notoriety than his earlier writing, although his written work is more vital in affording him an important niche in the history of African American protest.

In 1883, Fortune founded the *New York Age*, the paper with which he sought to "champion the cause" of his race. In time, the *Age* became the leading black journal of opinion in the United States. One of Fortune's early crusades was against segregation in the New York educational system.

Fortune was later responsible for coining the term "Afro-American" as a substitute for Negro in New York newspapers. He also set up the Afro-American Council, an organization which he regarded as the precursor of the Niagara Movement. In 1907 Fortune sold the *Age*, although he remained active in journalism as an editorial writer for several African American newspapers. He died on June 2, 1928.

Malvin R. Goode (1908–1995)
Television News Correspondent

Malvin Russell Goode had been with the *Pittsburgh Courier* for 14 years when in 1962 he joined ABC to cover the United Nations. His first test was the Cuban Missile Crisis, during which Goode distinguished himself with incisive TV and radio reports during the long hours of United Nations debate.

Goode was born in White Plains, Virginia, in 1908; educated in the public schools of Homestead, Pennsylvania; and graduated from the University of Pittsburgh in 1931. He worked for 12 years as a laborer in the steel mills while in high school and college and for five years after graduation. In 1936, he was appointed to a post in juvenile court and became boys work director of the Centre Avenue YMCA, where he led the fight to eliminate discrimination in Pittsburgh branches of the YMCA.

Goode served with the Pittsburgh Housing Authority for six years and in 1948 joined the *Pittsburgh Courier*. The following year he started a career in radio with station KQV, doing a 15-minute news show two nights each week. In 1950, he started a five-minute daily news program on WHOD.

Goode became news director at WHOD in 1952. He and his sister, the late Mary Dee, had the only brother-sister team in radio for six years. He was the first African American to hold membership in the National Association of Radio and TV News Directors and the first African American correspondent on TV network news.

For two months, in 1963, he joined with three colleagues to conduct courses in journalism for 104 African students in seminars at Lagos, Nigeria; Addis Ababa, Ethiopia; and Dar es Salaam, Tanzania.

On September 12, 1995, Goode died of a stroke in Pittsburgh.

Ed Gordon (1960–)

Television Anchor and Host

Born Edward Lansing Gordon III in Detroit, Michigan, the future journalist was inspired to achieve in part by his schoolteacher mother and Olympic gold medalist father, who unfortunately passed away when Gordon was eleven. After graduating with a degree in communications and political science from Western Michigan University in 1982, Gordon moved back to Detroit to launch his career in broadcasting.

Taking an unpaid internship with the city's public broadcasting affiliate in 1983 eventually landed him a job as host of its "Detroit Black Journal" a few years later. During that time, he also began freelance reporting from his hometown for an upstart cable network called Black Entertainment Television (BET). In 1988, the Washington, DC-based channel hired him as an anchor and chief correspondent for their weekly news program "BET News." Gordon left BET in 1996 to join NBC News as host of the Saturday edition of "Internight," a one-hour talk and interview program on MSNBC. He also serves as a daytime anchor for MSNBC and contributing correspondent for "Dateline NBC."

Gordon became an increasing presence on the well-regarded alternative to traditional network news, interviewing prominent African Americans on his "Conversations with Ed Gordon" show and hosting programs of special interest such as his "Black Men Speak Out: The Aftermath," which aired in the wake of the 1992 Los Angeles riots. During his tenure on "Conversations with Ed Gordon," he interviewed the last two sitting presidents and South African President Nelson Mandela, as well as more outspoken figures, such as the Rev. Al Sharpton and Nation of Islam leader Louis Farrakhan. He also hosted the BET staple "Lead Story," anchored several "BET News" specials on a wide range of topics, and hosted the critically acclaimed interview series "Personal Diary." Though the demands of the job at BET were arduous, Gordon derived a special satisfaction from his work in journalism when young African American males point out to him that they never were interested in news programs before his began airing.

Earl G. Graves (1935–)

Publisher and Media Executive

In the 1970s, Earl Graves emerged as one of America's leading publishers and exponents of black entrepreneurship. Within a few short years his magazine *Black Enterprise* was accepted as the authority on African Americans in business and as an important advocate for an active, socially responsive, African American middle class. Yearly sales of the magazine are currently over $17 million and increasing. *Black Enterprise* has a circulation of 250,000 and a readership of more than two million.

Born in Brooklyn in 1935, Graves graduated from Morgan State College in 1958 with a bachelor of arts degree in economics. In 1965, he was hired to a position on the staff of Robert Kennedy, then senator from New York. In 1968, he organized Earl Graves Associates, a firm which serves as a consultant on urban affairs and African American economic development and publishes *Black Enterprise*. Graves is also president and chief executive officer of Earl G. Graves Ltd., Earl G. Graves Marketing and Research Co., and Earl G. Graves Development Co. In December of 1998, he named his eldest son president of Earl G. Graves Publishing Company.

Graves wrote his autobiography *How to Succeed without Being White* in 1997. His other interests include being president of EGG Dallas Broadcasting, Inc., which operates KNOK-AM and KNOK-FM in Fort Worth, Texas. Graves is also chairman and president of Pepsi-Cola of Washington, DC.

Bryant Gumbel (1948–)

Television Anchor

Bryant Gumbel, the popular newscaster who gained fame as co-anchor of the "Today" show, was born in New Orleans, Louisiana, on September 29, 1948, but grew up in Chicago. He received a liberal arts degree from Bates College in Lewiston, Maine, in 1970.

Earl G. Graves (Earl G. Graves Publishing Co. Inc.)

Bryant Gumbel (AP/Wide World Photos, Inc.)

Before embarking on his career in television, Gumbel was a sportswriter. After submitting his first piece to *Black Sports* magazine in 1971, he was given additional freelance assignments and was soon hired as a staff writer. Within eight months, he was elevated to editor-in-chief.

Gumbel began his broadcasting career in October of 1972 when he became a weekend sportscaster for KNBC, the NBC station in Burbank, California. Within a year, he became weekday sportscaster and was appointed the station's sports director in 1976. He remained in that post until 1981. Gumbel made regular sports reports with NBC Sports as host of pre-game programming during coverage of the National Football League, Major League Baseball, and other sports broadcasts. Gumbel debuted as host of HBO's "Real Sports" program on April 2, 1995.

In January of 1982, Bryant Gumbel was named co-anchor of the "Today" show on NBC opposite Jane Pauley, selected as a replacement for Tom Brokaw. In 1997, at the height of the show's ratings, he relinquished his position after 15 years. During his tenure, he distinguished himself as a steadfast anchor, gifted interviewer, and role model for minority journalists. A bidding war for his services erupted between all major networks in the ensuing months following his departure. In the end, Gumbel signed a five-year contract with CBS News that netted him $5 million a year, his own prime-time news magazine "Public Eye With Bryant Gumbel," which was canceled in 1998, three specials each year, and his own company for syndicated programming development—not to mention CBS stock options. Early in 1999, CBS announced that Gumbel agreed to anchor "This Morning" beginning in the fall of 1999.

Greg Gumbel (1946–)

Radio and Television Sportcaster

The older brother of Bryant Gumbel, Greg Gumbel was born on May 3, 1946, in New Orleans, Louisiana. With his round, friendly face and affable disposition, Gumbel has graced the airways for over twenty years. He has covered local sports for WMAQ-TV in his hometown of Chicago, hosted ESPN's "Sports Center," done play-by-play for the Madison Square Garden Network, and served as host for CBS's "The NFL Today."

Currently employed as a sportcaster at NBC, Gumbel has worked with some of sports television's biggest names including Terry Bradshaw, John Madden, Mike

Ditka, Joe Montana, Bill Walton, and Joe Morgan. He has also worked on many large-scale sports events: Super Bowls, World Series, NBA and NCAA basketball championships, and the Olympics, both summer and winter.

Having addressed students at schools across the country, various chambers of commerce and town hall gatherings, as well as Boy Scout organizations, the Anti-Defamation League, and March of Dimes groups, Gumbel entertains and motivates audiences of all ages and types with his comments and videotaped sports highlights.

Ragan A. Henry (1934–)
Broadcast and Newspaper Executive

Ragan A. Henry is president of Broadcast Enterprises National Inc. and former publisher of *The National Leader*, an African American national newspaper launched in May of 1982, both headquartered in Philadelphia. Henry was also founder of U.S. Radio, the largest African American-owned radio group in the nation with 25 stations. In 1996, it was sold for $140 million to Clear Channel Communications of San Antonio, Texas. He is a partner in the Philadelphia law firm of Wolf, Black, Schorr, and Solis-Cohen.

Henry was born in Sadiesville, Kentucky, on February 2, 1934. He received his bachelor of arts degree from Harvard College in 1956 and his L.L.B. from Harvard Law School in 1961. He also attended Temple University Graduate School in 1963. Prior to joining his current law firm, he had been a partner in the Philadelphia firm of Goodis, Greenfield, Henry, and Edelstein from 1964 to 1977.

Henry was a lecturer at LaSalle College from 1971 to 1973 and has been a visiting professor at Syracuse University's S.I. Newhouse School of Communications since 1979. He serves on the boards of directors of Continental Bank, Abt Associates, Inc., National Association of Black Owned Broadcasters (president of the board), LaSalle College, and the Hospital of the University of Pennsylvania. He has been chairman of the John McKee Scholarship Committee Fellowships of the Noyes and Whitney Foundation.

Cheryl Willis Hudson (1948–)
Publishing Executive

Cheryl Willis Hudson, publisher, and Wade Hudson, president and chief executive officer, founded Just Us Books, Inc. in 1988 to publish children's books and learning material that focus on the African American experience.

Just Us Books, Inc. is now one of the leading publishers of African American interest books for young people. More than three dozen titles have been published with millions of copies in print. The company has garnered a number of awards and honors including The Parents' Choice Award, the Ben Franklin Award, the Multicultural Publisher's Exchange Award and the American Booksellers Association/Blackboard "Best Seller of 1994."

A native of Portsmouth, Virginia, Cheryl Willis Hudson graduated (cum laude) from Oberlin College in 1970. She also studied at Northeastern University, the Arts Students League, and Parsons School of Design. Prior to founding Just Us Books, she worked as an art editor and designer for several publishers including Houghton Mifflin, MacMillan Publishing, Arete Publishing, and Paperwing Press/Angel Entertainment.

Wade Hudson (1946–)
Publishing Executive

Wade Hudson is the president and chief executive officer of Just Us Books, Inc., a company that he co-founded with Cheryl Willis Hudson in 1988 to publish children's books and learning material that focus on the African American experience.

A native of Mansfield, Louisiana, he attended Southern University and has worked with numerous civil rights organizations including CORE, the Southern Christian Leadership Conference, and the Society for Opportunity, Unity and Leadership, which he co-founded. He also has worked as a public relations specialist for Essex County and Kean colleges in New Jersey.

As publishing professionals and advocates of diversity in literature, he and his wife conduct workshops and make presentations and appearances on panels across the country. They address topics such as: exploring books for the African American child; entrepreneurship in publishing; the nuts and bolts of building a publishing company; creative packaging of Afrocentric children's books; and publishing multicultural books for children and young adults.

Charlayne Hunter-Gault (1942–)
Journalist

Although now residing in Johannesburg, South Africa, Charlayne Hunter-Gault staked her claim as one of the leading journalists in the United States, having won many of the top honors in her field for excellence in investigative reporting. One of the springboards into her career came when she was the subject of a journalistic investigation at the height of the Civil Rights era. In 1961, she was one of two black students who first broke the color barrier at the University of Georgia. She later went on to receive a bachelor of arts degree from this institution in 1963.

Prior to joining the "MacNeil/Lehrer Report," subsequently renamed the "MacNeil/Lehrer NewsHour" and now "The NewsHour with Jim Lehrer" in 1978, Hunter-Gault held positions with the *New Yorker*, WRC-TV in Washington, DC, and *The New York Times*. She was the program's first woman anchor. In addition, her personal memoir *In My Place* was published in 1992.

Born on February 27, 1942, in Due West, South Carolina, Hunter-Gault built a reputation as a keen investigator of social injustice, especially among African Americans. Until 1997, she was the national correspondent for "The NewsHour with Jim Lehrer," the hour-long evening news program broadcast nightly on the Public Broadcasting Service (PBS). She also anchors "Rights and Wrongs: Human Rights Television," a weekly half-hour newsmagazine on PBS that incorporates news investigative reports, interviews, features, and cultural segments to examine human rights issues worldwide.

Hunter-Gault is the recipient of numerous awards including two national news and documentary Emmy awards and the prestigious George Foster Peabody Award for excellence in broadcast journalism for her work on the "NewsHour's Apartheid People" series on contemporary life in South Africa. She left PBS in the summer of 1997 to join her husband, Ronald Gault, managing director of J.P. Morgan, S.A., and to serve as the South Africa-based correspondent for National Public Radio.

Eugene D. Jackson (1943–)
Broadcast Executive

With over 25 years of experience in communications technology, Eugene D. Jackson began his entrepreneurial career in 1971 by raising $1 million to launch the Unity Broadcasting Network, parent company of the National Black Network (NBN). It is the first hourly news service that is distributed via satellite to over 125 African American-oriented radio stations. He is past president of Unity Broadcasting Network and four radio stations: WDAS-AM and WDAS-FM in Philadelphia and KATZ-AM and WZEN-FM in St. Louis.

Jackson was born in Waukomis, Oklahoma on September 5, 1943. He received a bachelor of science degree in electrical engineering from the University of Missouri at Rolla in 1967 and a master of business administration from Columbia University in 1971.

Jackson was an industrial engineer for Colgate-Palmolive from 1967 to 1968 and a production and project engineer for the Black Economic Union in New York City from 1968 to 1969. From 1969 to 1971, Jackson directed major industry programs for the Interracial Council for Business Opportunity in New York City.

Jackson serves on the boards of directors of the National Association of Broadcasters, the Council of Concerned Black Executives, Freedom National Bank, and Trans Africa (1977). He was a member of the Council on Foreign Relations in 1978 and on the board of governors of the International Radio and Television Society from 1974 to 1976.

Jackson recently divested his interest in broadcasting to develop and invest in cable television, the cellular telephone business, and the Internet. In 1993, he formed the World African Network of which he is chairman and chief executive officer. He is the vice chairman and the largest single shareholder in the Queens Inner-Unity Cable System (QUICS), the $63 million cable system that serves the borough of Queens in New York, as a joint venture with Time Warner, Inc.

John H. Johnson (1918–)
Publisher, Media Executive

One of America's foremost businessmen, John H. Johnson sits at the head of the most prosperous and powerful African American publishing company in the United States. Beginning with *Negro Digest* in 1942 and following with *Ebony* in 1945, Johnson built a chain of journalistic successes that now also includes *Jet*, *EM: Ebony Man*, and, most recently, *Ebony South Africa*, which marked the company's foray into international publishing.

Throughout the development of the above publications, he bought and sold three radio stations, started a book publishing division, and produced the former syndicated television show "Ebony/Jet Showcase." He also created two beauty care lines—Supreme Beauty Products and the world-renowned Fashion Fair Cosmetics—as well as the Ebony Fashion Fair, a spectacular traveling fashion show. In addition, he produces the annual American Black Achievement Awards for television, which first aired in 1978.

Born in Arkansas City, Arkansas, on January 19, 1918, Johnson, at age six, lost his father, a mill worker, and was raised by his mother and stepfather. He attended local segregated schools until the family moved to Chicago. Johnson attended DuSable High School in Chicago, excelling academically and in extracurricular activities, while writing for the yearbook and school paper.

After graduation, an insurance executive heard a speech delivered by Johnson and was so impressed that he offered him a partial scholarship at the University of Chicago. After two years, however, Johnson quit classes and entered the Northwestern School of Commerce in 1938, studying for an additional two years before joining the Supreme Liberty Life Insurance Company. While running the company's house organ, it occurred to Johnson that a digest of weekly or monthly news items

John H. Johnson with his daughter, Linda, in 1992 (AP/Wide World Photos, Inc.).

of special interest and importance to the African American community might achieve a wide African American readership. The idea resulted in the creation of *Negro Digest*, a periodical containing both news reprints and feature articles. Of the latter, perhaps the most beneficial to circulation was Eleanor Roosevelt's contribution to the feature "If I Were a Negro."

Buoyed by success, Johnson decided to approach the market with yet another offering, a pictorial magazine patterned after *Life*. The first issue of *Ebony* sold out its press run of 25,000 copies and soon became a permanent staple in the world of journalism as large companies began to advertise regularly in it.

In addition to serving as publisher and chief executive officer of Johnson Publishing Company, Inc., Johnson is chairman and chief executive officer of Supreme Life Insurance Company, chairman of WJPC-AM in Chicago and president of Fashion Fair Cosmetics. He has served on the boards of directors of the Greyhound Corporation, Verex Corporation, Marina Bank, Supreme Life Insurance Company, and Zenith Radio Corporation. Johnson also serves as a trustee for the Art Institute of Chicago and United Negro College Fund; on the advisory council of the Harvard Graduate School of Business; as a director for the Chamber of Commerce of the United States; on the advertising council of Junior Achievement and Chicago USO. He has received honorary doctoral degrees from numerous colleges and universities and many honors and awards from civil and professional organizations.

In 1989, Johnson wrote *Succeeding Against the Odds: The Autobiography of a Great American Business.*

Robert L. Johnson (1946–)

Cable Television Executive, Publisher, Businessman

Born on April 8, 1946, in Hickory, Mississippi, Robert L. Johnson graduated from the University of Illinois in 1968 and earned a master's degree in public administration in 1972 from Princeton University. He worked for the Washington, DC-based Urban League, the Corporation for Public Broadcasting, and as a press secretary for the Honorable Walter E. Fauntroy, congressional delegate from the District of Columbia, before joining the National Cable Television Association in 1976.

While serving as vice president of government relations for the association, Johnson came up with the idea of creating a cable channel aimed at African American viewers. In 1979, he took out a $15,000 personal loan to start Black Entertainment Television (BET), a component of the parent company BET Holdings, Inc. As the founder, chairman, and chief executive officer, Johnson molded the station into an extremely popular 24-hour cable station with shows that cater to the interests of African Americans. It reaches over fifty million homes.

BET Holdings, Inc. also operates four other major cable channels: BET On Jazz: The Cable Station; BET On Jazz International, a 24-hour jazz program service that reaches more than two million domestic and one million international subscribers; BET Movies, the first 24-hour, all-black movie channel; and BET Action pay-per-view, which reaches ten million subscribers.

BET Holdings, Inc. has also ventured into other businesses outside of the cable industry including a publishing division responsible for the following publications: *Emerge: Black America's News Magazine; BET Weekend*, the nation's third largest black publication with more than 1.2 million readers; *Heart & Soul*, a health, fitness and beauty magazine; and *Arabesque Books*, the only line of original African American romance novels written by African American authors. Other businesses include: MSBET, an interactive website based upon a joint venture with Microsoft Corporation; BET Soundstage, a new music theme restaurant; BET Soundstage Club, a joint venture with Walt Disney World Resort at Disney's Pleasure Island in Orlando,

Florida; and BET On Jazz Restaurant, a fine dining restaurant specializing in new world cuisine.

In 1998, Johnson announced that he would soon be starting a venture to make low-budget films with African American stars, financed and produced by African Americans, and largely aimed at the African American urban market. His initial plans included showcasing three motion pictures and ten made-for-television films a year based on the Arabesque books.

In addition to running BET, Johnson is on the board of directors of US Airways, the Hilton Hotels Corporation, the United Negro College Fund, the National Cable Television Association's Academy of Cable Programming, the American Film Institute, and the Advertising Council. He has received the following major awards: the Business Leader of the Year award from the *Washingtonian* magazine (1998); *Broadcasting & Cable* magazine's Hall of Fame Award (1997); the Business of the Year Award by the Washington, DC. Chamber of Commerce (1985); and the Pioneer award by the Capitol Press Club (1984). Other awards include an NAACP Image Award, a Distinguished Alumni Award from Princeton University, and the President's Award from the National Cable Television Association.

Clarence B. Jones (1931–)
Publishing Executive

Born in Philadelphia in 1931, Jones graduated from Columbia University and Boston University Law School and then practiced as an attorney, specializing in civil rights and copyright cases for a New York City law firm. During this period, he was counsel for Dr. Martin Luther King, Jr. and the Southern Christian Leadership Conference. In 1968 and again in 1972, he served as a delegate from New York State to the Democratic Convention. Jones was also an observer at Attica prison during the uprising there in 1971.

In 1971, Jones, as head of Inner City Broadcasting, led a group of investors in the purchase of the New York *Amsterdam News*, the nation's largest African American newspaper. Inner City Broadcasting also owned radio station WLIB and has full ownership of WBLS-FM.

Tom Joyner (1949?–)
Radio Personality and Announcer

The jingle "oh, oh, oh, it's the Tom Joyner Morning Show" can be heard in over 95 markets on the four-hour syndicated radio program "The Tom Joyner Morning Show." Debuting in January of 1994 and hosted by Joyner, it is estimated that over five million listeners tune in daily. In addition, his show reaches more African Americans in the country than any other electronic media. Known as the "Fly Jock, the hardest working man in radio" because he simultaneously hosted the morning show on KKDA in Dallas and the afternoon show for WGCI in Chicago in the 1980s, Joyner keeps audiences captivated with his educational and entertaining material.

Regular program highlights include: "Little Known Black History Facts;" the "It's Your World" soap opera; "Melvin's Lovelines;" comedy bits and news from his co-hosts J. Anthony Brown, Myra J., Ms. Dupree, and Sybil Wilkes; political commentary by Tavis Smiley, host of "BET Tonight with Tavis Smiley;" and the "Old School Breakfast Mix," a music medley of soul classics tailored to Joyner's over-thirty—in particular baby-boomer—audience. In addition, there are the "Thursday Morning Mom" and "Real Fathers, Real Men" segments in which people can send in a tribute to an exceptional parent and win that person $500.

Entering radio by accident, Joyner received a job as a newscaster at an African American-owned station in Montgomery, Alabama, not too long after graduating from Tuskegee University. While employed at the station and under the tutelage of Tracy Larkin, he learned that radio needs to be involved in the community. One example of the power of community radio occurred in the early 1970s when Joyner took to the airways to let people know that civil rights activist Stokely Carmichael and his South African wife, Miriam Makeba, needed a ride to a rally in Selma, Alabama. The next day, an entire local entourage was ready to escort them. A more recent example of Joyner's community activism would include the voter registration drive that he and Tavis Smiley coordinated in 1996 that attracted approximately 250,000 African Americans. Through this effort, both gentlemen believe that these additional voters helped to reelect U.S. House members Cynthia McKinney of Georgia and Bennie Thompson of Mississippi after redistricting put them in political jeopardy.

As a graduate of a historically black university, Joyner recently teamed up with the United Negro College Fund and established the Tom Joyner Foundation, a nonprofit organization, to award scholarships throughout the school year to college students in need of financial support to complete their education. Each month, he announces the college or university that will be the beneficiary.

Joyner is the first African American to be elected to the Radio Hall of Fame. He was inducted in 1998.

Delano Lewis (1938–)
Business and Broadcasting Executive

Born in Arkansas City, Kansas on November 12, 1938, Delano Eugene Lewis grew up in Kansas City, Kansas.

He received his bachelor or arts degree in political science and history from the University of Kansas in 1960 and a law degree from the Washburn University School of Law in 1963. Fresh out of law school, Lewis became one of only ten African American attorneys in the U.S. Department of Justice in Washington, DC. After two years, he took a post with the Equal Employment Opportunity Commission (EEOC), and after only one year, in 1966, he volunteered for the Peace Corps and went to Nigeria and Uganda. Returning from Africa in 1969, Lewis worked as legislative assistant to various senators and congressmen and donated his time to advisory boards and community service organizations.

In 1973, Lewis left government and entered the private sector. He joined the Chesapeake and Potomac Telephone Company (C&P), a subsidiary of Bell Atlantic, as a public affairs manager in 1973. Subsequently, he held positions of increasing authority and responsibility, culminating in his election as president in July of 1988. In January of 1990, he became the chief executive officer. He then vaulted from the top of the telephone company to the role of president and chief executive officer of National Public Radio (NPR) in 1994. NPR, a membership organization of nearly six hundred public radio stations nationwide, produces and distributes the award-winning programs "All Things Considered," "Talk of the Nation," "Weekend Edition," and "NPR's Performance Today." His goal was to make NPR "the leading provider of high quality news, information and cultural programming worldwide." During his tenure, he focused on three areas: top quality programming, financial strength, and customer service.

After a four-year stint as the president and chief executive officer of NPR, Lewis resigned on August 1, 1998 to pursue other interests including teaching, lecturing, and writing a book about his experiences.

At the invitation of Vice President Al Gore, Lewis served as a co-chair of the National Information Infrastructure Advisory Council (NIIAC) from 1994 to 1996. Its members consisted of business, industry, academic, and local government leaders. The NIIAC provided recommendations to the Clinton Administration on how best to develop America's communications network for full citizen participation by 2000.

Lewis serves on many boards of directors, such as Colgate-Palmolive, Black Entertainment Tonight, Hallburton, and Guest Services, Inc. He is the chairman of the board of the Eugene and Agnes Meyer Foundation, an honorary member of Mainstream, a national board member of Africare, and an emeritus member of the board of the Washington Performing Arts Society. He was named "Man of the Year" by the Greater Washington Board of Trade in 1992, named "Washingtonian of the Year" by *Washingtonian* magazine in 1978, named to the Sovereign Military Order of Malta in 1987, and was awarded the President's Medal from Catholic University in 1978.

Samuel Logan, Jr. (1933–)
Newspaper Publisher

As the publisher of the oldest and largest African American newspaper in Michigan, Samuel Logan, Jr. was born on August 31, 1933, in Louisiana. Now in its 63rd year of publication, the *Michigan Chronicle* is owned by Sengstacke Enterprises, whose headquarters are in Chicago. The company also produces the daily *Chicago Defender*, the *New Pittsburgh Courier*, and the *Tri-State Defender* in Memphis, Tennessee.

Initially having worked in the cotton fields of Louisiana, Logan moved to Detroit where he found employment in a factory. During the Korean War, he volunteered as a paratrooper with the United States Army, 82nd Airborne Division. After four years of service, he was honorably discharged in 1956. Upon his return to the United States, three men influenced his life: Frank Seymour, who eventually became his role model, Tom Cleveland, and Robert Leatherwood, both owners of Detroit's first African American advertising agency. Logan applied for a position with Cleveland and Leatherwood's agency and was hired to work as a "boy Friday" for $32 a week.

Seymour eventually sold his share of his business to Logan, whose performance had been impressive, which made him a full partner. Later on, he worked as a sales representative with radio stations WCHB-AM and WCHD-FM, founded by another African American pioneer, Dr. Haley Bell. His last move occurred when he joined the *Michigan Chronicle* as assistant to then-advertising manager, the late Tremaine Shearer. Rising steadily through the ranks, he held the following positions over the years: advertising manager, advertising director, vice president of marketing, and general manager. On his way to the top, Logan took time to acquire a bachelor of arts degree in business administration from the University of Detroit, now the University of Detroit-Mercy, in 1973.

The *Michigan Chronicle* has been voted the best African American newspaper in the country several times by the National Newspaper Publishers Association. In addition, Logan is a member of the NAACP, the Urban League, the Michigan Historical Commission, and the Central Michigan University Scholarship Fund. He has received awards from the Metropolitan Youth Foundation, The Optimist Club of Central Detroit, Omega Psi Phi Fraternity, Inc., the State of Michigan-Minori-

Norma Quarles (AP/Wide World Photos, Inc.)

ty Enterprises, and a host of others. In 1993, he was also voted "Publisher of the Year."

John Henry Murphy (1840–1922)
Publisher

John Henry Murphy was born a slave in Baltimore, Maryland, in 1840. He became superintendent of Bethel African Methodist Episcopal Church and founded the Sunday school newspaper, the *Sunday School Helper*. In 1892 he purchased the *Baltimore Afro-American* for $200. By 1922 the *Afro-American* had reached a circulation of 14,000, becoming the largest African American newspaper in the Northeast.

At first, Murphy set the paper's type himself, having acquired this skill in his forties. Throughout, he insisted that his paper maintain political and editorial independence. Murphy died April 5, 1922. The paper grew and is now under the control of Murphy's great-nephew, John H. Murphy III.

Norma Quarles (1936–)
Television News Correspondent

Born in New York City in 1936, Norma Quarles is an alumna of Hunter College and City College of New York. She first worked as a buyer for a New York specialty shop before moving to Chicago where she became a licensed real estate broker.

In 1965 she began her broadcast career in Chicago at WSDM Radio, working as a news reporter and disc jockey. She later returned to New York where she joined NBC in 1966 for a one-year training program. After three years with WKYC-TV in Cleveland, she was transferred to WNBC-TV in 1970, anchoring the early local news broadcasts during the "Today" show. In 1978, Quarles moved to NBC News as a correspondent based in Chicago, in addition to producing and reporting the "Urban Journal" series for WMAQ-TV. In 1988 Quarles left NBC after 21 years to join Cable News Network's New York bureau. Quarles served as a daytime anchor at CNN until 1990, when she became a correspondent.

Quarles is a member of the National Academy of Television Arts and Sciences, National Association of Broadcast Journalists, Sigma Delta Chi, and a board member of the Governor's National Academy of Television Arts and Sciences. In 1990, Quarles was inducted into the National Association of Black Journalists Hall of Fame.

Dudley Randall (1914–)
Publisher, Poet, Librarian

Dudley Randall was born in Washington, DC, on January 14, 1914, and was living in Detroit by the time he was nine years old. An early harbinger of Randall's poetic talent was the appearance of one of his poems in the *Detroit Free Press* at the early age of thirteen. After serving in the U.S. Army Signal Corps (1942–1946), Randall worked in the foundry at the Ford Motor Company and as a postal carrier and clerk while attending Wayne State University in Detroit. He received his bachelor of arts degree in 1949 and a master of arts degree in library science from the University of Michigan in 1951. He also did graduate work at the University of Ghana.

Randall worked in progressively responsible librarian positions at Lincoln University in Jefferson City, Missouri (1951 to 1954), Morgan State College in Baltimore, Maryland (1954 to 1956), and the Wayne County Federated Library System in Wayne, Michigan (1956 to 1969). From 1969 to 1975, he was a reference librarian and poet-in-residence at the University of Detroit. In 1969, he also served as a visiting lecturer at the University of Michigan.

Randall's love of poetry led to his founding of the *Broadside Press* in 1965. He wanted to make sure that African Americans had an outlet to "speak to and for their people." His works include *On Getting a Natural*

(1969) and *A Litany of Friends: New and Selected Poems* (1981). He retired from Broadside Press in 1993; however, it continues to publish new works. In 1980, he founded the Broadside Poets Theater and the Broadside Poetry Workshop.

Randall has been active in many Detroit cultural organizations and institutions including the Detroit Council for the Arts and the International Afro-American Museum in Detroit, now the Charles H. Wright Museum of African American History. In 1981, Randall received the Creative Artist Award in Literature from the Michigan Council for the Arts and in 1986, he was named the first poet laureate of Detroit by the late Mayor Coleman A. Young.

William J. Raspberry (1935–)

Commentator, Journalist

Born in Okolona, Mississippi, on October 12, 1935, Raspberry received his bachelor of science degree in history from Indiana Central College in 1958. While a student, he worked at the *Indianapolis Recorder* as a reporter, photographer, and editorial writer from 1956 through 1960. In 1960, Raspberry was drafted by the Army and served as a public information officer until his discharge in 1962. He began working for the *Washington Post* as a teletypist and soon worked his way up to reporter, assistant city editor, and finally a columnist in 1966. He continues writing today as a nationally syndicated columnist, appearing in 225 newspapers. Raspberry also teaches at Duke University, serving in the Knight Chair in Communications and Journalism.

Raspberry has also appeared as a television panelist and commentator and in 1965 was named Journalist of the Year by the Capital Press Club for his coverage of the Los Angeles Watts riot. In 1967, he received a Citation of Merit in Journalism from Lincoln University in Jefferson, Missouri, for distinction in improving human relations. He is generally regarded as an independent thinker, holding to no particular orthodoxy. His book *Looking Backward at Us*, published in 1991, is very similar to his other writings in that it deals with issues concerning the African American experience and social conditions and race relations in the United States.

Raspberry has taught journalism at Howard University and the University of Maryland School of Journalism. He is also a member of the Poynter Institute for Media Studies board of advisors and the Pulitzer Prize Board, Grid Iron Club, Capitol Press Club, Washington Association of Black Journalists, and Kappa Alpha Psi. Raspberry won the Pulitzer Prize in 1994 for Distinguished Commentary and the Lifetime Achievement Award from the National Association of Black Journalists (NABJ). In 1997, he was named one of the fifty most influential journalists in the national press corps by the *Washingtonian* magazine. In addition, he has been awarded honorary doctorates by 15 educational institutions.

William Raspberry (The Washington Post Writers Group)

Max Robinson (1939–1988)

Television News Correspondent

Born in Richmond, Virginia, on May 1, 1939, Max Robinson attended Oberlin College, Virginia Union University, and Indiana University. He began his career as a newsreader at WTOV-TV in Portsmouth, Virginia. In 1965, he worked as a studio floor director at WTOP-TV (now WUSA) in Washington, DC, before moving on to WRC-TV to work as a news reporter, and to WTOP-TV, where he worked as anchor.

In 1978, Robinson joined ABC "World News Tonight," becoming the first African American network anchor. Almost immediately, Robinson took it upon himself to fight racism at whatever cost necessary. ABC management became frustrated with Robinson and moved him to the post of weekend anchor. In 1983, Robinson left ABC for WMAQ-TV in Chicago, where he remained until 1985.

Robinson died of complications from acquired immune deficiency syndrome (AIDS) on December 20, 1988, in Washington, DC. He was the recipient of three

Emmy awards, the Capital Press Club Journalist of the Year Award, and the Ohio State Award, as well as an award from the National Education Association. He also taught at Federal City College, in Washington, DC, and the College of William and Mary in Williamsburg, Virginia.

Al Roker (1954–)
Weathercaster, Feature Reporter, Entrepreneur

Delighting visitors from across the country on the sidewalks outside of Studio 1-A with his humor, honesty, outgoing personality, and witty comments, Al Roker is the full-time weatherman for NBC's "Today" show and the weathercaster for News Channel 4's "Live at Five."

Born Albert Lincoln Roker on August 20, 1954, in New York, New York, Roker began his broadcasting career while still in college by landing a job as a weekend weatherman at WTVH-TV in Syracuse, New York, in 1974. After receiving a bachelor of arts degree in communications from the State University of New York at Oswego in 1976, he moved on to weathercasting jobs in Washington, DC (1976–1978) and Cleveland, Ohio (1978–1983), before becoming the weekend weathercaster at WNBC in New York in 1983. In 1998, his alma mater awarded him an honorary doctorate.

Besides his weathercasting duties, this six-time Emmy Award winner conducts celebrity interviews, cooking segments, and technology updates. Since 1985, he has hosted the annual "Christmas at Rockefeller Center" celebration. He has also co-hosted "The Macy's Thanksgiving Day Parade" and "The Rose Bowl Parade."

In 1994, Roker ventured into the world of entrepreneurship by creating Al Roker Productions, Inc. The multimedia company is involved in the development and production of network, cable, home video, and public televison projects. Two of the most successful projects include the critically acclaimed special on PBS about severe weather "Savage Skies" and a highly rated travel series called "Going Places." His website allows visitors to receive up-to-the-minute weather forecasts, peruse Roker's thoughts on a variety of subjects, laugh at his daily cartoon, write to him, and challenge the mind with some brain-twisting trivia. Another business venture, RokerWare, Inc., is a trademark line of merchandise all personally designed by Roker. Inspired by the recent birth of his baby girl, Roker introduced the WeatherBabies line as part of RokerWare, where fans can purchase a baby bib or baby t-shirt.

As an active member of the community, Roker has been honored by many civic and charitable organizations for his professional and community-minded activities and contributions. These include the Children's Defense Fund, the National Urban League Rainforest Alliance, Read Across America, the Arthur Ashe Institute for Urban Health, the Ronald McDonald House, the Hale House, and the Harlem Boys Choir. In addition, he is currently a member of the board of directors of Family AIDS Network and serves as honorary chair for the Susan G. Komen Breast Cancer Foundation Race for the Cure/Three Miles of Men.

Al Roker (AP/Wide World Photos, Inc.)

Carl Thomas Rowan (1925–)
Commentator, Journalist

Carl Rowan was born August 11, 1925 in Ravenscroft, Tennessee. He attended Tennessee A&I (now Tennessee State University) in Nashville and Washburn University in Topeka, Kansas. He received his bachelor of arts degree in mathematics from Oberlin College in 1947 and a master of arts degree in journalism from the University of Minnesota in 1948.

In 1948, Rowan went to work as a copyeditor, then later as a staff writer, for the *Minneapolis Tribune*, where he worked until 1961. In 1961, he was hired by the U. S. Department of State as deputy assistant secretary for public affairs. After three years with the Department of State, Rowan was appointed U. S. ambassador to

Carl Rowan (AP/Wide World Photos, Inc.)

Finland by President Lyndon Johnson in 1963, and in 1964 he was appointed director of the United States Information Agency (USIA), which operates overseas educational and cultural programs including the worldwide radio service "Voice of America." In 1965, Rowan resigned from the USIA to work as a columnist for the *Chicago Sun Times*.

Rowan has authored several books including *South of Freedom, Wait Till Next Year, Just Between Us Blacks, Dream Makers, Dream Breakers: The World of Justice Thurgood Marshall*, and a memoir entitled *Breaking Barriers*. He received the Alfred I. DuPont-Columbia University Silver Baton in 1987 for the television documentary "Thurgood Marshall: The Man." Rowan is a syndicated columnist and his work appears in numerous newspapers across the country.

Rowan has served as a political commentator for the Post-Newsweek Broadcasting Company and has been a frequent panelist on the NBC program "Meet the Press" and the syndicated programs "Agronsky & Co" and "Inside Washington."

Rowan is the founder of the Project Excellence program, a scholarship program for African American high school students. Scholarships are awarded to students who embrace academic achievement and resist negative peer pressure. Since its inception, the program has awarded more than $52 million in scholarships to more than 2,150 high school graduates.

In 1998, Rowan received the prestigious Victory Award from the National Rehabilitation Hospital in Washington, DC, for overcoming one of the biggest obstacles in his life—that of walking again after having his right leg amputated just below the knee because of a severe foot infection brought on by complications from diabetes. Established in 1986, the award is given to honor individuals who have coped with physical adversity in an exemplary way.

John B. Russwurm (1799–1851)
Newspaper Publisher

Born in Port Antonio, Jamaica, on October 1, 1799, Russwurm graduated from Bowdoin College in Brunswick, Maine in 1826. From Brunswick, Russwurm moved to New York, where on March 16, 1827, he and Samuel E. Cornish published the first edition of *Freedom's Journal*—the nation's first African American newspaper.

In 1829, Russwurm decided to immigrate to Monrovia, Liberia. From 1830 to 1835, he published the *Liberia Herald*. Cornish, who had left the paper in late 1827, resumed his role as editor in 1830, publishing the paper under the name *Rights of All*.

Russwurm went on to serve as superintendent of education in Monrovia and later as governor of a settlement. He died June 17, 1851.

John Herman Henry Sengstacke (1912–1997)
Publishing Executive

A nephew of the great publisher Robert Abbott, John Sengstacke was born in Savannah, Georgia, on November 25, 1912. He received a bachelor of arts degree from Hampton Institute, now Hampton University, in 1934. Upon graduation, he went to work with Robert Abbott, attended school to learn printing, and wrote editorials and articles for three Abbott papers. In 1934, he became vice president and general manager of the company.

During World War II, Sengstacke was an advisor to the U. S. Office of War Information during a period of severe tension between the government and the African American press. He also presided over the Chicago rationing board.

In 1940, after the death of his uncle, Sengstacke became president of the Robert S. Abbott Publishing Company. In 1956, Sengstacke founded the *Daily Defender*, one of only three African American dailies in the country. In 1940, he founded the Negro Newspaper Publishers' Association, now known as the National Newspaper Publishers Association, and served six terms as president. It is comprised of over two hundred African American newspapers. He was president of Tri-State Defender, Inc., Florida Courier Publishing Compa-

John Brown Russwurm (The Granger Collection Ltd.)

ny, New Pittsburgh Courier Publishing Company, Amalgamated Publishers, Inc., chairman of the Michigan Chronicle Publishing Company and Sengstacke Enterprises, Inc., and treasurer of Chicago Defender Charities, Inc.

Prior to his death on May 28, 1997, after an extended illness, Sengstacke served in leadership positions with many professional, educational, and civic organizations, received a number of presidential appointments, and was the recipient of several academic awards. He held the position of trustee at Bethune-Cookman College and chairman of the board at Provident Hospital and the Training School Association. He was a member of the board of directors of the American Society of Newspaper Editors, on the advisory board of the Boy Scouts of America, and a principal in Chicago United.

Bernard Shaw (1940–)

Television News Anchor

Bernard Shaw was born on May 22, 1940, in Chicago. He is the principal Washington anchor for "NewsStand: CNN & Time," a weekly primetime investigative newsmagazine on the Cable News Network (CNN). He also co-anchors "Inside Politics," the nation's only daily program devoted exclusively to political news. Shaw has been on board as the Washington anchor since the cable network went on the air on June 1, 1980. He has often reported first-hand on major international news stories. His reporting has taken him to 46 countries spanning five continents. The awards, honors, and accolades that Shaw has received over the years for his outstanding journalistic aptitude are too numerous to recount.

Bernard Shaw holding an Ace Award (AP/Wide World Photos, Inc.).

Shaw was present when the Chinese government's tanks rolled into Tiananmen Square in May of 1989, crushing the student-led pro-democracy movement. In January of 1991, Shaw, along with two other colleagues from CNN, were stranded in Baghdad when allied bombing attacks launched Operation Desert Storm. From their hotel room, Shaw and the others provided first-hand accounts of the bombing of the city. Shaw covered the outbreak of the Gulf War and the bombing of the Alfred P. Murrah Federal Building in Oklahoma City, Oklahoma, the worst act of terrorism in U.S. history.

As a result of his comprehensive coverage of "Operation Desert Storm," Shaw received numerous international, as well as national, awards and honors. In July of 1991, he received the Eduard Rhein Foundation's Cultural Journalistic Award, marking the first time that the foundation has presented this award to a non-German. In October of 1992, the Italian government honored him with its President's Award, presented to those leaders who have actively contributed to development, innovation, and cooperation. In December of the same year, Shaw was the recipient of the coveted David Brinkley Award for excellence in communication from Barry University.

Shaw's first job as a television journalist came in 1971 with CBS News at their Washington bureau where he conducted an exclusive interview with Attorney General John Mitchell at the height of the Watergate scandal. In 1977 he left CBS to join ABC News as Miami bureau chief and Latin American correspondent. Shaw was one of the first reporters to film from location on the Jonestown massacre story in Guyana, and his team provided the only aerial photos of the mass suicide-murder site. ABC sent Shaw to Iran to report on the 1979 hostage crisis at the American embassy in Teheran. He then returned to Washington as ABC's senior Capitol Hill correspondent.

Prior to joining CBS News, Shaw was a reporter for Group W, a Westinghouse Broadcasting Company, based first in Chicago and then in Washington (1966–1971). Shaw served as Group W's White House correspondent during the last year of the Johnson Administration (1968). His other assignments included local and national urban affairs, the struggles of the Mexican Americans and Puerto Ricans, and the plight of the American Indians in Billings, Montana. In 1968, he reported on the aftermath of the assassination of Dr. Martin Luther King, Jr. in Memphis and his funeral in Atlanta.

Shaw has been elected a Fellow of the Society of Professional Journalists (SPJ), the highest distinction the society gives to journalists for public service. In June of 1995, he was inducted into the SPJ Hall of Fame. In October of 1996, he received the Paul White Life Achievement Award from the Radio Television News Directors' Association, one of the industry's most coveted awards. One month later, he and his co-anchor Judy Woodruff garnered the 1996 ACE for Best Newscaster of the Year for "Inside Politics." In April of 1997, he was inducted into the Chicago Journalists Hall of Fame. In September of 1997, he was the inaugural recipient of the Congressional Medal of Honor Society's Tex McCrary Award for journalism, which honors the distinguished achievements of those in the field of journalism.

Carole Simpson (1940–)

Television News Anchor

Born on December 7, 1940, Carole Simpson graduated from the University of Michigan with a bachelor of arts degree in journalism and did graduate work in journalism at the University of Iowa. She first entered broadcasting in 1965 as a reporter for a local radio station, WCFL, in Morris, Illinois. In 1968, she moved to radio station WBBM in Chicago and in 1970, she went to work as a reporter for the Chicago television station WMAQ.

Carole Simpson (AP/Wide World Photos, Inc.)

Simpson made her first network appearance as a substitute anchor for NBC "Nightly News" in 1974 and as anchor on NBC's "Newsbreak" on weekends. In 1982, Simpson joined ABC in Washington as a general assignment correspondent. She is currently the anchor of "World News Sunday" and an Emmy Award-winning senior correspondent for "ABC News." She reports most frequently on family and social issues for "World News Tonight With Peter Jennings." Her reports have also appeared on "20/20," "Nightline," and other ABC news broadcasts and specials. She is an occasional contributor to "This Week" and has substituted for Peter Jennings on "World News Tonight."

Simpson has served as president of the Radio and Television Correspondents Association, as chairperson of the ABC Women's Advisory Board, and as a member of the board of directors of the Washington chapter of the Society of Professional Journalists. She is also a member of Theta Sigma Phi, the Radio Television News Directors Association, and the National Association of Black Journalists. She has been awarded the Media Journalism Award, the Milestone Award in broadcast journalism from the National Commission of Working Women, the Turner Broadcasting "Trumpet" Award for scholastic achievement, the Leonard Zeidenberg First Amendment Award from Radio and Television News Director Foundation, and the Silver Bell Award from the Ad Council. She was inducted into the University of Iowa Communications Hall of Fame and received the University of Missouri's distinguished journalist award. In 1992, she was named Journalist of the Year by the National Association of Black Journalists. She has established several college scholarships for women and minorities pursuing careers in broadcast journalism at the University of Michigan, as well as the Carole Simpson scholarship administered by the Radio and Television News Directors Foundation (RTNDF).

Tavis Smiley (1964–)

Host, Executive Producer, Political Commentator

Recognized for his tough interviewing tactics and strong emphasis on issues relevant to the African American community, *Time*selected Tavis Smiley as one of America's fifty most promising young leaders under the age of forty. *Ebony* profiled him as one of Black America's future leaders. *Newsweek* crowned him as among "20 people changing how Americans get their news" and dubbed him one of the nation's "captains of the airwaves." The accolades for the innumerable talents of Tavis Smiley, host of "BET Tonight with Tavis Smiley," a live one-hour news and entertainment program on Black Entertainment Television (BET), are endless.

Smiley, born on September 13, 1964 in Gulfport, Mississippi, is the author of *On Air: The Best of Tavis Smiley on the Tom Joyner Morning Show* and the critically acclaimed book *Hard Left: Straight Talk About the Wrongs of the Right.* Twice a week, he offers political commentary on the "Tom Joyner Morning Show," a nationally syndicated radio show. In this role, Smiley led several national radio campaigns which influenced national events, such as Fox Television's decision to return "Living Single" to the lineup, Christie's auction house donation of slavery artifacts to an African American museum, the Katz Radio Group's increased media buys on African American and Hispanic radio, and the honoring of Rosa Parks with the Congressional Medal. In addition to his other on-air roles, Smiley serves as a political analyst on CNN.

Smiley received a bachelor of arts degree in law and public policy at Indiana University in 1986. In 1988, he went to Los Angeles to work for the city's first African American mayor, Tom Bradley. In 1991, he started doing radio segment "The Smiley Report," which became so popular that it was nationally syndicated a year later. His popularity spread even further when he signed on as the political commentator on the "Tom Joyner Morning Show." The position was initially designed as a temporary assignment to help Joyner register people to vote. Smiley's few moments on the air were such a success that Joyner extended an invitation to him to regularly comment on the issues of the day.

Smiley is the recipient of the Mickey Leland Humanitarian Award, NAMIC (1998) and the NAACP Image Award for news, talk or information series (1999). He maintains memberships with Kappa Alpha Psi Fraternity, Inc., the National Association of Black Journalists, NAACP, and the American Federation of Television and Radio Artists (AFTRA).

Barbara Smith (1946–)

Publisher, Editor, Writer

Barbara Smith was born on November 16, 1946, in Cleveland, Ohio. She earned a bachelor of arts degree from Mount Holyoke College in 1969 and a master's degree from the University of Pittsburgh in 1971. She served as an instructor at the University of Massachusetts from 1976 until 1981, Barnard College in 1983, and New York University in 1985. Together with Myrna Bain, Cherríe Moraga, and Mariana Romo-Carmona, Smith operates Kitchen Table: Women of Color Press, the first publisher in the United States committed to publishing and distributing the work of Third World women.

Smith has co-authored and co-edited numerous books including *Yours in Struggle, Three Feminist Perspectives on Anti-Semitism and Racism, Home Girls, A Black Feminist Anthology,* and *But Some of Us Are Brave, Black Women's Studies.*

Chuck Stone (1924–)

Journalist, Educator

Chuck Stone was born in 1924 into a family that initially lived in luxurious surroundings due to his father's executive position with a hair care company; however, alcoholism resulted in divorce and Stone's mother moved him and his three younger sisters to Connecticut. After high school, he enrolled in the famed Tuskegee training program for African American bomber pilots during World War II and became a navigator with the U.S. Air Corps. After the war's end, Stone earned degrees from Wesleyan University and the University of Chicago, and for a time worked with an international development agency in Africa.

In 1959, Stone entered the profession of journalism after being hired at the *New York Age*, a Harlem paper. Within a short time, he had become its editor, as well as launched a career noted for his outspoken opinions. During the early 1960s, he became the White House correspondent for the *Washington Afro-American*, for which he often wrote critically of the Kennedy Administration's lack of progress on civil rights issues.

In 1965, Stone joined the staff of Adam Clayton Powell, Jr., the controversial Harlem activist who was then serving as a member of the U.S. House of Representatives. When Powell's political career ended amid charges of misuse of public funds two years later, Stone channeled his feelings of anger toward the white political establishment in the fictional chronicle of Powell, *King Strut.* It would be Stone's third book, after the 1968 collection of his newspaper columns, *Tell It Like It Is* and *Black Political Power in America* (1970).

Stone became a regular columnist for the *Philadelphia Daily News* in 1972 and spent the next several years lambasting the city's corrupt political machinery and heavy-handed police force. Equal in his criticisms unleashed first at the administration of former cop Frank Rizzo, and later at the city's first African American mayor, Wilson Goode, Stone's columns—which continued after he became senior editor in 1979—made him both a revered and feared civic personage. In an unusual development, his condemnations of police brutality toward Philadelphia's African American citizenry often prompted suspects to turn themselves in at the columnist's home or office first and wait for authorities to arrest them there.

After nearly two decades, Stone resigned from the *Philadelphia Daily News* to further pursue his career in academia. In 1991, he became the Walter Spearman Professor at the University of North Carolina at Chapel Hill's School of Journalism and Mass Communication. His column continues to be syndicated nationally in over one hundred newspapers, and in the spring of 1996 Stone was honored with the Missouri Honor Medal for Distinguished Service in Journalism from the University of Missouri. He joined an impressive roster of past recipients that included Walter Cronkite and Charlayne Hunter-Gault. Stone was also selected to be a torch carrier for the Olympic flame that journeyed across the nation before the opening of the 1996 Summer Games in Atlanta, Georgia.

Pierre Monte Sutton (1947–)

Broadcast Executive

Pierre Sutton is president of Inner City Broadcasting Corporation in New York City and president of its radio stations in New York and California. He is the son of Percy E. Sutton, chairman of the board of Inner City Broadcasting and former borough president of Manhattan. Inner City Broadcasting has several divisions including Inner City Cable, Inner City Artists Management, and Inner City Broadcasting Corporation-Television (ICBC-TV). ICBC-TV produces "Showtime at the Apollo," "Apollo Comedy Hour," and "New Music Report."

Susan Taylor (AP/Wide World Photos, Inc.)

Pierre Sutton was born in New York City on February 1, 1947. He received a bachelor of arts degree from the University of Toledo in 1968. Sutton began his career in 1971 as vice president of Inner City Research and Analysis Corporation, became executive editor of the *New York Courier* newspaper in 1971–1972, later served a public affairs director for WLIB radio from 1972 to 1975, was promoted to vice president of Inner City Broadcasting from 1975 to 1977, and eventually became president in 1977. He has served as a board member of the Minority Investment Fund, first vice president of the National Association of Black Owned Broadcasters, chairman of the Harlem Boy Scouts, member of the board and executive committee of the New York City Marathon, trustee of the Alvin Ailey Dance Foundation, board member of the Better Business Bureau of Harlem, and member of the board of the Hayden Planetarium.

Susan L. Taylor (1946–)

Editor

Susan Taylor was born in New York City on January 23, 1946 and received a bachelor of arts degree from Fordham University. Since 1980, Susan Taylor has been editor-in-chief of *Essence*, a magazine established in

Lemuel Tucker (AP/Wide World Photos, Inc.)

1970 for African American women. The publication has a monthly circulation of one million and a readership of 7.6 million—29% of which is male.

A former actress, cosmetologist, and founder of her own cosmetics company, Nequai Cosmetics, Taylor began her relationship with *Essence* magazine as a freelance writer. In 1971, she became the magazine's beauty and fashion editor. She held this position until 1980. Taylor, as editor-in-chief, is also executive coordinator of Essence Communications, Inc. (ECI). ECI is a major investor in Amistad Press, an African American-owned book publishing company. The company also has a licensing division that includes Essence Hosery, Essence Eyewear, and Essence Collection by Butterick. Essence Art Reproductions, a distributor of fine art created by African American artists; Essence Television Productions, Inc., producer of the Essence Awards, an annual salute to distinguished African Americans; and the Essence Music Festival, a three-day festival of cultural celebrations and empowerment seminars, also fall under the ECI umbrella.

Taylor is author of the "In the Spirit" column in *Essence* magazine. In 1993, she wrote a book entitled *In the Spirit: The Inspirational Writings of Susan L. Taylor*, a collection of inspirational essays named for and taken from her monthly Essence column. *In the Spirit* has sold over 350,000 copies since its publication. Her most recent book is *Lessons in Living.*

Lemuel Tucker (1938–1991)
Television News Correspondent

Born in 1938 in Saginaw, Michigan, Lemuel Tucker was a graduate of Central Michigan University. Tucker worked as a Washington bureau correspondent for CBS news from 1977 until 1988. Prior to that he was with ABC News as New York City correspondent, from 1972 until 1977. From 1965 through 1972, Tucker was with NBC News where he served for some of that time as assistant bureau chief in Vietnam. He was awarded an Emmy for his reporting on hunger in the United States, a series of seven reports broadcast during 1968 and 1969. He died in March of 1991 in Washington, DC.

Montel Williams (1956–)
Talk Show Host

A former naval intelligence officer who first gained prominence delivering highly-charged, popular motivational speeches to millions of children around the country, Montel Williams is now a talk show host with a non-traditional background. He began his professional career in the U.S. Marine Corps in 1974. In 1976, Williams became the first African American to attend the prestigious Naval Academy Prep School. At Annapolis, he studied Mandarin Chinese and graduated with a degree in general engineering. He has won numerous awards and distinctions over the course of his long and varied naval career including the Armed Forces Expeditionary Medal and two Meritorious Service Medals.

In 1988, Williams began informally counseling the wives and families of the servicemen in his command. He was later asked to speak to a local group of kids in Kansas City, Missouri, about the importance of leadership and overcoming obstacles. Thus, began his career in motivational speaking. Now, his daily hour-long talk show "The Montel Williams Show" is in its seventh season.

Williams's commitment to making a difference has resulted in his finding solutions to problems by tackling them. Through several episodes last year, "The Montel Williams Show" stressed the importance of AIDS education in communities across the country. As a result of the show's ongoing coverage of the AIDS epidemic, the White House Office of National AIDS Policy invited Williams to produce several public service announcements on AIDS prevention. In addition, his After-Care Program arranges for guests to attend psychological treatment, motivational camps, drug and alcohol rehabilitation, and treatment for eating disorders.

Montel Williams holding a Crystal Apple Award in 1996 (AP/ Wide World Photos, Inc.).

Oprah Winfrey (Archive Photos, Inc)

A recipient of several daytime Emmy awards—the most recent in 1996 for outstanding talk show host—"The Montel Williams Show" has been honored with several humanitarian awards. The Entertainment Industry Council, Inc. and the National Institute on Drug Abuse/National Institutes of Health presented the show with a PRISM Commendation for the episode "What Parents Need to Know about Teens and Drugs." The foundation of American Women in Radio and Television granted the show an honorable mention Gracie Award in recognition for excellence in programming for the positive and realistic portrayal of women. The show also received the Nancy Susan Reynolds Award for the episode "Teenagers Living with AIDS" and the Silver Angel Award for the episode "The Life and Times of Mother Theresa."

Oprah Winfrey (1954–)

Television Talk Show Host, Actress, Producer

Oprah Winfrey's rise to fame is an inspiring tale. She was born on January 29, 1954, in Kosciusko, Mississippi. Her name was supposed to have been "Orpah" after a biblical figure in the book of Ruth; sources vary as to the origin of the misspelling.

Winfrey was a precocious child who asked her kindergarten teacher to advance her to the first grade; she also skipped the second grade. Her parents, who were not married, separated when she was very young and sent her to live with her grandparents. At the age of six, Winfrey sent to Milwaukee to live with her mother. From the time that she was nine years old, she suffered sexual abuse at the hands of male family members and acquaintances; these events, which she did not discuss publicly until the 1980s, have had a profound effect on her life.

When she was 14 years old, Winfrey went to live with her father in Nashville, Tennessee, and it was there that she got her life back on track. Her father insisted on hard work and discipline as a means of self-improvement, and Winfrey complied, winning a college scholarship that allowed her to attend Tennessee State University. In 1971, she began working part-time as a radio announcer for WVOL in Nashville. Two years later, after receiving a bachelor of arts degree, she became a reporter at WTVF-TV in Nashville. From 1976 to 1983, she lived in Baltimore, working for the ABC affiliate WJZ-TV, progressing from news anchor to co-host of the popular show "People Are Talking." In 1984, she moved to Chicago and took over the ailing morning show "A.M. Chicago." By September of the next year, the show was so successful that it was expanded to an hour format and renamed "The Oprah Winfrey Show." Now in syndication across the country, "The Oprah Winfrey Show" is one of the most popular television programs in history. In 1986, Oprah founded Harpo, Inc., her own production company ("Harpo" is "Oprah" spelled backwards). As such, she is the first African American woman to host a nationally syndicated weekday show, own and produce her own television show, and own a film and a television production company.

A talented actress, Winfrey has appeared in the motion pictures *The Color Purple* (1985), *Native Son* (1986), and *Beloved* (1998). She has also appeared in the television movies *The Women of Brewster Place* (1989), *There Are No Children Here* (1993), and *Before Women Had Wings* (1997). As a producer, Winfrey has presented several television and movie specials, most notably *David and Lisa* (1998) and *The Wedding* (1998), both based on novels.

As a former victim of child abuse, Winfrey is a strong advocate of children's rights. When she heard the tragic story of a four-year-old Chicago girl's molestation and murder, she proposed federal child protection legislation designed to keep nationwide records on convicted child abusers. Her efforts on behalf of abused and neglected children came to fruition on December 20, 1993, when President Clinton signed the "Oprah Bill," a law designed to protect children from abuse.

"The Oprah Winfrey Show," now in its thirteenth season of syndication, continues to be the number one talk show on the air and broadcasts in over 130 international territories. It was recently renewed through the year 2000 in over 99 percent of the country, including the top ten markets, and through 2002 in 91 percent of the country. Reaching over twenty million homes a day, "The Oprah Winfrey Show" continues to enlighten, educate, and entertain viewers. In 1998, the show unveiled a new set; premiered a new theme song "Run On With Oprah" performed by Winfrey herself; and embarked on a new type of programming called "Change Your Life TV," designed to inspire viewers to make small adjustments so that they can create big results in their lives. In the spirit of her "Change Your Life TV" programming, she recently launched a website to empower viewers by enabling them to access the experts and use the information and advice offered on the show.

Famous for her candor, forthrightness, and willingness to go the distance, Winfrey successfully won a $12 million slander suit brought against her by Texas cattlemen in 1998. The cattlemen took Winfrey to court over a 1996 show in which one of her guests, an anti-meat activist, suggested that American beef industry practices could cause BSE, or mad cow disease. The cattlemen claimed that because of her influence with viewers, beef prices immediately slumped to a ten-year low. The jury of eight women and four men deliberated close to six hours before rejecting all claims brought by the cattlemen.

Winfrey continues to win numerous awards for her work in television and film. Recent accomplishments include receipt of the Horatio Alger Award in 1993 and induction into the Television Hall of Fame in 1994. At the end of the 1995–1996 television season, she received the George Foster Peabody Individual Achievement Award, one of broadcasting's most coveted awards. She was named among "America's 25 Most Influential People of 1996" by *Time* magazine and favorite female television performer at the 1997 and 1998 People's Choice Awards. She also received a Daytime Emmy Award for outstanding talk/service show host—one of many—in 1998. Earlier this year, she was nominated for an Image Award by the NAACP for outstanding lead actress in a motion picture for her portrayal of Sethe in *Beloved*.

◆ PRINT AND BROADCAST MEDIA

Publishers

Afram Press
PO Box 2262
Philadelphia, PA 19101
(610) 871-6992

Africa Fund
17 John St., 12th Fl.
New York, NY 10038
(212) 962-1210
Fax: (212) 964-8570

Africa World Press, Inc.
PO Box 1892
Trenton, NJ 08607
(609) 844-9583
Fax: (609) 844-0198

African-American Institute
380 Lexington Ave.
New York, NY 10168
(212) 949-5666
Fax: (212) 682-6174

African and Caribbean Imprint Library Services
236 Main St.
Falmouth, MA 02540
(508)540-5378
Fax: (508) 548-6801

African Studies Association Press
Credit Union Bldg.
Emory University
Atlanta, GA 30322
(404) 329-6410
Fax: (404) 329-6433

Africana Publishing Co.
160 Broadway, East Bldg.
New York, NY 10038
(212) 374-0100
Fax: (212) 374-1313

Afro-Am Publishing/Distributing Co., Inc.
1909 W. 95th St.
Chicago, IL 60643
(312)791-1611

Akili Books of America
PO Box 1291
South Gate, CA 90280
(213) 635-7191

Amen-Ra Publishing Co.
PO Box 328642
Columbus, OH 43232
(614)863-5189
Fax: (614) 445-8373

Ankh Enterprises
7850 Sunset Blvd., No. 105
Los Angeles, CA 90046
(213)850-7203

Arts and Communications Network Inc.
PO Box 435
Rosendale, NY 12472
(914) 687-0767
Fax: (914) 687-0267

Asante Publications
218 Main St., No. 425
Kirkland, WA 98033-6199
(619) 287-7926

Associated Publishers, Inc.
1407 14th St., NW
Washington, DC 20005-3704
(202) 265-1441
Fax: (202) 328-8677

Association of Caribbean Universities and Research Institutes
PO Box 11532
Caparra Heights Station
San Juan, Puerto Rico 00922
(809) 764-0000

Aye-Aye Press
31 Queen St.
PO Box 1122
Christiansted, VI 00821
(809) 778-8465
Fax: (809) 778-8465

Balamp Publishing
4205 Fullerton
Detroit, MI 48238
(313) 491-1950

Beckham House Publishers Group, Inc.
PO Box 4066
Silver Spring, MD 20914
(301) 384-7995
Fax: (301) 384-7995

Benin Press Ltd.
5225 S. Blackstone Ave.
Chicago, IL 60615
(312) 643-2363

Benin Publishing Co.
802 Columbus Dr.
Teaneck, NJ 07666
(201) 837-8641

Black Classic Press
PO Box 13414
Baltimore, MD 21203
(410) 358-0980
Fax: (410) 358-0987

Black Economic Research Team Inc.
PO Box 13513
Baltimore, MD 21203
(410) 366-7668

Black Entrepreneurs Press
4502 S. Congress Ave., Ste. 254
Austin, TX 78744
(512) 444-9962

Black Graphics International
PO Box 732, Linwood Station
Detroit, MI 48206
(313) 890-1128

Black Resource Guide, Inc.
501 Oneida Pl., NW
Washington, DC 20011
(202) 291-4373
Fax: (202) 291-4373

Blacklight Fellowship
128 S. Paulina St.
Chicago, IL 60612
(312) 563-0081
Fax: (312) 563-0086

Broadside Press
PO Box 04257
Detroit, MI 48204
(313) 963-8526
Fax: (313) 934-1231

Calaloux Publications
PO Box 812028
Wellesley, MA 02181-0012
(617) 237-2230

Carib House (USA)
11305 Goleta St.
Los Angeles, CA 91342
(818) 890-1056
Fax: (818) 897-7280

Carver Publishing, Inc.
PO Box 9353
Hampton, VA 23670-0353
(804) 838-1244

Charill Publishers
4468 San Francisco Ave.
St. Louis, MO 63115
(314) 382-4998
Fax: (314) 531-2627

Communicators Press
3636 Georgia Ave., Ste. B2
Washington, DC 20011
(202) 726-8618
Fax: (202) 291-9149

Detroit Black Writers' Guild, Inc.
5601 W. Warren
Detroit, MI 48210
(313) 897-2551
Fax: (313) 963-9138

Duncan and Duncan, Inc.
2809 Pulaski Hwy.
Edgewood, MD 21040
(410) 538-5579
Fax: (410) 538-5584

Essai Seay Publications
PO Box 55
East St. Louis, IL 62202-0055
(618) 271-7890

Famous Black Quotations
PO Box 64898
Chicago, IL 60664
(312) 667-2227

Freeland Publications
PO Box 18941
Philadelphia, PA 19119
(215) 226-2507

Gumbs and Thomas Publishers, Inc.
PO Box 381
New York, NY 10039
(212) 694-6677
Fax: (212) 694-0602

Heritage Press
PO Box 18625
Baltimore, MD 21216
(410) 728-8521

Holloway House Publishing Co.
8060 Melrose Ave.
Los Angeles, CA 90046
(323) 653-8060
Fax: (323) 655-9452

Institute for Southern Studies
2009 Chapel Hill Rd.
PO Box 531
Durham, NC 27702
(919) 419-8311
Fax: (919) 419-8315

Joint Center for Political and Economic Studies
1090 Vermont Ave. NW, Ste. 1100
Washington, DC 20005-4961
(202) 789-3500
Fax: (202) 789-6391

Just Us Books, Inc.
356 Gleenwood Ave., 3rd Fl.
East Orange, NJ 07017
(201) 676-4345
Fax: (201) 677-7570

Kitchen Table: Women of Color Press
PO Box 40-4920
Brooklyn, NY 12140
(718) 935-1082
Fax: (718) 935-1107

M.L. Williams Publishing Co., Inc.
PO Box 53552
1315 Walnut St., Ste. 1624
Philadelphia, PA 19105
(215) 735-1121
Fax: (215) 471-4550

Majority Press
PO Box 538
Dover, MA 02030
(508) 655-5636
Fax: (508) 655-1631

National Center for Urban Ethnic Affairs
PO Box 20
Washington, DC 20064
(202) 232-3600
Fax: (202) 319-6289

New Day Press, Inc.
Karamu House
2355 E. 89th St.
Cleveland, OH 44106
(216) 795-7070
Fax: (216) 795-7073

The Noble Press
213 W. Institute Pl., Ste. 508
Chicago, IL 60610
(312) 642-1168

Omenana
3227 Washington St., No. 2
Jamaica Plain, MA 02130
(617) 445-0161

Open Hand Publishing Inc.
PO Box 22048
Seattle, WA 98122
(206) 323-2187
Fax: (206) 323-2188

Path Press, Inc.
53 W. Jackson Blvd., Ste. 724
Chicago, IL 60604
(312) 663-0167
Fax: (312) 663-5318

Raw Ink Press
Southwest Sta., PO Box 70417
Washington, DC 20024-0417
(202) 686-4686

Red Sea Press, Inc.
11-D Princess Road
Lawrenceville, NJ 08648
(609) 844-9583
Fax: (609) 844-0198

Shamal Books, Inc.
GPO Box 16
New York, NY 10116

Third World Press
PO Box 19730
Chicago, IL 60619
(312) 651-0700
Fax: (312) 651-7286

Universal Black Writer Press
PO Box 5, Radio City Sta.
New York, NY 10101-0005

Urban Research Press, Inc.
840 E. 87th St.
Chicago, IL 60619
(312) 994-7200
Fax: (312) 994-5191

WREE (Women for Racial and Economic Equality)
198 Broadway, Rm. 606
New York, NY 10038
(212) 385-1103

Newspapers

Alabama

Birmingham Times
The Birmingham Times Publishing Co.
115 3rd Ave., W
PO Box 10503
Birmingham, AL 35202
(205) 251-5158
Circulation: 10,000.

Birmingham World
407 15th St., N
Birmingham, AL 35203-1877
(205) 251-6523
Fax: (205) 328-6729
Circulation: 12,600.

Campus Digest
Tuskegee University
Tuskegee, AL 36083
(205) 727-8263
Circulation: 2,000.

Greene County Democrat
Greene County Newspaper Co.
214 Boligee St.
PO Box 598
Eutaw, AL 35462
(205) 372-3373
Fax: (205) 372-2243
Circulation: 3,500.

National Inner City News
National Inner City Enterprises, Inc.
1318 Polaris Dr.
PO Box 1545
Mobile, AL 36633-1545
Circulation: 8,000.

Mobile Beacon
2311 Costarides St.
PO Box 1407
Mobile, AL 36633
Circulation: 4,952.

Montgomery-Tuskegee Times
880 S. Court St., Ste. A
Montgomery, AL 36104
(205) 262-5026
Circulation: 10,000.

The New Times
New Times of Mobile
PO Box 40536
Mobile, AL 36640-0536
(205) 432-0356
Fax: (205) 432-8320
Circulation: 5,000.

Shoals News Leader
PO Box 427
Florence, AL 35631
(205) 766-5542
Circulation: 10,000.

Speakin' Out News
1300 Meridian St.
PO Box 2826
Huntsville, AL 35804
(205) 551-1020
Circulation: 24,000.

Arizona

Arizona Informant
1746 E. Madison, No. 2
Phoenix, AZ 85034
(602) 257-9300
Fax: (602) 257-0547
Circulation: 1,800.

Arkansas

Arkansas State Press
Carney Publishing Corp.
221 W. Second, Ste. 208
Little Rock, AR 72201
(501) 371-9991
Circulation: 5,000.

California

Bakersfield News Observer
1219 20th St.
Bakersfield, CA 93301
(805) 324-9466
Fax: (805) 324-9472

Berkeley Tri City Post
The Alameda Publishing Corp.
PO Box 1350
Oakland, CA 94604
(510) 763-1120
Fax: (510) 763-9670
Circulation: 20,000.

Black Voice News
PO Box 1581
Riverside, CA 92502
(909) 682-6070
Fax: (909) 276-0877
www.eee.org/bus/bvn/
Circulation: 7,500.

California Advocate
1715 E St., No. 108
PO Box 11826
Fresno, CA 93775
(209) 268-0941
Circulation: 22,500.

California Voice
270 Francisco St.
San Francisco, CA 94133
(941) 133-2012
Circulation: 37,325.

Carson Bulletin
Rapid Publishing
349 W. Compton
PO Box 4248
Compton, CA 90224
(213) 774-0018
Circulation: 8,000.

Central Star/Journal Wave
Central News-Wave Publications
2621 W. 54th St.
Los Angeles, CA 90043
(213) 290-3000
Fax: (213) 291-0219
Circulation: 35,292.

Compton/Carson Wave
Central News-Wave Publications
2621 W. 54th St.
Los Angeles, CA 90043
(213) 290-3000
Fax: (213) 291-0219
Circulation: 40,183.

Compton Bulletin
Rapid Publishing
349 W. Compton
PO Box 4248
Compton, CA 90224
(213) 774-0018
Circulation: 22,000.

Compton Metropolitan Gazette
First-Line Publishers
14621 Titus St., Ste. 228
Van Nuys, CA 91402
(818) 782-8695
Fax: (818) 782-2924
Circulation: 60,000.

Culver City Star
Central News-Wave Publications
2621 W. 54th St.
Los Angeles, CA 90043
(213) 290-3000
Fax: (213) 291-0219
Circulation: 29,109.

Firestone Park News/Southeast News Press
4053 Marlton Ave.
PO Box 19027A
Los Angeles, CA 90008
(213) 291-9486
Fax: (213) 291-2123
Circulation: 18,000.

Herald Dispatch
4053 Marlton Ave.
PO Box 19027A
Los Angeles, CA 90008
(213) 291-9486
Fax: (213) 291-2123
Circulation: 35,000.

Inglewood/Hawthorne Wave
Central News-Wave Publications
2621 W. 54th St.
Los Angeles, CA 90043
(213) 290-3000
Fax: (213) 291-0219
Circulation: 45,332.

Inglewood Tribune
Rapid Publishing
349 W. Compton
PO Box 4248
Compton, CA 90244
(213) 774-0018
Circulation: 10,000.

L.A. Metropolitan Gazette
First-Line Publishers/L.A. Metro Group
14621 Titus St., Ste. 228
Van Nuys, CA 91402
(818) 782-8695
Circulation: 60,000.

Long Beach Express
First-Line Publishers/L.A. Metro Group
14621 Titus St., Ste. 228
Van Nuys, CA 91402
(818) 782-8695
Fax: (818) 782-2924
www.xtra99.com
Circulation: 60,000.

Los Angeles Sentinel
3800 S. Crenshaw
PO Box 11456
Los Angeles, CA 90008
(213) 299-3800
Fax: (213) 299-3890
Circulation: 18,664.

Lynwood Journal
Rapid Publishing
349 W. Compton
PO Box 4248
Compton, CA 90224
(213) 774-0018

Lynwood Press
Central News-Wave Publications
2621 W. 54th St.
Los Angeles, CA 90043
(213) 290-3000
Fax: (213) 291-0219
Circulation: 24,006.

Mesa Tribune Wave
Central News-Wave Publications
2621 W. 54th St.
Los Angeles, CA 90043
(213) 290-3000
Circulation: 31,609.

Metro Reporter
270 Francisco St.
San Francisco, CA 94133-2120
(415) 391-2030
Fax: (415) 391-2527
Circulation: 108,895.

Metro Star
42353 47th St. W.
Lancaster, CA 93534

New Bayview
Double Rock Press
1624 Oakdale Ave.
PO Box 24477
San Francisco, CA 94124-0477
(415) 826-1484
Circulation: 12,000.

Oakland Post
The Alameda Publishing Corp.
PO Box 1350
Oakland, CA 94604-1350
(510) 763-1120
Circulation: 62,496.

Pasadena Gazette
First-Line Publishers/L.A. Metro Group
14621 Titus St., Ste. 228
Van Nuys, CA 91402
(818) 782-8695
Fax: (818) 782-2924
Circulation: 60,000.

Precinct Reporter
1677 W. Baseline St.
San Bernardino, CA 92411
(909) 889-0597
Fax: (909) 889-1706
Circulation: 55,000.

Richmond Post, Alameda Publishing Corp.
The Alameda Publishing Corp.
PO Box 1350
Oakland, CA 94604-1350
(510) 763-1120
Fax: (510) 763-9670
Circulation: 21,900.

Sacramento Observer
The Observer Newspapers
PO Box 817
San Leandro, CA 94577
(510) 483-7119
Circulation: 49,090.

San Bernardino American News
1583 W. Baseline St.
San Bernardino, CA 92411-1756
(909) 889-7677
Fax: (909) 889-2882
Circulation: 5,000.

San Diego Voice and Viewpoint
1729 N. Euclid Ave.
San Diego, CA 92112-0095
(619) 266-2233
Fax: (619) 266-0533
Circulation: 13,000.

San Fernando Gazette Express
First-Line Publishers/L.A. Metro Group
14621 Titus St., Ste. 228
Van Nuys, CA 91402
(818) 782-8695
Circulation: 60,000.

San Francisco Post
The Alameda Publishing Corp.
PO Box 1350
Oakland, CA 94604-1350
(510) 763-1120
Fax: (510) 763-9670
Circulation: 18,289.

Seaside Post News-Sentinel
The Alameda Publishing Corp.
1244A Broadway Ave.
PO Box 670
Seaside, CA 93955
(408) 394-6632
Circulation: 8,316.

Southwest News Wave
Central News-Wave Publications
2621 W. 54th St.
Los Angeles, CA 90043
(213) 290-3000
Fax: (213) 291-0219
Circulation: 38,932.

Southwest Topics/Sun Wave
Central News-Wave Publications
2621 W. 54th St.
Los Angeles, CA 90043
(213) 290-3000
Circulation: 30,223.

Sun-Reporter
Reporter Publications
1791 Vancroft Ave.
San Francisco, CA 94124
(415) 931-5778
Circulation: 11,249.

Watts Star Review
Firestone Park News/Southwest News Press
4053 Marlton Ave.
PO Box 19027A
Los Angeles, CA 90008
(213) 291-9486
Fax: (213) 291-2123
Circulation: 30,000.

Wilmington Beacon
Rapid Publishing
349 W. Compton
PO Box 4248
Compton, CA 90224
(213) 774-0018

Colorado

Denver Weekly News
PO Box 5008
Denver, CO 80217-5008
(303) 292-5158
Circulation: 17,500.

Hartford Inquirer
Inquiries Newspaper Group
PO Box 1260
Hartford, CT 06143
(860) 522-1462
Fax: (860) 522-3014
Circulation: 125,000.

The Inner City Newspaper
50 Fitch St.
New Haven, CT 06515
(203) 387-0354
Circulation: 35,000.

Delaware

The Defender
1702 Locust St.
Wilmington, DE 19802
(302) 656-3252
Fax: (302) 471-1130
Circulation: 14,000.

District of Columbia

Metro Chronicle
529 14th St., Ste. 1143
Washington, DC 20045
(202) 347-1114

The Washington New Observer
811 Florida Ave., NW
Washington, DC 20001
(202) 232-3060
Fax: (202) 232-1711
Circulation: 20,000.

Washington Capital Spotlight Newspaper
2112 New Hampshire Ave., Ste. B2
Washington, DC 20009
(202) 745-7858
(202) 745-7860
Circulation: 60,000.

Washington Informer
3117 Martin Luther King, Jr. Ave., SE
Washington, DC 20032
(202) 561-4100
Fax: (202) 574-3785
Circulation: 27,000.

New Observer
811 Florida Ave., NW
Washington, DC 20001
(202) 232-3060
Fax: (202) 232-1711
Circulation: 20,000.

Florida

Black Miami Weekly
PO Box F
Miami, FL 33147

The Bulletin
2490 Dr. M.L. King, Jr. Way
PO Box 2560
Sarasota, FL 34230-2560
(813) 953-3990
Circulation: 16,500.

Capital Outlook
602 N. Adams St.
Tallahassee, FL 32301
(904) 681-1852
Fax: (904) 681-1093
Circulation: 11,333.

Daytona Times
Daytona Times, Inc.
427 S. Dr. M.L. King Blvd.
Daytona Beach, FL 32114
(904) 253-0321
Fax: (904) 254-7510
Circulation: 20,150.

Famuan
Florida A and M University
Tallahassee, FL 32307
(904) 599-3159
Fax: (904) 561-2570
Circulation: 5,000.

Florida Sentinel-Bulletin
2207-21st Ave.
PO Box 3363
Tampa, FL 33601
(813) 248-1921
Fax: (813) 248-4507
Circulation: 23,345.

Florida Star Times
PO Box 40629
Jacksonville, FL 32203
(904) 766-8834
Fax: (904) 765-1673
Circulation: 2,400.

Florida Sun Review
LMH Publications
702 18th St.
Orlando, FL 32802
(407) 423-1156
Fax: (407) 849-1286
Circulation: 16,500.

Ft. Pierce Chronicle
1527 Ave. D
Fort Pierce, FL 34950
(407) 461-7093
Circulation: 10,500.

Miami Times
900 NW 54th St.
Miami, FL 33127
(305) 757-1147
Fax: (305) 757-5770
Circulation: 16,464.

News Reporter
1610 N. Howard Ave.
Tampa, FL 33607
(813) 254-2608
Circulation: 9,694.

Orlando Times
4403 Vineland Rd., Ste. B-5
PO Box 555339
Orlando, FL 32855-5339
(407) 841-3710
Fax: (407) 849-0434
Circulation: 11,000.

Pensacola Voice
213 E. Yonge St.
Pensacola, FL 32503
(904) 434-6963
Fax: (904) 469-8745
Circulation: 35,896.

Voice
Bethune-Cookman College
640 2nd Ave.
Daytona Beach, FL 32115
(904) 255-1401
Fax: (904) 258-8951
Circulation: 3,000.

Weekly Challenger
2500 9th St. S.
Saint Petersburg, FL 33705
(813) 896-2922
Circulation: 32,000.

Westside Gazette
PO Box 5304
Fort Lauderdale, FL 33310
(954) 523-5115
Fax: (954) 522-2553
Circulation: 7,000.

Georgia

Atlanta Daily World
145 Auburn Ave. NE
Atlanta, GA 30335-1201
(404) 659-1110
Circulation: 18,000.

Fort Valley Herald
Atlantic Communications of Georgia, Inc.
315 N. Camellia Blvd.
PO Box 899
Fort Valley, GA 31030
(912) 822-9714
Fax: (912) 232-8666
Circulation: 6,000.

Metro Courier
PO Box 2385
Augusta, GA 30903
(404)724-6556
Fax: (404) 722-7104
Circulation: 23,660.

Southeastern News
302 W. 16th Ave., Ste. D
Cordele, GA 31015
(912) 273-6714

The Atlanta Inquirer
947 Martin Luther King Jr. Dr. NW
Atlanta, GA 30314
(404) 523-6086
Fax: (404) 523-6088
www.mindspring.com/cweem/inq.html
Circulation: 61,082.

Atlanta Voice
633 Pryor St. SW
Atlanta, GA 30314-0405
(404) 524-6426
Fax: (404) 523-7853
Circulation: 133,000.

The Columbus Times
2230 Buena Vista Rd.
PO Box 2845
Columbus, GA 31993-2999
(706) 324-2404
Fax: (706) 596-0657
Circulation: 20,000.

The Herald
PO Box 486
Savannah, GA 31401-8022
(912) 232-4505
Fax: (912) 232-4079
Circulation: 8,000.

Savannah Tribune
Savannah Tribune, Inc.
916 Montgomery St.
PO Box 2066
Savannah, GA 31402
(912) 233-6128
Fax: (912) 233-6140
Circulation: 8,000.

Illinois

Chatham-Southeast Citizen
Citizen Newspapers
412 E. 87th St.
Chicago, IL 60619
(312) 487-7700
Fax: (312) 487-7931
Circulation: 20,597.

Chicago Crusader
Crusader Newspapers
6429 S. Martin Luther King Dr.
Chicago, IL 60637
(312) 752-2500
Fax: (312) 752-2817
Circulation: 57,000.

Chicago South Shore Scene
7426 S. Constance
Chicago, IL 60649
(773) 363-0441
Circulation: 20,000.

Chicago Citizen
Citizen Newspapers
412 E. 87th St.
Chicago, IL 60619
(312) 487-7700
Fax: (312) 487-7931

Chicago Independent Bulletin
2037 W. 95th St.
Chicago, IL 60643
(312) 783-1040
Circulation: 64,000.

Chicago Metro News
3437 S. Indiana Ave.
Chicago, IL 60616-3840
(312) 842-5950
Circulation: 84,000.

Chicago Shoreland News
AJA Enterprise
11740 S. Elizabeth
Chicago, IL 60643
(773) 568-7091
Fax: (773) 928-6056
Circulation: 38,000.

Chicago Standard News
Standard Newspapers
615 S. Halsted
Chicago Heights, IL 60411
(708) 755-5021
Fax: (708) 755-5020
www.standardnewspaper.com
Circulation: 15,000.

Chicago Weekend
Citizen Newspapers
412 E. 87th St.
Chicago, IL 60619
(312) 487-7700
Fax: (312) 487-7931
Circulation: 22,583.

Decatur Voice of the Black Community
625 E. Wood St.
Decatur, IL 62523
(217) 423-2231
Fax: (217) 423-2231
Circulation: 16,000.

East St. Louis Crusader
10th and State St.
East Saint Louis, IL 62205
(618) 271-2000

East St. Louis Monitor
East St. Louis Monitor Publishing, Inc.
1501 State St.
Box 2137
East Saint Louis, IL 62205
(618) 271-0468
Circulation: 22,500.

Hyde Park Citizen
Citizen Newspapers
412 E. 87th St.
Chicago, IL 60619
(312) 487-7700
Fax: (312) 487-7931
Circulation: 17,000.

Muslim Journal
Muslim Journal Enterprises, Inc.
929 W. 171st St.
Hazel Crest, IL 60429-1901
(708) 647-9600
Fax: (708) 647-0754
www.worldforum.com/muslimj
Circulation: 16,000.

Observer
6040 S. Harper St.
Chicago, IL 60637
(312) 288-5840
Circulation: 30,000.

South End Citizen
Citizen Newspapers
412 E. 87th St.
Chicago, IL 60619
(312) 487-7700
Fax: (312) 487-7931
Circulation: 19,586.

South Suburban Standard
Citizen Newspapers
615 S. Halstead
Chicago, IL 60411
(708) 755-5021
Fax: (708) 755-5020
www.standardnewspaper.com
Circulation: 25,000.

The Final Call
734 W. 79th St.
Chicago, IL 60620
(312) 602-1230
Fax: (312) 602-1013
www.aol.org
Circulation: 400,000.

Mississippi Enterprise
540 1/2 N. Farish St.
PO Box 87236
Chicago, IL 60680-0236
Circulation: 2,800.

Tri-City Journal
7115 W. North Ave., No. 308
Chicago, IL 60302-1002
(312) 346-8123
Fax: (312) 606-0860
Circulation: 50,000.

Indiana

Frost Illustrated
Frost, Inc.
3121 S. Calhoun
Fort Wayne, IN 46807-1901
(219) 745-0552
Circulation: 1,342.

Gary American
PO Box 1199
Gary, IN 46407
(219) 883-4903
Circulation: 10,000.

Gary New Crusader
1549 Broadway
Gary, IN 46407
(219) 885-4357
Fax: (219) 885-4359
Circulation: 27,000.

Info
Info Printing and Publishing, Inc.
1953 Broadway
Gary, IN 46401
(219) 882-5591
Fax: (219) 886-1090
Circulation: 18,640.

Indianapolis Recorder
The George P. Stewart Printing, Inc.
2901 N. Tacoma Ave.
PO Box 18499
Indianapolis, IN 46218
(317) 924-5143
Fax: (317) 924-5148
Circulation: 10,281.

Iowa

New Iowa Bystander
PO Box 762
Des Moines, IA 50303

Kansas

Kansas City Voice
2727 N. 13th St.
Kansas City, KS 66104
(913) 371-0303

Kentucky

Louisville Defender
1720 Dixie Hwy.
Louisville, KY 40201
(502) 772-2591
Fax: (502) 775-8655
Circulation: 2,270.

Suspension Press
PO Box 2064
Covington, KY 41012
Circulation: 38,000.

Louisiana

Baton Rouge Community Leader
1010 North Blvd.
Baton Rouge, LA 70802
(504) 343-0544
Circulation: 21,700.

Community Leader
1210 North Blvd.
Baton Rouge, LA 70802

Louisiana Weekly
1001 Howard Ave., Ste. 2600
New Orleans, LA 70113
(504) 524-5563
Fax: (504) 527-5826
Circulation: 10,000.

New Orleans Data News Weekly
Data Enterprises, Inc.
3501 Napoleon Ave.
New Orleans, LA 70125
(504) 822-4433
Fax: (504) 821-0320
Circulation: 20,000.

Alexandria News Weekly
PO Box 608
Alexandria, LA 71309
(318) 443-7664
Circulation: 13,750.

Shreveport Sun
The Shreveport Sun, Inc.
PO Box 38357
Shreveport, LA 71133-8357
(318) 631-6222
Circulation: 5,000.

Maryland

Baltimore Afro-American, Afro-American Co.
The Afro-American Co.
2519 N. Charles St.
Baltimore, MD 21218
(410) 554-8200
Fax: (410) 554-8213
Circulation: 15,127.

Every Wednesday
The Afro-American Co.
2519 N. Charles St.
Baltimore, MD 21218
(410) 554-8200
Fax: (410) 554-8213
Circulation: 42,777.

Washington Afro-American
The Afro-American Co.
2519 N. Charles St.
Baltimore, MD 21218
(410) 554-8200
Fax: (410) 554-8213
Circulation: 12,552.

Massachusetts

Bay State Banner
925 Washington St.
Dorchester, MA 02124
(617) 288-4900
Circulation: 21,252.

Boston Greater News
PO Box 497
Roxbury, MA 02119-0004
(617) 445-7063
Circulation: 12,300.

Michigan

Ecorse Telegram
4122 10th St.
PO Box 4585
Ecorse, MI 48229
(313) 928-2955
Circulation: 12,000.

Blazer News
PO Box 806
Jackson, MI 49204
(517) 788-4600
Fax: (517) 788-5300
Circulation: 6,100.

Michigan Chronicle
Sengstacke Newspaper Corp.
479 Ledyard St.
Detroit, MI 48201
(313) 963-5522
Fax: (313) 963-8788
Circulation: 47,428.

Michigan Citizen
New Day Publishing Enterprises
211 Glendale, Ste. 216
Highland Park, MI 48203
(313) 869-0033
Circulation: 51,442.

Detroit Journal
B and Y Publications
11000 W. McNichols, Ste. 210
Detroit, MI 48221
(313) 342-1717
Circulation: 20,000.

The Grand Rapids Times
PO Box 7258
Grand Rapids, MI 49510
(616) 245-8737
Fax: (616) 245-1026

Michigan Sentinel
27350 Southfield Rd., No. 127
Lathrup Village, MI 48076
(313) 559-1010
Circulation: 18,000.

Minnesota

Minneapolis Spokesman
3744 4th Ave. S.
Minneapolis, MN 55409
(612) 827-4021
Fax: (612) 827-0577
Circulation: 3,790.

St. Paul Recorder
590 Endicott Ave.
St. Paul, MN 55114
(612) 827-4021

Twin Cities Courier
84 S. 6th St., Ste. 501
Minneapolis, MN 55402
(612) 332-3211

Mississippi

Jackson Advocate
Natchez Democratic Inc.
PO Box 3708
Jackson, MS 39207-3708
(601) 948-4122
Fax: (601) 948-4125
Circulation: 20,000.

Mississippi Memo Digest
2511 5th St.
Box 5782
Meridian, MS 39301
(601) 693-2372
Circulation: 3,050.

Missouri

Call
Kansas City Call Inc.
PO Box 410-477
Kansas City, MO 64141
(816) 842-3804
Fax: (816) 842-4420
Circulation: 17,156.

Kansas City Globe
Jordan Communications Co., Inc.
615 E. 29th St.
PO Box 090410
Kansas City, MO 64109
(816) 531-5253
Fax: (816) 531-5256
Circulation: 30,000.

The St. Louis Metro Evening Whirl
Thomas Publication Co.
PO Box 5088
Saint Louis, MO 63115
(314) 535-4033
Fax: (314) 535-4280
Circulation: 40,000.

St. Louis American
American Publishing Co.
4144 Lindell Blvd., Ste. 13-5
Saint Louis, MO 63108-2927
(314) 533-8000
Fax: (314) 533-0038
Circulation: 1,442.

St. Louis Argus
4595 Martin Luther King Dr.
Saint Louis, MO 63113
(314) 531-1323
Fax: (314) 361-6421
Circulation: 33,000.

St. Louis Crusader
4371 Finney Ave.
Saint Louis, MO 63113
(314) 531-5860
Circulation: 9,000.

St. Louis Sentinel Newspaper
Woods Publications
2900 N. Market
Saint Louis, MO 63106
(314) 531-2691
Fax: (314) 531-4442
Circulation: 23,200.

Nevada

Las Vegas Sentinel-Voice
900 E. Charleston Blvd.
Las Vegas, NV 89104
(702) 380-8100
Circulation: 5,000.

New Jersey

Afro-American
429 Central Ave.
East Orange, NJ 07108
(201) 672-9102

Black Voice/Carta Boricua
Rutgers University
Student Activities Center
Box 50
George St.
New Brunswick, NJ 08901
(908) 463-1626
Fax: (908) 463-1702
Circulation: 4,000.

New Jersey Afro-American
PO Box 22162
Newark, NJ 07103
(201) 242-5364
Circulation: 20,000.

New York

Afro-American Times
The Challenge Group
1195 Atlantic Ave.
Brooklyn, NY 11216
(718) 636-9500
Fax: (718) 857-9115
Circulation: 55,000.

Afro-Americans in New York Life and History
Afro-American Historical Association of the Niagara Frontier, Inc.
PO Box 63
Buffalo, NY 14216
(716) 694-5096
Circulation: 600.

Amsterdam News
2340 Frederick Douglass Blvd.
New York, NY 10027
(212) 932-7400
Fax: (212) 222-3842
Circulation: 22,152.

Big Red News
Smith Haj Enterprises
155 Water St., 4th Fl.
Brooklyn, NY 11201
(718) 852-6001
Circulation: 53,766.

Black American
Cool Magazine, Inc.
310 Lenox Ave., No. 304
New York, NY 10027-4411
(212) 564-5110
Circulation: 177,000.

Brooklyn New York Recorder
86 Bainbridge St.
Brooklyn, NY 11233
(718) 493-4616

Buffalo Criterion
623 William St.
Buffalo, NY 14206
(716) 882-9570

Buffalo Fine Print News
806 Fillmore Ave.
Buffalo, NY 14212
(716) 855-3810
Circulation: 10,000.

Communicade
Okang Communications Corp.
104 Magnolia St.
PO Box 60739
Rochester, NY 14606
(716)235-6695
Circulation: 2,800.

Daily Challenge
1360 Fulton St.
Brooklyn, NY 11216
(718) 643-1162
Fax: (718) 857-9115
Circulation: 79,000.

Hudson Valley Black Press
PO Box 2160
Newburgh, NY 12550
(914) 562-1313
Circulation: 42,500.

Jamaica Shopping and Entertainment Guide
North American Publications
164-11 89th Ave., Ste. 190
Jamaica, NY 11432
(718) 591-7777
Circulation: 30,000.

NY Carib News
15 W. 39th St.
New York, NY 10018
(212) 944-1991
Fax: (212) 944-2089
Circulation: 67,000.

The Challenger
1303 Fillmore Ave.
Buffalo, NY 14211
(716) 897-0442
Fax: (716) 897-3307
Circulation: 10,000.

City Sun
The City Sun Publishing Co., Inc.
GPO 560
Brooklyn, NY 11202
(718) 624-5959
Fax: (718) 596-7429
Circulation: 8,728.

New York Voice-Harlem U.S.A.
175-61 Hillside Ave., Ste. 201
Jamaica, NY 11432
(718) 206-9866
Circulation: 70,000.

Westchester County Press
PO Box 1631
White Plains, NY 10602
(914) 684-0006
Circulation: 20,000.

Westchester Observer
542 E. 3rd St.
Mount Vernon, NY 10553

North Carolina

Carolina Peacemaker
400 Summit Ave.
Greensboro, NC 27420-0853
(919) 274-6210
Fax: (919) 273-5103
Circulation: 5,490.

Iredell County News
PO Box 407
Statesville, NC 28687
(704) 873-1054
Circulation: 2,500.

Star of Zion
A.M.E. Zion Publishing House
401 E. 2nd St.
Charlotte, NC 28230
(704) 377-4329
Fax: (704) 377-2809
Circulation: 7,500.

The 'M' Voice Newspaper
PO Box 8361
Greenville, NC 27834
(919) 757-0365
Circulation: 16,000.

The Carolina Times
PO Box 3825
Durham, NC 27702
(919) 682-2913
Circulation: 5,800.

The Carolinian
PO Box 25308
Raleigh, NC 27611
(919) 834-5558
Fax: (919) 832-3243
Circulation: 12,000.

The Charlotte Post
1531 Camden Rd.
PO Box 30144
Charlotte, NC 28230
(704) 376-0496
Fax: (704) 342-2160
www.thepost.mindspring.com
Circulation: 11,500.

Fayetteville Black Times
The Black Press, Inc.
108 Webb St.
PO Box 863
Fayetteville, NC 28302

The Public Post
PO Box 53798
Fayetteville, NC 28305
(919) 875-8938
Circulation: 1,000.

Wilmington Journal
412 S. 7th St.
PO Box 1020
Wilmington, NC 28401
(919) 762-5502
Fax: (919) 343-1334
Circulation: 9,000.

Winston-Salem Chronicle
617 N. Liberty St.
PO Box 1636
Winston-Salem, NC 27101
(336) 722-8624
Fax: (336) 723-9173
Circulation: 17,500.

Ohio

Call and Post
1949 E. 105 St.
Cleveland, OH 44106
(216) 791-7600
Fax: (216) 791-6568
Circulation: 43,283.

Cincinnati Herald
Porter Publishing
354 Hearne Ave.
Cincinnati, OH 45229
(513) 961-3331
Fax: (513) 961-0304
Circulation: 24,500.

South East Times
3249 E. 137th St.
Cleveland, OH 44120
(216) 921-2788

Akron Reporter
1046 S. Arlington
PO Box 2042
Akron, OH 44309
(330) 773-4196
Fax: (330) 535-7333
Circulation: 17,000.

Buckeye Review
William Publishing Co.
1555 Belmont Ave.
Youngstown, OH 44501-0287
(216) 743-2250
Circulation: 5,000.

Toledo Journal
3021 Douglas Rd.
PO Box 2536
Toledo, OH 43606
(419) 472-4521
Fax: (419) 472-1602
Circulation: 19,000.

Oklahoma

The Black Chronicle
PO Box 17498
Oklahoma City, OK 73136
(405) 424-4695
Fax: (405) 424-6708
Circulation: 28,927.

Oklahoma Eagle
PO Box 3267
Tulsa, OK 74101
(918) 582-7124
Circulation: 12,800.

Oregon

Portland Observer
PO Box 3137
Portland, OR 97211
(503) 288-0033
Circulation: 10,000.

The Portland Skanner
Skanner Group Inc.
PO Box 5455
Portland, OR 97228-5455
(503) 285-5555
Fax: (503) 285-2900
Circulation: 20,000.

Pennsylvania

New Pittsburgh Courier
Sengstac Newspapers
315 E. Carson St.
Pittsburgh, PA 15219
(412) 481-8302
Fax: (412) 481-1360
Circulation: 30,000.

Philadelphia New Observer
1930 Chestnut St., Ste. 900
PO Box 30092
Philadelphia, PA 19103
(215) 665-8400
Circulation: 81,000.

The Leader
The New Hope Gazette
6220 Ridge Ave
Philadelphia, PA 19178
(215) 862-9435
Circulation: 29,000.

The Lincolnian
Lincoln University
Office of Communications
Lincoln University, PA 19352
(215) 932-8300
Circulation: 1,500.

The Philadelphia Tribune
524-526 S. 16th St.
Philadelphia, PA 19146
(215) 546-1006
Fax: (215) 735-3612
Circulation: 33,890.

Rhode Island

Ocean State Grapevine
PO Box 16333
Rumford, RI 02916-0693

South Carolina

Charleston Black Times
South Carolina Black Media Group
1310 Harden
Columbia, SC 29211
(803) 799-5252
Fax: (803) 799-7709
Circulation: 6,883.

Columbia Black News
South Carolina Black Media Group
PO Box 11128
Columbia, SC 29211
(803) 799-5252
Fax: (803) 799-7709
Circulation: 22,834.

Florence Black Sun
1310 Harden
PO Box 11128
Columbia, SC 29204
(803) 799-5252
Fax: (803) 799-7709
Circulation: 5,734.

Greenville Black Star
South Carolina Black Media Group
1310 Harden
Columbia, SC 29204
(803) 799-5252
Fax: (803) 799-7709
Circulation: 6,849.

Orangeburg Black Voice
PO Box 11128
Columbia, SC 29211
(803) 799-5252
Fax: (803) 799-7709
Circulation: 5,365.

The Black News
South Carolina Black Media Group
1310 Harden
PO Box 11128
Columbia, SC 29204
(803) 799-5252
Fax: (803) 799-7709
Circulation: 5,164.

Sumter Black Post
1310 Harden
Columbia, SC 29204
(803) 799-5252
Circulation: 5,355.

Charleston Chronicle
Chronicle Communications Corp.
1109 King St.
PO Box 20548
Charleston, SC 29413-0548
(803) 723-2785
Fax: (803) 577-6099
Circulation: 3,000.

The Coastal Times
701 E. Bay St.
BTC Box 1407
Charleston, SC 29403
(803) 723-5318
Circulation: 4,580.

View South News
PO Box 1849
Orangeburg, SC 29116
(803) 531-1662
Fax: (803) 531-1662
Circulation: 5,000.

Tennessee

The Catholic Mentor
Winston Derek Publishers, Inc.
1722 W. End Ave.
Nashville, TN 37203
(615) 321-0535

Fisk News
Fisk University
1000 17th Ave. N.
Nashville, TN 37208
(615) 329-8710
Circulation: 1,000.

Memphis Silver Star News
3144 Park Ave.
Memphis, TN 38111

Tri-State Defender
PO Box 2065
Memphis, TN 38103-4598
(901) 523-1818
Fax: (901) 523-1820
Circulation: 15,000.

Texas

Dallas Examiner
424 Centre St.
Dallas, TX 75208
(214) 948-9175
Fax: (214) 948-9176
Circulation: 50,000.

Dallas Post Tribune
2726 S. Beckley
Dallas, TX 75224
(214) 946-7678
Fax: (214) 946-6823
Circulation: 20,000.

Houston Forward Times
Forward Times Publishing Co.
4411 Almeda Rd.
PO Box 8346
Houston, TX 77288-8346
(713) 526-4727
Fax: (713) 526-3170
Circulation: 60,000.

The Informer & Texas Freeman
PO Box 3086
Houston, TX 77253
(713) 218-7400
Fax: (713) 218-7077
Circulation: 30,000.

Houston Defender
PO Box 8005
Houston, TX 77288
(713) 663-7716
Fax: (713) 663-7116
Circulation: 23,000.

Houston Sun
1520 Isabella
PO Box 600603
Houston, TX 77004
(713) 524-4474
Circulation: 80,000.

Lubbock Southwest Digest
902 E. 28th St.
Lubbock, TX 79404
(806) 762-3612
Fax: (806) 749-6303
Circulation: 3,137.

Dallas Weekly Newspaper
Ad-Mast Publishing, Inc.
Anthony T. Davis Bldg.
3101 Martin Luther King, Jr. Blvd.
Dallas, TX 75215
(214) 428-8958
Fax: (214) 428-2807
Circulation: 15,236.

The Villager
1223-A Rosewood Ave.
Austin, TX 78702
(512) 476-0082
Fax: (512) 476-0179
Circulation: 6,000.

Waco Messenger
Smith Printing Co.
PO Box 2087
Waco, TX 76703
(817) 799-6911
Circulation: 3,000.

Virginia

Journal and Guide
362 Campostella Rd.
Norfolk, VA 23523-2204
(804) 543-6531
Circulation: 25,000.

Richmond Afro-American
The Afro-American Co.
2519 N. Charles St.
Richmond, VA 23219
(804) 649-8478
Fax: (804) 649-8477

Roanoke Tribune
PO Box 6021
Roanoke, VA 24017
(540) 343-0326
Fax: (540) 343-0326
Circulation: 5,200.

Washington

Facts Newspaper
2765 E. Cherry St.
PO Box 22015
Seattle, WA 98122
(206) 324-0552
Fax: (206) 324-1007
Circulation: 42,650.

Northwest Dispatch
PO Box 5637
Tacoma, WA 98415
(206) 272-7587
Circulation: 7,700.

Seattle Medium
Piloven Publishing
2600 S. Jackson
Seattle, WA 98144
(206) 323-3070
Fax: (206) 322-6518
Circulation: 37,000.

Tacoma True Citizen
Piloven Publishing
2600 S. Jackson St.
Seattle, WA 98144
(206) 323-3070
Fax: (206) 322-6518
Circulation: 13,500.

West Virginia

West Virginia Beacon Digest
PO Box 981
Charleston, WV 25324
(304) 342-4600
Circulation: 35,861.

Wisconsin

Milwaukee Community Journal
Community Journal, Inc.
3612 N. Martin Luther King Dr.
Milwaukee, WI 53212
(414) 265-5300
Fax: (414) 265-1536
Circulation: 39,960.

Milwaukee Courier
2431 W. Hopkins St.
Milwaukee, WI 53206
(414) 449-4860
Fax: (414) 449-4872
Circulation: 15,000.

Milwaukee Star
3815 N. Teutonia Ave.
Milwaukee, WI 53206
(414) 449-4870
Fax: (414) 449-4872
Circulation: 5,000.

Milwaukee Times
2254 MLK Jr. Dr.
Milwaukee, WI 53212
(414) 263-5008
Fax: (414) 263-4445
Circulation: 7,500.

Magazines and Journals

A and T Register
North Carolina Agricultural and Technical University
Box E25
Greensboro, NC 27411
(919) 334-7700
www.aurora.ncat.edu/~register
Circulation: 7,000.

About. . . Time
About. . . Time Magazine, Inc.
283 Genesee St.
Rochester, NY 14611
(716) 235-7150
Fax: (716) 235-7195
Circulation: 56,000.

African American Review
Indiana State University
Dept. of English
Terre Haute, IN 47809
(812) 237-2968
Fax: (812) 237-3156
Circulation: 4,200.

Alternative Press Index
PO Box 33109
Baltimore, MD 21218
(410) 243-2471
Fax: (410) 235-5325
www.nisc.com
Circulation: 550.

American Visions
1156 15th St. NW, Ste. 615
Washington, DC 20005
(202) 496-9593
Fax: (202) 496-9851
www.americanvisions.com
Circulation: 125,000.

Atlanta Tribune
L and L Communications, Inc.
875 Old Roswell Rd., Ste. C-100
Roswell, GA 30076
(404) 587-0501
Fax: (404) 642-6501
www.mindspring.com
Circulation: 22,000.

AUC Digest
Atlanta University Center
PO Box 3191
Atlanta, GA 30302
(404) 523-6136
Fax: (404) 523-5467
Circulation: 15,100.

Black Careers
Project Magazine, Inc.
PO Box 8214
Philadelphia, PA 19101-8214
(215) 387-1600
Circulation: 100,000.

Black College Sports Review
Winston-Salem Chronicle
617 N. Liberty St.
Winston-Salem, NC 27101-2912
(336) 722-8624
Fax: (336) 723-9173
Circulation: 135,000.

Black Collegian
Black Collegiate Services, Inc.
140 Carondelet St.
New Orleans, LA 70130-2526
(504) 523-0154
Fax: (504) 523-0271
www.black.collegian.com
Circulation: 108,184.

Black Employment and Education Magazine
Hamdani Communications Inc.
2625 Piedmont Rd.
Bldg. 56, Ste. 282
Atlanta, GA 30324
(404) 469-5891
Circulation: 175,000.

Black Enterprise
Earl Graves Publishing
130 5th Ave.
New York, NY 10011
(212) 242-8000
Fax: (212) 886-9610
Circulation: 325,045.

Black Family
Kent Enterprises, Inc.
Box 1046
Herndon, VA 22070-1046
Circulation: 200,000.

Black Health
Altier and Maynard Communications, Inc.
53 Oakwood Dr.
Madison, CT 06443-1823
(203) 431-3494
Circulation: 26,000.

Black News Digest
U.S. Dept. of Labor
Office of Public Affairs
200 Constitution Ave. NW
Washington, DC 20210
(202) 523-8743
Fax: (202) 523-8740

Black Scholar
Black World Foundation
PO Box 2869
Oakland, CA 94618
(510) 547-6633
Fax: (510) 547-6679
Circulation: 70,000.

Black Tennis Magazine
PO Box 210767
Dallas, TX 75211
(214) 670-7618
Fax: (214) 330-1318
Circulation: 5,000.

Black Lace
BLK Publishing Company
Box 83912
Los Angeles, CA 90083-0912
(310) 410-0808
Fax: (310) 410-9250
www.blk.com/blk
Circulation: 60,000.

Callaloo
The Johns Hopkins University Press
University of Virginia
Dept. of English
Wilson Hall
Charlottesville, VA 22903
(804) 924-6616
Circulation: 1,740.

Chocolate Singles
Chocolate Singles Enterprises, Inc.
PO Box 333
Jamaica, NY 11413
(718) 978-4800
Fax: (718) 978-4819

Christian Index
The Christian Methodist Episcopal Publishing House
PO Box 2018
Memphis, TN 38101
(901) 345-1173
Fax: (901) 332-2269
Circulation: 6,000.

Class Magazine
R.E. John-Sandy Communications Ltd.
900 Broadway
New York, NY 10003
(212) 677-3055
Fax: (212) 677-3341
Circulation: 187,345.

Confrontation/Change Review
3955 Denlinger Rd.
Dayton, OH 45426
(513) 837-0498
Fax: (513) 837-5888
Circulation: 3,200.

The Crisis
NAACP/Crisis Publishing
6565 Sunset Blvd.
Los Angeles, CA 90028-7206
(212) 481-4100
Fax: (212) 779-9277
Circulation: 350,000.

Dollars and Sense Magazine
National Publications Sales Agency, Inc.
1610 E. 79th St.
Chicago, IL 60649
(312) 375-6800
Fax: (312) 375-7149
Circulation: 286,346.

Ebony
Johnson Publishing Co., Inc.
820 S. Michigan Ave.
Chicago, IL 60605
(312) 322-9200
Fax: (312) 322-9375
Circulation: 1,819,431.

EM: Ebony Man
Johnson Publishing Co.
820 S. Michigan Ave.
Chicago, IL 60605
(312) 322-9200
Fax: (312) 322-9375
Circulation: 171,391.

Emerge
Emerge Communications Inc.
1700 N. Moore St., Ste. 2200
Arlington, VA 22209
(703) 875-0430
Fax: (703) 516-6406
Circulation: 165,095.

Essence
Essence Communications, Inc.
1500 Broadway 6th Fl.
New York, NY 10036
(212) 642-0600
Fax: (212) 921-5173
www.essence.com
Circulation: 1,000,273.

Ivy Leaf
Alpha Kappa Alpha Sorority, Inc.
5656 S. Stony Island Ave.
Chicago, IL 60637
(312) 684-1282
Fax: (312) 288-8251
www.aka1908.com
Circulation: 40,000.

Jet
Johnson Publishing Co., Inc.
820 S. Michigan Ave.
Chicago, IL 60605
(312) 322-9200
Fax: (312) 322-9375
Circulation: 923,414.

Journal of Black Studies
Sage Periodicals Press
2455 Teller Rd.
Thousand Oaks, CA 91360
(805) 499-0721
Fax: (805) 499-0871
Circulation: 1,650.

Journal of Negro Education
Howard University
PO Box 311
Washington, DC 20059
(202) 806-8120
Fax: (202) 806-8434
Circulation: 2,200.

Journal of Negro History
Association for the Study of Afro-American Life and History
Morehouse College
Box 20
Atlanta, GA 30314
(404) 215-2620
Fax: (404) 215-2715
Circulation: 3,700.

Journal of the National Medical Association
Slack, Inc.
6900 Grove Rd.
Thorofare, NJ 08086-9447
(609) 848-1000
Fax: (609) 853-5991
Circulation: 24,500.

Lincoln Review
The Lincoln Institute for Research and Education, Inc.
1001 Connecticut Ave. NW, Ste. 1135
Washington, DC 20036
(202) 223-5112
Circulation: 7,000.

Living Blues
Center for the Study of Southern Culture
University of Mississippi
301 Hill Hall
University, MS 38677
(601) 232-5993
Fax: (601) 232-7842
www.cssc.olemiss.edu
Circulation: 25,000.

Message
Review and Herald Publishing Assn.
55 W. Oak Ridge Dr.
Hagerstown, MD 21740
(301) 393-3000
Fax: (301) 393-3292
Circulation: 78,273.

Minority Business Entrepreneur
3528 Torrance Blvd., Ste. 101
Torrance, CA 90503-4826
(310) 540-9398
Fax: (310) 792-8263
Circulation: 40,000.

Minority Business Social and Cultural Directory
The Augusta Focus
PO Box 10112
Augusta, GA 30903
(706) 722-7327
Fax: (706) 724-6969
Circulation: 21,000.

Negro History Bulletin
The Assn. for the Study of Afro-American Life and History, Inc.
1407 14th St. NW
Washington, DC 20005-3704
(202) 667-2822
Fax: (202) 387-9802
Circulation: 10,000.

New Visions
16360 Broadway
Maple Heights, OH 44137
(216) 581-7070
Fax: (216) 581-7072

NSBE Magazine
NSBE Publications
1454 Duke St.
Alexandria, VA 22314
(703) 549-2207
Fax: (703) 683-5312
Circulation: 22,934.

Players
Players International Publications
8060 Melrose Ave.
Los Angeles, CA 90046
(213) 653-8060
Fax: (213) 682-2932
Circulation: 175,000.

Right On!
Sterling/Macfadden Partnership
233 Park Ave., S., 6th Fl.
New York, NY 10003
(212) 780-3500
Fax: (212) 780-3555
Circulation: 350,000.

SENGA
Megasin Publications
7501 Morrison Rd.
New Orleans, LA 70126
(504) 242-6022

Shooting Star Review
Shooting Star Productions Inc.
7123 Race St.
Pittsburgh, PA 15208-1424
(412) 731-7464
Circulation: 1,500.

Sophisticate's Black Hairstyles and Care Guide
Associated Publications Inc.
875 N. Michigan Ave., Ste. 2434
Chicago, IL 60611-1901
(312) 266-8680
Circulation: 158,478.

Upscale
Upscale Communications
594 Fielding Ln.
Atlanta, GA 30311
(404) 758-1467
Fax: (404) 758-2314
Circulation: 200,000.

US Black Engineer
Career Communications Group, Inc.
729 E. Pratt St., Ste. 504
Baltimore, MD 21202
(410) 244-7101
Fax: (410) 752-1837
www.ccgmag.com
Circulation: 15,300.

Voice of Missions
A.M.E. Sunday School Union
475 Riverside Dr., Rm. 1926
New York, NY 10115
(212) 870-2258
Fax: (212) 870-2242

Washington View
Viewcomm, Inc.
6856 Eastern Ave. NW, No. 309
Washington, DC 20012
(202) 371-1313
Circulation: 40,000.

The Western Journal of Black Studies
PO Box 645910
Pullman, WA 99164-5910
(509) 335-8681
Fax: (509) 335-8568
Circulation: 400.

Word Up!
Word Up! Publications, Inc.
63 Grand Ave.
River Edge, NJ 07661
(201) 487-6124
Fax: (201) 487-7965
Circulation: 92,513.

Radio Networks

African Time Broadcasting, Inc.
421 7th Ave., Ste. 1012
New York, NY 10001
(212) 244-2760
Fax: (212)244-2761

American-Urban Radio Network
463 7th Ave.
New York, NY 10018
(212) 714-1000
Fax: (212)714-2349

Black Radio Network
166 Madison Ave., 6th Fl.
New York, NY 10016
(212) 686-6850
Fax: (212)686-7308

Radio Stations

Alabama

KDKO-FM
PO Box 350
Evergreen, AL 36401
(334) 578-3693
Fax: (334) 578-5399

WAJF-FM
1301 Central Pkwy., SW
Decatur, AL 35601-4817
(205) 340-1490
Fax: (205) 351-1234

WAJO-AM
PO Box 930
Marion, AL 36756
(205) 683-6168
Fax: (205) 683-9926

WAPZ–AM
2821 US Hwy. 231
Wetumpka, AL 36092
(205) 567-2251
Fax: (205) 567-7971

WBIL-FM
PO Box 869
Tuskegee, AL 36083
(205) 727-2100
Fax: (205) 727-9169

WBLX-FM
1204 Dauphin St.
Mobile, AL 36604
(205) 432-7609
Fax: (205) 432-2054

WDLT-FM
PO Box 180426
Mobile, AL 36618-0426
(334) 380-9098
Fax: (334) 380-9029

WENN-FM
424 16th St. N.
PO Box 697
Birmingham, AL 35203-0697
(205) 254-1820
Fax: (205) 254-1833

WEUP-AM
PO Box 11398
Huntsville, AL 35814
(205) 837-9387
Fax: (205) 837-9404

WGOK-AM
PO Box 1425
Mobile, AL 36633-1425
(334) 432-8661
Fax: (334) 432-1921

WJLD-AM
1449 Spaulding Ishkooda Rd.
Birmingham, AL 35211
(205) 942-1776
Fax: (205) 942-4814

WKXN-FM
PO Box 369
Greenville, AL 36037
(334) 382-6555
Fax: (334) 382-6555

WMMV-FM
PO Box 901
Spanish Fort, AL 36527-0901

WNPT-FM
229 3rd St.
Northport, AL 35476
(205) 758-3311
Fax: (205)349-4824

WRAG-AM
Hwy. 17 S.
PO Box 71
Carrollton, AL 35447-0071
(205) 367-8136
Fax: (205) 367-8689

WSBM-AM
624 Sam Phillips St.
PO Box 932
Florence, AL 35631
(205) 764-8121
Fax: (205) 764-1869

WSLY-FM
11474 U.S. Hwy. 11
York, AL 36925
(205) 392-5234
Fax: (205) 392-5234

WTSK-FM
142 Skyland Blvd.
Tuscaloosa, AL 35405-4015
(205) 345-7200
Fax: (205) 349-1715

WTUG-FM
142 Skyland Blvd.
Tuscaloosa, AL 35405-4015
(205) 345-7200
Fax: (205) 349-1715

WZMG-AM
915 Saugahatchee Lake Rd.
PO Box 2329
Opelika, AL 36803
(334) 745-4656
Fax: (334) 749-1520

WZZA-AM
1570 Woodmont Dr.
Tuscumbia, AL 35674
(205) 381-1862

Arizona

KISO-AM
840 N. Central Ave.
Phoenix, AZ 85004
(602) 258-8181
Fax: (602) 420-9916

KRIM-FM
200 W. Frontier, Ste. P
Payson, AZ 85547-2579
(602) 423-9255
800-638-1039
Fax: (602) 423-9382

Arkansas

KCAT-AM
PO Box 8808
Pine Bluff, AR 71611-8808
(501) 534-5001

KCTL-FM
307 Hwy. 49B
PO Box 2870
West Helena, AR 72390
(501) 572-9506
Fax: (501) 572-1845

KIPR-FM
415 N. McKinley, Ste. 920
Little Rock, AR 72205
(501) 663-0092
Fax: (501) 664-9201

KMZX-FM
1403 Main St.
North Little Rock, AR 72114-4128

KXAR-FM
PO Box 320
Hope, AR 71801-0320
(501) 777-3601
Fax: (501) 777-3535

California

KACD-FM
1425 5th St.
Santa Monica, CA 90401
(310) 458-1031
Fax: (310) 393-2443

KALI-FM
5723 Melrose Ave.
Hollywood, CA 90038-3898
(213) 466-6161
Fax: (213) 466-9464

KBLA-AM
1700 N. Alvarado St.
Los Angeles, CA 90026
(213)665-1580
Fax: (213) 660-1507

KDIA-AM
384 Embarcadero W., No. 3rd.
Oakland, CA 94607-3734
(510) 251-1400
Fax: (510) 251-2110

KJLH-FM
161 N. LaBrea Ave.
Inglewood, CA 90301
(213) 330-2200
Fax: (213) 330-2244

KKBT-FM
6735 Yucca St.
Hollywood, CA 90028
(213) 466-9566
Fax: (213) 466-2592

KMCG-AM
550 Laguna Dr.
Carlsbad, CA 92008
(619) 729-5945
(888) 570-1957
Fax: (619) 729-7067

KQEQ-AM
139 W. Olive Ave.
Fresno, CA 93728
(209) 233-8803
Fax: (209) 233-8871

KXBT-AM
3267 Sonoma Blvd.
Vallejo, CA 94590
(707) 644-8944
800-488-5842
Fax: (707) 644-3736

Colorado

KKMG-FM
6805 Corporate Dr., Ste. 130
Colorado Springs, CO 80919-1977

KWVF-FM
PO Box 5557
Pagosa Springs, CO 81147
(970) 264-1400
Fax: (970) 264-1063

Connecticut

WKND-AM
544 Windsor Ave.
PO Box 1480
Windsor, CT 06095
(203) 688-6221
Fax: (203) 688-0711

WNHC-AM
112 Washington Ave.
North Haven, CT 06473-1707
(203) 234-1340
Fax: (203) 239-6712

WQTQ-FM
Weaver High School
415 Granby St.
Hartford, CT 06112
(860) 722-8661
Fax: (860) 286-9909

WYBC-FM
165 Elm St.
PO Box 209050
New Haven, CT 06520
(203) 432-4118
Fax: (203) 432-4117

District of Columbia

WHUR-FM
529 Bryant St., NW
Washington, DC 20059
(202) 806-3500
Fax: (202) 806-3522

Florida

WAMF-FM
Florida A & M University
PO Box 6202
Tallahassee, FL 32312
(904) 599-3083
Fax: (904) 561-2829

WEDR-FM
Box 551748
Carol City, FL 33055
(305) 623-7711
Fax: (305) 624-2736

WEXY-AM
412 W. Oakland Park Blvd.
Fort Lauderdale, FL 33311-1712
(305) 561-1520
Fax: (305) 561-9830
800-648-8063

WHBT-AM
109B Ridgeland Rd.
Tallahassee, FL 32312
(904) 385-1156
Fax: (904) 224-8329

WHBX-FM
109-B Ridgeland Rd.
Tallahasse, FL 32312
(904) 385-1156
Fax: (904) 224-8329

WHQT-FM
1401 N. Bay Causeway
Miami, FL 33141
(305) 759-4311
Fax: (305) 759-8491

WJHM-FM
37 Skyline Dr., Ste. 4200
Lake Mary, FL 32746
800-299-4102
Fax: (407) 333-2919

WJLQ-FM
6565 N. W St.
Pensacola, FL 32505
(904) 478-6011
Fax: (904) 478-3971

WJWA-AM
PO Box 189
West Palm Beach, FL 33402

WPJS-AM
3033 Riviera Dr., No. 200
Naples, FL 33940-4134
(813) 248-9040

WPOM-AM
5033 Okeechobee Blvd.
West Palm Beach, FL 33417-4533
(407) 844-6200
Fax: (407) 840-0061

WPUL-AM
PO Box 4010
South Daytona, FL 32121-4010
(904) 767-1131
Fax: (904) 254-7510

WRBD-AM
PO Box 626
Stuart, FL 34995-0626
(954) 731-4800
Fax: (954) 739-7917

WRBQ-AM
5510 W. Gray St., Ste. 130
Tampa, FL 33609
(813) 287-1047
Fax: (813) 287-0041

WRNE-AM
312 E. Nine Mile Rd., Ste. 27
Pensacola, FL 32514-1475
(904) 478-6000
Fax: (904) 484-8080

WRXB-AM
1700 34th St. S.
St. Petersburg, FL 33711-3833
(813) 327-9792
Fax: (813) 321-3025

WSWN-AM
2001 State Rd. 715
PO Box 1505
Belle Glade, FL 33430
(561) 996-2063
Fax: (561) 996-1852

WTCL-AM
PO Box 157
Chattahoochee, FL 32324-0814
(904) 663-2323

WTMP-AM
5207 Washington Blvd.
Tampa, FL 33619
(813) 620-1300
Fax: (813) 628-0713

WWAB-AM
1203 W. Chase St.
PO Box 65
Lakeland, FL 33802-0065
(813) 682-2998
Fax: (813) 687-4000

Georgia

WAKB-FM
PO Box 10003
Augusta, GA 30903
(706) 854-0440
Fax: (706) 854-1055

WALR-FM
209 CNN Center
Atlanta, GA 30303
(404) 688-0068
Fax: (404) 688-4262

WBKZ-AM
548 Hawthorne Ave.
PO Box 88
Athens, GA 30606
(706) 548-8800
Fax: (706) 549-8800

WCLA-FM
316 N. River St.
Box 427
Claxton, GA 30417
(912) 739-3035
Fax: (912) 739-0050

WCNN-AM
209 CNN Center
Atlanta, GA 30303-2705
(404) 688-0068
Fax: (404) 688-4262

WFXM-FM
Atl Hwy. 341
Fort Valley, GA 31030
(912) 827-1273
Fax: (912) 742-8299

WGOV-AM
2973 U.S. 84 W.
Valdosta, GA 31601
(912) 242-4513
Fax: (912) 247-7676

WHCJ-FM
PO Box 20484
Savannah, GA 31402-9716
(912) 356-2399
Fax: (912) 356-2996

WHGH-AM
Box 2218
Thomasville, GA 31799
(912) 228-4124
Fax: (912) 225-9508

WJGA-FM
PO Box 3878
Jackson, GA 30233
(770) 775-3151
Fax: (770) 775-3151

WPGA-FM
PO Drawer 980
Perry, GA 31069-0980
(912) 987-2980
Fax: (912) 987-7595

WSNT-AM
PO Box 150
Sandersville, GA 31082
(912) 552-5182
Fax: (912) 553-0800

WXRS-AM
Box 1590
Swainsboro, GA 30401
(912) 237-1590
Fax: (912) 237-3559

Illinois

WBCP-AM
PO Box 1023
Champaign, IL 61820
(217) 359-1580
Fax: (217) 359-1583

WEJM-FM
800 S. Wells, Ste. 250
Chicago, IL 60607
(312) 360-9000
Fax: (312) 306-9070

WEMG-AM
12844 S. Halsted St.
Chicago, IL 60628
(312) 468-1060

WESL-AM
149 S. 8th St.
East St. Louis, IL 62201
(618) 271-7687
Fax: (618) 875-4315

WGCI-AM
332 S. Michigan Ave., Ste. 600
Chicago, IL 60604-4301
(312) 427-4800
Fax: (312) 987-4453

WGCI-FM
332 S. Michigan Ave., Ste. 600
Chicago, IL 60604
(312) 427-4700
Fax: (312) 427-7410

WJPC-AM
800 S. Wells, Ste. 250
Chicago, IL 60607
(312) 360-9000
Fax: (312) 360-9070

WLUV-FM
2272 Elmwood
Rockford, IL 61103
(815) 877-9588
Fax: (815) 877-9649

WVAZ-FM
800 S. Wells, Ste. 250
Chicago, IL 60607
(312) 360-9000
Fax: (312) 360-9070

Indiana

WPZZ-FM
2021 E. 52nd St., No. 200
Indianapolis, IN 46205-1405
(317) 736-4040
Fax: (317) 736-7998

WSYW-AM
8203 Indy Ct.
Indianapolis, IN 46214-2300
(317) 271-1111
Fax: (317) 273-1507

WTLC-FM
2126 N. Meridan St.
Indianapolis, IN 46202
(317) 923-1456
Fax: (317) 924-9684

Iowa

KBBG-FM
918 Newell St.
Waterloo, IA 50703
(319) 234-1441
Fax: (319) 234-6182

KUCB-FM
1404 6th Ave.
Des Moines, IA 50314
(515) 246-1588
Fax: (515) 246-0480

Kentucky

WLBN-AM
Box 680
Lebanon, KY 40033
(502) 692-3126
Fax: (502) 692-6003

WNVL-AM
108 N. Main St.
PO Box 247
Nicholasville, KY 40340-0247
(606) 885-6031
Fax: (606) 887-4650

WQKS-AM
400 Hammond Plz.
Hopkinsville, KY 42240-4969
(502) 886-1480
Fax: (502) 886-6286

Louisiana

KBCE-FM
Box 69
Boyce, LA 71409
(318) 793-4003
Fax: (318) 793-8888

KFXZ-FM
3225 Ambassador Caffery Pkwy.
Lafayette, LA 70506-7214
(318) 981-0106
Fax: (318) 988-0443

KGRM-FM
Drawer K
Grambling, LA 71245
(318) 274-2345
Fax: (318) 274-3245

KJCB-AM
413 Jefferson St.
Lafayette, LA 70501-7057
(318) 233-4262

KMEZ-FM
1450 Poydras St.
New Orleans, LA 70112
(504) 593-2171
Fax: (504) 593-1865

KNEK-FM
PO Box 598
Washington, LA 70589
(318) 826-3921
Fax: (318) 826-3206

KRUS-AM
Box 430
500 N. Monroe St.
Ruston, LA 71270
(318) 255-2530
Fax: (318) 225-2100

KVOL-FM
123 E. Main St.
Lafayette, LA 70501
(318) 233-1330
Fax: (318) 237-7733

KXZZ-AM
311 Alamo St.
Lake Charles, LA 70601
(318) 436-7277
Fax: (318) 436-7278

KYEA-FM
516 Martin St.
West Monroe, LA 71292
(318) 322-1491
Fax: (318) 325-7203

WQUE-FM
2228 Gravier
New Orleans, LA 70119
(504) 827-6000
Fax: (504) 827-6047

WWOZ-FM
PO Box 51840
New Orleans, LA 70151-1840
(504) 568-1234
Fax: (504) 558-9332

WXOK-AM
7707 Waco Ave.
Baton Rouge, LA 70806
(504) 926-1106
Fax: (504) 928-1606

Maryland

WESM-FM
University of Maryland, Eastern Shore
Backbone Rd.
Princess Anne, MD 21853
(410) 651-2816
Fax: (410) 651-2819

WJDY-AM
1633 N. Division St.
Salisbury, MD 21801-3805
(410) 742-5191
Fax: (410) 749-9079

WPGC-FM
6301 Ivy Ln., Ste. 800
Greenbelt, MD 20770
(301) 441-3500
Fax: (301) 499-9555

WWIN-FM
100 St. Paul St.
Baltimore, MD 21202
(410) 332-8200
Fax: (410) 752-2252

WXYV-FM
1829 Reistertown Rd.
Baltimore, MD 21208
(410) 653-2200
Fax: (410) 486-8057

WYRE-AM
112 Main St.
Annapolis, MD 21401
(410) 626-0103
Fax: (410) 267-7634

Massachusetts

WAIC-FM
1000 State St.
Springfield, MA 01109
(413) 736-7662
Fax: (413) 737-2803

WILD-AM
90 Warren St.
Boston, MA 02119
(617) 427-2222
Fax: (617) 427-2677

WJMN-FM
235 Bear Hill Rd.
Waltham, MA 02154-1014
(617) 290-0009
Fax: (617) 290-0722

Michigan

WCHB-AM
32790 Henry Ruff Rd.
Inkster, MI 48141
(313) 278-1440
Fax: (313) 722-8495

WDOZ-AM
PO Box 1310
15001 Michigan Ave.
Dearborn, MI 48121
(313) 846-8500
Fax: (313) 846-1068

WDZZ-FM
120 E. 1st St., Ste. 1830
Flint, MI 48502
(810) 767-7300
Fax: (810) 238-7310

WGPR-FM
3146 E. Jefferson Ave.
Detroit, MI 48207
(313) 259-8862
Fax: (313) 259-6662

WHPR-FM
15851 Woodward Ave.
Highland Park, MI 48203
(313) 868-8812
Fax: (313) 868-8725

WJLB-FM
645 Griswold St., Ste. 633
Detroit, MI 48226-4177
(313) 965-2000
Fax: (313) 965-9970

WKBZ-FM
592 W. Pontaluna Rd.
Muskegon, MI 49444
(616) 798-2141
Fax: (616) 798-3677

WKWM-AM
2610 Horizon SE, Ste. F
Grand Rapids, MI 49546
(616) 956-3323
Fax: (616) 956-9321

WMHG-AM
875 E. Summit Ave.
Muskegon, MI 49444
(616) 733-1616
Fax: (616) 739-9037

WMXD-FM
645 Griswold
Detroit, MI 48226
(313) 965-2000
Fax: (313) 965-9970

WQBH-AM
Penobscot Bldg.
Detroit, MI 48226
(313) 965-4500
Fax: (313) 965-4608

WQHH-FM
101 Northcrest Rd., Ste. 4
Lansing, MI 48906-1262
(517) 484-9600
Fax: (517) 484-9699

WTLZ-FM
126 N. Franklin St., Ste. 514
Saginaw, MI 48607
(517) 754-1071
Fax: (517) 754-4292

WXLA-AM
101 Northcrest Rd., Ste. 4
Lansing, MI 48906-1262
(517) 484-9600
Fax: (517) 484-9699

Minnesota

KMOJ-FM
501 Bryant Ave. N
Minneapolis, MN 55405
(612) 377-0594
Fax: (612) 377-6919

KSGS-AM
11320 Valley View Rd.
Eden Prairie, MN 55344
(612) 941-5774
Fax: (612) 941-8750

Mississippi

WACR-AM
1910 14th Ave. N
PO Box 1078
Columbus, MS 39703
(601) 328-1050
Fax: (601) 328-1054

WACR-FM
1910 14th Ave. N
Columbus, MS 39703
(601) 328-1050
Fax: (601) 328-1054

WAID-FM
112 Le Flore Ave.
Box 668
Clarksdale, MS 38614
(601) 627-2281
Fax: (601) 624-2900

WALT-AM
3436 Hwy. 45 N
PO Box 5797
Meridian, MS 39302
(601) 693-2661
Fax: (601) 483-0826

WBAD-FM
PO Box 4426
Greenville, MS 38704-4426
(601) 335-9265
Fax: (601) 335-5538

WBFN-AM
Drawer 70
Quitman, MS 39355
(601) 776-3327
Fax: (601) 776-6762

WCLD-FM
Drawer 780
Cleveland, MS 38732
(601) 843-4091
Fax: (601) 843-9805

WESE-FM
PO Box 3300
Tupelo, MS 38803
(601) 842-1067
Fax: (601) 842-0725

WESY-AM
7 Oaks Rd.
PO Box 5804
Greenville, MS 38704-5804
(601) 378-9405
Fax: (601) 335-5538

WGVM-AM
1383 Pickett St.
Greenville, MS 38701
(888) 808-8644
Fax: (601) 332-1315

WJMG-FM
1204 Gravel Line St.
Hattiesburg, MS 39401
(601) 544-1941
Fax: (601) 544-1947

WKRA-FM
Hwy. 4 East-C
PO Box 398
Holly Springs, MS 38635
(601) 252-6692

WKXG-AM
Browning Rd.
PO Box 1686
Greenwood, MS 38930
(601) 453-2174
Fax: (601) 455-5733

WKXI-AM
731 S. Tear Orchird, Ste. 27
Ridgeland, MS 39157
(601) 957-1300
Fax: (601) 956-0516

WMXU-FM
PO Box 1076
Columbus, MS 39703
(601) 327-1183
Fax: (601) 328-1122

WNBN-AM
1290 266-23rd St.
Meridian, MS 39301
(601) 483-7930

WORV-AM
1204 Graveline
Hattiesburg, MS 39401
(601) 544-1941
Fax: (601) 544-1947

WQFX-FM
Security Bldg., Penthouse Ste.
PO Box 789
Gulfport, MS 39502
Fax: (601) 374-4967

WROX-AM
317 Delta Ave.
Clarksdale, MS 38614
(601) 627-7343
Fax: (601) 627-1000

WTYJ-FM
20 E. Franklin
Natchez, MS 39120
(601) 442-2522
Fax: (601) 446-9918

WURC-FM
Rust College
150 E. Rust Ave.
Holly Springs, MS 38635
(601) 252-5881
Fax: (601) 252-8869

Missouri

KIRL-AM
3713 Hwy. 94 N
St. Charles, MO 63132
(314) 692-5108
Fax: (314) 692-5127

KMJM-FM
10155 Crsecent Sq. Dr.
St. Louis, MO 63108
(314) 361-1108
Fax: (314) 361-2276

Nebraska

KBBX-AM
4807 Dodge St.
Omaha, NE 68132
(402) 556-6700
Fax: (402) 556-9427

Nevada

KCEP-FM
330 W. Washington St.
Las Vegas, NV 89106-3327
(702) 648-4218
Fax: (702) 647-0803

New Mexico

KANW-FM
2020 Coal Ave. SE
Albuquerque, NM 87106
(505) 242-7163

New York

WBLK-FM
712 Main St., Ste. 112
Buffalo, NY 14202
(716) 852-5955
Fax: (716) 852-6605

WBLS-FM
3 Park Ave.
New York, NY 10016
(212) 447-1000
Fax: (212) 447-5194

WDKX-FM
683 E. Main St.
Rochester, NY 14605
(716) 262-2050
Fax: (716) 262-2626

WGMC-FM
Box 300
North Greece, NY 14515
(716) 621-9233

WRKS-FM
395 Hudson St. 7th Fl.
New York, NY 10014
(212) 242-9870
Fax: (212) 929-8559

WWRL-AM
41-30 58th St.
Woodside, NY 11377
(718) 335-1600
Fax: (718) 651-9749

North Carolina

WBAV-AM
520 Hwy. 29 N
Concord, NC 28025
(704) 342-2644
Fax: (704) 343-9820

WBCG-FM
PO Box 38
Murfreesboro, NC 27855
(919) 398-4111
Fax: (919) 332-8329

WFXC-FM
5400 S. Miami Blvd., No. 116
Morrisville, NC 27560
(919) 941-0700
Fax: (919) 941-1074

WFXK-FM
3209 Gresham Lake Rd., Ste. 160
Raleigh, NC 27615
800-332-1043
Fax: (919) 954-1975

WIDU-AM
145 Roman St.
Drawer 2247
Fayetteville, NC 28302
(910) 483-6111
Fax: (910) 483-6601

WIKS-FM
207 Glenburnie Dr.
PO Box 12684
New Bern, NC 28561-2815
(919) 633-1500
Fax: (919) 633-0718

WJMH-FM
7819 National Service Rd., Bldg. 401
Greensboro, NC 27409
(910) 605-5200
Fax: (910) 855-5899

WLLE-AM
649 Maywood Ave.
Raleigh, NC 27603
(919) 833-3874
Fax: (919) 832-1126

WNAA-FM
NC A & T State University
Price Hall, Ste. 200
Greensboro, NC 27411
(910) 334-7936
Fax: (910) 334-7960

WOOW-AM
310 Evans St. Mall
Greenville, NC 27834
(919) 757-0365
Fax: (919) 757-1793

WQOK-FM
8601 Six Forks Rd., Ste. 609
Raleigh, NC 27615
(919) 848-9736
Fax: (919) 848-4724

WRVS-FM
PO Box 800
Elizabeth City, NC 27909
(919) 335-3517
Fax: (919) 335-3745

WSMY-AM
PO Box 910
Roanoke Rapids, NC 27870
(919) 536-3115
Fax: (919) 536-3045

WSNC-FM
Winston-Salem State University
601 MLK Junior Dr.
Winston-Salem, NC 27101
(910) 750-2324
Fax: (910) 750- 2329

Ohio

WCIN-AM
3540 Reading Rd.
Cincinnati, OH 45229
(513) 281-7180
Fax: (513) 281-6125

WCKX-FM
510 E. Mound St.
Columbus, OH 43215-5539
(614) 464-0020
Fax: (614) 464-2960

WDIG-AM
4039 Sunset Blvd.
Steubenville, OH 43952
(614) 264-1760
Fax: (614) 282-1473

WIZF-FM
7030 Reading Rd., No. 316
Cincinnati, OH 45237-3839
(513) 351-5900
Fax: (513) 351-0020

WJTB-AM
105 Lake Ave.
Elyria, OH 44035
(216) 327-1844
Fax: (216) 322-8942

WLPM-AM
188 Katy Ln.
Englewood, OH 45322-2466

WLQR-AM
2965 Pickle Rd.
PO Box 167581
Oregon, OH 43616
(419) 691-1470
Fax: (419) 691-0396

WVKO-AM
4401 Carriage Hill Ln.
Columbus, OH 43220-3800
(614) 451-2191
Fax: (614) 821-9595

WZAK-FM
2510 St. Claire Ave.
Cleveland, OH 44114
(216) 621-9300
Fax: (216) 771-4164

WZIP-FM
157 University Ave.
Akron, OH 44325-1004
(216) 972-7105
Fax: (216) 972-5521

Oklahoma

KIRQ-FM
PO Box 1050
Lawton, OK 73502
(405) 355-1050
Fax: (405) 355-1056

KVSP-AM
1528 NE 23rd St.
Oklahoma City, OK 73111
(405) 427-5877
Fax: (405) 424-6708

KXOJ-AM
2448 E. 81st St., Ste. 5950
Tulsa, OK 74137
(918) 492-2660
Fax: (918) 492-8840

Pennsylvania

WDAS-FM
Belmont Ave. at Edgely Rd.
Philadelphia, PA 19131
(215) 878-2000
Fax: (215) 877-3931

WHAT-AM
2471 N. 54th St.
Philadelphia, PA 19131
(215) 581-5161
Fax: (215) 581-5185

WKDU-FM
3210 Chestnut St.
Philadelphia, PA 19104
(215) 895-5920
Fax: (215) 895-1414

WLIU-FM
Office of Student Activities
Lincoln University, PA 19352
(215) 932-8300
Fax: (215) 932-1905

WPHI-FM
100 Old York Rd., Ste. A-1
Jenkintown, PA 19046
(215) 884-9400
Fax: (215) 884-2608

WTCY-AM
PO Box 104
Harrisburg, PA 17108
(717) 238-5122
Fax: (717) 234-7780

WUSL-FM
440 Domino Ln.
Philadelphia, PA 19128
(215) 483-8900
Fax: (215) 483-5930

South Carolina

WASC-AM
840 Wofford
PO Box 5686
Spartanburg, SC 29304
(803) 585-1530
Fax: (803) 573-7790

WBAW-AM
PO Box 447
Barnwell, SC 29812
(803) 259-3507
Fax: (803) 259-2691

WDOG-AM
PO Box 442
Allendale, SC 29810
(803) 259-3507

WDOG-FM
PO Box 442
Allendale, SC 29810
(803) 584-3500

WFXA-FM
104 Bennett Ln.
North Augusta, SC 29841
(803) 279-2330
Fax: (803) 279-8149

WGCD-AM
PO Box 746
Chester, SC 29706
(803) 581-1490

WLBG-AM
Box 1289
Laurens, SC 29360
(803) 984-3544
Fax: (803) 984-3545

WMTY-FM
PO Box 459
Greenwood, SC 29648
(864) 223-4300
Fax: (803) 223-4096

WPAL-AM
1717 Wappoo Rd.
Charleston, SC 29407
(803) 763-6330
Fax: (803) 769-4857

WQKI-FM
Riley Road
St. Matthews, SC 29135
(803) 874-2777

WWDM-FM
PO Box 9127
Columbia, SC 29290
(803) 495-2558
Fax: (803) 695-8605

WYNN-FM
170 E. Palmetto St.
PO Box 100531
Florence, SC 29501-0531
(803) 662-6364
Fax: (803) 669-2654

Tennessee

KJMS-FM
80 N. Tillman
Memphis, TN 38111
(901) 323-0101
Fax: (901) 320-1754

WABD-AM
150 State Line Rd.
Clarksville, TN 37042
(615) 431-5555
Fax: (615) 431-4986

WBOL-AM
PO Box 191
Bolivar, TN 38008
(901) 658-3690
Fax: (901) 658-3408

WDBL-AM
Box 606
Springfield, TN 37172
(615) 384-5541
Fax: (615) 384-9325

WDIA-AM
112 Union Ave.
Memphis, TN 38103
(901) 529-4300
Fax: (901) 529-9557

WFKX-FM
425 E. Chester
Jackson, TN 38301
(901) 427-9616
Fax: (901) 427-9302

WHRK-FM
112 Union Ave.
Memphis, TN 38103
(901) 529-4300
Fax: (901) 529-9557

WJTT-FM
409 Chestnut St., Ste. A154
Chattanooga, TN 37402
(423) 265-9494
Fax: (423) 266-2335

WNOX-FM
108 A.W. Inskip Dr.
Knoxville, TN 37912
(423) 281-9999
Fax: (423) 688-0375

WQQK-FM
1320 Brick Church Pike
PO Box 70085
Nashville, TN 37207
(615) 227-1470
Fax: (615) 227-2740

WVOL-AM
1320 Brick Church Pike
PO Box 70085
Nashville, TN 37207
(615) 227-1470
Fax: (615) 227-2740

Texas

KALO-AM
7700 Gulfway
Port Arthur, TX 77642
(409) 963-1276
Fax: (409) 963-1640

KAZI-FM
8906 Wall St., Ste. 202
Austin, TX 78754-4542
(512) 836-9544
Fax: (512) 836-1146

KCOH-AM
5011 Almeda Rd.
Houston, TX 77004
(713) 522-1001
Fax: (713) 521-0769

KHRN-FM
219 N. Main, Ste. 600
Bryan, TX 77803
(409) 779-3337
Fax: (409) 779-3444

KIIZ-AM
Box 2469
Harker Heights, TX 76543
(817) 699-5000
Fax: (817) 628-8840

KJCE-AM
4301 Westbank Dr.
Bldg. B, Ste. 350
Austin, TX 78746
800-366-8696
Fax: (512) 329-6252

KKDA-FM
PO Box 530860
Grand Prairie, TX 75053
(214) 263-9911
Fax: (214) 554-0010

KMHT-FM
PO Box 330
Huntsville, TX 77342-0330

KMJQ-FM
24 Greenway Plaza, No. 1508
Houston, TX 77046
(713) 623-0102
Fax: (713) 623-0106

KPVU-FM
PO Box 156
Prairie View, TX 77446-0156
(409) 857-4511
Fax: (409) 857-2729

KRBV-FM
7901 Carpenter Frwy.
Dallas, TX 75247
(214) 630-3011
Fax: (214) 688-7760

KSJL-AM
217 Alamo Plaza, Ste. 200
San Antonio, TX 78205
(210) 271-9600
Fax: (210) 271-0489

KZEY-AM
PO Box 4248
Tyler, TX 75712
(903) 593-1744
Fax: (903) 593-2666

Utah

KTCE-FM
PO Box 10
Provo, UT 84603-0010
(801) 371-9000
Fax: (801) 465-3299

Virginia

WARR-AM
553 Michigan Dr.
Hampton, VA 23669-3899
(804) 723-1270

WCDX-FM
2809 Emerywood Pkwy., Ste. 300
Richmond, VA 23294
(804) 672-9299
Fax: (804) 672-9314

WCHV-AM
1140 Rose Hill Dr.
Charlottseville, VA 22903
(804) 977-5566
Fax: (804) 977-0747

WHOV-FM
Hampton Institute
Hampton, VA 23668
(804) 727-5670
Fax: (804) 727-5084

WILA-AM
865 Industrial Ave.
PO Box 3444
Danville, VA 24543
(804) 792-2133
Fax: (804) 792-2134

WJJS-AM
1105 Main St.
Madison Heights, VA 24572
(804) 847-1266
Fax: (804) 845-4385

WJWS-AM
PO Box 216
South Hill, VA 23970
(804) 447-4007
Fax: (804) 447-4789

WKBY-AM
12932 US Hwy. 29
Chatham, VA 24531
(804) 432-8108
Fax: (804) 432-1523

WMYK-FM
645 Church St., Ste. 400
Norfolk, VA 23510
(804) 622-9723
Fax: (804) 624-6515

WPAK-AM
446 Old Plank Rd.
Farmville, VA 23901
(804) 392-8114
Fax: (804) 392-1080

WPLZ-FM
2809 Emerywood Pkwy., No. 300
Richmond, VA 23294
(804) 672-9300
Fax: (804) 672-9314

WVST-FM
Virginia State University
PO Box 9067
Petersburg, VA 23806
(804) 524-5932
Fax: (804) 524-5826

Washington

KKFX-AM
1509 Queen Anne Ave., No. 612
Seattle, WA 98109-5730
(206) 728-1250
Fax: (206) 728-1949

KRIZ-AM
2600 S. Jackson St.
Seattle, WA 98144
(206) 329-7880
Fax: (206) 322-6518

KZIZ-AM
c/o KRIZ-AM
2600 S. Jackson St.
Seattle, WA 98144
(206) 627-1103
Fax: (206) 322-6518

Wisconsin

WBZN-AM
2400 S. 102nd St.
West Allis, WI 53227
(414) 321-1007
Fax: (414) 321-2231

WKKV-FM
2400 S. 102nd St.
West Allis, WI 53227
(414) 321-1007
Fax: (414) 321-2231

WNOV-AM
3815 N. Teutonia Ave.
Milwaukee, WI 53206
(414) 449-9668
Fax: (414) 449-9945

Cable Television Networks

BET (Black Entertainment Television)
BET Holdings, Inc.
1900 W. Pl, NE
Washington, DC 20018
(202) 608-2100
Fax: (202) 608-2597

Television Stations

California

KNTV-TV
645 Park Ave.
San Jose, CA 95110
(408) 286-1111
Fax: (408) 295-5461

KSEE-TV
5035 E. McKinley
Fresno, CA 93727
(209) 454-2424
Fax: (209) 454-2485

District of Columbia

WHMM-TV
2222 4th St., NW
Washington, DC 20059
(202) 806-3200
Fax: (202) 806-3300

Florida

WTVT-TV
3213 W. Kennedy Blvd.
Tampa, FL 33609
(813) 876-1313
Fax: (813) 875-8329

Georgia

WFLI-TV
4654 Varnell Rd.
PO Box 302
Cohutta, GA 30710
(706) 694-3337
Fax: (706) 694-4112

WGXA-TV
559 Martin Luther King, Jr.
Macon, GA 31201
(912) 745-2424
800-592-4240
Fax: (912) 750-4347

WRDW-TV
PO Drawer 1212
Augusta, GA 30903-1212
(912) 278-1212
Fax: (912) 279-8316

Illinois

WEEK-TV
2907 Springfield Rd.
Peoria, IL 61611
(309) 698-2525
Fax: (309) 698-9335

Indiana

WPTA-TV
3401 Butler Rd.
Box 2121
Ft. Wayne, IN 46801
(219) 483-0584
Fax: (219) 484-8240

Louisiana

WNOL-TV
1661 Canal St., Ste. 1200
New Orleans, LA 70112-2861
(504) 525-3838
Fax: (504) 569-0908

Maine

WVII-TV
371 Target Industrial Circle
PO Box 1101
Bangor, ME 04401
(207) 945-6457
Fax: (207) 942-0511

Michigan

WWMT-TV
590 W. Maple St.
Kalamazoo, MI 49008
(616) 388-3333
Fax: (616) 388-8322

Minnesota

KBJR-TV
230 E. Superior St.
Duluth, MN 55802
(218) 727-8484
Fax: (218) 727-9699

New York

WKBW-TV
7 Broadcast Plaza
Buffalo, NY 14202
(716) 845-6100
Fax: (716) 842-1855

WTVH-TV
980 James St.
Syracuse, NY 13203
(315) 425-5555
Fax: (315) 425-5513

Tennessee

WFLI-AM
621 O'Grady Dr.
Chattanooga, TN 37409
(615) 821-3555
Fax: (423) 821-3557

Texas

KEYE-TV
10700 Metric Blvd.
Austin, TX 78758
(512) 835-0042
Fax: (512) 837-6753

Wisconsin

WJFW-TV
S. Oneida Ave.
PO Box 858
Rhinelander, WI 54501
(715) 369-4700
Fax: (715) 369-1910

20

Film and Television

◆ African Americans in Film ◆ African Americans in Television
◆ Filmography of Selected Feature Films and Documentaries
◆ Actors, Filmmakers, and Film and Television Executives

by Gil L. Robertson IV

As the foremost medium for creative expression, cinema yields a great deal of power and influence in defining images that shape humanity. Although primarily seen as a form of entertainment, it plays a significant role in the manner in which society views itself and the world around it. With regards to the representation of African Americans in cinema, the medium has largely failed in illuminating images that reflect the complete diversity of that experience. Instead, it has largely focused on images that devalue African Americans by confining their representation within an ideological web of myths, stereotypes, and caricatures.

The experiences of African Americans in television have been somewhat less limiting than those realized in film. This has been due, in part, to the fact that television sought to capture an African American audience from the outset. In fact, many of the medium's earliest participants such as Steve Allen publicly stated that the medium's success would certainly benefit by the inclusion of African American performers. Therefore, beginning with the medium's widespread use in the late 1940s and into the present day, television has provided some unique avenues of expression for African Americans in acting, production, and executive roles.

◆ AFRICAN AMERICANS IN FILM

The Silent Film Era

Beginning with the inception of the "moving camera" in the 1890s, African American images in cinema have been positioned, marginalized, and subordinated in every possible manner to glorify and relentlessly hold to America's status quo. In 1898, the first African Americans appeared in film as soldiers heading for battle in the Spanish–American War. Soon afterwards though, the depiction of African Americans began to mirror the racial stereotypes of that time, appearing as criminals, ministers, and, during the period in which American society grew sentimental for the Civil War era, as slaves. The most provocative film of the era in which African Americans were depicted in servitude was D.W. Griffith's *The Birth of a Nation* (1915).

Released at the end of the silent film era, *The Birth of a Nation* unleashed a tremendous amount of ire and controversy that is still discussed in cinematic circles. Although its release represented a technical and artistic triumph for the film community, its unabashed message of racial intolerance and embellished, stereotypical images of African Americans has become symbolic of the tremendous obstacles that African Americans face in cinema. Although other films such as *Uncle Tom's Cabin* (1909) and *The Nigger* (1915) drew upon the same anti-African American propaganda, *The Birth of a Nation*, due to its technological significance, stands out as a fundamental reference to cinema's position on African American images.

Redefining African American Images

In response to the popularity of such films, African Americans during the 1910s and 1920s formed independent film projects and production companies in order to create more realistic images of the African American culture.

Perhaps the best known African American filmmaker of this period is Oscar Micheaux, who managed to generate financial profits from more than thirty silent and sound features that his private studio released. Utilizing a similar distribution system to that created by African American film producer Noble Johnson, Micheaux personally delivered films to movie theaters across the country, edited films on the road, and obtained money from theater owners by having actors give private performances from scenes of upcoming releases. Despite the fact that many of his films suffered from poor technical skills, Micheaux's expert abilities as a promoter earned him a sizeable following. (Always daring, Micheaux turned the tables on Hollywood by casting his light-skinned actors to play whites in several of his films.) In 1924 the Micheaux movie *Body and Soul* featured Paul Robeson in his film debut.

After recovering from bankruptcy, Micheaux released *The Exile* in 1931—the first African American feature-length sound movie—and *God's Stepchildren* (1937), among other "talkies." As taste began to shift from what were called "race productions" though, Micheaux saw his audience dwindle. His final film released in 1948, a three-hour epic titled *The Betrayal*, was a commercial failure. While many of his films have been lost, Micheaux maintained control of his prized works, ensuring that they were protected as the legal property of his wife.

There were other African American pioneer filmmakers of this time period—some of whose efforts pre-dated Micheaux's. William "Bill" Foster began using "all-colored" casts in a number of short films in 1913. Through his Foster Photoplay Company, he released several films, the most notable of which were *The Railroad Porter*, *The Butler*, and *The Grafter and the Maid*. Although Foster genuinely believed in the viability of launching an African American movie company, attempting to secure technical and financial support not to mention distribution outlets soon brought about his company's demise.

Headed by Noble Johnson, the Lincoln Motion Picture Company, which was established in the summer of 1915, was perhaps the first company to produce significant films featuring black performers for African American audiences. The company released several films that depicted African Americans in a common, natural manner. In response to distribution problems that often plagued African American studios, Johnson worked out a commission system that engaged African American media personnel across the United States to utilize their business relationships with movie theater owners and show his films. By doing so, Johnson was able to produce such films as *The Realization of a Negro's Ambition* (1916), *The Trooper of Company K* (1917), and *The Law of Nature* (1918). Though somewhat successful, this system could not compete with major Hollywood studios, and after Johnson's defection to Universal Films, the company soon folded.

Another early African American film pioneer was Emmett J. Scott. A former secretary to Tuskegee Institute founder Booker T. Washington, Scott believed that African American cinema could be financially supported through the sale of stock in his production company. Incorporated in July 1916, his Birth of a Race Photoplay Corporation produced *The Birth of a Race* and released the film in December 1918. Although the film did not meet original expectations, it did succeed in establishing a capital-raising tool that would prove instrumental to future African American filmmakers.

In addition, many other African American entrepreneurs took the gamble on producing films with varying degrees of success. The Frederick Douglass Film Company premiered its first film *The Colored American Winning His Suit* in 1916. In 1920, the Royal Gardens Film Company presented *In the Depths of Our Hearts*, and in 1921 the ex-heavyweight champion Jack Johnson starred in *As the World Rolls On* for Andlauer Productions. In each case, however, the African American entrepreneurs behind these ventures succumbed to the insurmountable obstacles dealt to them because of racism.

Breaking into Mainstream Sound Films

Prior to the sound era of cinema, many film producers used white actors in "blackface," or burnt-cork makeup, to portray blacks. As a means of capturing the distinctive dialect and cadence of African Americans though, most producers began to employ African American actors for such limited roles during the new era of sound film. Though short "talkies" by other white filmmakers depicted African Americans in a more authentic manner, little else changed for African American performers, generally appearing as criminals and domestic servants, among other roles. In fact, the film widely heralded for utilizing sound in film *The Jazz Singer* (1927) starred ex-vaudevillian Al Jolson singing in "blackface."

One favorable change for African American performers during this era was the establishment of the movie musical. From the late 1920s through the 1940s, countless movie musicals were made and featured African American performers. For the fortunate few, singing in a film was a real achievement—not only did it guarantee work on a project, but it also enabled performers to showcase broader talents. As the film community reveled in its latest trend, many multi-talented African American performers—such as Lena Horne—were discovered.

Lena Horne (Schomburg Center for Research in Black Culture)

Hattie McDaniel (AP/Wide World Photos, Inc.)

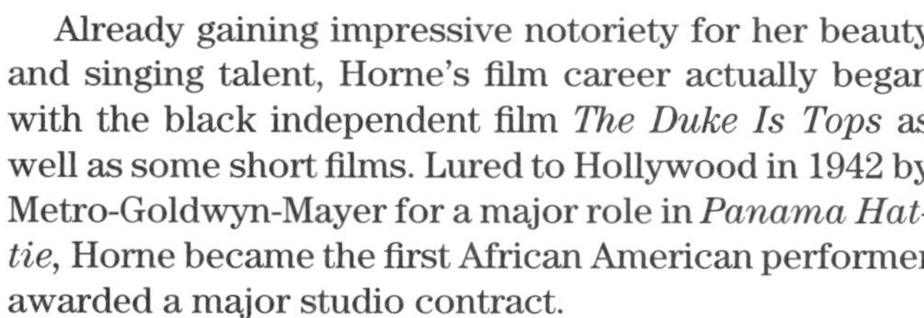

Already gaining impressive notoriety for her beauty and singing talent, Horne's film career actually began with the black independent film *The Duke Is Tops* as well as some short films. Lured to Hollywood in 1942 by Metro-Goldwyn-Mayer for a major role in *Panama Hattie*, Horne became the first African American performer awarded a major studio contract.

Lena Horne faced some unusual circumstances in Hollywood, though, due to her physical appearance. As a light-skinned African American with long flowing hair, she was viewed by many as something other than black. However, as a staunch supporter of her ethnicity, the actress refused to sacrifice pride in her heritage—such as playing demeaning roles as a slave or servant—for greater opportunities of film stardom. As a result, Horne only appeared in two other major films *Cabin In The Sky* and *Stormy Weather*. Beyond these works, Horne's brief film career mostly consisted of musical numbers that could easily be edited in order to appease Southern viewing audiences.

Another notable performer whose breakthrough came during this era was actor Paul Robeson. Widely respected for his work as a stage actor, Robeson went on to play important roles in nine feature films between 1929 and 1942. By sheer force of talent and charisma, Robeson succeeded where many others had failed in consistently securing roles that were central to the theme of the film. In such classic dramas as *Emperor Jones*, the musical *Show Boat*, and the British film *The Proud Valley*, Robeson created characters that challenged film barriers of that time. Unfortunately, the barriers of prejudice and stereotype continued to exist, and Robeson, after consistently being denied roles worthy of his talent, abandoned Hollywood to pursue a concert career.

African American Actors Endure Racial Stereotypes

Throughout the pantheon of early Hollywood cinema perhaps no other African American caricature was as well-entrenched as the "mammy" figure. Often the source of comic relief, these characters populated films from around 1914 through the late 1950s. No two performers better embodied that image than Louise Beavers and Hattie McDaniels, since physically, they both met the industry's standards. Although Beavers and McDaniels both enjoyed lengthy film careers, neither was able to discard this stereotype. Beavers, who is best known for her role in the 1934 film version of *Imitation Of Life*,

Dorothy Dandridge (AP/Wide World Photos, Inc.)

Sidney Poitier (AP/Wide World Photos, Inc.)

also appeared in over 120 films. McDaniels, who earned an Academy Award in 1939 for her role in *Gone With the Wind*, appeared in more than 300 films. Despite the stereotypical roles that each performed, Beavers and McDaniels were both well-respected and seen as successful members of the Hollywood film community.

Between the late 1920s through the mid-1940s, many other African American performers were successful in establishing film careers. Although virtually all had to suffer through gross indignities in pursuit of careers, they nevertheless contributed to the growing African American presence in mainstream films. These actors and actresses included Earl "Rochester" Anderson, Rex Ingram, Ethel Waters, and Nina Mae McKinney.

World War II Propaganda Films Strive for Racial Harmony

With the advent of World War II, leaders of the Civil Rights movement of the early twentieth century seized the opportunity to press the U.S. government to address racial injustice including providing equal opportunity in wartime industry and the military. At the same time, such activist groups as the National Association for the Advancement of Colored People (NAACP) lobbied Hollywood for better film roles for African Americans.

In response, the U.S. War Department produced the groundbreaking film *The Negro Soldier* in 1944. At the same time, Hollywood produced movies that depicted a racially-integrated military, years before President Truman's Executive Order No. 9981 mandated desegregation of the armed forces. For example, in *Crash Dive*, African American actor Ben Carter is shown saving the life of the film's star, Tyrone Power. In the film *Lifeboat* African American actor Canada Lee is shown among a shipwrecked group of civilians whose ship has been destroyed by enemy fire.

Later in the war, the U.S. government commissioned several short civilian films that expressed the theme of racial harmony. One such effort was *The House I Live In*, which won an Oscar Award for best short film in 1947. Documentaries of this period also reflected a liberal attitude toward race relations shortly after wartime. For example, documentarians Loeb and Levitt produced the work *The Quiet One* in 1948 that depicted the concerted effort put forth by white social workers in dealing with disadvantaged black juveniles.

Blacks in Postwar American Films

Films made in post-war America began to feature African Americans in multi-dimensional roles, as well as more integrated into American life. In fact, a number of films that were released in the late 1940s through the mid-1960s presented African Americans with families, careers, and working towards goals of a better life. Thus, Hollywood films sought, if only slightly, to broaden the scope of the African American experience. One significant cause was the increasing degree of political and economic influence wielded by the African American community.

Making his film debut in the 1950 drama *No Way Out* Sidney Poitier became the cinematic model for integration. Consistently depicted as an educated, intelligent, and well-mannered black man, Hollywood was quick to capitalize on Poitier's appeal. With film credits that include *Cry, the Beloved Country* (1951), *The Defiant Ones* (1958), *A Raisin in the Sun* (1961), *Guess Who's Coming to Dinner* (1967), and *In the Heat of the Night* (1967), Poitier became Hollywood's first bonafide African American film star. In 1963, he won the Academy Award in the best actor category—the first by an African American—for his lead role in *Lilies of the Field.*

Though Poitier's success symbolized the changing industry standards for African American performers during the course of the next two decades, his stardom did not come without a price. Although positioned as a leading actor, Poitier's characterizations often lacked human dimension. For instance, in all but three of the films made during this period, Poitier was never allowed to exhibit any degree of sexuality. Nonetheless, Poitier's career heralded greater acceptance of black actors as equals to their white counterparts.

In 1954, film actress Dorothy Dandridge became the first African American woman to be nominated for an Academy Award in the best actress category for her role in *Carmen Jones.* With unrivaled talent and beauty, it seemed that Dandridge would become the female counterpart to Poitier's leading African American man. However, she was unable to ever find a subsequent role offering the same dimensions as Carmen Jones. While Dandridge repeatedly demonstrated dramatic ability and landed a respectable contract with Twentieth Century Fox, the industry mainly only cast her in films as an exotic native. When the pressures of battling the film industry proved too much, Dandridge drifted from the Hollywood scene and in 1965 died of an apparent suicide.

In the case of actor Harry Belafonte, Hollywood was faced with another dilemma. A naturally romantic hero, the film industry found it difficult to contain Belafonte's sexuality. Similar to Dandridge whom he starred opposite in *Carmen Jones* and *Island in the Sun*, Belafonte's career was therefore largely confined to playing an island native and other unflattering roles. After performing in *Odds Against Tomorrow*, *The World, the Flesh, and the Devil*, and *Buck and the Preacher*, Belafonte began a successful career as a concert performer and prominent civil rights spokesperson, selecting future film projects only with great discretion.

Many other actors and actresses enjoyed success in films and mainstream acceptance. Among those who made a real impact during this period were Diana Sands, Ruby Dee, and Brock Peters. Along with Poitier, Dandridge, and Belafonte, their films marked the advent of the 1960s Civil Rights movement.

Blaxploitation Films

During the 1960s Civil Rights movement and the war in Vietnam, American society was in the midst of a cultural revolution. As a result, films began to reflect the political and social changes brought about by the period's harsh, challenging ideology. Director Melvin Van Peebles's seminal 1971 African American-action film *Sweet Sweetback's Baadasssss Song* seemed to define, more than any other film, this era—one marked with contempt for white social order and its police.

In wake of the enormous success of Peebles's films, Hollywood rushed to produce similar movies that would capture this new African American audience. Although some of the African American action films, most notably *Shaft* (1971), *Superfly* (1972), and *Coffy* (1973), experienced a great deal of commercial success, this trend was soon dubbed "blaxploitation" by the African American media. In pursuit of increased profits though, Hollywood even remade blaxploitation films from classic horror movies—*Blacula* and *Blackenstein*, both in 1972.

Along with the popularity of African American action films was the emergence of a new wave of serious African American-oriented dramas. While most of these films failed to meet their initial expectations, a number of others did—the 1969 releases of *The Learning Tree*, *Slaves*, *Putney Swope*, and *Sounder* (1972) to a few.

Finally, more African Americans worked in Hollywood than ever before during this period—many behind the camera as well. Such screenwriters as Richard Wesley, Bill Gunn, and Lonne Elder and directors Gordon Parks, Sr., Gordon Parks, Jr., Michael Schultz, and Stan Lathan were all called upon to participate in the making of major studio films.

Harry Belafonte (Belafonte Enterprises, Inc.)

Transitions in African American Film

Although Motown founder Berry Gordy Jr.'s impact on the American music industry is legendary, little credit has been given to him as a film producer/director. Under his Motown Films banner, Gordy produced several films, the most successful being the 1972 release *Lady Sings the Blues* starring Diana Ross and Billy Dee Williams. Gordy's pairing of them was the first time that African American performers were presented as romantic icons. Gordy's 1976 film *Mahogany* was also the first to feature an African American actress as glamorous, independent, and sexual.

African American comedians were enjoying enormous film success as well. Richard Pryor emerged in the late 1970s as a film icon. Best known for his often provocative, iconoclastic stand-up routines, Pryor rose to superstardom through supporting role appearances. After appearing opposite Gene Wilder in the 1976 buddy film *Silver Streak*, Pryor continued to exhibit box-office clout in such films as *Greased Lightning*, *Which Way is Up*, and *Bustin' Loose*. He later returned to the stage where his two live concert films permanently sealed his position in film history. Other comedians, notably Eddie Murphy in the terrifically successful movie *48 Hours* (1982) later benefitted from Pryor's success.

New African American Cinema Emerges

Towards the mid-1980s African American actors and actresses appeared to be running on empty. With the roles offered by the blaxploitation era long gone, stereotypes of the past began to reemerge. The tragic mulatto, a well-used cinematic device once again appeared as such actresses as Rae Dawn Chong (*American Flyers*), Jennifer Beals (*Flashdance*), and Lisa Bonet (*Angel Heart*) were cast in roles that made no discernable mention of their ethnicity. In addition, the African American musical made a brief resurgence in the films *Beat Street*, *Krush Groove*, *The Last Dragon*, *The Cotton Club*, and *Purple Rain*.

Another trend that enjoyed renewed popularity in cinema was "buddy movies." Although cinematic history is filled with various pairing of black and white performers, the film industry in the 1980s perfected the trend with enormous box-office success. Some notable buddy film pairings included Carl Weathers and Sylvester Stallone in the *Rocky* films and Danny Glover and Mel Gibson in the *Lethal Weapon* series.

Meanwhile, a low-budget independent film was released by a recent New York University Film School graduate named Spike Lee. The release *She's Gotta Have It* resulted in the resurgence of African American cinema. Lee managed to gain large audiences for most of his commercial ventures and directed a string of successful Hollywood films including one of the most politically-charged films of the era, *Do the Right Thing* (1989).

Spike Lee's box-office successes, coupled with the achievements of University of Southern California Film School graduate John Singleton (*Boyz N the Hood*, *Poetic Justice*, and *Rosewood*) and comedian turned actor/director Robert Townsend, (*Hollywood Shuffle* and *The Five Heartbeats*) seemed to guarantee a viable future for African American filmmakers. Along with the filmmakers, African American actors in Hollywood began to gain steady work.

Promising Future Awaits African Americans in Film

As the twentieth century drew to a close, other African American performers, most notably Angela Bassett, Laurence Fishburne, Morgan Freeman, Denzel Washington, and Lynn Whitfield have demonstrated enormous staying power and marketability. As more African American performers gain responsibility for defining African American images in cinema, it looks as if opportunities for African Americans actors, filmmakers, and industry executives during the twenty-first century will be very promising.

◆ AFRICAN AMERICANS IN TELEVISION

The Early Years of Television

Largely due to the fact that many of the new medium's early stars were lifted from popular radio programs, African American performers began to make advancements within television almost from the start. For example, entertainer and pianist Bob Howard was included in the CBS network's evening broadcast. Another gifted entertainer, jazz pianist Hazel Scott, had her own 15-minute broadcast three days a week. African American performers also appeared on variety and game shows, such as "Your Show of Shows," "All Star Revue," "Strike it Rich," and "High Finance," throughout the late 1940s and into the 1950s. On the ABC television network, musician Billy Daniels was given his own short-lived variety show in the fall of 1952.

Although television did not make use of all the same stereotypes that cinema employed, many negative caricatures did arise. As the medium began to rebroadcast feature films and shorts that appeared in theaters, many grossly unflattering portrayals of African Americans began to appear on television. In fact, such shorts as Hal Roach's *Our Gang/Little Rascals* became television mainstays.

In 1950, veteran actress Ethel Waters appeared on the first television show in which an African American was the central figure. As the star of "Beulah" for the first two seasons, the popular show centered on the weekly trials and tribulations of a black maid or "mammy"—a supporting character on the popular "Fibber McGee and Molly" radio show. ("Beulah" ran until 1953, when protests by the NAACP and other activist groups forced its cancellation.)

Other numerous former radio performers quickly followed in Water's wake including Eddie "Rochester" Anderson who played opposite Jack Benny on "The Jack Benny Show" and Willie Best who was a regularly featured performer on "The Trouble with Father" and "Oh My Little Margie." In 1953 actress Lillian Randolph began to reprise the role of a maid that she played on radio for the television series "Make Room for Daddy." Later, she appeared in the television show "Great Gildersleeve."

Perhaps no other television show, though, created as much controversy for its negative stereotyping of African Americans as the "Amos n' Andy" show. Based on the very popular 1930s and 1940s radio show "Amos n' Andy" ran from 1951 to 1953. The show was perceived

Diahann Carroll posing on the set of "Julia" in 1970 (Corbis Corporation [Bellevue]).

by many, both black as white, as an offensive reminder of the past, and the NAACP initiated lawsuits and boycott threats that were critical in forcing the show's cancellation. After the series was cancelled though, it continued to appear in syndication until the mid-1960s.

Thoughout the early 1950s, variety shows hosted by veteran white entertainers, such as Ed Sullivan, Milton Berle, and Steve Allen, occasionally featured African American entertainers. But in 1956, NBC took the bold step of creating a slot for the variety program "The Nat King Cole Show." Although the variety format had always been very popular with television viewers, and Cole's recording success was undeniable, the network was unable to secure regular sponsors, especially after Cole touched the arm of a white female guest. The show was cancelled after its first season.

Commercial Television Reacts to the 1960s

Throughout the late 1950s and into the 1960s, African Americans appeared in many serious documentaries concerning rural poverty, segregation, and the Civil Rights movement led by the Reverend Martin Luther King, Jr. The powerful medium of television provided

King and the other leaders the opportunity to increase the white viewing audience's awareness of their civil rights cause.

Commercial television reacted to the changing political, social, and economic climate in the United States much the same way that cinema did—by including more African American performers in its programming. Ensemble television shows soon began to feature African American performers: Otis Young appeared in "The Outcast;" Greg Morris starred in "Mission Impossible;" and Nicelle Nicholas was featured in "Star Trek." However, the most dramatic changes in television's positioning of African American talent occurred when Sheldon Leonard hired Bill Cosby as one of two leads to star in the 1965 television show "I Spy" and actress Diahann Carroll was featured as a widowed nurse and single mother in the drama "Julia."

While the show only lasted three seasons, "I Spy" marked the first time that an African American television actor was so widely accepted by television viewers—primarily for his inoffensive, perfect image. Consequently, Cosby earned three Emmy Awards for his portrayal of the character, Alexander Scott. Lasting from 1968 to 1971, "Julia" presented Carroll as an African American woman seemingly detached from the reality of the lives led by most African Americans. Though popular with the majority viewing audience, the show was criticized for its bland depiction of an African American. Others, however, viewed Carroll's character as an improvement over past characterizations of African Americans on television.

Blacks also began to appear on television in roles opposite whites in ways that had never before been possible. "Harlem Detective" featured black and white actors cast as equals on the police force. "Eastside/Westside" and "The Nurses" featured African American actresses Cicely Tyson and Hilda Simms, respectively, in regularly featured roles. Praised for its more balanced portrayal of African Americans, "Eastside/Westside" unfortunately lasted only one season.

As the first successful African American television variety show, "The Flip Wilson Show" was the first weekly program by an African American to feature "racial comedy" as a form of general audience entertainment. The show's rousing success paved the way for the development of the future African American situation comedies.

The Presence of African Americans on Television Expands

During the 1970s television producers, such as Norman Lear with "All in the Family," "Sanford and Son," and "Good Times" and Bud Yorkin with "What's Happenin'" and "Carter Country," created comedy programming to appeal to African American audiences. Though these shows flourished and made the African American presence on television commonplace, critics referred to them as "new ministrelsy" and derided their perpetuation of stereotypical aspects of African American humor.

One of the most significant changes occurred in children's television programming. The public television series "Sesame Street" featured a multiracial mix of children and adults interacting and learning. In addition, animated programs or cartoons, such as Bill Cosby's "Fat Albert and the Cosby Kids" (1972–1989) and the "Jackson Five," depicted events in the lives of young African American characters.

In the category of drama, notably made-for-television movies and miniseries, two productions stood out among the rest in the 1970s—"The Autobiography of Miss Jane Pittman" (1974) and "Roots" (1977). Starring actress Cicely Tyson, "The Autobiography of Miss Jane Pittman" was set in 1962 and spanned the life of a 110-year old African American woman from the era of slavery to the 1960s Civil Rights movement. For her outstanding efforts, Tyson was awarded an Emmy for best lead actress in a drama-special program. Based on the Alex Haley novel, "Roots" was the highest-rated miniseries ever, attracting an estimated 130 million viewers. Featuring such prominent African American actors as Louis Gossett, Jr., Cicely Tyson, and Maya Angelou, the eight-part epic movie traced Haley's family history from Africa to slavery in the American South.

The Cosby Decade

Throughout the late 1970s and early 1980s, African American actors continued to appear in stereotypical comedies or made-for-television movies with few exceptions. In 1984, however, veteran entertainer Bill Cosby returned to television with a half-hour series called "The Cosby Show." Although expected to do well, few could have predicted the level of the show's popularity. Consistently rated the top weekly television program, "The Cosby Show" ran for eight seasons and created tremendous opportunities for African American performers. While the phenomenal success of the "Roots" miniseries had proven that all-African American television vehicles could attract a large viewing audience, "The Cosby Show" demonstrated that an audience of similar proportions would also regularly support an entertaining, family-oriented program centered on African Americans as well.

In the wake of "The Cosby Show's" success, an increasing number of African Americans began produc-

Cicely Tyson and Maya Angelou performing in *Roots,* the hugely popular made-for-television movie of the 1970s (AP/Wide World Photos, Inc.).

ing more African American-themed shows in the late 1980s. Actor Frank Reid produced and starred in the short-lived, Emmy Award-winning show "Frank's Place." Choreographer Debbie Allen produced "The Cosby Show" spin-off "A Different World," which depicted academic life at a historical African American university. In addition, Quincy Jones's produced "Fresh Prince of Bel Air" starring rap artist Will Smith, and "In Living Color," which was produced by comedian Keenan Ivory Wayans and featured many talented members of the Wayans family.

Burgeoning Television Networks Target African American Audiences

Black Entertainment Television (BET) Holdings, Inc., which began operations in the 1980s, became the first African American-controlled cable entertainment company listed on the New York Stock Exchange in the 1990s. Led by industry giant Robert Johnson, BET targets an estimated 45 million subscribers nationwide by providing original programming on its three cable television channels—BET Cable Network, BET on Jazz, and BET Movies/Starz!3. In addition, the company has diversified its holdings by publishing magazines, marketing clothes and cosmetics, and forming a partnership with Microsoft to offer MSBET, an online service that provides entertainment information to the growing number of African Americans using the Internet.

Clearly understanding the financial gain that could result, such upstart television networks as Fox, Warner Brothers, and United Paramount Network (UPN) began to vigorously court the African American audiences in the 1990s. Such highly-rated programs as "Roc," "Living Single," "Martin," as well as many others were major hits with both black and young white television viewers. However, on the major television networks, African American programs have become an increasing rarity as the networks have begun to concentrate on offerings that deliver them the widest possible audience share.

Finally, in the areas of daytime and late night talk shows, several African Americans attained widespread acceptance for the first time in television history: Oprah Winfrey and Montel Williams have produced Emmy Award-winning daytime shows, while Arsenio Hall successfully led many imitators in attempting to revitalize late night talk show.

The Future of African Americans in Television

As television industry headed into the twenty-first century, more African Americans than ever before were involved in television—in acting, production, and executive roles. However, while African Americans have continued to enjoy success in comedic television vehicles, no primetime dramatic series has made it beyond a full television season since the 1970s. Instead, the trend is for African American performers to be cast in ensemble shows, such as "ER," "Touched by an Angel," and "NYPD Blue." Although most of these show integrate their African American cast members into their stories well, many African American performers fear that their singular voice is being diluted by an increasingly multiethnic array of characters. It remains to be seen if African Americans can find a significant place in television's new diverse cast blend.

◆ FILMOGRAPHY OF SELECTED FEATURE FILMS AND DOCUMENTARIES

The following filmography includes more than two hundred selected feature films and documentaries that are remarkable for their depiction of themes and issues related to the experiences of African Americans throughout history. Ranging from the early silent movie era through major studio releases, documentaries, and made-for-television movies of the 1990s, many of these cinematic works also represent significant milestones for African Americans in the film and television industries.

Africans in America: America's Journey through Slavery
(1998)

A four-part television documentary that chronicles the history of racial slavery in the United States from the start of the Atlantic slave trade in the sixteenth century to the end of the American Civil War in 1865. The work examines slavery from philosophical, societal, and economic viewpoints.

America's Dream
(1995)

Trilogy of short stories covering African American life from 1938 to 1958: "Long Black Song," based on a short story by Richard Wright; "The Boy Who Painted Christ Black," based on a story by John Henrich Clarke; and Maya Angelou's "The Reunion."

Amistad
(1997)

Director Steven Spielberg creates an epic that relates the 1839 account of African captives aboard the slaveship Amistad, led by a Mende tribesman named Cinque (Djimon Hounsou), who free themselves and take over the ship in a bloody mutiny. Lengthy legal battles eventually reach the Supreme Court, where the Africans are found to be rightfully freed individuals in the eyes of the law.

The Autobiography of Miss Jane Pittman
(1974)

The history of African Americans in the South is seen through the eyes of a 110-year-old former slave. From the Civil War through the Civil Rights movement, Miss Pittman (Cicely Tyson) relates every piece of African American history, allowing the viewer to experience the injustices. Received nine Emmy Awards; adapted by Tracy Keenan Wynn from the novel by Ernest J. Gaines.

Beloved
(1998)

Oprah Winfrey's pet project (she had owned the film rights for ten years) is a faithful adaptation of Toni Morrison's Pulitzer Prize-winning novel.

Beverly Hills Cop
(1984)

When a close friend of smooth-talking Detroit cop Axle Foley (Eddie Murphy) is brutally murdered, he traces the murderer to the posh streets of Beverly Hills. There he must stay on his toes to keep one step ahead of the killer and two steps ahead of the law. First of three action-comedies.

Bingo Long Traveling All-Stars & Motor Kings
(1976)

Set in 1939, this film follows the comedic adventures of a lively group of African American baseball players (Billy Dee Williams, James Earl Jones, and Richard Pryor) who have defected from the old Negro National League. The All-Stars travel the country challenging local white teams.

Bird
(1988)

The richly textured biography of jazz saxophone great Charlie Parker (Forest Whitaker), from his rise to stardom to his premature death via extended heroin use. The soundtrack, which features Parker's own solos remastered from original recordings, earned an Academy Award for best sound. Whitaker earned the Cannes Film Festival Award for best actor, while Clint Eastwood garnered the Golden Globe Award for best director.

Birth of a Race
(1918)

Emmet J. Scott's film offers a positive depiction of African Americans during the Civil War. Although the film did not meet original expectations, it proved an inspiration to many African Americans.

Black Girl
(1972)

Directed by Ossie Davis, this intense drama examines the relationship between an African American woman, who feels that she is a failure, and her children.

Black Like Me
(1964)

Based on John Howard Griffin's successful book about how Griffin turned his skin black with a drug and traveled the South to experience prejudice firsthand. Features Roscoe Lee Brown.

Black Rodeo
(1972)

Documentary directed by Jeff Kanew provides a glimpse of an all-African American rodeo held at Triborough Stadium in New York in September, 1971.

Blackboard Jungle
(1955)

Well-remembered urban drama about an idealistic teacher (Sidney Poitier) in a slum area who fights doggedly to connect with his unruly students. Bill Hailey's "Rock Around the Clock" over the opening credits was the first use of rock music in a mainstream feature film.

Blacula
(1972)

The African Prince Mamuwalde (William Marshall) stalks the streets of Los Angeles trying to satisfy his insatiable desire for blood. Mildly successful melding of blaxploitation and horror that spawned a sequel "Scream, Blacula, Scream."

Blood of Jesus
(1941)

A sinful husband accidentally shoots his newly baptized wife, causing an uproar in their rural town. Director Spencer Williams, Jr. later starred as Andy on the "Amos n' Andy" television series. Due to its rare treatment of African American religion, the film was named to the National Film Registry in 1991.

Blue Collar
(1978)

An auto assembly line worker, tired of the poverty of his life, hatches a plan to rob his own union. Starring Richard Pryor and Yaphet Kotto, the film is a study of the working class and the robbing of the human spirit.

Body and Soul
(1924)

The first screen appearance of Paul Robeson has him cast in a dual role as a conniving preacher and his good brother. The preacher preys on the heroine, making her life a misery. Objections by censors to the preacher's character caused him to be redeemed and become worthy of the heroine's love. Directed by African American filmmaker Oscar Micheaux.

Boyz N the Hood
(1991)

Singleton's debut as a writer and director is an astonishing picture of young African American men, four high school students with different backgrounds, aims, and abilities trying to survive Los Angeles gangs and bigotry. Excellent acting throughout, with special nods to Laurence Fishburne and Cuba Gooding, Jr. Musical score by Stanley Clarke. Singleton was the youngest director ever nominated for an Oscar.

The Brother from Another Planet
(1984)

A black alien (Joe Morton) escapes from his home planet and winds up in Harlem, where he is pursued by two alien bounty hunters. The humor arises from cultural and racial misunderstandings. Independently-made morality fable by John Sayles.

Brother John
(1970)

An early look at racial tensions and labor problems. An angel (Sidney Poitier) goes back to his hometown in Alabama to see how things are going. Directed by James Goldstone and musical score by Quincy Jones.

Buck and the Preacher
(1972)

A trail guide (Sidney Poitier) and a con man preacher (Harry Belafonte) and wife (Ruby Dee) join forces to help a wagon train of former slaves who are seeking to homestead out West. Poitier's debut as a director.

Cuba Gooding Jr. (Archive Photos, Inc.)

Buffalo Soldiers
(1997)

Post-Civil War western concerns the all-black cavalry troops created by Congress in 1866 to patrol the American West. A former slave and by-the-book Army man, Sgt. Washington Wyatt (Danny Glover), leads the chase for Apache warrior Victorio (Harrison Lowe) across the New Mexico Territory while trying to deal with the common degradation suffered by his troops at the hands of white officers.

The Bus
(1964)

Documentary covers Martin Luther King, Jr.'s epic 1963 March on Washington.

Cabin in the Sky
(1943)

Based on a Broadway show and featuring an all-African American cast—Ethel Waters, Eddie Anderson, Lena Horne, and Rex Ingram. Lively dance numbers and a musical score with contributions from Louis Armstrong and Duke Ellington.

Carmen Jones
(1954)

George Bizet's tale of femme fatale Carmen with an all-African American cast—Dorothy Dandridge, Harry Belafonte, Diahann Carroll, and Brock Peters. Dandridge's Oscar nomination for best actress was first ever by an African American in a lead role. The film earned the 1955 Golden Globe Award for best film and was named to the National Film Registry in 1992.

Change of Mind
(1969)

Directed by Robert Stevens, the film portrays an African American male (Raymond St. Jacques) who has a white man's brain transplanted into his head. After the operation, he is accepted by the brain donor's wife as her husband. Music by Duke Ellington.

Charlotte Forten's Mission: Experiment in Freedom
(1985)

Fact-based story set during the Civil War. A wealthy, educated African American woman (Melba Moore), determined to prove to President Lincoln that blacks are equal to whites, journeys to a remote island off the coast of Georgia. There she teaches freed slaves to read and write.

Chuck Berry: Hail! Hail! Rock 'n' Roll
(1987)

Engaging, energetic portrait of one of rock's founding fathers, via interviews, behind-the-scenes footage, and performance clips of Berry at sixty years of age. Songs featured: "Johnny B. Goode," "Roll Over Beethoven," "Maybelline," and more. Appearances by Etta James, Bo Diddley, and Robert Cray, among others.

Claudine
(1974)

Directed by John Berry, the film depicts a single mother (Diahann Carroll) who attempts to maintain her family of six children. James Earl Jones plays a trash collector and her boyfriend.

Cleopatra Jones
(1973)

Federal government agent (Tamara Dobson) with considerable martial arts prowess takes on loathsome drug lords. Followed by *Cleopatra Jones and the Casino of Gold.*

Clockers
(1995)

Strike (Mekhi Phifer), leader of a group of drug dealers ("clockers"), engages in a power struggle with his boss (Delroy Lindo), his do-the-right-thing brother Victor (Isaiah Washington), and his own conscience. He is also suspected of murder by relentless narcotics cop Rocco Klein (Harvey Keitel). Poignant and compelling street drama is based on the Richard Price novel. Music by Terence Blanchard.

Color Adjustment
(1991)

Narrated by Ruby Dee, the film documents the modern history of race relations in the United States in the arena of television. Traces the progress of African Americans from caricatures to victims to mainstream as portrayed by television.

The Color Purple
(1985)

Adaptation of Alice Walker's acclaimed book features strong lead from Whoopi Goldberg (her screen debut which earned the 1986 Golden Globe Award for best actress in a drama) and talk show host Oprah Winfrey (also her film debut), among others. Brilliant musical score by co-producer Quincy Jones compliments this strong film.

The Cool World
(1963)

Tough-talking docudrama, set on the streets of Harlem, focuses on a 15-year-old African American youth whose one ambition in life is to own a gun and lead his gang. Named to the National Film Registry in 1994.

Cooley High
(1975)

African American high school students in Chicago go through the rites of passage in their senior year during the 1960s. Film is funny, smart, and much acclaimed. Great soundtrack featuring Motown hits of the era is a highlight. Sequel to the TV series "What's Happenin'."

Cornbread, Earl and Me
(1975)

Directed by Joe Manduke, a high school basketball star from the ghetto is mistaken for a murderer by cops and is shot, causing a subsequent furor of protest and racial hatred. Music by Donald Byrd.

Cosmic Slop
(1994)

Three-part anthology: "Space Traders," based on a story by Derrick Bell; "The First Commandment;" and "Tang," based on a story by Chester Himes.

The Cotton Club
(1984)

An African American musician playing at The Cotton Club falls in love with gangster Dutch Schultz's girlfriend. A black tap dancer falls in love with a member of the chorus line who can pass for white. These two love stories are told against a background of mob violence and music during the early jazz era.

Cotton Comes to Harlem
(1970)

A successful mix of crime and comedy about a suspicious preacher's back-to-Africa scheme that detectives (Godfrey Cambridge and Raymond St. Jacques) suspect is a swindle. Based on the novel by Chester Himes, the film serves as the directorial debut of Ozzie Davis.

The Court Martial of Jackie Robinson
(1990)

True story of a little known chapter in the life of the famous athlete. During his stint in the Army, Robinson (played by Andre Braugher) refused to take a back seat on a bus and subsequently faced the possibility of court martial.

Crisis at Central High
(1980)

A dramatic television recreation of the events leading up to the 1957 integration of Central High in Little Rock, Arkansas. Based on teacher Elizabeth Huckaby's journal.

Crooklyn
(1994)

Director Spike Lee profiles an African American middle-class family growing up in 1970s Brooklyn and focuses on the only girl (Zelda Harris) coming of age. Music by Terence Blanchard.

Darktown Jubilee
(1914)

One of the earliest feature films to star an African American actor-comedian Bert Williams. This film was controversial because it portrayed African Americans in a positive manner.

Daughters of the Dust
(1991)

Five women of a Gullah family living on the Sea Islands off the Georgia coast in 1902 contemplate moving to the mainland in this emotional tale of change. Family bonds and memories are celebrated with a quiet narrative and beautiful cinematography in Julie Dash's feature-film directorial debut. Honored by the Sundance Film Festival for best cinematography.

The Defiant Ones
(1958)

Thought-provoking story about racism revolves around two black and white escaped prisoners (Sidney Poitier and Tony Curtis) from a chain gang in the rural South. Their societal conditioning to hate each other dissolves as they face constant peril together. Earned several cinematic honors including Academy Awards for best story, screenplay, and best black & white cinematography, as well as the Golden Globe Award for best film—drama.

Devil in a Blue Dress
(1995)

Easy Rawlins (Denzel Washington), an unemployed aircraft worker in 1948 Los Angeles, is hired to find mystery woman Daphne (Jennifer Beals) by a shady businessman. Realism and accuracy in period detail enhance solid performance by Washington. Based upon the Walter Mosley novel.

Do the Right Thing
(1989)

An uncompromising, brutal comedy written and directed by Spike Lee about the racial tensions surrounding a white-owned pizzeria in the Bed-Stuy section of Brooklyn on the hottest day of the summer, and the violence that eventually erupts.

Down in the Delta
(1998)

Chicago matriarch Rosa Lynn (Mary Alice) tries to prevent her jobless, single-mom daughter Loretta (Alfre Woodard) from succumbing to destructive forces by sending Loretta and her two grandchildren to her brother's home (Morgan Freeman) in the Mississippi delta. Poet-novelist Maya Angelou's first outing as a director skillfully demonstrates the importance of connecting to one's heritage.

A Dream for Christmas
(1973)

Earl Hamner, Jr. (best known for writing the "The Waltons") wrote this moving made-for-television story of an African American minister whose church in Los Angeles is scheduled to be demolished.

Driving Miss Daisy
(1989)

Tender and sincere portrayal of a 25-year friendship between an aging Jewish woman and the African American chauffeur forced upon her by her son. The film subtly explores the effects of prejudice in the South. Earned numerous Academy and Golden Globe Awards.

The Duke Is Tops
(1938)

In singer Lena Horne's earliest existing film appearance, she attempts to make the "big-time," while her boyfriend joins a traveling medicine show. The film helped to the begin the 1940s swing era.

Dutchman
(1967)

Film presentation of Amiri Baraka's one-act play depicting the claustrophobic reality of the African American male's situation in the late 1960s. Starring Al Freeman, Jr., the film earned best honors at the 1967 Cannes Film Festival.

Eight Trey Gangster: The Making of a Crip
(1993)

A provocative documentary that explores the experiences and social environment influencing the life decisions of an African American gang member in Los Angeles.

Emperor Jones
(1933)

Loosely based on Eugene O'Neill's play, the film portrays the rise and fall of a railroad porter (Paul Robeson) whose exploits take him from a life sentence on a chain gang to emperor of Haiti.

Eve's Bayou
(1997)

Set in Louisiana 1962 and told in flashback, the film presents a mesmerizing and complex story with haunting visuals about the upper middle-class Batiste family.

Impressive, multi-layered directorial debut from Kasi Lemmons. Music by Terence Blanchard.

Eyes on the Prize
(1986)

A comprehensive six-part series on the history of the Civil Rights movement from World War II to the present. Includes Rosa Parks and the bus boycott, the leadership of Martin Luther King, Jr., and the last great march in Selma, among other moments.

Eyes on the Prize II: America at the Racial Crossroads (1965–1985)
(1987)

The Civil Rights movement, from the mid-1960s to mid-1980s, is traced in this four-volume documentary.

A Family Thing
(1996)

Racial issues are addressed in this character-driven story of two brothers in which Southerner Earl Pilcher (Robert Duvall) learns his biological mother was black and that he also has a half brother, Ray (James Earl Jones), who is black and living in Chicago. The two brothers slowly find common ground.

Fear of a Black Hat
(1994)

A good-natured comedy in which the trio known as NWH (Niggaz With Hats) are touring in support of their album and trying to convince filmmaker Nina Blackburn (Kasi Lemmons) of their street credibility. However, the more the gangsta rappers explain themselves, the less sense they make.

The Five Heartbeats
(1991)

Well-told story of five African American singers in the 1960s, their successes and failures as a group and as individuals. Skillfully directed by Robert Townsend who did research by talking to the Dells. Music by Stanley Clarke.

For Love of Ivy
(1968)

Sidney Poitier is a trucking executive who has a gambling operation on the side. Ivy (Abbey Lincoln) is the black maid of a rich white family who is about to leave her job to look for romance. The two are brought together but the road to true love does not run smooth. Based on a story by Poitier; music by Quincy Jones.

For Us, The Living
(1988)

The life and assassination of civil rights activist Medgar Evers are dramatically presented in this adaptation of the biography written by Evers's widow. Provides insight into Evers's character, not just a recording of the events surrounding his life.

48 Hrs.
(1982)

An experienced San Francisco cop (Nick Nolte) springs a convict (Eddie Murphy) from jail for 48 hours to find a vicious murdering-escaped con. Film marks Murphy's screen debut.

Fresh
(1994)

Enterprising young man (Sean Nelson) who sells drugs draws life lessons from chess-hustler father (Samuel L. Jackson) and heroin-dealing mentor (Giancarlo Esposito), so he looks for a way out of the dead-end business. First time director Boaz Yakin was awarded the Filmmakers Trophy and Special Jury Prize at the 1994 Sundance Film Festival.

Fundi: The Story of Ella Baker
(1986)

Ella Baker's nickname "Fundi" comes from the Swahili word for a person who passes skills from one generation to another. This film documents Baker's work in the Civil Rights movement of the 1960s, and her friendship with Dr. Martin Luther King, Jr.

Get On the Bus
(1996)

Spike Lee looks at the personal side of the Million Man March through a fictional group of men who board a bus in south central Los Angeles and head for Washington, DC. Practically ignoring the event itself, Lee and writer Reggie Rock Bythewood focus on the men who participated, their reasons, and their interaction with each other.

Ghosts of Mississippi
(1996)

Director Rob Reiner tells the story of civil rights leader Medgar Evers, murdered in 1963, and the three trials of Byron De la Beckwith (James Woods), who was finally convicted (after two hung juries) in 1994. Whoopie Goldberg plays the role of Evers's widow, Myrlie; Evers's sons, Darrell and Van, play themselves; and daughter Reena appears as a juror while her character is played by Yolanda King, the daughter of slain civil rights leader Martin Luther King, Jr.

Glory
(1989)

A rich, historical spectacle chronicling the 54th Massachusetts, the first African American volunteer infantry unit in the Civil War. Winner of Academy Awards for best cinematography and best sound, the film offers stunning performances throughout, with exceptional work from Morgan Freeman and Denzel Washington who earned both Academy and Golden Globe Awards for best supporting actor.

Go, Man, Go!
(1954)

This film depicts the Harlem Globetrotters at a time when few African Americans competed in professional basketball and the traveling team worked to find its place in American sports with its players amazing skills and showmanship.

Go Tell It on the Mountain
(1984)

Young African American boy tries to gain the approval of his stern stepfather in this fine adaptation of James Baldwin's semi-autobiographical novel set in the 1930s.

Gone Are the Days
(1963)

Adaptation of the play *Purlie Victorious*. An African American preacher (Ossie Davis) stands up to a segregationist plantation owner from whom he obtains money to establish a church.

Gone with the Wind
(1939)

Based on Margaret Mitchell's novel, this epic Civil War drama traces Scarlett O'Hara's (Vivien Leigh) survival through the tragic history of the South during the Civil War and Reconstruction Period. Hattie McDaniel became the first African American to win an Academy Award for her portrayal of the loyal maid, Mammy. The multiple Academy Award-winning film was named to the American Film Institute Top 100 list in 1998.

Greased Lightning
(1977)

The story of the first African American auto racing champion, Wendell Scott (Richard Pryor), who had to overcome racial prejudice to achieve his success. Co-written by Melvin Van Peebles, the film also starred Pam Grier and Cleavon Little.

The Great White Hope
(1970)

A semi-fictionalized biography of boxer Jack Johnson, played by James Earl Jones, who became the first African American heavyweight world champion in 1910. Jane Alexander makes her film debut as the boxer's white lover, as both battle the racism of the times.

The Greatest
(1977)

Autobiography of Cassius Clay, the boxer who would later become the internationally recognized Muhammad Ali. Ali plays himself, and George Benson's hit "The Greatest Love of All" is introduced.

Green Pastures
(1936)

An adaptation of Marc Connelly's Pulitzer Prize-winning play that attempts to retell biblical stories in black English vernacular of the 1930s. Southern theater owners boycotted the controversial film which had an all-African American cast.

Guess Who's Coming to Dinner
(1967)

Controversial in its time, a young white woman (Katharine Houghton) brings her black fiancé (Sidney Poitier) home to meet her parents (Katharine Hepburn and Spencer Tracy). The situation truly tests their open-mindedness and understanding. Named to the American Film Institute Top 100 list in 1998.

Hallelujah!
(1929)

The first all-African American feature film and the first talkie for director King Vidor was given the go-ahead by MGM production chief Irving Thalberg, though he knew the film would be both controversial and get minimal release in the Deep South. Great music included traditional spirituals and songs by Irving Berlin.

Hangin' with the Homeboys
(1991)

Although the Bronx does not offer much for any of them, they have little interest in escaping its confines, four young men are more than willing to complain. With characters insightfully written and well-portrayed, the film earned honors for best screenplay at the 1991 Sundance Film Festival.

Hank Aaron: Chasing the Dream
(1995)

Docudrama combines archival footage, interviews, and reenactments to tell the story of the life and career of Henry Aaron, baseball's all-time home run king. Emphasis on personal and societal issues, as well as on-the-field accomplishments.

Harlem Nights
(1989)

Two Harlem nightclub owners in the 1930s battle comically against efforts by the mob and crooked cops to take over their territory. High-grossing effort from Eddie Murphy, who directed, wrote, produced, and starred in this film. Music by Herbie Hancock.

Having Our Say: The Delany Sisters' First 100 Years
(1999)

A made-for-television movie based on the true story of the Delany sisters (played by Ruby Dee and Diahann Carroll), who lived well beyond the age of 100 after having built successful careers at a time when most women, and most African Americans, were being denied opportunities. Produced by Camille O. Cosby.

A Hero Ain't Nothin' but a Sandwich
(1978)

A young urban African American teenager (Larry B. Scott) gets involved in drugs and is eventually saved from ruin. Based on Alice Childress's novel.

Higher Learning
(1994)

Malik (Omar Epps), Kristen (Kristy Swanson), and Remy (Michael Rapaport) are college freshmen who confront issues of racial prejudice and emerging sexuality. Laurence Fishburne plays an instructor in this John Singleton film.

Hollywood Shuffle
(1987)

Robert Townsend's autobiographical comedy about a struggling African American actor in Hollywood trying to find work and getting nothing but stereotypical roles. Written, directed, and financed by Townsend who created this often clever and appealing film on a $100,000 budget.

Home of the Brave
(1949)

A black soldier is sent on a top secret mission in the South Pacific, but finds that he must battle with his white comrades as he is subjected to subordinate treatment and constant racial slurs. Hollywood's first outstanding statement against racial prejudice.

Hoodlum
(1996)

Highly fictionalized tale of 1930s gangster "Bumpy" Johnson (Laurence Fishburne, reprising his role from *The Cotton Club*), who refuses to allow Dutch Schultz (Tim Roth) and Lucky Luciano (Andy Garcia) to muscle into the Harlem numbers rackets.

Hoop Dreams
(1994)

Exceptional documentary follows two inner-city basketball phenoms' lives through high school as they chase their dreams of playing in the NBA. Offers plenty of game footage, but the more telling and fascinating parts of the film deal with the kids' families and home life. Both players encounter dramatic reversals of fortune on and off the court, demonstrating the incredibly long odds they face. Earned numerous honors including the Audience Award at the 1994 Sundance Film Festival.

House Party
(1990)

Light-hearted, African American hip hop version of a 1950s teen comedy with rap duo Kid 'n' Play. Features real-life music rappers and some dynamite dance numbers. Earned best cinematography honors at the 1990 Sundance Film Festival.

How Stella Got Her Groove Back
(1998)

A flipside to the May-December romance that is based on the novel by Terry McMillan. Stars Angela Bassett and Whoopi Goldberg, among others.

How U Like Me Now?
(1992)

Daryll Robert's second directorial effort offers a fresh look at African Americans on film with plenty of lively supporting characters and witty dialogue. Music by Chuck Webb.

I Know Why the Caged Bird Sings
(1979)

An African American writer's memories of growing up in the rural South during the 1930s. Strong performances from Esther Rolle and Constance Good. Based on the book by Maya Angelou.

I'll Make Me a World: A Century of African American Arts
(1999)

PBS documentary produced by famed documentarian Henry Hampton that honors the achievements of twentieth-century African American writers, dancers, painters, actors, filmmakers, musicians, and other artists who changed forever who Americans are as a nation and culture.

I'm Gonna Git You Sucka
(1988)

Parody of "blaxploitation" films popular during the 1960s and 1970s. A number of stars who made "blaxploitation" films, including Jim Brown, take part in the gags.

Imitation of Life
(1934)

Fannie Hurst novel tells the story of widowed Beatrice Pullman (Claudette Colbert) who uses maid Delilah's (Louise Beaver) recipe for pancakes in order to have the women open a restaurant, which becomes a success. Both mothers suffer at the hands of their willful teenaged daughters.

In the Heat of the Night
(1967)

An African American homicide expert (Sidney Poitier) is asked to help solve the murder of a wealthy industrialist in a small Mississippi town, despite resentment on the part of the town's chief of police (Rod Steiger). Powerful script with underlying theme of racial prejudice is served well by taut direction and powerhouse performances. Won several Academy and Golden Globe Awards.

Intruder in the Dust
(1949)

A small Southern community develops a lynch mob mentality when a black man is accused of killing a white man. Powerful, but largely ignored portrait of race relations in the South. Adapted from a novel by William Faulkner.

Jack Johnson
(1971)

Documentary discusses the life of the first African American heavyweight boxing champion, Jack Johnson. Brock Peters provides the voice of Johnson and Miles Davis the musical score.

The Jackie Robinson Story
(1950)

Chronicles Robinson's rise from UCLA to his breakthrough as the first African American man to play baseball in the major league. Robinson plays himself; the film deals honestly with the racial issues of the time.

Jason's Lyric
(1994)

Director Doug McHenry's intense drama focuses on the stormy relationship between two brothers (Allen Payne and Bokeem Woodbine) whose lives in a impoverished Houston neighborhood lead them along different paths.

Jefferson in Paris
(1994)

Thomas Jefferson (Nick Nolte) confronts the personal and political issues of slavery in America, as well as his feelings for Sally Hemings (Thandie Newton), a Monticello slave brought to Paris by Jefferson's daughter.

Jo Jo Dancer, Your Life Is Calling
(1986)

Pryor directed and starred in this semi-autobiographical price-of-fame story of a comic, hospitalized for a drug-related accident, who must reevaluate his life. A serious departure from Pryor's slapstick comedies. Music by Herbie Hancock.

Joey Breaker
(1993)

Small picture works large message with sense of humor and sincere performances. Dedicated to Fred Fondren who died of AIDS in 1992. Filmed in New York City and St. Lucia.

The Josephine Baker Story
(1990)

Made-for-television biography of exotic entertainer/activist Josephine Baker (played by Lynn Whitfield), an African American woman from St. Louis who found superstardom in pre-WWII Europe, but repeated racism and rejection in the United States.

Juice
(1992)

Day-to-day street life of four Harlem youths as they try to earn respect ("juice") in their neighborhood. The gritty look and feel of the drama comes naturally to Ernest R. Dickerson in his directorial debut.

Lynn Whitfield (Corbis Corporation [Bellevue])

Jungle Fever
(1991)

Married black architect's affair (played by Wesley Snipes) with his white secretary (Annabella Sciorra) provides the backdrop for a cold look at interracial love. Written, produced, and directed by Spike Lee, the film focuses more on the discomfort of friends and families than with the intense world created by the lovers for themselves. Samuel L. Jackson plays a drug-addicted brother.

Kansas City
(1995)

Robert Altman mixes music, politics, crime and the movies in this bittersweet homage to his hometown, set in the jazz-driven 1930s. Styled to imitate the brilliant jazz scores played by the likes of Joshua Redman and James Carter.

King
(1978)

Docudrama with terrific cast follows the life and career of one of the greatest non-violent civil rights leaders of all time, Martin Luther King, Jr.

Lady Sings the Blues
(1972)

Jazz artist Billie Holiday's life (depicted by singer Diana Ross) becomes a musical drama depicting her struggle against racism and drug addiction in her pursuit of fame and romance. Billy Dee Williams, Richard Pryor, and Scatman Crothers head the supporting cast.

Laurel Avenue
(1993)

Looks at the life of an extended working-class African American family in St. Paul, Minnesota, over a busy weekend.

Lean on Me
(1989)

Depicts the career of Joe Clark, a tough New Jersey teacher who became the principal of the state's toughest, crime-plagued school and, through controversial hard-line tactics, turned it around.

The Learning Tree
(1969)

A beautifully photographed adaptation of Gordon Park, Sr.'s biographical novel about a 14-year-old African American boy in 1920s Kansas. The first feature film financed by a major Hollywood studio to be directed by an African American.

Lethal Weapon
(1989)

Danny Glover and Mel Gibson work well together as a pair of cops whom uncover a heroin smuggling ring run. Packed with plenty of action, violence, and humorous undertones.

The Liberation of L.B. Jones
(1970)

In this dramatic study of Southern race relations, a wealthy black undertaker (Roscoe Lee Brown) wants a divorce from his wife (Lola Falana) who is having an affair with a white policeman.

Lilies of the Field
(1963)

Five East German nuns enlist the aid of a free-spirited U.S. Army veteran (Sidney Poitier). They persuade him to build their chapel and teach them English. Poitier is excellent as the itinerant laborer and became the first African American man to win an Academy Award for best actor.

Listen Up!: The Lives of Quincy Jones
(1991)

A biography of the music legend responsible for various movie scores, record productions, and arrangements for the industry's top stars.

The Long Walk Home
(1989)

Whoopi Goldberg stars in this dramatic story about the relationship between a rich white housewife (Sissy Spacek) and her black maid whom she drives to work during the 1956 Montgomery bus boycott.

Look Out Sister
(1948)

Louis Jordan and an all-African American cast star in this musical satire of westerns. Lots of African American culture, slang, and music from 1940s.

Losing Isaiah
(1994)

A controversial and emotionally-moving story of a social worker (Jessica Lange) who adopts the title character, an African American baby abandoned by his drug-addicted mother (Halle Berry). Four years later, now clean and sober, the natural mother enlists the aid of a lawyer (Samuel L. Jackson) to regain custody of her child.

Lost Boundaries
(1949)

Respected physician Scott Carter (debut role for Mel Ferrer) and his family live and work in a small New Hampshire town, hiding the fact that they are black, passing for white, in their segregated society. But then the truth becomes known. Canada Lee also stars in this film based on a true story.

Love Jones
(1996)

A contemporary Chicago nightclub, the Sanctuary, is the gathering spot for middle-class African American urbanites looking for romance. Earned the Audience Award at the 1997 Sundance Film Festival.

The Mack
(1973)

The Mack is a pimp who comes out of retirement to reclaim a piece of the action in Oakland, California. Violent blaxploitation film was a box-office dynamite at time of release.

Malcolm X
(1992)

Marked by strong direction from Spike Lee and good performances (notably Freeman Jr. as Elijah Muhammad), it is Denzel Washington's convincing performance in the title role that truly brings this stirring tribute to the controversial African American activist film alive. Based on "The Autobiography of Malcolm X" by Malcolm X and Alex Haley.

The Man
(1972)

James Earl Jones plays the president pro tem of the U.S. Senate who becomes the first African American president when all the office holders above him in the presidential succession become victims of accidents and illnesses.

Menace II Society
(1993)

Critically acclaimed portrayal of African American teens living in Watts during the 1990s is realistically captured by 21-year-old twin directors, Allen and Albert Hughes, in their big-screen debut.

Miss Evers' Boys
(1997)

Wrenching docudrama covers a forty-year U.S. Public Health Service study in which African American men suffering from syphilis were monitored but not treated for the disease. Alfre Woodward earned the Emmy Award for outstanding lead actress in a miniseries or special for her role as nurse Eunice Evers.

Mississippi Masala
(1992)

This film portrays an interracial romance that sets off a cultural collision and escalates racial tensions in a small Southern town when Mina (Sarita Choudhury), a sheltered young Indian woman, falls in love with Demetrius (Denzel Washington), an ambitious African American man with his own carpet-cleaning business.

Mo' Better Blues
(1990)

Bleek Gilliam (Denzel Washington) is a handsome, accomplished self-interested jazz trumpeter who divides his limited time between two female lovers (Cynda Williams and Joie Lee). What is interesting is subtle racial issues his life draws into focus. The Branford Marsalis Quartet provides the music for Bleek's group,

Denzel Washington in the title role of Spike Lee's film *Malcolm X* (Archive Photos, Inc).

scored by Lee's dad, Bill (on whose life the script is loosely based).

Mr. & Mrs. Loving
(1996)

Fact-based movie, set in the 1960s, follows the interracial romance, marriage, and struggle of Richard Loving (Timothy Hutton) and Mildred "Bean" Jeter (Lela Rochon) and their landmark Supreme Court decision concerning miscegenation laws.

Native Son
(1986)

This second film adaptation of the classic Richard Wright novel tells the story of a poor African American man who accidentally kills a white woman and then hides the body.

New Jack City
(1991)

Director Mario Van Peebles stars in his own film as a police detective who assigns two undercover officers (Ice-T and Judd Nelson) to capture a wealthy Harlem drug lord (Wesley Snipes). Music by Johnny Gill, 2 Live Crew, Ice-T, and others.

No Maps on My Taps
(1979)

A unique African American art form—jazz tap dancing—is shown in rare photos and Hollywood film clips from the 1930s, and in intimate portraits of three surviving dancers: Sandman Sims, Chuck Green, and Bunny Briggs.

No Way Out
(1950)

Sidney Poitier plays an outstanding young actor who treats two white criminals who are wounded in an attempted robbery. After one of the men dies, the other accuses the doctor of murder.

Norman, Is That You?
(1976)

Film adaptation based on the Broadway play about the confused black parents of a homosexual son and his white lover.

Nothing but a Man
(1964)

Duff Anderson (Ivan Dixon) portrays an African American laborer trying to make a life in a small Alabama town. Abbey Lincoln, Yaphet Kotto, and Gloria Foster also star in this unsentimental depiction of the times. Named to the National Film Registry in 1993.

Once Upon a Time . . . When We Were Colored
(1995)

Actor Tim Reid makes a fine directorial debut with the story of an African American youngster growing up parentless in 1950s Mississippi. Nostalgic, sensitive, and heartwarming adaptation of Clifton Taulbert's autobiographical book.

One False Move
(1991)

Not a typical crime thriller, first-time feature director Carl Franklin is more interested in a psychological character study of racism and small-town mores. Earned the 1993 Independent Spirit Award for best director.

One Potato, Two Potato
(1964)

The story of an interracial marriage between white laborer Julie Cullen (Barbara Barrie) and Frank Richards (Bernie Hamilton), an African American man that she meets at the plant where she works.

Panther
(1995)

A highly controversial, fictionalized account of the Black Panther movement in the late 1960s. Directed by Melvin Van Peebles. Music by Stanley Clarke.

Paris Is Burning
(1991)

Jennie Livingston's documentary portrayal of New York City's transvestite balls between 1985 and 1989. This is a compelling look at a subculture of primarily African American and Hispanic men and the one place they can truly be themselves. Winner of the 1991 Sundance Film Festival Grand Jury Prize.

Pastime
(1991)

A bittersweet baseball elegy set in the minor leagues in 1957. A boyish 41-year-old pitcher cannot face his impending retirement and pals around with the team pariah, a 17-year-old African American rookie. Splendidly written and acted, the film won the 1991 Sundance Film Festival Audience Award.

A Patch of Blue
(1965)

A kind-hearted blind girl (Elizabeth Hartman) falls in love with an African American man (Sidney Poitier) without acknowledging racial differences.

Paul Robeson: Tribute to an Artist
(1980)

A documentary that features a look at the tremendous life of actor Paul Robeson.

The Piano Lesson
(1994)

Adaptation of August Wilson's 1990 Pulitzer Prize-winning play set in 1936 concerning the prized heirloom of the Charles family—an 80-year-old, ornately carved upright piano.

Pinky
(1949)

Early Hollywood treatment of the tragic choice made by some African Americans to pass as white in order to attain a better life for themselves and their families. Based on the novel *Quality* by Cyd Ricketts Sumner.

Poetic Justice
(1993)

John Singleton's second directorial effort is about Justice (Janet Jackson in her film debut), a young hairdresser who copes with her boyfriend's brutal murder by writing poetry (provided by poet Maya Angelou). Production stopped on the South Central Los Angeles set during the 1992 riots, but the aftermath provided poignant pictures for later scenes.

Porgy and Bess
(1992)

The Glyndebourne production of Gershwin's folk opera about the denizens of Catfish Row. Simon Rattle conducts the London Philharmonic.

Posse
(1993)

Set during the Spanish-American War, this film revolves around a group of African American soldiers. Following their escape from Cuba with a fortune in gold, they travel towards Freemanville, where the group's

Sidney Poitier, Ruby Dee, and others in the production of *A Raisin In the Sun* (Corbis Corporation [Bellevue]).

leader (director Mario Van Peebles) avenges the death of his father.

Purple Rain
(1984)

A quasi-autobiographical film tells the tale of Prince's struggle for love, attention, acceptance, and popular artistic recognition in Minneapolis. Earned the 1984 Academy Award for best original song score and/or adaptation.

Putney Swope
(1969)

Comedy about a token African American ad man mistakenly elected chairman of the board of a Madison Avenue ad agency who turns the company upside down.

The Quiet One
(1948)

Explores the ghetto's psychological effects on a ten-year-old African American child. The film's commentary was written by James Agee.

Race to Freedom: The Story of the Underground Railroad
(1994)

Story of four fugitive slaves, in 1850, who struggle to get from North Carolina to the safety of Canada through a network of safe houses and people willing to risk smuggling them to asylum.

A Rage in Harlem
(1991)

Set in Harlem in 1956, this film portrays the tale of a beautiful con women named Imabelle (Robin Givens). Adapted from a book by Chester Himes.

Ragtime
(1981)

From the E.L. Doctorow novel set in 1906 America, a small, unthinking act represents all the racist attacks on an African American man who refuses to back down this time.

A Raisin in the Sun
(1961)

Outstanding story of a black family trying to make a better life for themselves in an all-white neighborhood in Chicago. Based on the Broadway play by Hansberry who also wrote the screenplay.

Rebound: The Legend of Earl "The Goat" Manigault
(1996)

The film stars Earl "The Goat" Manigault (Don Cheadle) as a 1960s Harlem playground basketball phenom who turn his life around to found his own basketball tournament in Harlem, after dropping out of college, turning to heroin, and eventually winding up in prison. Music by Kevin Eubanks.

Richard Pryor: Live on the Sunset Strip
(1982)

Filmed live at the Hollywood Palladium, this film captures Richard Pryor at his funniest including his segment about "Pryor on Fire."

The River Niger
(1976)

James Earl Jones is riveting and Cicely Tyson is good in this adaptation of the Tony-award winning play about African American ghetto life. Directed by Krishna Shaw,

Don Cheadle (AP/Wide World Photos, Inc.)

the film depicts believable characters expressing realistic emotions.

Roots
(1977)

The complete version of Alex Haley's made-for-television saga that follows an African American man's search for his heritage, revealing an epic panorama of America's past. Music by Quincy Jones.

Roots: The Gift
(1988)

A made-for-television movie based on the Alex Haley characters featuring Louis Gossett and LeVar Burton, among others.

Roots: The Next Generation
(1979)

Sequel to the landmark television miniseries continuing the story of author Alex Haley's ancestors from the Reconstruction era of the 1880s to 1967, culminating with Haley's visit to West Africa where he is told the story of Kunta Kinte.

Rosewood
(1996)

Based on the true story of the well-off African American community of Rosewood, Florida, which was destroyed by a white mob in 1923. Directed by John Singleton and starring Ving Rhames, the film accurately shows the tensions present between blacks and whites of the time.

Say Amen, Somebody
(1982)

Documentary about gospel music and two of its greatest legends—Willie Mae Ford Smith and Thomas A. Dorsey. Aptly demonstrates the power of music sung from the heart.

School Daze
(1988)

Director/writer/star Spike Lee's second outing is a rambunctious comedy set at an African American college in the South.

Separate But Equal
(1991)

A powerful dramatization of the 1954 *Brown v. The Board of Education, Topeka* case that resulted in a landmark civil rights decision of the Supreme Court. Features Sidney Poitier as NAACP attorney Thurgood Marshall.

Sergeant Rutledge
(1960)

The story of a court-martial, told in flashback, about an African American cavalry officer on trial for rape and murder. A detailed look at overt and covert racism handled by master director John Ford. Based on the novel *Captain Buffalo* by James Warner Bellah.

Set It Off
(1996)

This film finds four female friends (Jada Pinkett, Queen Latifah, Vivica A. Fox, and Kimberly Elise) in Los Angeles pushed over the edge and taking up bank robbery to escape poverty and strike a blow against "the system."

Shadows
(1960)

Director John Cassavettes's first independent feature revolves around jazz player Hugh (Hugh Hurd), his brother Ben (Ben Carruthers), and sister Lelia (Lelia Goldoni). Light-skinned enough to pass for white, Lelia gets involved with the white Tony (Anthony Ray) who leaves when he finds out her true heritage. Music by Charles Mingus. The film was named to the National Film Registry in 1993.

Shaft
(1971)

Gordon Parks, Sr. directed this sophisticated action film featuring Richard Roundtree as the African American private eye, John Shaft. Academy Award-winning theme song by Isaac Hayes, the first music award from the Academy to an African American. Adapted from the novel by Ernest Tidyman.

She's Gotta Have It
(1986)

Spike Lee wrote, directed, edited, produced, and starred in this very popular romantic comedy about an independent-minded African American girl in Brooklyn and the three men and one woman who compete for her attention. Awarded the 1987 Independent Spirit Award for best first feature.

Show Boat
(1936)

The second of three film versions of the Kern/Hammerstein musical (based on the Edna Ferber novel) about a Mississippi showboat and the life and loves of its denizens. The film's musical numbers include Paul Robeson's immortal rendition of "Old Man River." Named to the National Film Registry in 1996.

Silver Streak
(1976)

Energetic Hitchcock parody features successful first pairing of Richard Pryor and Gene Wilder.

Skin Game
(1971)

A fast-talking con artist (James Garner) and his African American partner (Lou Gossett, Jr.) travel throughout the antebellum South setting up scams. Finely acted comedy-drama.

Slam
(1998)

After being jailed for possession and suspicion of murdering his supplier, street-smart, low-level drug dealer Ray (Saul Williams) relies on spoken word poetry that he composes to see him through life's challenges. Awarded the Sundance Film Festival Grand Jury Prize in 1998.

Slaves
(1969)

Ossie Davis appears in this remake of *Uncle Tom's Cabin.* Directed by Herbert J. Biberman.

A Soldier's Story
(1984)

An African American U.S. Army attorney (Howard E. Rollins, Jr.) is sent to a Southern military base to investigate the murder of an unpopular sergeant. From the Pulitzer-prize winning play by Charles Fuller, with most of the Broadway cast. Fine performances from Denzel Washington and Adolph Caesar. Music by Herbie Hancock.

Sophisticated Gents
(1981)

Nine boyhood friends, members of an African American athletic club, reunite after 25 years to honor their old coach and see how each of their lives has been affected by being black men in American society. Based on the novel "The Junior Bachelor Society" by John A. Williams.

Soul Food
(1997)

Film depicts the lives of three sisters (Vanessa Williams, Vivica A. Fox, and Nia Long) who struggle to hold their family together by keeping up their mother's Sunday dinner tradition after she becomes ill. Boasts many promising debuts including director/writer George Tillman, Jr. Produced by music producer Kenneth "Babyface" Edmonds.

Soul of the Game
(1996)

Television movie follows the lives of three talented players in the Negro League during the 1945 season as they await the potential integration of baseball: Flashy, aging pitcher Satchel Paige (Delroy Lindo); mentally unstable catcher Josh Gibson (Mykelti Williamson); and the young, college-educated Jackie Robinson (Blair Underwood).

Sounder
(1972)

The film depicts the struggles of a family of African American sharecroppers in rural Louisiana during the Depression. Cicely Tyson brings strength and style to her role with fine help from Paul Winfield. Adapted from the novel by William Armstrong. Nominated for several Oscars at the 1972 Academy Awards. Music by Taj Mahal.

South Central
(1992)

A low-budget urban drama set in a gang-infested Los Angeles neighborhood. Feature debut of director Steve Anderson. Based on the novel *Crips* by Donald Bakeer.

Stormy Weather
(1943)

In this cavalcade of African American entertainment, the plot is overshadowed by the nearly non-stop array of musical numbers, showcasing this stellar cast (Lena Horne, Bill Robinson, Fats Waller, Dooley Wilson, and Cab Calloway) at their performing peak.

Straight Out of Brooklyn
(1991)

A bleak, nearly hopeless look at a struggling African American family in a Brooklyn housing project. An up-close and raw look at part of society seldom shown in mainstream film. Music by Harold Wheeler. Awarded the Sundance Film Festival Special Jury Prize in 1991.

Sudie & Simpson
(1990)

Heartwarming tale of friendship between a twelve-year-old white girl and an adult black man set in rural 1940s Georgia. Based on Sara Flanigan Carter's autobiographical novel.

Sugar Hill
(1994)

Two brothers (Michael Wright and Wesley Snipes) are heroin dealers who have built their own crime empire in the Sugar Hill section of Harlem. Snipes is moved to reconsider his career options when he falls for an aspiring actress (Theresa Randle). Music by Terence Blanchard and Larry Joshua.

Superfly
(1972)

Controversial upon release, pioneering blaxploitation film of the 1970s has Harlem dope dealer (Ron O'Neal) attempt to leave the profession after one last big score. Directed by Gordon Parks, Jr. Excellent period tunes by Curtis Mayfield.

Sweet Sweetback's Baadasssss Song
(1971)

An African American man kills two white policemen who beat up a black militant. He uses his streetwise survival skills to elude the law and escape to Mexico. Directed by Melvin Van Peebles.

Take a Giant Step
(1959)

An African American youth (Johnny Nash) struggles with society's attitude towards race and seeks the comfort of his family's maid (Ruby Dee). Directed by Philip Leacock.

A Time to Kill
(1996)

Powerful story of revenge, racism, and the question of justice in the "new South." Based on the John Grisham novel. Samuel L. Jackson earned a Golden Globe Award nomination for best supporting actor.

To Kill a Mockingbird
(1962)

Faithful adaptation of Harper Lee's powerful novel. Gregory Peck's performance as Southern lawyer defending a black man (Brock Peters) accused of raping a white woman is flawless, earning him the Academy and Golden Globe Awards for best actor. The film was named to the National Film Registry in 1995 and the Top 100 list of the American Film Institute in 1998.

To Sir, with Love
(1967)

Skillful and warm performance by Sidney Poitier as an idealistic teacher who wins over his unruly students in London's tough East End. Based on the novel by E.R. Braithwaite.

To Sleep with Anger
(1990)

Danny Glover's best performance as a stranger from the South whose visit divides an African American middle-class family living in Los Angeles.. Insightful look into the conflicting values of black America. The film earned the Sundance Film Festival Special Jury Prize in 1990.

The Tuskegee Airmen
(1995)

Made-for-television drama based on the formation and World War II achievements of the U.S. Army Air Corps' first squadron of African American combat fighter pilots, the "Fighting 99th" of the 332nd Fighter Group. Based on a story by former Tuskegee airman, Robert W. Williams.

Uncle Tom's Cabin
(1914)

Satisfying version of Harriet Beecher Stowe's tale from the view of a founder of the Underground Railroad. Sam Lucas was the first African American actor to garner a lead role. Subsequent versions of this film were made in 1927 and 1987 (first sound version).

Uptight
(1968)

In a story set in Cleveland, actor Raymond St. Jacques leads a group of African American well-armed revolutionaries shortly following the assassination of Martin Luther King, Jr. Ruby Dee and Julian Mayfield serve as co-stars.

Uptown Saturday Night
(1974)

Two working men (Sidney Poitier and Bill Cosby) attempt to recover a stolen lottery ticket from the African American underworld after being ripped off at an illegal gambling place. Directed by Sidney Poitier.

Waiting to Exhale
(1995)

Popular adaptation of Terry McMillan's novel about four African American women (Whitney Houston, Angela Bassett, Loretta Devine, and Lela Rochon) hoping to enter the right romantic relationship. Music by producer Kenneth "Babyface" Edmonds.

The Walking Dead
(1994)

Preston A. Whitmore II's directorial debut depicts the Vietnam War from the perspectives of four black and one white Marine assigned to rescue prisoners of war from a North Vietnam camp in 1972.

Watermelon Man
(1970)

The tables are turned for a bigoted white man when he wakes up one morning to discover he has become a black man. Godrey Cambridge takes on both roles. Directed by Melvin Van Peebles.

What's Love Got to Do with It?
(1993)

Energetic biographical film of powerhouse songstress Tina Turner (Angela Bassett) and her abusive relationship with husband, Ike (Laurence Fishburne). Based on "I, Tina" by Turner and Kurt Loder. For her performance, Bassett earned the Golden Globe Award for best actress in 1994. Music by Stanley Clarke.

The Wiz
(1978)

An African American version of the long-time favorite "The Wizard of Oz," based on the Broadway musical. Features all-star cast—Diana Ross, Michael Jackson, Lena Horne, Nipsey Russell, and Richard Pryor. Music by Quincy Jones.

The Women of Brewster Place
(1989)

Excellent, complex script gives each actress in a fine ensemble headed by executive producer Oprah Winfrey (in her dramatic television debut) time in the spotlight. Pilot for the series "Brewster Place." Based on the novel by Gloria Naylor.

The Wood
(1999)

Based on writer-director Rick Famuyiwa's real life story, the ensemble comedy flashes back between the middle and high school days of three male friends growing up in Inglewood, California, and an eventful wedding day in the late 1990s. Captures the mood and nostalgia of the 1980s through memorable rhythm and blues and hip hop music.

The World, the Flesh, and the Devil
(1959)

Three survivors of a nuclear holocaust form an uneasy alliance and deal with issues of survival and racism. Features actor Harry Belafonte.

Zebrahead
(1992)

Outstanding performances by the young and largely unknown cast, particularly Michael Rapaport and N'Bushe Wright, and an excellent musical score by Taj Mahal enriches the action. Awarded the Sundance Film Festival Filmmakers Trophy.

Zooman
(1995)

The film offers a hard-hitting message on violence and responsibility and features performances by Louis Gossett, Jr. and Vondie Curtis-Hall. Based on Fuller's 1978 play *Zooman and the Sign.*

◆ ACTORS, FILMMAKERS, AND FILM AND TELEVISION EXECUTIVES

(To locate biographical profiles more readily, please consult the index at the back of the book.)

Angela Bassett (1959?–)

Actress

Born in St. Petersburg, Florida, in the late 1950s, Angela Bassett was one of two daughters of a single mother and grew up in public housing. Inspired to the acting craft after witnessing a stage performance by James Earl Jones when she was a teenager, Bassett earned top grades and enrolled in Yale University. After receiving a master's degree from its prestigious school of drama in the early 1980s, Bassett settled in New York City and began winning acting roles in an industry not particularly known for a wealth of interesting, non-stereotypical roles offered to African American women.

Bassett found work in television commercials, the CBS daytime television drama "The Guiding Light" and debuted on Broadway in the acclaimed musical *Ma Rainey's Black Bottom.* Film roles were next on the horizon; in 1991, she appeared in two notable films, John Singleton's *Boyz N the Hood*—a casting that came with the good word of her friend, actor Larry Fishburne—and John Sayles's *City of Hope.* Her work attracted the attention of filmmaker Spike Lee, who cast her as Betty Shabazz, wife of Malcolm X, in his 1992 film biography of the slain leader. Bassett's portrayal won high marks from critics for its intensity and sensitivity.

Once again voicing strong support for his acting colleague, Fishburne agreed to play the role of 1960s soul musician Ike Turner in a film on the condition that Bassett won its starring role based on Tina Turner's autobiography. The 1993 film *What's Love Got to Do With It* catapulted Bassett into major stardom and won her rave reviews from critics for the vivid depiction of some of the more harrowing years of the singer's life. She won a Golden Globe Award for her efforts as well as two NAACP Image Awards. Late in 1995, Bassett appeared in a lead role in the cyberspace thriller *Strange Days,* opposite Ralph Fiennes and in the Eddie Murphy comedy *Vampire in Brooklyn.* Later that same year the actress won further critical acclaim for her ensemble-cast part in 1995's *Waiting to Exhale,* the box-office hit based on novelist Terry McMillan's tale of a close-knit quartet of African American women. In 1998 she starred as an older women who falls in love with a much younger man in *How Stella Got Her Groove Back.* During that same year, she also served as series narrator for the acclaimed PBS documentary titled "Africans in America: America's Journey through Slavery." In 1999, Bassett began work on a science fiction movie with director Walter Hill titled *Supernova.*

Harry Belafonte (1927–)

Singer, Actor

Born on March 1, 1927, in New York City, Harry Belafonte moved to the West Indies at the age of eight. At 13, Belafonte returned to New York, where he attended high school. Belafonte joined the Navy in 1944; after his discharge, while working as a janitor in New York, he became interested in drama. He studied acting at Stanley Kubrick's Dramatic Workshop and with Erwin Piscator at the New School for Social Research, where his classmates included Marlon Brando and Walter Matthau. A successful singing engagement at The Royal Roost, a New York jazz club, led to other engagements around the country. But Belafonte, dissatisfied with the music he was performing, returned to New York, opened a restaurant in Greenwich Village, and studied folk singing. His first appearances as a folk singer in the 1950s "helped give folk music a period of mass appeal," according to John S. Wilson in a 1981 *New York Times* article. During his performances at the Palace Theater in New York, Belafonte had audiences calypsoing in the aisles.

Belafonte produced the first integrated musical shows on television, which both won him two Emmy awards and resulted in his being fired by the sponsor. The famous incident in which white British singer Petula Clark touched his arm while singing a song caused a national furor in pre-civil rights America. When Dr. Martin Luther King, Jr. marched on Montgomery, Alabama, and Washington, DC, Harry Belafonte joined him and brought along a large contingent of performers. Touring in the stage musical *Three for Tonight* in which he had appeared on Broadway in 1955, Belafonte was forced to flee in the middle of a performance in Spartanburg, South Carolina, and be rushed to the airport in the mayor's car. Word had come that the Ku Klux Klan was marching on the theater.

Belafonte also appeared on Broadway in John Murray Anderson's *Almanac* (1953), and his movies include: *Carmen Jones* (1954); *Island in the Sun* (1957); *The World, the Flesh, and the Devil* (1958); *Odds against Tomorrow* (1959); *The Angel Levine* (1969); *Buck and the Preacher* (1972); and *Uptown Saturday Night* (1974); and *White Man's Burden* (1995). He also directed the film *Port Chicago,* in 1994.

In the 1980s, Belafonte appeared in his first dramatic role on television in the NBC presentation of "Grambling's White Tiger" and, in 1981, Columbia Records released his first album in seven years, *Loving You Is Where I Belong*, consisting of mostly ballads. He has received numerous awards and honors including the 1982 Martin Luther King, Jr. Nonviolent Peace Prize and three honorary doctorates. Belafonte received the Thurgood Marshall Lifetime Achievement Award in 1993 and the National Medal of Arts in 1994.

Halle Berry (1968–)
Actress, Model

Halle Berry was born in Cleveland, Ohio, to an interracial family. After winning the Miss Teen Ohio beauty pageant, Berry enrolled in Cleveland's Cuyahoga Community College in 1986 to study broadcast journalism. She decided to become an actor and moved to Chicago, where she studied acting and worked as a model.

She relocated to Manhattan in 1988 and landed her first TV role on the television series "Paper Dolls." Her big break came when she was selected by director Spike Lee to appear in his 1991 film *Jungle Fever* in which she played a crack addict.

Berry was cast in the 1991 social satire *Strictly Business*. Some of her notable film roles include the 1996 action film *Executive Decision*, the 1997 comedy *B.A.P.S.*, and the 1997 made for television movie *Solomon & Sheba*, where she starred playing the Queen of Sheba. She also starred as Dorothy Dandridge in the HBO film *Introducing Dorothy Dandridge* and in the 1998 film *Bulworth*. Her high profile marriage to baseball star David Justice ended in 1996 in divorce.

Halle Berry (Archive Photos, Inc.)

Andre Braugher (1962?–)
Actor

A Chicago native, Andre Braugher began his career in the highly popular "Kojak" television movies. He received a B.A. from Stanford University and a M.F.A. from the Juilliard School. He has performed numerous productions of Shakespeare in New York for the New York Shakespeare Festival and at the Joseph Papp Public Theatre.

He gained national recognition for his starring role as Detective Frank Pembleton on the long-running serial drama "Homicide: Life on the Street." In 1998, Braugher earned an Emmy Award for outstanding lead actor in a drama series.

Braugher's other notable television and film roles include *Glory*, *Murder in Mississippi*, *Simple Justice*, *The Tuskegee Airmen*, *Get on the Bus*, *Primal Fear*, *City of Angels*, and *Passing Glory*. Most recently Braugher finished filming *All The Rage* and *Duets*, opposite Gwyneth Paltrow. In 1999, Braugher made his directorial debut with one vignette of the ShowTime trilogy "Love Songs."

Diahann Carroll (1935–)
Actress, Singer

Diahann Carroll was born in the Bronx on July 17, 1935, the daughter of a subway conductor and a nurse. As a child, she was a member of the Abyssinian Baptist Church choir; at the age of ten, Carroll won a Metropolitan Opera scholarship. Singing lessons held little appeal for her, however, so she continued her schooling at the High School of Music and Art. As a concession to her parents, Carroll enrolled at New York University, where she was to be a sociology student, but stage fever led her to an appearance on a television talent show, which netted her $1,000. A subsequent appearance at the Latin Quarter Club launched her professional career.

In 1954, Carroll appeared in *House of Flowers*, winning favorable press notices. In that year, she also appeared in a film version of *Carmen Jones*, in the role of Myrt.

Movie and television appearances kept Carroll busy until 1958, the year she was slated to appear as an Asian in Richard Rodgers's *Flower Drum Song.* The part did not materialize. Three years later, Rodgers cast her in *No Strings* as a high fashion model, a role for which she earned a Tony award in 1962.

In the late 1960s, Carroll was cast as lead in the television series "Julia," in which she played a nurse and war widow. She also appeared in the films *Porgy and Bess* (1959), *Goodbye Again* (1961), *Paris Blues* (1961), *Claudine* with James Earl Jones (1974), *Sister, Sister* (1982), and *The Five Heartbeats* (1991). She has been featured in the television series "Dynasty" and "A Different World" and has written an autobiography.

From 1996 to 1997, Carroll appeared on stage in the Broadway musical *Sunset Boulevard.*

Rupert Crosse (1928–1973)

Actor

Born in Nevis, British West Indies, on November 29, 1928, Rupert Crosse moved to Harlem at an early age. Crosse returned to Nevis at the age of seven, after the death of his father. Reared by his grandparents and strongly influenced by his grandfather, a schoolmaster, Crosse received a solid education before returning to New York, where he attended Benjamin Franklin High School. Crosse also later worked at odd jobs before interrupting high school to spend two years in military service in Germany and Japan. Once out of service, Crosse finished high school and entered Bloomfield College and Seminary in New Jersey. Though he intended to become a minister, it was obvious from the jobs he had held—machinist, construction worker, and recreation counselor—that his career plans were not yet definite.

Crosse subsequently enrolled at the Daykarhanora School, studying acting and appearing in the Equity Library Theatre off-Broadway production *Climate of Eden.* He then transferred to John Cassavetes's workshop, where he helped to create *Shadows* (1961), winner of a Venice Film Festival Award. Crosse's first Hollywood role was in a Cassavetes movie *Too Late Blues* (1962). His most important film role was as Ned McCaslin in the screen adaptation of William Faulkner's Pulitzer Prize-winning novel *The Reivers* (1969). Crosse was nominated for an Academy Award as best supporting actor for this outstanding performance. His other film credits include *The Wild Seed* and *Ride in the Whirlwind.*

Crosse's stage credits are also numerous including appearances in *Sweet Bird of Youth, The Blood Knot,* and *Hatful of Rain.* Television viewers saw Crosse in "Dr. Kildare," "I Spy," and "The Man from U.N.C.L.E.," as well as several other series.

Rupert Crosse died of cancer on March 5, 1973, at the age of 45 at his sister's home in Nevis.

Dorothy Dandridge (1922–1965)

Actress

Dorothy Dandridge was born on November 9, 1922, in Cleveland, Ohio; her mother was the actress Ruby Dandridge. As children, Dorothy and her sister, Vivian, performed as "The Wonder Kids," touring the United States. In 1934, they were joined by a third performer, Etta Jones, and the trio became the Dandridge Sisters. The Dandridge Sisters were a popular act, performing at the Cotton Club in Harlem and in the motion picture *A Day at the Races* (1937). By the 1940s, Dorothy Dandridge had struck out on her own, appearing in the "soundies" (musical shorts) *Easy Street, Yes, Indeed, Cow Cow Boogie, Jungle Jig, Paper Doll,* and *Sing for My Supper.*

Dandridge married Harold Nicholas (of the famed Nicholas Brothers dance team) in 1942, and had a daughter, Harolyn, in 1943. Harolyn was diagnosed as having a severe developmental disability and was sent to an institution; shortly thereafter, Dandridge divorced Nicholas. She carried on a fairly successful career as a nightclub singer during the 1940s and 1950s. Her greatest triumph, however, came as a film actress, particularly in the all-African American musical *Carmen Jones* (1954) for which she received an Oscar nomination for best actress, becoming the first African American woman to receive this nomination. Another important role was in *Island in the Sun* (1957), where she was paired romantically with a white man, John Justin—a breakthrough in desegregating the screen. In 1959, Dandridge played Bess opposite Sidney Poitier's Porgy in the movie version of *Porgy and Bess.* Ultimately, she appeared in over 25 films.

Dandridge married the white Las Vegas restaurateur Jack Dennison in 1959, but three years later divorced and declared personal bankruptcy. She died of an overdose of a prescription antidepressant on September 8, 1965.

Ossie Davis (1917–)

Actor

Ossie Davis grew up in Waycross, Georgia, and attended Howard University in Washington, DC, where Dr. Alain Locke suggested he pursue an acting career in New York. After completing service in the Army, Davis landed his first role in 1946 in the play *Jeb,* where he met Ruby Dee, whom he married two years later.

After appearing in the movie *No Way Out* (1950), Davis won Broadway roles in *No Time for Sergeants, Raisin in the Sun,* and *Jamaica.* In 1961, he and Dee starred in *Purlie Victorious,* which Davis himself had written. Two years later, they repeated their roles in the movie version *Gone Are the Days*.

Davis's other movie credits from this period include *The Cardinal* (1963), *Shock Treatment* (1964), *The Hill* (1965), *A Man Called Adam* (1966), and *The Scalphunter* (1968).

Davis then directed such films as *Cotton Comes to Harlem* (1970) and *Black Girl* (1972). His play *Escape to Freedom: A Play about Young Frederick Douglass*, had its debut at Town Hall in New York and later was published by Viking Junior Books. Davis has also been involved with television scripts and educational programming. "The Ruby Dee/Ossie Davis Story Hour" was produced for television in 1974. The arts education television series "With Ossie and Ruby" appeared in 1981. Davis and Ruby Dee also founded the Institute of New Cinema Artists and the Recording Industry Training Program.

Davis's continued movie appearances include roles in *Let's Do It Again* (1975), *Hot Stuff* (1979), and *Nothing Personal* (1979). Recent film credits include *Harry and Son* (1984) and Spike Lee's *School Daze* (1988) and *Do the Right Thing* (1989). In addition, Davis has appeared on such television series as "The Defenders," "The Nurses," "East Side, West Side," and "Evening Shade." In 1993, Davis starred in the TV miniseries "Queen," the sequel to the classic miniseries "Roots." He also appeared in the TV movie *The Android Affair* in 1995.

Davis is also the author of *Just Like Martin*, a novel for young adults.

Sammy Davis, Jr. (1925–1990)

Actor, Comedian, Dancer, Singer

Sammy Davis Jr. was often called "the world's greatest entertainer," a title that attested to his remarkable versatility as singer, dancer, actor, mimic, and musician.

Davis was born in New York City on December 8, 1925. Four years later he was appearing in vaudeville with his father and "uncle" in the Will Mastin Trio. In 1931, Davis made his movie debut with Ethel Waters in *Rufus Jones for President;* this was followed by an appearance in *Season's Greetings*.

Throughout the 1930s, the Will Mastin Trio continued to play vaudeville, burlesque, and cabarets. In 1943, Davis entered the Army and served for two years by writing, directing, and producing camp shows. After his discharge, he rejoined the trio, which in 1946 cracked the major club circuit with a successful Hollywood engagement.

Davis recorded a string of hits ("Hey There," "Mr. Wonderful," "Too Close for Comfort") during his steady rise to the top of show business. In November 1954, he lost an eye in an automobile accident, which fortunately did not interfere with his career. He scored a hit in his first Broadway show *Mr. Wonderful* (1956) and later repeated this success in *Golden Boy* (1964).

In 1959, Davis played Sportin' Life in the movie version of *Porgy and Bess*. Other Davis movies from this period include *Oceans 11* (1960) and *Robin and the Seven Hoods* (1964). His 1966 autobiography *Yes, I Can* became a best seller, and he starred in his own network television series. In addition, he spent time with a coterie of entertainers dubbed "The Rat Pack," who were fixtures of top-dollar nightspots in Los Angeles and Las Vegas throughout the decade.

In 1968, the NAACP awarded Davis its Spingarn Medal. In the 1970s, Davis appeared in films, television, and nightclubs. In 1972, he was involved in a controversy over his support of Richard Nixon which was publicized by a famous photograph of Nixon hugging Davis at the 1972 Republican Convention. In 1974, Davis renounced his support of Nixon and Nixon's programs. In the same year, his television commercials for Japan's Suntory Whiskey won the grand prize at the Cannes Film Festival, and the National Academy of TV Arts and Sciences honored him for his unique contributions to television.

In 1975, Davis became host of an evening talk and entertainment show. In 1980, he marked his fiftieth anniversary as an entertainer and the Friars Club honored him with its Annual Life Achievement Award. During that same decade, Davis embarked on a hugely successful revue tour with Frank Sinatra and Liza Minelli. In 1989, he appeared in his final film *Tap* with Gregory Hines and Harold Nicholas. Later that year, he was diagnosed with throat cancer and died on May 16, 1990. Shortly before his death though, he was honored with a television special devoted to his life.

Davis married three times. His first marriage was in 1959 to singer Loray White. He married his second wife, actress Mai Britt, in 1961; she is the mother of his three children. In 1970, he married dancer Altovise Gore.

Suzanne de Passe (1948–)

Producer, Entrepreneur

Suzanne de Passe was born in 1948 in Harlem. She graduated from Manhattan High School and attended Syracuse University. She left without receiving her degree and became a booking agent for a New York theater. It was there that Motown Records founder Barry Gordy found de Passe and hired her as his creative assistant. Having discovered the Jackson 5 and the Commodores while working for Motown, de Passe developed a reputation for spotting talent.

In 1973 she received an Oscar nomination for co-writing the screenplay of the movie *Lady Sings the Blues*. In the early 1980s, she became the head of Motown Productions, the film and television division of Motown. Her production of "Motown 25," an anniversary show for the company, earned several Emmy Awards. In 1989, de Passe produced the miniseries "Lonesome Dove," which won seven Emmy Awards, a Golden Globe, and a Peabody Award. She also served as executive producer to the many spinoffs of the this award-winning miniseries. In 1999, she produced "The Temptations," the well-received docudrama based on the famous Motown singing group.

De Passe is the CEO of her own production company, de Passe Entertainment. The company has produced the WB shows "Sister, Sister" and "Smart Guy." In 1986, she was the subject of a study by the Harvard Business School. She has consistently taken less than the normal fee accorded to producers in order to get her projects funded, believing visibility is more important than profit. In 1995 de Passe was awarded the Charles W. Fries Producer of the Year Award for her outstanding contribution to the television industry. She is married to Paul Le Mat.

Ruby Dee (1924–)

Actress

Ruby Dee was born in Cleveland on October 27, 1924, but grew up in Harlem, attending Hunter College in New York. In 1942, she appeared in *South Pacific* with Canada Lee. Five years later, she met Ossie Davis while they were both playing in *Jeb*. They were married two years later.

Ruby Dee's movies roles from this period include parts in *No Way Out* (1950), *Edge of the City* (1957), *Raisin in the Sun* (1961), Genet's *The Balcony* (1963), and *Purlie Victorious* (1963), written by Davis. Since 1960, she has appeared often on network television.

In 1965, Ruby Dee became the first African American actress to appear in major roles at the American Shakespeare Festival in Stratford, Connecticut. Appearances in movies including *The Incident* (1967), *Uptight* (1968), *Buck and the Preacher* (1972), *Black Girl* (directed by Davis) (1972), and *Countdown at Kusini* (1976) followed. Her musical satire *Take It from the Top*, in which she appeared with her husband in a showcase run at the Henry Street Settlement Theatre in New York, premiered in 1979.

As a team, Ruby Dee and Ossie Davis have recorded several talking story albums for Caedmon. In 1974, they produced "The Ruby Dee/Ossie Davis Story Hour," which was sponsored by Kraft Foods and carried by more than sixty stations of the National Black Network. Together they founded the Institute of New Cinema Artists to train young people for jobs in films and television, and then the Recording Industry Training Program to develop jobs in the music industry for disadvantaged youths. In 1981, Alcoa funded a television series on the Public Broadcasting System titled "With Ossie and Ruby," which used guests to provide an anthology of the arts. Recent film credits include *Cat People* (1982) and, with Ossie Davis, Spike Lee's *Do the Right Thing* (1989). In 1998, she narrated the PBS special "God's Gonna Trouble the Waters."

Ruby Dee holding an Emmy Award in 1991 (AP/Wide World Photos, Inc.).

Bill Duke (1943–)

Actor, Producer, Director

Bill Duke was born in Poughkeepsie, New York. He graduated with a B.A. in 1964 from Boston University and in 1968 with an M.A. from New York University. Duke began his career directing off-Broadway plays including the New York Shakespeare Festival's production of "Unfinished Business" for which he won the 1974 Adelco Award.

He made his film debut with *American Gigolo* in 1980, and has worked as an actor in a number of projects for film and television that include *Predator* (1987), *Commando* (1985), *Bird on a Wire* (1990), and *Action Jackson* (1988).

As a director his films include *A Rage in Harlem* (1991), *Deep Cover* (1992), *The Cemetery Club* (1992), *Sister Act 2: Back in the Habit* (1993), and *Hoodlum* (1997).

In 1994, he completed *Black Light: The African American Hero*, a book of photo essays celebrating ninety of the greatest African American heroes of the twentieth century. His most recent work as an author was a 1998 inspirational book entitled *The Journey*. He is currently the head of the School of Performing Arts at Howard University.

Tracey Edmonds (1967–)

Producer

As the President and CEO of Edmonds Entertainment, Tracey Edmonds is involved in virtually every aspect of the entertainment business. With divisions that include a record label, music publishing, film and television production and artist management, Edmonds's power and influence is unique for an African American female in entertainment.

A Southern California native, Edmonds is a 1987 Stanford graduate and former real estate executive who, in 1993, parlayed her business smarts and connections to create Yab Yum Entertainment. Originally established as a music publishing house, the company expanded into filmmaking with the 1996 release *Soul Food*. Grossing $43 million dollars at the box office, the film paved the way for Edmonds's entry into film. Since, Edmonds has produced the romantic comedy *Hav' Plenty*, and teen drama *Light it Up*. Married to R&B/pop superstar Kenneth "Babyface" Edmonds, Tracey Edmonds has a son.

Stepin Fetchit (1902–1985)

Actor

Stepin Fetchit's place in movie history is a controversial one. Praised by some critics as an actor who opened doors for other African Americans in Hollywood, he has been berated by others for catering to racist stereotypes and doing little to raise the status of African American actors. His characters—lazy, inarticulate, slow-witted, and always in the service of whites—have become so uncomfortable to watch that his scenes are sometimes cut when films in which he appeared are shown on television. Even at the height of his career, civil rights groups protested his roles, which they considered demeaning caricatures.

Born Lincoln Theodore Monroe Andrew Perry in Key West, Florida, on May 30, 1902, Stepin Fetchit's early career was in the Royal American Shows plantation revues. He and his partner, Ed Lee, took the names "Step 'n' Fetchit: Two Dancing Fools from Dixie." When the duo broke up, Fetchit appropriated "Stepin Fetchit" for himself.

Fetchit appeared in numerous motion pictures in the 1920s and 1930s including *In Old Kentucky* (1927), *Salute* (1929), *Hearts in Dixie* (1929), *Show Boat* (1929), *Swing High* (1930), *Stand Up and Cheer* (1934), *David Harum* (1934), *One More Spring* (1936), and *Zenobia* (1939). Fetchit earned a great deal of income from these films and spent it wildly. His extravagant lifestyle ended when he filed for bankruptcy in the 1930s.

Fetchit made sporadic appearances in films later in his life, among them *Miracle in Harlem* (1949), *Bend of the River* (1952), *Amazing Grace* (1974), and *Won Ton Ton, The Dog Who Saved Hollywood* (1976).

Laurence Fishburne (1961–)

Actor

Laurence Fishburne made his stage debut at age ten with the Negro Ensemble Theatre. The Augusta, Georgia, native made television history as member of daytime television's first African American family on "One Life to Live." Making his film debut at the age of 12 in *Cornbread, Earl and Me*, (1975) Fishburne moved to the Philippines for two years to co-star in the Francis Ford Coopla's war classic *Apocalypse Now*. Other notable roles for the actor include: *Rumble Fish* (1983); *The Cotton Club* (1984); *Gardens of Stone* (1987); *King of New York* (1990); *Class Action* (1991); *Deep Cover* (1992); and *Searching for Bobby Fischer* (1993).

Following his star making performance in director John Singleton's *Boyz N the Hood*, Fishburne was nominated for an Oscar for his portrayal of 1960s pop icon Ike Turner in the 1993 film *What's Love Got to Do With It*. In 1995, Fishburne became the first African American to play the title role in the film adaptation of the Shakespeare classic *Othello*. On Broadway, the actor has starred in the August Wilson production *Two Trains Running* and , most recently, finished a run in the play. In film, Fishburne's recent projects include *Fled* (1996), *Hoodlum* (1997), *Event Horizon* (1998), and *The Matrix* (1999).

Morgan Freeman (1937–)

Actor

Born in Memphis, Tennessee, on June 1, 1937, Morgan Freeman grew up in Greenwood, Mississippi. He joined the U.S. Air Force in 1955, but left a few years later to pursue an acting career in Hollywood, taking classes at Los Angeles City College. He moved to New York City in the 1960s.

Laurence Fishburne (Archive Photos, Inc.)

Morgan Freeman (AP/Wide World Photos, Inc.)

Freeman's first important role was in the short-running off-Broadway play *The Nigger-Lovers* in 1967. Soon thereafter, he appeared in the all-African American version of the musical *Hello, Dolly!*

Americans who grew up in the 1970s remember Freeman fondly as a regular on the public television program "The Electric Company" in which he appeared from 1971–1976; his most notable character was the hip Easy Reader. More theater roles followed in productions of *The Mighty Gents* (1978), *Othello* (1982), *The Gospel at Colonus* (1983), and *The Taming of the Shrew* (1990).

In 1987, Freeman was cast in the Broadway play *Driving Miss Daisy.* He won an Obie Award for his portrayal of Hoke, the chauffeur for a wealthy white woman in the American South. Freeman recreated his Broadway role for the 1989 movie version of the play, receiving an Academy Award nomination for best actor. In the same year, Freeman appeared in the highly successful movie *Glory* about an all-African American Union regiment in the Civil War. Other film credits include: *Clean and Sober* (1988), *Lean on Me* (1989), *Johnny Handsome* (1989), *Unforgiven* (1993), *The Shawshank Redemption* (1994), *Outbreak* (1995), and *Seven* (1995). Freeman also directed the 1993 film *Bopha!.* In 1995, Freeman was nominated again for an Academy Award for his role in *The Shawshank Redemption.* In 1998, Freeman starred in *Deep Impact.*

Danny Glover (1947–)
Actor

Born on July 22, 1947, in San Francisco, California, Danny Glover attended San Francisco State University and trained at the Black Actors Workshop of the American Conservatory Theatre.

Glover went on to appear in many stage productions including *Island*, *Macbeth*, *Sizwe Banzi is Dead*, and New York productions of *Suicide in B Flat*, *The Blood Knot*, and *Master Harold . . . and the Boys*, which won him a Theatre World Award.

Glover's film credits include: *Escape from Alcatraz* (1979); *Chu Chu and the Philly Flash* (1984); *Iceman* (1984); *Witness* (1985); *Places in the Heart* (1985); *The Color Purple* (1985); *Mandela* (1987); *Lethal Weapon* (1987)and its sequels; *Bat 21* (1988); *Predator 2* (1990); *To Sleep With Anger* (1990); *Flight of the Intruder* (1991); *A Rage in Harlem* (1991); *Pure Luck* (1991);

Danny Glover (AP/Wide World Photos, Inc.)

Louis Gossett, Jr. (AP/Wide World Photos, Inc.)

Grand Canyon (1991); *Bopha!* (1993); *The Saint of Fort Washington* (1993); *Angels in the Outfield* (1994); *Operation Dumbo Drop* (1995); and *Lethal Weapon 4*.

On television, Glover appeared in the hit series "Hill Street Blues," the miniseries "Chiefs," "Lonesome Dove," and other projects including "Many Mansions," "Face of Rage," "A Place at the Table," "Mandela," and "A Raisin in the Sun."

Louis Gossett, Jr. (1936–)
Actor

Born in Brooklyn on May 27, 1936, Louis Gossett began acting at the age of 17 when a leg injury prevented him from pursuing his first love—basketball. In 1953, he won out over 445 contenders for the role of a black youngster in *Take A Giant Step*, for which he received a Donaldson Award as best newcomer of the year.

While performing in *The Desk Set* in 1958, Gossett was drafted by the professional basketball team the New York Knicks, but decided to remain in theater. Ultimately, he would appear in more than sixty stage productions including such plays as *Lost in the Stars*, *A Raisin in the Sun*, *The Blacks*, and *Murderous Angels*.

On television, Gossett played characters roles in such series as "The Nurses," "The Defenders" and "East Side, West Side." In 1977, he won an Emmy for his performance in the acclaimed miniseries "Roots." He also starred in such films as *Skin Game* (1971), *The Deep* (1977), *Officer and a Gentleman* (1983), *Iron Eagle* (1986), *Iron Eagle II* (1988), and *Diggstown* (1993). In 1989, Gossett starred in his own television series "Gideon Oliver."

Gossett has also starred in television movies such as *Father and Son: Dangerous Relations* and *Ray Alexander: A Taste for Justice*.

Pam Grier (1949–)
Actress

Pamala Suzette Grier was born May 26, 1949, in Winston-Salem, North Carolina. Her father's military career kept the family moving. Grier spent her early years in Europe, until the age of 14, when her family returned to the United States. They settled in Denver, Colorado, where she would enroll in Metropolitan State College with aspirations of a future career in medicine.

In 1967, Grier entered the Miss Colorado Universe contest in hopes of winning prize money to battle the rising tuition costs. There she attracted the attention of an agent with her second place finish. David Baumgarten, who handled many great talents, invited her to Hollywood to begin a career in acting. Grier was disinclined to go, but she was encouraged by her mother to take the agent up on his offer.

After signing with the Agency of Performing Arts, Grier attended acting classes and worked the office switchboard. Acting roles did not come right away, but she eventually landed a small part in 1969's *The Bird Cage*. Throughout the 1970s, she was a box-office draw, often appearing in blaxploitation movies such as *Coffy* and *Foxy Brown*. Though she was usually cast as a strong, independent woman and enjoyed being one of the few actresses given the chance to create such portrayals, she felt hemmed in by the stereotypes these films encouraged. One of the few bankable female stars of the time, Grier unofficially retired. Then in 1981, she co-starred in *Fort Apache: The Bronx*.

A demanding film, Grier felt validated by the success of her difficult performance. Since then, Grier has appeared on stage, in films, and on television. She was recognized by the NAACP Image Awards as the best actress in 1986 for *Fool for Love*. In 1993, she received awards from the National Black Theatre Festival and the African American Film Society. In 1997 she made a comeback in Quentin Tarentino's *Jackie Brown*.

Henry Hampton (1940–1998)
Documentary Filmmaker

As a force behind the library of documentaries that primarily seek to address the African American experience, Henry Hampton used his vast understanding of the film medium as a tool to bring cultures together. A St. Louis native and son of a prominent surgeon, Hampton received his B.A. in literature in 1961 from Washington University. He has also taught at Tufts University.

In 1968, Hampton founded his production house, Blackside Inc., and initially produced industrial and documentary films. With a focus towards achieving social change through entertainment, Blackside Inc. has produced more than sixty films and media projects since its inception. Notable projects include *The Great Depression*, *America's War on Poverty*, *Code Blue*, and "Malcolm X: Make It Plain," an *American Experience* biography. However, Hampton is best known for the critically acclaimed, 14-hour documentary on the Civil Rights movement, *Eyes on the Prize*.

Hampton perfected the art of mixing archival news footage with contemporary interviews, thus giving the events more meaning to his audience. During his career he received numerous awards including six Emmys, an Academy Award nomination, and the dupont/Columbia Award for excellence in journalism. At the time of his death, he was working on the documentary *I'll Make Me A World*, a six-hour series on African American creative artists which was presented on PBS in memoriam to Hampton in 1999.

Rex Ingram (1895–1969)
Actor

A major movie and radio personality during the 1930s and 1940s, Rex Ingram was born on October 20, 1895, in Cairo, Illinois, aboard the *Robert E. Lee*, a Mississippi riverboat on which his father was a stoker.

Ingram attended military schools, where he displayed an interest in acting. After working briefly as a cook for the Union Pacific Railroad and as head of his own small window-washing business, Ingram gravitated to Hollywood, where in 1919 he appeared in the original Tarzan film. Roles in such classics as *Lord Jim*, *Beau Geste* (1926), *King Kong* (1933), *The Green Pastures* (1936), and *Huckleberry Finn* (1939) followed. During the late 1920s and early 1930s, Ingram also appeared prominently in theater in San Francisco. During the late 1930s, he starred in daytime radio soap operas and in Works Progress Administration theater projects.

Ingram continued with a distinguished career on the New York stage and in film and television. In 1957, he played Pozzo in *Waiting for Godot*. Later film credits include *Elmer Gantry* (1960), *Your Cheating Heart* (1964), *Hurry Sundown* (1967), and *Journey to Shiloh* (1968). He died on September 19, 1969.

Samuel L. Jackson (1949?–)
Actor

Samuel Jackson was born in Chattanooga, Tennessee in c. 1949. As a child, Jackson active imagination had him recreating scenes from his favorite movies. He also acted in various school plays. His first serious involvement in acting came as a student at Morehouse College in Atlanta. After deciding on drama as a major, Jackson began to enroll in theater classes at Morehouse's sister school Spellman College.

After receiving his Dramatic Arts degree, Jackson and his wife-to-be, La Tanya Richardson, moved to New York City. Jackson performed in various shows and films between the years of 1976 and 1981. As a cast member of Charles Burnett's *A Soldier's Play*, Jackson began to make connections. Morgan Freeman and Spike Lee both encouraged Jackson to keep pursuing his goals. Several years later, Jackson and Lee collaborated on the first of many films the two would film together.

School Daze and *Do the Right Thing* set the stage for the film that would create Jackson's reputation. *Jungle Fever*, also directed by Lee, displayed Jackson's versa-

Rex Ingram (Corbis Corporation [Bellevue])

Samuel L. Jackson (Archive Photos, Inc.)

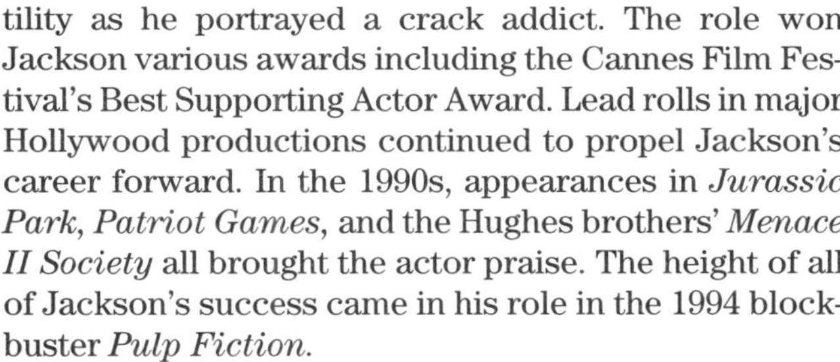

tility as he portrayed a crack addict. The role won Jackson various awards including the Cannes Film Festival's Best Supporting Actor Award. Lead rolls in major Hollywood productions continued to propel Jackson's career forward. In the 1990s, appearances in *Jurassic Park*, *Patriot Games*, and the Hughes brothers' *Menace II Society* all brought the actor praise. The height of all of Jackson's success came in his role in the 1994 blockbuster *Pulp Fiction*.

Despite the accolades and success his films produced, Jackson desired to work on-stage again. His wish came true as he was cast lead male in the play *Distant Fires*. Demand for Jackson's work has kept him busy. Movies such as *Die Hard with a Vengeance* and *The Great White Hype* have kept the actor busy in the mid-1990s. In 1999, he starred in the much anticipated prequel to *Star Wars*, *The Phantom Menace*.

James Earl Jones (1931–)
Actor

Jones (whose father Robert Earl Jones was featured in the movie *One Potato, Two Potato*) was born in Tate County, Mississippi, on January 17, 1931, and raised by his grandparents on a farm near Jackson, Michigan. He turned to acting after a brief period as a premedical student at the University of Michigan (from which he graduated cum laude in 1953) and upon completion of military service with the Army's Cold Weather Mountain Training Command in Colorado.

After moving to New York, Jones studied at the American Theatre Wing, making his off-Broadway debut in 1957 in *Wedding in Japan*. Since then, he has appeared in numerous plays, on and off-Broadway, including *Sunrise at Campobello* (1958), *The Cool World* (1960), *The Blacks* (1961), *The Blood Knot* (1964), and *Anyone, Anyone*.

Jones's career as an actor progressed slowly until he portrayed Jack Jefferson in the Broadway smash hit *The Great White Hope*. The play was based on the life of Jack Johnson, the first black heavyweight champion. For this performance, Jones received the 1969 Tony Award for the best dramatic actor in a Broadway play and a Drama Desk Award for one of the best performances of the 1968–1969 New York season.

By the 1970s, Jones was appearing in roles traditionally performed by white actors including the title role in *King Lear* and an award-winning performance as Lenny in Steinbeck's *Of Mice and Men*.

James Earl Jones holding two Emmy Awards in 1991 (AP/Wide World Photos, Inc.).

In 1978, Jones appeared in the highly controversial *Paul Robeson*, a one-man show on Broadway. Many leading African Americans advocated a boycott of the show because they felt it did not measure up to the man himself. However, many critics gave the show high praise.

In 1980, Jones starred in Athol Fugard's *A Lesson from Aloes*, a top contender for a Tony Award that year. He also appeared in the Yale Repertory Theater Production of *Hedda Gabler*. In the spring of 1982, he co-starred with Christopher Plummer on Broadway in *Othello*, a production acclaimed as among the best ever done. In 1987, Jones received a Tony award for his performance in August Wilson's Pulitzer Prize-winning play *Fences*.

Jones's early film credits include *Dr. Strangelove* (1964), *River Niger* (1976), and *The Greatest* (1977). He was the screen voice of Darth Vader in *Star Wars* (1977) and its sequels *The Empire Strikes Back* (1980) and *The Return of Jedi* (1983). Jones has also appeared in the following movies: *Conan the Barbarian* (1982); *Allan Quartermain and the Lost City of Gold* (1986); *Soul Man* (1986); *Matewan* (1987); *Coming to America* (1988); *Field of Dreams* (1989); *Three Fugitives* (1989); *The Hunt for Red October* (1990); *Patriot Games* (1992); *Sommersby* (1993); *The Sandlot* (1993); *Excessive Force* (1993); *The Meteor Man* (1993); *Clean Slate* (1994); *Clear and Present Danger* (1994); *Jefferson in Paris* (1995); *Cry, the Beloved Country* (1995); and *A Family Thing* (1996).

Among numerous television appearances, Jones portrayed author Alex Haley in "Roots: The Next Generation" (1979) and has narrated documentaries for the Public Broadcasting System. During the early 1990s, Jones appeared in the television series "Gabriel's Fire" and the television movies *Percy and Thunder* and *The Vernon Johns Story*. He starred in the CBS series "Under One Roof" in 1995.

In 1976, Jones was elected to the Board of Governors of the Academy of Motion Picture Arts and Sciences. In 1979, New York City presented him with the "Mayor's Award of Honor for Arts and Culture." He received an honorary Doctorate of Humane Letters from the University of Michigan in 1971 and the New York Man of the Year Award in 1976. In 1985, he was inducted into the Theater Hall of Fame.

Canada Lee (1907–1952)

Actor

Canada Lee was born Leonard Corneliou Canagata in Manhattan, New York, on May 3, 1907. After studying violin as a young boy, he ran off to Saratoga to become a jockey. Failing in this endeavor, he returned to New York and began a boxing career. In 1926, after winning ninety out of one hundred fights, including the national amateur lightweight title, he turned professional. Over the next few years, he won 175 out of some 200 fights against such top opponents as Jack Britton and Vince Dundee. In 1933, a detached retina brought an end to his ring career. He had acquired the name Canada Lee when a ring announcer could not pronounce his real name.

In 1934, Lee successfully auditioned at the Harlem YMCA for his first acting role which was in a Works Progress Administration production of *Brother Moses*. In 1941, Orson Welles, who had met Lee in the Federal Theatre's all-African American production of *Macbeth*, chose him to play Bigger Thomas in the stage version of Richard Wright's famed novel *Native Son*.

In 1944, Lee served as narrator of a radio series called "New World A-Comin'"—the first such series devoted to racial issues. That same year, he also appeared in Alfred Hitchcock's film *Lifeboat* and in the Broadway play *Anna Lucasta*. He also worked for the NBC radio network as master of ceremonies for various war-related programming.

Lee's political activism eventually ended his career. He campaigned against racism and discriminatory hiring practices. He also signed a petition urging the expulsion of Mississippi racist Theodore Bilbo from the Senate. Eventually, these efforts led to his blacklisting by the Hollywood establishment for suspicion of being a communist agent. In 1950, he starred in the British production of *Cry, the Beloved Country*—the first film to challenge apartheid and the wretched living conditions of blacks in South Africa. However, the emotional stress of the blacklisting affected his health and in 1952, he died of a heart attack.

Spike Lee (1957–)
Filmmaker

Lee was born March 20, 1957, in Atlanta, Georgia. His family moved briefly to Chicago before settling in New York in 1959. Lee received a B.A. in mass communication in 1979 from Morehouse College. After a summer internship at Columbia Pictures in Burbank, California, Lee enrolled in New York University's prestigious Institute of Film and Television. He received an M.A. in filmmaking in 1983. While at New York University he wrote and directed *Joe's Bed-Sty Barbershop: We Cut Heads* for which he won the 1982 Student Academy award given by the Academy of Motion Picture Arts and Sciences. The movie was later shown on public television's Independent Focus Series.

Spike Lee directing the film *Crooklyn* (Archive Photos, Inc.).

Notable films by Lee include: *She's Gotta Have It* (1986), which resulted in the resurgence of African American cinema; *School Daze* (1988); *Do The Right Thing* (1989); *Mo' Better Blues* (1990); *Jungle Fever* (1991); *Malcolm X* (1992); *Crooklyn* (1994); *Clockers* (1995); *Girl 6* (1996); *He Got Game* (1998); and *Summer of Sam* (1999). *She's Gotta Have It* won the Los Angeles Film Critics New Generation award and the Prix de Juenesse at the Cannes Film Festival.

Lee has also written two books: *Spike Lee's Gotta Have It: Inside Guerilla Filmmaking* (1987) and *Uplift the Race* (1988). He has established a fellowship for minority filmmakers at New York University and is a trustee of Morehouse College. Lee's production company, Forty Acres and a Mule Filmworks is located in Brooklyn, New York.

Byron Lewis (1931–)
Producer

Byron Lewis was born in Newark, New Jersey. He received his B.A. in 1953 from Long Island University. He founded the Uni-World corporation in 1969. Lewis recognized early on the power behind the buying potential of African Americans and ethnic markets. As the marketing agency for accounts that include powerhouse corporations such as Burger King, Mars Inc.. and Quaker Oats, Uni-World generated over two hundred million dollars in revenue in 1998.

Lewis is the executive producer of the widely syndicated television show "America's Black Forum" and the founder and executive producer of the Acapulco Black Film Festival. Lewis is a member of the National Urban League and has won many honors for his role in advertising and as a producer.

Hattie McDaniel (1898–1952)
Actress

Hattie McDaniel was born on June 10, 1898, in Wichita, Kansas, and moved to Denver, Colorado, as a child. After a period of singing for Denver radio as an amateur, she entered vaudeville professionally, and by 1924 was a headliner on the Pantages circuit.

By 1931, McDaniel had made her way to Hollywood. After a slow start, during which she supported herself as a maid and washer woman, she gradually began to get more movie roles. Her early film credits included *Judge Priest* (1934), *The Little Colonel* (1935), *Showboat* (1936), *Saratoga* (1937), and *Nothing Sacred*. Her portrayal of a "mammy" figure in *Gone with the Wind*, a role for which she received an Oscar award in 1940 as best supporting actress, is still regarded as a definitive interpretation. McDaniel was the first African American to receive an Oscar award.

McDaniel subsequently appeared in films such as *The Great Lie* (1941), *In This Our Life* (1942), *Johnny Come Lately* (1943), *Since You Went Away* (1944), *Margie* (1946), *Never Say Goodbye* (1946), *Song of the South* (1946), *Mr. Blandings Builds His Dream House* (1948), *Family Honeymoon* (1948), and *The Big Wheel* (1949).

In addition to her movie roles, McDaniel enjoyed success in radio, in the 1930s, as Hi-Hat Hattie and in the 1940s in the title role of the very successful "Beulah" series. McDaniel died on October 26, 1952.

Butterfly McQueen (1911–1995)
Actress

Butterfly McQueen's portrayal of Prissy in *Gone with the Wind* (1939) rivals Hattie McDaniel's Oscar-winning role as the "mammy," and is certainly as popular with audiences as Vivien Leigh's Scarlett O'Hara or Clark Gable's Rhett Butler.

Born Thelma McQueen on January 8, 1911, in Tampa, Florida, McQueen began her career in the 1930s performing as a radio actress in "The Goldbergs," "The Danny Kaye Show," "The Jack Benny Show," and "The Beulah Show." She also appeared on stage in *Brown Sugar* (1937), *Brother Rat* (1937), and *What a Life* (1938).

After her role in *Gone with the Wind* in 1939, McQueen was cast in other motion pictures such as *I Dood It* (1943), *Cabin in the Sky* (1943), *Mildred Pierce* (1945), and *Duel in the Sun* (1947). She appeared as Oriole on the television series "Beulah" from 1950 to 1952.

Given her outspokenness against racism and discrimination and her refusal to play stereotyped servant roles, McQueen's appearances after this period were sporadic. In 1968, she won accolades for her performance in the off-Broadway play *Curley McDimple*. She was cast in the television program "The Seven Wishes of Joanna Peabody" in 1978, and the film *Mosquito Coast* in 1986. McQueen received a B.A. in Spanish from New York City College in 1975.

On December 22, 1995, McQueen died after being critically burned when a kerosene heater in her cottage caught fire.

Butterfly McQueen (Archive Photos, Inc.)

Oscar Deveraux Micheaux (1884–1951)
Filmmaker, Author

Micheaux was born in 1884 in Metropolis, Illinois. Little is known about his early years other than he left home at 17 and worked briefly as a pullman porter. In 1904 he began homesteading in Gregory County, South Dakota.

Micheaux was a hard-working farmer who loved to read and had a flair for writing. In 1913 he wrote, published, and promoted *The Conquest: Story of a Negro Pioneer*. This novel was followed by *Forged Note: Romance of the Darker Races* in 1915 and *The Homesteader* in 1917. Much of his writing was melodramatic and probably autobiographical.

In 1918 the Lincoln Picture Company, an independent African American film production company, tried to buy the film rights to *The Homesteader*. When Micheaux insisted that he direct the planned movie, the deal fell through. Micheaux went to New York where he formed the Oscar Micheaux Corp. Between 1919 and 1937 Micheaux made about thirty films including *Body and Soul*, a 1924 movie in which Paul Robeson made his first cinematic appearance.

Although Micheaux was an excellent self-promoter of his books and films, his company went into bankruptcy in 1928. By 1931 however, Micheaux was back in the film business producing and directing *The Exile* (1931), and *Veiled Aristocrats* (1932). Between 1941 and 1943 he wrote four more books *Wind From Nowhere, Case of*

Mrs. Wingate, *Masquerade*, and *Story of Dorothy Stansfield*. In 1948 he made his last film *The Betrayal*. While none of Micheaux's films achieved critical acclaim, they were quite popular with black audiences and attracted a limited white following. While his characters broke with the African American stereotypes of the day, the themes of his movies ignored racial injustice and the day-to-day problems of African Americans.

Micheaux was known as a hard worker and a natty dresser who consumed neither alcohol or tobacco. Although he made a great deal of money, all of it was squandered away. Micheaux died penniless in Charlotte, North Carolina. Conflicting dates are given for his death—March 26, 1951 and April 1, 1951.

Clarence Muse (1889–1979)

Actor, Director

Born on October 14, 1889, Clarence Muse was perhaps best known for his film acting, He was, however, also successful as a director, playwright, and actor on the stage.

The Baltimore native's parents came from Virginia and North Carolina, and his grandfather from Martinique. After studying law at Dickinson University in Pennsylvania, Muse sang as part of a hotel quartet in Palm Beach, Florida. A subsequent job with a stock company took him on tour through the South with his wife and son. Coming to New York, he barely scraped a living together, mostly performing as a vaudevillian.

After several plays with the now-famous Lincoln Theatre group and the Lafayette Players in Harlem, and a Broadway stint in *Dr. Jekyll and Mr. Hyde*, where having white roles played by blacks in white face created quite a controversy, Muse had established himself as an actor and singer.

Muse's first movie role was in *Hearts in Dixie* (1929), produced at the William Fox Studio, in which Muse played a ninety-year-old man. Later, he returned to the stage for the role of a butler in the show that was to be called *Under the Virgin Moon*. After Muse wrote the theme song, the title was changed to his *When It's Sleepy Time Down South*. Both the song and the show were hits.

When the Federal Theatre Project in Los Angeles presented Hall Johnson's *Run Little Chillun*, Muse directed the show. After its successful two-year run, Muse made the screen adaption *Way Down South* (1939).

During Muse's career, he appeared in 219 films, and was at one time one of the highest paid African American actors, often portraying faithful servant "Uncle Tom" characters. His movie credits include: *Huckleberry Finn* (1931); *Cabin in the Cotton* (1932); *Count of Monte Cristo* (1934); *So Red the Rose* (1935); *Showboat* (1936); *The Toy Wife* (1938); *The Flame of New Orleans* (1941); *Tales of Manhattan* (1942); *Heaven Can Wait* (1943); *Night and Day* (1946); *An Act of Murder* (1948); *Porgy and Bess* (1959); *Buck and the Preacher* (1971); and *Car Wash* (1976). His last film was *Black Stallion* in 1979. He also appeared over the years in concerts and on radio.

Muse died October 13, 1979, the day before his ninetieth birthday. He had lived in Perris, California on his Muse-a-While Ranch.

Sidney Poitier (1927–)

Actor

Sidney Poitier was born on February 20, 1927, in Miami, but moved to the Bahamas with his family at a very early age. At age 15, he returned to Miami; he later rode freight trains to New York City, where he found employment as a dishwasher. After the attack on Pearl Harbor, he enlisted in the Army and served on active duty for four years.

Back in New York, Poitier auditioned for the American Negro Theater, but was turned down by director Frederick O'Neal. After working diligently to improve his diction, Poitier was accepted in the theater group, receiving acting lessons in exchange for doing backstage chores.

In 1950, Poitier made his Hollywood debut in *No Way Out*, followed by successful appearances in *Cry, the Beloved Country* (1952), *Red Ball Express* (1952), *Go, Man, Go* (1954), *Blackboard Jungle* (1956), *Goodbye, My Lady* (1956), *Edge of the City* (1957), *Band of Angels* (1957), *Something of Value* (1957), and *Porgy and Bess* (1959), among others. Poitier starred on Broadway in 1959 in Lorraine Hansberry's award-winning *Raisin in the Sun*, and repeated this success in the movie version of the play in 1961.

In 1965, Poitier became the first African American to win an Oscar for a starring role, receiving this award for his performance in *Lilies of the Field*. Seven years earlier, Poitier had been the first African American actor nominated for the award for his portrayal of an escaped convict in *The Defiant Ones*.

Subsequent notable film appearances include performances in *To Sir with Love* (1967), *Heat of the Night* (1967), *Guess Who's Coming to Dinner* (with Spencer Tracy and Katharine Hepburn) (1968), *Buck and the Preacher* (1972), and *A Warm December* (1973), in both of which he acted and directed, *Uptown Saturday Night* (1974), and *A Piece of the Action* (1977). After years of inactivity, Poitier performed in two additional films *Little Nikita* and *Shoot To Kill*, both released in 1988. His directing ventures include *Stir Crazy* (with Richard Pryor and Gene Wilder) (1980), *Hanky Panky* (with

Gilda Radner) (1982), and the musical *Fast Forward* (1985).

Poitier spent two years writing his memoirs *This Life* published by Knopf in 1980. In 1981, Citadel Press published *The Films of Sidney Poitier* by Alvin H. Marill.

In 1993, Poitier won the Thurgood Marshall Lifetime Achievement Award and the Living Legend Award from the National Black Theater Festival. On December 3, 1995, he was presented with one of the Kennedy Center Honors.

Phylicia Rashad (1948–)

Actress

Known to millions as Claire Huxtable from "The Cosby Show," Phylicia Rashad has led a distinguished acting career on television and the stage. She was born on June 19, 1948, in Houston, Texas, and until 1985 was known as Phylicia Ayers-Allen. Her sister is the famous Debbie Allen; both sisters received early instruction in music, acting, and dance. Phylicia graduated magna cum laude from Howard University in 1970 with a B.F.A. in theater.

Early in her career, Rashad played the character Courtney Wright in the soap opera "One Life to Live." Her big break came with "The Cosby Show" in which she and Bill Cosby presided over the Huxtable family for seven years, from 1985 to 1992. In 1997, she and Cosby began the new sitcom "Cosby." Rashad has also appeared in Broadway and off-Broadway productions of *The Cherry Orchard*, *The Wiz*, *Zora*, *Dreamgirls*, *A Raisin in the Sun*, and *Into the Woods*.

Rashad has received two honorary doctorates, one from Providence College in Rhode Island and one from Barber-Scotia College in North Carolina. In 1995, Rashad was named spokesperson for the American Diabetes Association. She and her husband Ahmad Rashad, a sportscaster for NBC, live in Westchester County, New York.

Richard Roundtree (1942–)

Actor

Richard Roundtree is best known as John Shaft, the tough, renegade detective from the movie *Shaft* (1971). Born in New Rochelle, New York, on July 9, 1942, Roundtree graduated from New Rochelle High School, and attended Southern Illinois University on a football scholarship. After brief stints as a suit salesman and a model, he began a stage career with the Negro Ensemble Company. With *Shaft* (1971) and its sequels *Shaft's Big Score* (1972) and *Shaft in Africa* (1973), Roundtree reached the peak of his career and became a pop icon.

Richard Roundtree (Archive Photos, Inc)

Roundtree's subsequently appeared in the films *Embassy* (1972), *Charley One Eye* (1973), *Earthquake* (1974), *Diamonds* (1975), and *Man Friday* (1976). He appeared in the television miniseries "Roots" (1977) and continues to be cast in various television programs and motion pictures.

In 1995, Roundtree appeared in the films *Seven* and *When We Were Colored.* He has also served as host of the TV show "Cop Files." He also appeared on the WB network in 1997 in "Rescue 77," a paramedic-based drama.

John Singleton (1968–)

Filmmaker

Singleton was born in Los Angeles in 1968. After graduating from high school in 1986, he enrolled in the University of Southern California's prestigious Film Writing Program, which is part of their School of Cinema-Television. While there he formed an African American Film Association and did a six month director's internship for the "Arsenio Hall Show." He twice won the school's Jack Nicholson Award for best feature length screenplay. Before graduating in 1990, he signed with the well known Creative Artists Agency.

John Singleton (Corbis Corporation [Bellevue])

Singleton was soon approached by Columbia Pictures to sell the film rights to *Boyz N the Hood*, his original screenplay and college thesis. Singleton agreed, but only if he would be the movie's director. The movie was released in July of 1991 to mixed critical reviews. Although its first showings were marred by theater violence, it garnered Singleton an Academy Award nomination for best director. He became the first African American and the youngest person to be so honored.

Since *Boyz N the Hood*, Singleton has done a short cable television film for Michael Jackson entitled *Remember the Time*. His second film *Poetic Justice* was released in the summer of 1993. His third film *Higher Learning* was released in 1995 followed the next year by *Rosewood*.

Wesley Snipes (1962–)

Actor

Born in Orlando, Florida, on July 31, 1962, Wesley Snipes spent his childhood in the Bronx, New York. At the age of 12, he appeared in his first off-Broadway production, a minor role in the play *The Me Nobody Knows*. His interest in dance led him to enroll in New York's High School for the Performing Arts. However, before completing the curriculum, his mother sent him back to Orlando to finish school, where he continued to study drama.

Upon high school graduation, Snipes was awarded a scholarship to study theater at the State University of New York at Purchase. Snipes subsequently appeared in on and off-Broadway productions including Wole Soyinka's *Death and the King's Horsemen*, Emily Mann's *Execution of Justice*, and John Pielmeier's *The Boys of Winter*. He has also appeared in Michael Jackson's video "Bad" and in the HBO production *Vietnam War Story* for which he received cable television's best actor award.

Snipes's film appearances include roles in *Wildcats* (1986), *Streets of Gold* (1986), *Major League* (1989), and *King of New York* (1990). In 1990 Snipes appeared in Spike Lee's *Mo' Better Blues*, with Denzel Washington. This was followed by a role in Mario Van Peebles's *New Jack City* (1991) and in Spike Lee's *Jungle Fever* (1991). His most recent films include *White Men Can't Jump*, *Passenger 57*, *Rising Sun*, *Sugar Hill*, *One Night Stand*, and *Blade*.

Robert Townsend (1957–)

Director, Actor

Robert Townsend began his career as an actor with bit parts in such films as *Cooley High* and *A Soldier's Story*. He was born in Detroit, Michigan, and worked as a stand-up comedian before coming to Hollywood to try acting.

In 1987 Townsend responded to the paucity of film roles available to African American actors by creating and financing his own project *Hollywood Shuffle*. The film's success launched Townsend into prominence as a director. Other notable Townsend films include the Eddie Murphy concert film *Raw* (1987), *The Five Heart Beats* (1991), *The Meteor Man* (1993), and *B.A.P.S.* (1997).

Townsend has won two Cable Ace Awards and multiple NAACP Image Awards. He is best known for his role as the patriarch on the long-running sitcom "Parenthood." Townsend also served as host on the syndicated variety show "Motown Live." He also recently completed a starring role in the suspense drama *Fraternity Boys*. As a director Townsend recently finished work on the dramatic trilogy *Love Songs* and the Lifetime cable network made-for-television movie *Jackie's Back*.

Cicely Tyson (1939–)

Actress

During the early 1970s, Cicely Tyson emerged as America's leading black dramatic star. She achieved this through two sterling performances—as Rebecca, the

Wesley Snipes (AP/Wide World Photos, Inc.)

wife of a Southern sharecropper in the film *Sounder* and as the lead in a television special "The Autobiography of Miss Jane Pittman," the story of an ex-slave who, past her one hundredth year, challenges racist authority by deliberately drinking from a "white only" water fountain as a white deputy sheriff watches.

Cicely Tyson was born in New York City on December 19, 1939, and raised by a very religious, strict mother, who associated movies with sin and forbade Cicely to go to movie theaters. Blessed with poise and natural grace, Tyson became a model and appeared on the cover of America's two foremost fashion magazines *Vogue* and *Harper's Bazaar* in 1956. Interested in acting, she began to study drama and in 1959 appeared on a CBS culture series "Camera Three" with what is believed to be the first natural African hair style worn on television.

Tyson won a role in an off-Broadway production of Jean Genet's *The Blacks* (1961), for which she received the 1962 Vernon Rice Award. She then played a lead part in the CBS series "East Side, West Side." Tyson subsequently moved into film parts, appearing in *The Comedians* (1967) and *The Heart Is a Lonely Hunter* (1968). Critical acclaim led to her role as Rebecca in *Sounder* (1972), for which she was nominated for an Academy award and named best actress by the National Society of Film Critics. She won an Emmy television acting trophy for "Jane Pittman" (1974).

Tyson's other film appearances include *The Blue Bird* (1976) and *The River Niger* (1976). On television, she has appeared in "Roots" (1977), "King" (1978), and "Wilma" (1978). She portrayed Harriet Tubman in "A Woman Called Moses," and Chicago schoolteacher Marva Collins in a made-for-television movie in 1981. Recent television appearances include "Cry Freedom" (1987) and "The Women of Brewster Place" (1989). In 1995, Tyson starred in the television series "Sweet Justice."

In 1979, Marymount College presented Tyson with an honorary Doctor of Fine Arts. Tyson owns a house on Malibu Beach in California. In November 1981, she married jazz trumpeter Miles Davis, but the couple divorced before Davis's death.

Melvin Van Peebles (1932–)

Filmmaker, Actor, Writer

Melvin Van Peebles was born on August 21, 1932, in Chicago, Illinois. As a child, Van Peebles's family moved to Phoenix, Illinois, where he graduated from high school. Studied English literature, Van Peebles received his Bachelor in Arts from Wesleyan University in 1953. After spending three and a half years as a flight navigator for the U.S. Air Force, Van Peebles settled in San Francisco.

While in San Francisco, Van Peebles began to dabble in filmmaking. *Three Pickup Men for Herrick*, completed in 1958, is the best known of his early work, but with success in his sight, Van Peebles took his films to Hollywood. Several rejections frustrated Van Peebles, prompting a move to Holland. There Van Peebles's luck changed for a short while. He acted with the Dutch National Theater while studying astronomy at the University of Amsterdam, but troubles with his wife forced Van Peebles to move again. He found a home in Paris, where wrote several novels in self-taught French.

Experiences in France led to Van Peebles's first international film success. *Three Day Pass* received generally positive criticism as it premiered at the San Francisco International Film Festival. This led to Van Peebles directing a string of films including *Watermelon Man* and *Sweet Sweetback's Baadasssss Song*, which he wrote, directed, and produced. A smash, the film grossed nearly $14 million dollars. This film used a mostly black crew and became controversial for its violence, earning an X rating. However, the money the film earned launched the "blaxploitation" film movement in Hollywood.

In 1971, Van Peebles turned his attention toward Broadway. His productions of *Ain't Supposed to Die a Natural Death* and *Don't Play Us Cheap* received mixed reviews. Despite the lack of critical enthusiasm for his work *Ain't Supposed to Die a Natural Death* closed as the fifth-longest running show on Broadway and *Don't Play* received first prize during a Belgian Festival. Throughout the 1970s, Van Peebles continued to write and direct for films, plays, and television. In 1987, his teleplay *The Day They Came to Arrest the Book* received an Emmy Award.

After a hiatus, Van Peebles returned to directing, for the film *Identity Crisis*, featuring his son Mario, who also penned the film. In 1993, the father-son team reversed roles in the film *Posse*, which Mario directed and in which Melvin acted. In the mid-1990s, they continued to develop a variety of projects together including *Panther*, a fictionalized motion picture of the history of The Black Panthers.

Denzel Washington (1954–)
Actor

Born on December 28, 1954, in Mt. Vernon, New York, Denzel Washington attended an upstate private high school, the Oakland Academy, and then entered Fordham University as a pre-med major. Washington did not originally intend to become an actor, but when he auditioned for the lead role in a student production of Eugene O'Neill's *The Emperor Jones*, he won the part over theater majors. His performance in that play, and later in a production of *Othello*, led his drama instructor to encourage Washington to pursue an acting career.

Denzel Washington holding a Golden Globe Award in 1990 (AP/Wide World Photos, Inc.).

Washington's first major role was in the off-Broadway drama *A Soldier's Story*. Washington re-created his role when the play was adapted into a motion picture in 1984. He played Dr. Phillip Chandler on the television series "St. Elsewhere" and appeared in a string of films including *Carbon Copy* (1980), *Cry Freedom* (in which he portrayed South African activist Steven Biko) (1987), *The Mighty Quinn* (1989), *Glory* (which won him an Academy Award for best supporting actor) (1989), *Mo' Better Blues* (1990), *Mississippi Masala* (1992), and *Malcolm X* (1992). Washington also starred in *Philadelphia* (1993), playing an attorney for an HIV-positive lawyer played by Oscar winner Tom Hanks. Later, he starred in *Crimson Tide*, *Devil in a Blue Dress*, *Virtuosity*, *Courage Under Fire*, and *He Got Game*.

In addition to winning an Oscar for *Glory*, Washington won the Silver Beard Award at the Berlin International Film Festival in 1993. Washington is married to actress Pauletta Pearson.

Billy Dee Williams (1937–)
Actor

A screen, television, and stage actor with impressive credits, Billy Dee Williams has starred in some of the most commercially popular films ever released.

Born William December Williams in Harlem on April 6, 1937, Williams was a withdrawn, overweight youngster who initially planned to become a fashion illustrator. While studying on scholarship at the School of Fine Arts in the National Academy of Design, a CBS casting director helped him secure bit parts in several television shows including "Lamp Unto My Feet" and "Look Up And Live."

Williams then began to study acting under Sidney Poitier and Paul Mann at the Actors Workshop in Harlem. He made his film debut in *The Last Angry Man* (1959), and then appeared on stage in *The Cool World* (1960), *A Taste of Honey* (1960), and *The Blacks* (1962). He later appeared briefly on Broadway in *Hallelujah Baby* (1967) and in several off-Broadway shows including *Ceremonies in Dark Old Men* (1970).

Williams's next major role was in the acclaimed television movie *Brian's Song* (1970), a performance for which he received an Emmy nomination. Motown's Berry Gordy then signed Williams to a seven-year contract after which he starred in *Lady Sings the Blues* (1972) and *Mahogany* (1976) with Diana Ross. His last movie for Gordy was *The Bingo Long Traveling All-Stars and Motor King* (1976).

In the early 1980s, Williams appeared in two of George Lucas's *Star Wars* adventures *The Empire Strikes Back* and *Return of the Jedi*. He has appeared in numerous television movies including *Scott Joplin*, *Christmas Lilies of the Field*, and the miniseries "Chiefs." When he was cast opposite Diahann Carroll in the prime time drama "Dynasty" his reputation as a romantic lead was secured. At the end of the decade, he starred in action films such as *Oceans of Fire* and *Number One With a Bullet*.

In 1995, Williams played a detective in the TV murder mystery "Falling for You." He also hosted the Black Theatre Festival in Winston-Salem, North Carolina and the Infiniti Sports Festival. Some of Williams's paintings were featured in a computer screensaver program "Art in the Dark: Extraordinary Works by African American Artists."

Billy Dee Williams (AP/Wide World Photos, Inc.)

Vanessa Williams (1963–)
Model, Singer, Actress

A native of New York City, Vanessa Williams made history in 1983, when she became the first African American woman to be chosen Miss America, and again in 1984, when she was forced to relinquish her title after Penthouse published nude photos of her taken years before her crowning.

In the wake of the pageant controversy Williams has gone on to achieve success, signing in 1987 with Mercury/Wing Records. Her debut project *The Right Stuff* achieved gold record status fueled by hit singles such as the titled track and the ballad "Dreamin." More hits have followed in 1992 including "Saving the Best for Last" and "Colors of the Wind," the theme song from the blockbuster Disney animated film *Pocahontas* which went on to win Academy, Golden Globe, and Grammy awards.

Williams made her film debut with *Under the Gun* in 1986, and has gone on to star opposite Arnold Schwarzenegger in *Eraser* (1996) and *Hoodlum*, (1997) along side Laurence Fishburne. Some of her other notable film roles include: the highly successful family drama *Soul Food* (1997) and the romantic dance musical

Dance With Me (1998). On television, Williams has starred in "Stopin' at the Savoy," "The Jacksons: An American Dream," "The Odyssey," and, most recently, "Future Sport." Williams made her Broadway debut in June 1994 in the hit musical "Kiss of the Spider Woman."

Paul Winfield (1941–)
Actor

Born in Los Angeles on May 22, 1941, Paul Winfield grew up in a poor family. Excelling in school, he attended a number of colleges—the University of Portland, Stanford University, Los Angeles City College, and the University of California at Los Angeles—but left UCLA before graduation to pursue his acting career.

Winfield appeared on television shows in the late 1960s and early 1970s—most notably as one of Diahann Carroll's boyfriends in the series "Julia." His great success in that period was in the film *Sounder* (1972), in which he played a sharecropper father in the nineteenth-century American South. For this role, he received an Academy Award nomination for best actor.

Winfield subsequently appeared in the motion pictures *Gordon's War* (1973), *Conrack* (1974), *Huckleberry Finn* (1974), and *A Hero Ain't Nothing But a Sandwich* (1978). He received accolades for his portrayal of Dr. Martin Luther King, Jr. in the NBC movie *King* (1978), for which he received an Emmy nomination. His second Emmy nomination came with his role in the television miniseries "Roots: The Next Generation" (1979).

In the 1980s, Winfield kept busy with appearances on television in "The Charmings," "The Women of Brewster Place," "Wiseguy," and "227;" on film in *Star Trek II: The Wrath of Khan* (1982), *Damnation Alley* (1983), and *The Terminator* (1984); and on the stage in *A Midsummer Night's Dream*, *Othello*, and *The Seagull*. In 1990, he played the sarcastic Judge Larren Lyttle in the movie *Presumed Innocent* and in 1992 appeared on Broadway in the cast of *A Few Good Men*.

Winfield has won several major awards including an NAACP Image Award and election to the Black Filmmakers Hall of Fame. In 1995, Winfield won an Emmy for best guest actor on a drama series for his work in "Picket Fences: Enemy Lines."

21

Drama, Comedy, and Dance

◆ The Origins of African American Performance Art ◆ Minstrelsy
◆ Reclaiming the Black Image: 1890 to 1920
◆ African American Dramatic Theater in the Twentieth Century
◆ African American Musicals in the Twentieth Century
◆ African American Comedy in the Twentieth Century
◆ African American Dance in the Twentieth Century
◆ Stage Actors, Comedians, Choreographers, and Dancers

by Bernadette A. Meier

For more than two hundred years, African American performers have appeared on the American stage. Despite the prejudices that they have had to face both within the theater community and from the entertainment-seeking public, they have made significant contributions to American performance art. The artistic heritage of today's African American actors, dancers, and comedians can be traced back to the last decades of the eighteenth century.

◆ THE ORIGINS OF AFRICAN AMERICAN PERFORMANCE ART

The Earliest Plays with African American Actors

The first performances by African American actors on the American stage were in plays authored by white playwrights who provided blacks with narrow opportunities to portray shallow characters. Often blacks were cast in the role of the buffoon in order to appeal to the sensibilities of a bigoted public. In 1769, for example, the cast of Lewis Hallam's comedy *The Padlock* included a West Indian slave character named Mongo, who was a clown to be played by a black. Other white-authored plays from the period that depicted blacks in demoralizing roles were *Robinson Crusoe, Harlequin* (1792), and *The Triumph of Love* (1795) by John Randolph, which included the native black character named Sambo. Thus, the earliest appearances of blacks on the American stage were as characters void of intellectual and moral sensibilities.

The African Grove Theatre

New York City's free African American community founded the first African American theater in 1821—the African Grove Theatre, located at Mercer and Bleecker streets "in the rear of the one-mile stone on Broadway." A group of amateur African American actors organized by Henry Brown presented *Richard III* at the theater on October 1, 1821. The African Grove Theatre subsequently produced *Othello, Hamlet,* and such lighter works as *Tom and Jerry* and *The Poor Soldier, Obi.*

One of the principal actors at the African Grove Theatre was James Hewlet, a West Indian-born black who distinguished himself in roles in *Othello* and *Richard III.* Hewlet later toured England and billed himself as "The New York and London Colored Comedian." Ira Aldridge, who later distinguished himself as one of the great Shakespearean tragic actors, was also a member of the permanent group that performed at the African Grove Theatre. Aldridge was cast in comic and musical roles as well as in Shakespearean tragedies.

The African Grove Theatre also featured the first play written and produced by an African American. The play was Henry Brown's *The Drama of King Shotaway,* which was presented in June of 1823.

Because of disturbances created by whites in the audience, the local police raided the African Grove Theatre on several occasions. The theater evidently was wrecked by police and hoodlums during one of these raids, which forced its closing in late 1823. The group of black actors affiliated with the African Grove Theatre, determined to preserve their company, continued for several years to present plays at different rented locations throughout New York City.

◆ MINSTRELSY

Talented slaves were among the earliest African American entertainers in colonial and antebellum America. On plantations throughout the South, slave performers—using clappers, jawbones, and blacksmith rasps—danced, sang, and told jokes for the entertainment of their fellow slaves as well as their masters, who often showcased their talents at local gatherings. Some masters hired out talented slaves to perform in traveling troupes.

During the late 1820s and early 1830s, white entertainers, exposed to the artistry of black performers, began to imitate blacks in their routines. Blackening their faces with cork, these white entertainers performed jigs, songs, and jokes with topical allusions to blacks in their lyrics. Thus, the art of minstrelsy as theatrical material was born.

White minstrel troupes in blackface became very popular on the American stage in the 1830s. Among some of the more famous white minstrel performers were Thomas Dartmouth Rice, "Daddy Rice," the original "Jim Crow," Edwin Forrest and Dan Emmett, and the Christy Minstrels.

Some traveling white minstrel troupes used black performers to enhance the authenticity of their productions. One such troupe was the Ethiopian Minstrels, whose star performer was William Henry Lane, an African American dancer who used the stage name "Master Juba." Lane was one of the greatest dancers of his generation. Throughout the United States and England, "Master Juba" was enthusiastically praised by audiences and critics alike. One anonymous English critic, quoted by dance historian Marian Hannah Winter, wrote the following critique of one of Lane's performances:

> Juba exceeded anything ever witnessed in Europe. The style as well as the execution is unlike anything seen in this country. The manner in which he beats time with feet, and the extraordinary command he possesses over them, can only be believed by those who have been present at the exhibition. ("Juba and American Minstrelsy." *Chronicles of the American Dance*, edited by Paul Magriel.)

Traveling African American minstrels began to appear in the 1850s, serving as a precursor to stage performers (Schomburg Center for Research in Black Culture).

Although black minstrel troupes began to appear in the 1850s, it was not until after the Civil War that they became established on the American stage. Although black minstrels inherited the negative stereotypes of blacks that white minstrels had established, the African American performer won a permanent place on the American stage, providing a training ground for the many black dancers, comedians, singers, and composers to come. Notable among these stage personalities were dancer-comedians Billy Kersands, Bert Williams, Bob Height, Dewey "Pigmeat" Martin, and Ernest Hogan; singers such as Gertrude "Ma" Rainey and Bessie Smith; and composers James Bland and William Christopher Handy. To a great extent, black minstrelsy created a national appreciation for the talent of black stage entertainers, drawing audiences to black shows and other forms of black entertainment for generations to come.

◆ RECLAIMING THE BLACK IMAGE: 1890 TO 1920

By the 1890s, African American producers, writers, and stage performers sought to reform the demeaning images of blacks that were prevalent on the American stage. *The Creole Show*, cast by African American producer Sam Jack in 1891, was the first all-black musical to depart from minstrelsy. *The Creole Show*, which was also notable for its inclusion of a chorus line, premiered in Boston in 1891 and later played at the Chicago World's Fair for the entire season. In 1895 African American producer John W. Ishaw presented *The Octoroon*, another all-black musical that moved away from the minstrel tradition. *Oriental America*, which Ishaw also produced, broke further from minstrel conventions by not closing with the traditional walkaround, but with an operatic medley.

Between 1898 and 1911, 13 all-black musicals opened on Broadway, showcasing the talents of African American musicians, lyricists, directors, producers, and writers.

Trip to Coontown, written and directed by Bob Cole in 1898, completely broke away from the minstrel tradition. The plot of this all-black performance piece was presented completely through music and dance. The first musical produced, written, and performed by African Americans on Broadway, it ushered in a new era for blacks on the American stage.

The highly popular *Clorinda: The Origin of the Cakewalk*, with music by composer Will Marion Cook and lyrics by poet Paul Laurence Dunbar, opened in 1898 at the Casino Roof Garden and featured comedian-singer Ernest Hogan. Hogan would later appear on Broadway in both *Rufus Rastus* and *Oyster Man* (1902). Bob Cole, J. Rosamond Johnson, and James Weldon Johnson wrote and performed in *The Shoo-Fly Regiment*, another musical that opened on Broadway in 1902.

The comic-dance duo of Bert Williams and George Walker premiered their first Broadway musical *The Policy Players* in 1899. This success was followed by Williams and Walker's *Sons of Ham*, which played on Broadway for two seasons beginning in September of 1900. Their *In Dahomey* premiered on Broadway in 1903 and, after a long run, toured successfully in England. *The Southerners*, with music by Will Marion Cook, opened on Broadway in 1904 with an interracial cast starring Abbie Mitchell. The Williams and Walker team returned to Broadway in 1906 with a new musical *Abyssinia*, which consistently played to a full house. Williams and Walker appeared in their last Broadway production together entitled *Bandanna Land* in 1908. George Walker fell into ill health after the show closed and died in 1911.

Bert Williams (Corbis Corporation [Bellevue])

Bert Williams went on to appear in *Mr. Lord of Koal* on Broadway in 1909, and later he was the star comedian performer in the *Ziegfield Follies*. The last black musical to open on Broadway before the 1920s was *His Honor the Barber* in 1911, with S. H. Dudley in the lead.

Black Vaudeville

The unique world of black vaudeville employed dancers, comics, and pantomimes who, denied access to the American legitimate stage, developed their own revues and routines that reflected the African American popular culture. The white owners of the Theater Owners Booking Association (T.O.B.A.), hired the entertainers to play to black audiences in large and small towns across America from the early 1900s until the Great Depression.

Vaudeville was the stage where dancers such as Bert Williams and Bill (Bojangles) Robinson polished their craft that helped them eventually move into the mainstream white theater. Comic Dewey "Pigmeat" Markham developed his legendary "Here Come Da Judge" routine. Tim Moore was wildly popular, later to be seen on "Amos n' Andy" as the incorrigible "Kingfish."

The plantation-derived black dance that became the cakewalk was said to be a parody by black slaves of the showy party manners of slaveowner families, but its mimicry delighted the masters and mistresses. The cakewalk became a national and worldwide rage at the end of the nineteenth century, even though the black bourgeoisie condemned it as vulgar.

Just as the cakewalk was developed to make fun of a white dancing style, ragtime was a response to European classical music. Ragtime was derived from minstrel show tunes and New Orleans street marches. Pianists Ben Harvey and Scott Joplin made its distinctive rhythmic syncopation popular in the 1890s. One of the earliest examples of the form is the "Harlem Rag" of 1895.

Humor was used to cope with the pain and frustration of everyday life. Markham's "Here Come Da Judge" routine was a critical farce on a legal system that afforded no justice or protection for African Americans. Ventriloquist Johnnie Woods with his sidekick Little Henry played the circuit as a dapper, prosperous gentleman berating and chiding the incorrigible dummy, dressed in a red check suit with bad manners and poor breeding. These comedy styles were later imitated by white performers such as Eddie Cantor, Al Jolson, and Abbott and Costello, who were a success on the white stage where blacks were not allowed.

What white folks derided as demeaning and vulgar became grist for the comic and satiric black player. They took the white notions of low-class and made a joke of it. The subject of race on the black stage was ground for debate, commiseration, derision, and mockery. But they also condemned bad manners and attitudes among themselves.

Although black performers were often able to bridge the gap from folk and vaudeville entertainment to the musical classics and drama, white audiences typically expected them to restrict themselves to the more "Negroid" comedy routines and minstrel styles. However, the privileged few of high society saw some of the best of the black players at the "colored clubs" such as the Cotton Club, Connie's Inn, and the Club Alabam' in New York. The Cotton Club boasted a Chorus Line of "tall, tan and terrific" black women as well as the hottest black entertainment.

The Black Performer in Europe 1900 to 1920

Many black performers who struggled on the American circuit found great success in Europe. The "black craze" of African American art, music, and dance took Paris by storm in the 1920s. Ballroom dancers such as Fredi Washington and Al Moore, the singers Bessie Smith and Josephine Baker, and producers such as Claude Hopkins found a receptive audience amongst Roaring Twenties Parisians. Europe was not as color-conscious as the United States. The elegant and refined Washington and Moore were so light-skinned that they were not totally accepted on the black circuit with their "white style" act. However, Europe welcomed their sophisticated artistry and style.

Hopkins introduced singer Josephine Baker to Paris where she developed her flamboyant and provocative act before appreciative Europeans. The Folies Bergère of Paris allowed Baker to push the boundaries of nudity and innuendo in her singing and dancing, and she remained an international sensation throughout her career.

The dancer and pantomime Johnny Hudgins was an enormous hit with black and white audiences both in the United States and Europe. He was filmed by Jean Renoir in a short entitled *Charleston* in the 1920s and left behind a detailed account of his act. His characters included the Ballroom Dancer, the Ice Skater, and the Pullman Porter. One of his more notable numbers involved him performing the Charleston in a lady's feather-plumed straw hat.

◆ AFRICAN AMERICAN DRAMATIC THEATER IN THE TWENTIETH CENTURY

The Dramatic Theater from 1900 to 1940

Black actors on the American dramatic stage, like the performers in all-black musicals, struggled to shed the demeaning image of the African American projected by most white-produced minstrelsy and drama. The presentation of three plays—*The Rider of Dreams*, *Granny Maumee*, and *Simon the Cyrenian*—by white playwright Ridgely Torrence at the Garden Theatre in Madison Square Garden on April 5, 1917, was an exceptional and highly successful effort to objectively portray the African American on the dramatic stage.

During the Harlem Renaissance years, the African American dramatic actor remained less active than the black performer in musicals, and the image of blacks projected by white playwrights was generally inadequate. For example, when Charles Gilpin starred in Eugene O'Neill's *Emperor Jones* at the Provincetown Theatre in 1920, critic Loften Mitchell noted that:

> This play, while offering one of the most magnificent roles for a Negro in the American theater, is the first in a long line to deal with the Negro on this level. O'Neill obviously saw in the Negro rich subject matter, but he was either incapable or

Josephine Baker (AP/Wide World Photos, Inc.)

unwilling to deal directly with the matter. (*Black Drama, the Story of the American Negro in the Theatre*, 1967.)

Nonetheless, African American actors and actresses had to accept the roles in which they were cast by white playwrights. In 1924, the O'Neill play *All God's Chillun' Got Wings* opened at the Provincetown Theatre with Paul Robeson and Mary Blair to mixed reviews because of its interracial theme. Rose McClendon starred in Paul Green's Pulitzer Prize-winning *In Abraham's Bosom* in 1926 and was ably supported by Abbie Mitchell and Jules Bledsoe. Marc Connelly's *Green Pastures* opened on Broadway on February 26, 1930; with Richard B. Harrison playing "De Lawd," it ran for 557 performances and was taken on an extensive road tour.

Three plays by Langston Hughes that did treat the African American objectively were produced successfully on Broadway in the 1930s. *Mulatto*, which opened in 1935 and starred Rose McClendon and Morris McKenney, had the longest Broadway run of any play written by an African American in the history of the American theater with 373 consecutive performances. It was followed by *Little Ham* (1935) and *Troubled Island* (1936).

The Federal Theater Project

In the mid-1930s the Works Progress Administration (WPA) sponsored one of the greatest organized efforts to assist and encourage American actors, especially African American actors. The Federal Theater Project employed a total of 851 African American actors to work in 16 segregated units of the project in Chicago, New York, and other cities from 1935 until 1939, when Congress ended the project. While the project was in operation, African American actors appeared in 75 plays including classics, vaudeville routines, contemporary comedies, children's shows, circuses, and "living newspaper" performances. Notable among the African American actors who worked in the project—and later became stars on Broadway and in film—were Butterfly McQueen, Canada Lee, Rex Ingram, Katherine Dunham, Edna Thomas, Thomas Anderson, and Arthur Dooley Wilson.

In the wake of the Federal Theater Project, The American Negro Theater was established in Harlem by Abram Hill, Austin Briggs-Hall, Frederick O'Neal, and Hattie King-Reeves. Its objective was to authentically portray African American life and to give African American actors and playwrights a forum for their talents. Some of their productions eventually made it to Broadway. In 1944 the theater produced *Anna Lucasta* in the basement of the 135th Street Library in Harlem. It was successful enough to move to Broadway and featured Hilda Simms, Frederick O'Neal, Alice Childress, Alvin Childress, Earle Hyman, and Herbert Henry. Abram Hill's *Walk Hard* opened in Harlem in 1946 and became a Broadway production with Maxwell Glanville in the lead. The American Negro Theater provided a training ground for many African American actors who later became stars on Broadway and in Hollywood including Ruby Dee, Ossie Davis, Harry Belafonte, and Sidney Poitier.

Dramatic Theater in the 1950s

The rise of television in the 1950s generally had an adverse affect on the American theater. Employment for all actors fell sharply, especially for African American actors. Ethel Waters did, however, open on Broadway in 1950 as the lead in *Member of the Wedding*, which was well-received. Louis Peterson's *Take a Giant Step* opened on Broadway in September of 1953 to critical praise; in the cast were Frederick O'Neal, Helen Martin, Maxwell Glanville, Pauline Myers, Estelle Evans, and Louis Gossett, Jr.

One of the most successful all-black plays to appear on Broadway opened in March of 1959: Lorraine Hansberry's *Raisin in the Sun*, which won the New York Drama Critics Circle Award. It was directed by the

Ossie Davis with co-star Ruby Dee in the play *Purlie Victorious* (AP/Wide World Photos, Inc.).

legendary African American director Lloyd Richards. Its cast included Sidney Poitier, Ruby Dee, Diana Sands, Claudia McNeil, Louis Gossett, Jr., Ivan Dixon, Lonnie Elder III, and Douglas Turner Ward. *Raisin in the Sun* indicated the future of African Americans in the theater.

The Dramatic Theater Since 1960

As the Civil Rights movement challenged the national conscience in the 1960s, every facet of African American life changed, including black performing arts. More plays about African Americans by both black and white playwrights were produced, providing increased employment for black actors.

Three events in the 1960s signaled trends that would affect African American dramatic actors for the next thirty years: the production of Jean Genet's play *The Blacks;* the staging of the Leroi Jones's (Imamu Amiri Baraka) play *The Dutchman;* and the founding of the Negro Ensemble Company.

On May 4, 1961, *The Blacks*, by French playwright/author Jean Genet, opened off-Broadway at the St. Mark's Theater. A play about black Americans written for white audiences, *The Blacks* provided employment for a host of African American actors including Roscoe Lee Browne, James Earl Jones, Louis Gossett, Jr., Helen Martin, Cicely Tyson, Godfrey Cambridge, Raymond St. Jacques, Maya Angelou, Charles Gordone, and many others who appeared in its road tours. Subsequently, African American dramatic actors appeared on and off-Broadway in several major plays by white playwrights. Notable among them were: *In White America* by Judith Rutherford Marechal (1968), with Gloria Foster and Moses Gunn; *The Great White Hope* by William Sackler (1968), starring James Earl Jones; and *So Nice, They Named It Twice* by Neil Harris (1975), featuring Bill Jay and Veronica Redd.

On May 23, 1961, when the Leroi Jones play *The Dutchman* opened at the Cherry Lane Theatre, the black revolutionary play was introduced to theater audiences. African American actors were provided with the opportunity to perform in roles that not only affirmed blackness, but portrayed black political militancy. Several black revolutionary plays followed that afforded opportunities for African American actors including James Baldwin's *Blues for Mr. Charlie* (1964), with Al Freeman, Jr. and Diana Sands; and *The Toilet/The Slave*, (1964) by Leroi Jones, starring James Spruill, Walter Jones, Nan Martin, and Al Freeman, Jr. In the 1990s, black revolutionary plays such as *General Hag's Skeezag* (1991) continued to provide important roles for African American actors.

Perhaps most beneficial to African American actors was the founding of the Negro Ensemble Company in New York in 1967. This theatrical production company, initially financed by a three-year grant of $1,200,000 from the Ford Foundation, was the brainchild of playwright/actor Douglas Turner Ward. Housed originally at the St. Mark's Theater and currently at Theater Four, the Negro Ensemble is headed by actor Robert Hooks as executive director, Gerald Krone as administrative director, and Douglas Turner Ward as artistic director. The Negro Ensemble's objective is to develop African American managers, playwrights, actors, and technicians.

The Negro Ensemble has staged more than one hundred productions including the work of forty African American playwrights, and provided work for countless aspiring and seasoned African American actors. Several plays produced by the Negro Ensemble have eventually gone to Broadway including Douglas Turner Ward's *The River Niger* (1973), which won a Tony Award and an Obie Award, and Charles Fuller's Pulitzer Prize-winning *The Soldier's Play* (1981). A plethora of outstanding African American actors and actresses have appeared in Negro Ensemble productions including Marshall Williams, Denise Nichols, Esther Rolle, Roxie Roker, Adolph

Ceasar, Denzel Washington, Moses Gunn, and Barbara Montgomery.

Several African American playwrights had plays successfully produced on Broadway independently of the Negro Ensemble Company. Ntozake Shange's widely acclaimed *For Colored Girls Who Have Considered Suicide/When the Rainbow Is Enuf* (1972) had a cast of seven African American actresses. August Wilson's *Fences*, which opened on March 26, 1987, and featured James Earl Jones, won the 1987 Pulitzer Prize in drama. Wilson's *Two Trains Running*, which opened April 13, 1992 and starred Roscoe Lee Browne and Laurence Fishburne, received the New York Drama Critic's Award for 1992. *The Piano Lesson*, which opened in 1990, earned Wilson his second Pulitzer Prize, and his *Seven Guitars* premiered in 1996. Wilson is one of the strongest voices for the African American in theater at the end of the twentieth century.

August Wilson (AP/Wide World Photos, Inc.)

◆ AFRICAN AMERICAN MUSICALS IN THE TWENTIETH CENTURY

Between 1898 and 1911, 13 all-black musicals opened on Broadway. The performances showcased the talents of Ernest Hogan and the comic-dance duo of George Walker and Bert Williams. For nearly a decade after the close of *His Honor the Barber* though, the Broadway stage did not carry exclusively African American musicals.

On May 23, 1921, *Shuffle Along* signaled the return of black musicals to "The Great White Way" and the arrival of the Harlem Renaissance on the American stage. Featuring the talented singer-dancer Florence Mills, *Shuffle Along* was written by Noble Sissle, Eubie Blake, Flournoy Miller, and Aubrey Lyles. Mills quickly became a sought-after performer, appearing in *The Plantation Revue*, which opened on Broadway on July 17, 1922, and later toured England. In 1926, Mills returned to Harlem and played the lead in *Black Birds* at the Alhambra Theatre for a six-week run. Subsequently, Mills performed in Paris for six months.

Noble Sissle and Eubie Blake returned to Broadway on September 24, 1924, with their new musical *Chocolate Dandies*. Two years later, in 1926, Flournoy Miller and Aubrey Lyles opened on Broadway in *Runnin' Wild*, which introduced the Charleston to the country. Bill "Bojangles" Robinson, starring in *Blackbirds of 1928*, dazzled Broadway audiences with his exciting tap dancing style. Several other black musicals opened on Broadway during the 1920s including *Rang Tang* (1927), *Keep Shuffling* (1928), and *Hot Chocolates* (1929).

Porgy and Bess, opening on Broadway in 1935, became the major all-black musical production of the 1930s. With music by George Gershwin, this adaptation of the novel and play by DuBose and Dorothy Heyward was an immediate success as a folk opera. Todd Duncan was cast as Porgy, with Ann Brown as Bess, and comedian-dancer John Bubbles as the character Sportin' Life.

In the 1940s, black musicals were scarce on Broadway. *Cabin in the Sky*, starring Ethel Waters, Dooley Wilson, Todd Duncan, Rex Ingram, J. Rosamond Johnson, and Katherine Dunham and her dancers, ran for 165 performances after it opened on October 25, 1940. *Carmen Jones*, perhaps the most successful all-black musical of the decade, opened in 1943 with Luther Saxon, Napoleon Reed, Carlotta Franzel, and Cozy Cove; it had a run of 231 performances and was taken on tour. In 1946 *St. Louis Woman*, featuring Rex Ingram, Pearl Bailey, Juanita Hall, and June Hawkins, played a short run to mixed reviews.

The years from 1961 to the mid-1980s constituted one of the most active periods for African American performers in musical theater. Many of the black musicals produced during these years, both on and off-Broadway, enjoyed substantial runs and extended road tours.

Langston Hughes's musical *Black Nativity* opened on Broadway on December 11, 1961. Directed by Vinette

Carroll, the cast was headed by gospel singers Marion Williams and the Stars of Faith and also featured Alex Bradford, Clive Thompson, Cleo Quitman, and Carl Ford. Although it ran for only 57 performances on Broadway, it went on to tour extensively throughout the United States and abroad.

In 1964, Sammy Davis, Jr. dazzled Broadway in Clifford Odets's *Golden Boy*. Davis was supported by a brilliant cast which included Robert Guillaume, Louis Gossett, Jr., Lola Falana, and Billy Daniels. *Golden Boy* ran for 586 performances.

Leslie Uggams and Robert Hooks appeared in *Hallelujah Baby*, which opened in New York's Martin Beck Theater on April 26, 1967. *Hallelujah Baby*, a musical look at five decades of black history, received a Tony Award and ran for 293 performances.

Purlie, based on Ossie Davis's 1961 play *Purlie Victorious* opened on May 9, 1970, with Melba Moore and Robert Guillaume in lead roles. *Purlie* received good reviews and enjoyed a run of 688 performances.

Micki Grant's *Don't Bother Me, I Can't Cope*, starring Micki Grant and Alex Bradford, opened on April 19, 1972, to rave reviews. For this musical, which ran for 1,065 performances, Micki Grant received a Drama Desk Award and an Obie Award.

Virginia Capers, Joe Morton, and Helen Martin opened *Raisin*, based on Lorraine Hansberry's play *Raisin in the Sun* on October 13, 1973. *Raisin* received the Tony Award for the best musical in 1974 and had a run of 847 performances.

Despite initially poor reviews, *The Wiz*, a black musical version of *The Wizard of Oz*, became a highly successful show. Opening on Broadway on January 5, 1975, *The Wiz* featured an array of talented performers including Stephanie Mills, Hinton Battle, Ted Ross, Andre De Shields, Dee Dee Bridgewater, and Mabel King. *The Wiz* swept the Tony Award ceremonies in 1975 and became the longest-running black musical in the history of Broadway with 1,672 performances.

Ain't Misbehavin', another popular black musical of the 1970s, opened on May 8, 1978. Based on a cavalcade of songs composed by Thomas "Fats" Waller, *Ain't Misbehavin'* starred Nell Carter, Andre DeShields, Armelia McQueen, Ken Page, and Charlene Woodard. It played to Broadway audiences for 1,604 performances, and Nell Carter received a Tony Award as best featured actress.

Two spectacular black musicals premiered on Broadway in the 1980s. *Dream Girls*, which opened at the Imperial Theater on December 20, 1981, captivated Broadway audiences with a cast that included Jennifer Holiday, Cleavant Derricks, Loretta Devine, and Cheryl Alexander. *Dream Girls* ran for 1,522 performances on Broadway and had an extensive road tour. Jennifer Holiday won a Tony Award for her role as Effie Melody White. On April 27, 1986, Debbie Allen opened in the lead role of *Sweet Charity*. Reviews were favorable and the musical enjoyed a run of 386 performances, establishing Debbie Allen as a musical theater actress.

Sammy Davis, Jr. (AP/Wide World Photos, Inc.)

A few new all-black musicals opened in the early 1990s including *Five Guys Name Moe*, a tribute to musician Louis Jordan with Clarke Peters and Charles Augin, and *Jelly's Last Jam*, featuring Gregory Hines as the adult Jelly Roll Morton who won the Tony Award for best actor in a musical in 1992.

Young African American musical stars have hit it big on Broadway in the 1990s. The monumental hit *Bring in 'Da Noise/Bring in 'Da Funk* opened in 1995 starring young tap wizard Savion Glover and directed by George C. Wolfe. It celebrates three hundred years of African American history in poetry, music, song and dance. The musical won four Tony Awards, one each for Glover and Wolfe, and continued a long run on Broadway while mounting a highly successful touring company.

Savion Glover performs with *Bring in 'Da Funk, Bring in 'Da Noise* fellow cast members (AP/Wide World Photos, Inc.).

A lavish production of *Carousel* opened on Broadway in 1994 for which the young African American actress and singer Audra McDonald won a Tony Award as best featured actress. For her role in *The Master Class*, she won another Tony. She then starred in the musical *Ragtime* in 1997 and won a third Tony for her performance.

African American choreographer Garth Fagan won the Tony Award for his work on the Disney-produced spectacle *The Lion King*, which also took the Tony for best musical in 1997.

◆ AFRICAN AMERICAN COMEDY IN THE TWENTIETH CENTURY

The earliest black comedians in America, like other early black entertainers, were slaves who in their free time entertained themselves and their masters. In the early minstrel shows, white comedians in blackface created comic caricatures of blacks, whom they referred to as "coons." When African Americans began appearing in minstrel shows shortly after the Civil War, they found themselves burdened with the "coon" comic caricatures created by white performers. The dance-comedy team of Bert Williams and George Walker were the most famous of the early black comedians, appearing in numerous black musicals between 1899 and 1909.

In the all-black musicals of the 1920s, a new comic movement emerged: the comedy of style which emphasized such antics as rolling the eyes or shaking the hips. The venom and bite of black folk humor was replaced by a comedy of style that was more acceptable to the white audiences of these all-black musicals.

Real black folk humor, however, did survive and thrive in black nightclubs and black theaters such as the Apollo in Harlem and the Regal in Chicago in the 1930s, 1940s, and 1950s. In these settings, known as the "Chitterling Circuit," such African American comedians as Tim Moore, Dusty Fletcher, Butterbeans and Susie, Stepin Fetchit, Jackie "Moms" Mabley, Redd Foxx, and Slappy White performed without restrictions.

African American comedians enjoyed greater exposure during the 1960s. No longer confined to the "Chitterling Circuit," comedians such as Jackie "Moms" Mabley, Redd Foxx, and Slappy White began to perform to audiences in exclusive white clubs as well as to audiences within the black community. They used black

Redd Foxx, Jr. (AP/Wide World Photos, Inc.)

folk humor to comment on politics, civil rights, work, sex, and a variety of other subjects. Jackie "Moms" Mabley made two popular recordings: *Moms Mabley at the UN* and *Moms Mabley at the Geneva Conference.* In January of 1972, Redd Foxx premiered on television as Fred Sanford in "Sanford and Son," which remains one of the most popular syndicated shows.

Several younger African American comedians came into prominence in the early 1960s. Dick Gregory used black folk humor to make political commentary. Bill Cosby specialized in amusing chronicles about boyhood in America. Godfrey Cambridge, although successful, did not rely on black folk humor. During the late 1960s and the early 1970s, Flip Wilson, who parodied historical and social experience by creating black characters who lived in a black world, became extremely popular on television. His cast of characters, which included "Freddy the Playboy," "Sammy the White House Janitor," and "Geraldine," were the epitome of black folk humor as commentary on an array of issues.

Another pivotal African American comedian who began his career in the 1960s was Richard Pryor. His well-timed, risque, sharp folk humor quickly won him a large group of faithful fans. Pryor, who has recorded extensively, has starred successfully in several films including *Lady Sings the Blues*, *Car Wash*, and *Stir Crazy*.

During the 1980s, numerous African American comedians became successful in the various entertainment media. Eddie Murphy made his first appearance on the television show "Saturday Night Live" on November 15, 1980. From television, Murphy went on to Hollywood, making his movie debut in the film *48 Hours* in 1982. Starring roles followed in such films as *Beverly Hills Cop*, which was the highest-grossing comedy film in history, and *Trading Places*. Murphy has established his own company, Eddie Murphy Productions, to create and produce television and film projects. His recent projects include *The Nutty Professor*, *Dr. Dolittle*, and *Life*. Arsenio Hall came to prominence in 1987 as a successful interim guest host on the now defunct "The Late Show," which won him a lucrative movie contract with Paramount Pictures. In 1988, Hall was featured with Eddie Murphy in the film *Coming to America* and hosted his own highly successful late-night talk show.

Richard Pryor (AP/Wide World Photos, Inc.)

After achieving success on the stand-up circuit, several African Americans earned opportunities on television and in films in the 1990s. Keenan Ivory Wayans and his brother Damon starred with several of their siblings in the critically acclaimed sketch-comedy show "In Living Color," which provided a vehicle for social commentary. Martin Lawrence appealed to audiences in a self-titled television show that featured him performing not only as himself but also as his mother and another female character, Sheneneh. Chris Rock gained popularity on "Saturday Night Live" with brash, politically-informed characters that helped him earn roles in such movies as *New Jack City* (1991) and *Boomerang* (1992). Newcomers such as Jamie Foxx, Steve Harvey, and Chris Tucker indicate a strong future for black comedians.

◆ AFRICAN AMERICAN DANCE IN THE TWENTIETH CENTURY

Black dance, like other forms of black entertainment, had its beginnings in Africa and on the plantations of early America, where slaves performed to entertain themselves and their masters. White minstrels in blackface incorporated many of these black dance inventions into their shows, while dancers in black minstrelsy like "Master Juba" (William Henry Lane) thrilled audiences with their artistry.

Many performers in the early black musicals that appeared on Broadway from 1898 through 1910 were expert show dancers, such as George Walker and Bert Williams. Similarly, in the all-black musicals of the 1920s, performers such as Florence Mills and Bill "Bojangles" Robinson captivated audiences with their show dancing. The musical *Runnin' Wild* (1926) was responsible for creating the Charleston dance craze of the Roaring Twenties.

By the early 1930s, African American pioneers of modern dance were appearing on the dance stage. Four of these African American innovators were Hemsley Winfield, Asadata Dafore, Katherine Dunham, and Pearl Primus.

Hemsley Winfield presented what was billed as "The First Negro Concert in America" in Manhattan's Chanin Building on April 31, 1931. Two suites on African themes were performed, along with solos by Edna Guy and Winfield himself. In 1933, Winfield became the first African American to dance for the Metropolitan Opera, performing the role of the Witch Doctor in *Emperor Jones*.

Austin Asadata Dafore Horton, a native of Sierra Leone, electrified audiences in New York with his 1934 production of *Kykunkor*. Dance historian Lynne Fauley Emery concluded that *Kykunkor* "was the first performance by black dancers on the concert stage which was entirely successful. It revealed the potential of ethnic material to black dancers, and herein lay Dafore's value as a great influence on black concert dance" (1988, *Black Dance from 1619 to Today*).

Katherine Dunham (Corbis Corporation [Bellevue])

Katherine Dunham had her first lead dance role in Ruth Page's West Indian ballet *La Guiablesse* in 1933. In 1936, Dunham received a master's degree in anthropology from the University of Chicago; her thesis *The Dances of Haiti* was the result of her on-site study of native dances in the West Indies. For the next thirty years, Dunham and her dance company toured the United States and Europe, dazzling audiences with her choreography. During the 1963–64 season, Dunham choreographed the Metropolitan Opera's production of *Aida*, becoming the first African American to do so.

Pearl Primus, like Katherine Dunham, was trained in anthropology. Her research in primitive African dance inspired her first composition performed as a professional dancer entitled *African Ceremonial*, which she presented on February 14, 1943. On October 4, 1944, Primus made her Broadway debut at the Belasco Theater in New York. Her performance included dances of West Indian, African, and African American origin; the concert was widely acclaimed and launched her career as a dancer. Primus has traveled to Africa many times to research African dances; in 1959 she was named director of Liberia's Performing Arts Center. She later opened the Primus-Borde School of Primal Dance with her husband, dancer Percival Borde, and is currently involved with the Pearl Primus Dance Language Institute in New Rochelle, New York.

By the late 1950s, several African American dancers and dance companies were distinguishing themselves on the concert stage. Janet Collins was the "premiere danseuse" of the Metropolitan Opera Ballet from 1951 until 1954. Arthur Mitchell made his debut as a principal dancer with the New York City Ballet in 1955. Alvin Ailey established his company in 1958. In addition, Geoffrey Holder, who made his Broadway debut in 1954 in *House of Flowers*, became a leading choreographer.

Since the early 1960s, two of the leading dance companies in the United States have been headed by African American males and composed largely of African American dancers. They are the Alvin Ailey American Dance Theater and the Dance Theater of Harlem. In the 1970s, several prominent African American women dancers established schools and trained young dancers in regional companies throughout the United States.

The Alvin Ailey American Dance Theater

The Alvin Ailey American Dance Theater, since its founding in 1958, has performed before more people throughout the world than any other American dance company. With a touring circuit that has included 48 states and 45 countries on all continents, the Alvin Ailey American Dance Theater has been seen by more than 15 million people. Today, the Alvin Ailey organization consists of three components: the Alvin Ailey American Dance Theater, the Alvin Ailey Repertory Ensemble, and the Alvin Ailey American Dance Center.

Between 1958 and 1988, the Alvin Ailey Dance Theater performed 150 works by 45 choreographers, most of whom were African American. Notable among these African American choreographers have been Tally Beatty, Donald McKayle, Louis Johnson, Eleo Romare, Billy Wilson, George Faison, Pearl Primus, Judith Jamison, Katherine Dunham, Ulysses Dove, Milton Myers, Kelvin Rotardier, Geoffrey Holder, and Gary DeLoatch. More than 250 dancers, again mostly African American, have performed with the dance theater. Among its star performers have been Judith Jamison, Clive Thompson, Dudley Williams, Donna Wood, Gary DeLoatch, George Faison, and Sara Yaraborough. A prolific choreographer, Alvin Ailey created numerous works for his dance theater and other dance companies including: *Revelations* (1958); *Reflections in D*, with music by Duke Ellington (1962); *Quintet* (1968); *Cry* (1971); *Memoria* (1974); and *Three Black Kings* (1976). Alvin Ailey choreographed *Carmen* for the Metropolitan Opera in 1973 and *Precipice* for the Paris Opera in 1983.

The Alvin Ailey Repertory Ensemble (AARE) was established in 1974 as a training and performing company. Many of its graduates advance to the dance theater or perform with other dance companies. In 1988, the AARE had more than one hundred members.

Alvin Ailey (The Library of Congress)

Alvin Ailey died in December of 1989, and his belief that a company should exhibit the works of many artists has allowed the three troupes to flourish in the ten years since his death. Judith Jamison has taken over as artistic director and has expanded on Ailey's concept of extending dance opportunities as fully as possible.

The Alvin Ailey American Dance Center is the official school of the Ailey organization. It attracts students from across the United States and abroad and offers a certificate in dance. The center's curriculum includes training in ballet, the Dunham Technique, jazz, and modern dance. In 1998, a fully staffed school in New York City had an enrollment of 3,500 students; three intensive summer camps in urban locations taught dance to preteens and awarded scholarships, and a new affiliation with Fordham University offers a bachelor in fine arts to eligible dance students.

The Alvin Ailey American Dance Theater celebrated its fortieth year in December of 1998 by presenting the works of many choreographers including artistic director Judith Jamison, two current company members, and

Arthur Mitchell

a French guest. Long-time Ailey choreographer Geoffrey Holder redesigned and restaged his lavish 1967 production of *The Prodigal Prince*, the story of a Haitian folk artist and voodoo priest who painted with a feather, for the anniversary celebration.

The Dance Theater of Harlem

In 1969, Arthur Mitchell, who had established himself as one of the leading ballet dancers in the United States, and Karel Shook, a white ballet teacher, founded the Dance Theater of Harlem. It was established after Martin Luther King, Jr.'s death to provide the arts of dance and theater to young people in Harlem. The Dance Theater of Harlem made its formal debut in 1971 at the Guggenheim Museum in New York City. Three of Mitchell's works were premiered at this concert: *Rhythmetron; Tones;* and *Fete Noire.*

Today, the dance theater's repertory is wide-ranging. It includes works in the Balanchine tradition such as *Serenade*, as well as black-inspired works such as *Dougla.*

Among the most spectacular works performed by the theater are *Firebird*, *Giselle*, *Scheherazade*, and *Swan Lake*. Some of the dancers who have had long associations with the theater are Lowell Smith, Virginia Johnson, Shelia Rohan, and Troy Game. Many of the theater's graduates have gone on to perform with other dance companies in the United States and Europe. The Dance Theater of Harlem's school currently has about one thousand students.

Black Regional Dance Schools

While Ailey and Mitchell built their companies in New York, African American women such as Joan Myers Brown, Ann Williams, Cleo Parker Robinson, Lula Washington, and Jeraldyne Blunden established young, mostly African American dance companies in major American cities. Robinson founded her Cleo Parker Robinson Dance Ensemble in 1970 in her native Denver, the same year that Blunden created her company in Dayton, Ohio, and Brown opened her school in Philadelphia. In 1976, Williams founded the Dallas Black Dance Theater, and in 1980 Washington created a troupe in Los Angeles that is now known as the Lula Washington Dance Theater.

Each institution began as a school with deep roots in African American urban communities they never left behind. They all started on a shoestring with a few eager young dancers. Their focus was on the discipline of dance and the values of integrity and intelligence. Today these troupes are nationally known for the high quality of their dancing and for repertories that include modern dance classics, some by African American choreographers. These five women have developed a cooperative network through which they exchange ideas and dancers. Collectively, they have trained thousands of dancers, some of whom have gone on to major companies.

In 1997, they were honored with a daylong tribute entitled *Dance Women: Living Legends*, in which all five companies performed and celebrated the efforts of these five women in the pursuit of dance.

Between 1960 and 1999, many African American dancers have led distinguished careers in concert dance and show dancing. Among them have been Eleo Pomare, Debbie Allen, Rod Rogers, Fred Benjamin, Pepsi Bethel, Eleanor Hampton, Charles Moore, Garth Fagan, Carmen de Lavallade, and Mary Hinkson. Fagan earned a Tony Award in 1997 for his choreographic work in the stage production of Disney's *The Lion King*. Foremost among African American choreographers have been Geoffrey Holder, Louis Johnson, Donald McKayle, Bebe Miller, and Donald Byrd. Prominent among the African American dancers who are reviving the tap dance tradition are Buster Brown, Honi Coles, Hinton Battle, Gregory Hines, Lavaughn Robinson, Nita Feldman, and Savion Glover. Glover came to prominence in the 1995 Broadway production of *Bring in 'Da Noise/Bring in 'Da Funk*.

◆ STAGE ACTORS, COMEDIANS, CHOREOGRAPHERS, AND DANCERS

(To locate biographical profiles more readily, please consult the index at the back of the book.)

Alvin Ailey (1931–1989)
Dancer, Choreographer

Alvin Ailey was born in Rogers, Texas, on January 5, 1931. He was the founder of the Alvin Ailey Dance Theater and won international fame as both dancer and choreographer. Ailey studied dancing after graduating from high school, where he was a star athlete. After briefly attending college, Ailey joined the stage crew of the Lester Horton Theater in Los Angeles, for which Ailey eventually performed as a dancer. In 1953, after Horton's death, Ailey became the company choreographer. In 1954, Ailey performed on Broadway as the lead dancer in *House of Flowers*.

Ailey formed his own dance group in 1958 and began giving four performances annually. In 1962, the Ailey troupe made an official State Department tour of Australia, receiving accolades throughout the country. One critic called Ailey's work "the most stark and devastating theatre ever presented in Australia."

After numerous appearances as a featured dancer with Harry Belafonte and others, Ailey performed in a straight dramatic role with Claudia McNeil in Broadway's *Tiger, Tiger Burning Bright*. Other Broadway appearances included roles in *Ding Dong Bell*, *Dark of the Moon*, and *African Holiday*. Ailey also choreographed or staged several operas including Samuel Barber's *Anthony and Cleopatra* (1966), Leonard Bernstein's *Mass* (1971), and Georges Bizet's *Carmen*. In addition, Ailey created works for various international ballet stars and companies.

In 1965, Ailey took his group on one of the most successful European tours ever made by an American dance company. In London, it was held over six weeks to accommodate the demand for tickets, and in Hamburg it received an unprecedented 61 curtain calls. A German critic called this performance "a triumph of sweeping, violent beauty, a furious spectacle. The stage vibrates. One has never seen anything like it." In 1970, Ailey's company became the first American modern dance group to tour the Soviet Union.

During the mid-1970s Ailey, among his other professional commitments, devoted much time to creating special jazz dance sequences for America's Bicentennial celebration. Among numerous honors including several honorary degrees, Ailey was awarded the NAACP's Spingarn Medal in 1976. Ailey died on December 1, 1989.

Ira Aldridge (1807–1867)
Actor

Born on July 24, 1807, in New York City, Ira Aldridge was one of the leading Shakespearean actors of the nineteenth century. Although he was denied the opportunity to perform before the American public in his prime, the fame that he won abroad established him as one of the prominent figures of international theater.

Aldridge's early dramatic training centered around the African Grove Theatre in New York in 1821. His first role was in *Pizarro*, and he subsequently played a variety of small roles in classical productions before accepting employment as a steward on a ship bound for England.

After studying briefly at the University of Glasgow in Scotland, Aldridge went to London in 1825 and appeared in the melodrama *Surinam, or a Slave's Revenge*. In 1833, he appeared in London's Theatre Royal in the title role of *Othello*, earning wide acclaim. For the next three decades, he toured the continent with great success, often appearing before European royalty.

Aldridge died in Lodz, Poland, on August 7, 1867. He is honored by a commemorative tablet in the New Memorial Theatre in Stratford-upon-Avon, England.

Debbie Allen (AP/Wide World Photos, Inc.)

Debbie Allen (1950–)
Actress, Singer, Dancer, Director

Debbie Allen was born on January 16, 1950, in Houston, Texas. From the age of three, she trained as a dancer with the Ballet Nacional de Mexico, the Houston Ballet, and the National Ballet School. A cum laude graduate of Howard University, she became head of the Dance Department at the Duke Ellington School of Performing Arts.

Allen began her career on the Broadway stage in the chorus line of the hit musical *Purlie* (1972). She then portrayed Beneatha in the Tony and Grammy award-winning musical *Raisin* (1973). Other early stage roles were in the national touring company of *Guys and Dolls* and the drama *Anna Lucasta* performed for the New Federal Theatre at the Henry Street Settlement in New York.

Allen was subsequently selected to star in an NBC pilot "3 Girls 3" and then appeared on other television hits including "Good Times" and "The Love Boat." At this time, her talent as a choreographer recognized, she worked on such television projects as "Midnight Special" as well as two films *The Fish that Saved Pittsburgh* (1979) and *Under Fire* (1981).

The year of 1982 was pivotal for Allen. She appeared in the film *Ragtime* and the television series "Fame," as well as the Joseph Papp television special "Alice at the Palace." Allen also starred in a dance performance for the Academy Awards ceremonies.

Allen's career continued with roles in the television special "Ben Vereen . . . His Roots" and the miniseries *Roots: The Next Generation* (1979). She also appeared on stage again in *Ain't Misbehavin'* (1979) and a revival of *West Side Story* (1980), which earned her a Tony Award nomination and a Drama Desk Award.

As each season passed on "Fame," Allen became more involved as choreographer and was soon regularly directing episodes of the series. In 1988, she was selected by the producers to become director of the television sitcom "A Different World." In another acknowledgment of her stature as a performer and creative talent, she starred in her own television special during the 1988-89 season. She choreographed the Academy Awards telecasts for several years in the 1990s.

In 1998, Allen co-produced the historic film *Amistad* with Steven Spielberg directing, after she had spent ten years looking for someone to champion it. *Amistad* chronicles the 1839 revolt on board a slave ship bound for America. It highlights the courtroom drama about Joseph Cinque, the enslaved African who led the revolt played by Djimon Hounsou.

In 1995, Allen appeared with LL Cool J in the television show "In the House." She also worked as director of the television program "Out of Sync."

Allen is an Executive Committee member of UCLA's School of Theatre, Film and Television. She was awarded an honorary doctorate from her alma mater, Howard University, and the North Carolina School of the Arts.

Eddie "Rochester" Anderson (1905–1977)
Comedian

For many years, Eddie Anderson was the only African American performing regularly on a network radio show. As the character Rochester on the Jack Benny program, he became one of the best-known African American entertainers.

Anderson was born in Oakland, California, on September 18, 1905, the son of "Big Ed" Anderson, a minstrel performer, and Ella Mae, a tightwire walker. During the 1920s and early 1930s, Anderson traveled throughout the Middle and Far West singing, dancing, and performing as a clown in small clubs. On Easter Sunday, 1937, he was featured on Jack Benny's radio show, in what was supposed to be a single appearance; Anderson was such a hit that he quickly became a regular on the program.

Anderson is best known for his work with Benny (in television as well as on radio), but he also appeared in a number of movies including *What Price Hollywood?* (1932), *Cabin in the Sky* (1943), and *It's a Mad, Mad, Mad, Mad World* (1963).

Anderson died on February 28, 1977, at the age of 71.

Pearl Bailey (1918–1990)
Singer, Actress

Born on March 29, 1918, in Newport News, Virginia, Pearl Bailey moved to Philadelphia with her family in 1933. She sang at small clubs in Scranton, Pennsylvania, and in Washington, DC, before becoming the vocalist for the band of Cootie Williams and later for Count Basie. In the early 1940s, Bailey had her first successful New York engagements at the Village Vanguard and the Blue Angel. During World War II, she toured with the USO. Bailey made her New York stage debut in 1946 in *St. Louis Woman*, for which she won a Donaldson Award as the year's most promising new performer. She also appeared in the films *Variety Girl* (1947) and *Isn't It Romantic?* (1948).

During the 1950s Bailey appeared in the movies *Carmen Jones*, *That Certain Feeling*, and *Porgy and Bess*, and on Broadway in *House of Flowers*. In the 1950s and 1960s, she worked as a recording artist, nightclub headliner, and television performer. In 1967, she received a special Tony Award for her starring role on Broadway in *Hello, Dolly*. In 1969, she published an autobiography *The Raw Pearl*. Her other books include: *Talking to Myself* (1971); *Pearl's Kitchen* (1973); *Duey Tale* (1975); and *Hurry Up, America, and Spit* (1976).

In 1975, Bailey was named a special adviser to the United States Mission to the United Nations. In 1976, she appeared in the film *Norman, Is That You?*, with Redd Foxx, and on stage in Washington, DC, in *Something To Do*, a musical saluting the American worker. She also received an award in 1976 from the Screen Actors Guild for outstanding achievement in fostering the finest ideals of the acting profession. Georgetown University made her an honorary doctor of humane letters in 1977.

In January of 1980, Bailey gave a one-night concert at Radio City Music Hall in New York. In 1981, she performed as the voice of the cartoon character "Owl" in the Disney movie *The Fox and the Hound*.

Bailey married the jazz drummer Louis Bellson in 1952. She died on August 17, 1990, in Philadelphia.

Josephine Baker (1906–1975)
Dancer, Singer

Born in St. Louis on June 3, 1906, Josephine Baker received little formal education; she left school at the age of eight to supplement the family income by working as a kitchen helper and baby-sitter. While still in elementary school, she took a part-time job as a chorus girl. At 17, she performed as a chorus girl in Noble Sissle's musical comedy *Shuffle Along*, which played in Radio City Music Hall in 1923. Her next show was *Chocolate Dandies*, followed by a major dancing part in *La Revue Nègre*, an American production that introduced *le jazz hot* to Paris in 1925.

In Paris, Baker left the show to create her most sensational role, that of the "Dark Star" of the Folies Bergère. In her act, she appeared topless on a mirror, clad only in a protective waist shield of rubber bananas. The spectacular dance made her an overnight star and a public figure with a loyal following. In true "star" tradition, she catered to her fans by adopting such flamboyant eccentricities as walking pet leopards down the Champs-Elysées.

In 1930, after completing a world tour, Baker made her debut as a singing and dancing comedienne at the Casino de Paris. Critics called her a "complete artist, the perfect master of her tools." In time, she ventured into films, starring alongside French idol Jean Gabin in *Zouzou* (1934), and into light opera, performing in *La Créole* (1934), an operetta about a Jamaican girl.

During World War II, Baker served first as a Red Cross volunteer, and later did underground intelligence work through an Italian Embassy attaché. After the war, the French government decorated her with the Legion of Honor. She returned to the entertainment world, regularly starring at the Folies Bergère, appearing on French television, and going on another extended international tour. In 1951, in the course of a successful American tour, Baker made headlines by speaking out against discrimination and refusing to perform in segregated venues.

Beginning in 1954, Baker earned another reputation—not as a lavish and provocative entertainer, but as a progressive humanitarian. She used her fortune to begin adopting and tutoring a group of orphaned babies of all races and retired from the stage in 1956 to devote all her time to her "rainbow family." Within three years, however, her "experiment in brotherhood" had taken such a toll on her finances that she was forced to return to the stage, starring in *Paris, Mes Amours*, a musical based in part on her own fabled career.

Baker privately, and without voicing discouragement, survived numerous financial crises. Illness hardly managed to dampen her indomitable spirit. Through her long life, she retained her most noteworthy stage attributes—an intimate, subdued voice, coupled with an infectiously energetic and vivacious manner.

Baker died in Paris on April 12, 1975, after opening a gala to celebrate her fiftieth year in show business.

James Hubert "Eubie" Blake (1883–1983)

Musician, Composer

Eubie Blake was born in Baltimore on February 7, 1883. The son of former slaves, Blake was the last of ten children and the only one to survive beyond two months. His mother worked as a laundress, his father as a stevedore.

At the age of six, Blake started taking piano lessons. He studied under the renowned teacher Margaret Marshall and subsequently learned musical composition from Llewelyn Wilson, who at one time conducted an all-black symphony orchestra sponsored by the city of Baltimore. At the age of 17, Blake was playing for a Baltimore night club.

In 1915, Blake collaborated with Noble Sissle. That year, Blake and Sissle sold their first song "It's All Your Fault" to Sophie Tucker, and her introduction of the song started them on their way. Blake and Sissle moved to New York and, together with Flournoy Miller and Aubrey Lyles, created one of the pioneer black shows *Shuffle Along* in 1921; the show was produced again on Broadway in 1952. *Chocolate Dandies* and *Elsie* followed in 1924.

Eubie Blake performing at the piano during the 1979 Newport Jazz Festival (AP/Wide World Photos, Inc.).

During the early 1930s, Blake collaborated with Andy Razaf and wrote the musical score for Lew Leslie's *Blackbirds*. Out of this association came the hit *Memories of You*. During World War II, Blake was appointed musical conductor for the United Services Organization's (USO) Hospital Unit. In 1946 he announced his retirement and enrolled in New York University.

For many years, Blake's most requested song was "Charleston Rag," which he composed in 1899 and which was written down by someone else because Blake could not then read music. Among his most famous songs were "How Ya' Gonna Keep 'Em Down on the Farm," "Love Will Find a Way," and "You're Lucky to Me." Some of his other works include "I'm Just Wild About Harry," "Serenade Blues," "It's All Your Fault," and "Floradora Girls," with lyrics by Sissle.

Though known as a master of ragtime, Blake always most loved the music of the classical masters. In the intimacy of his Brooklyn studio, Blake rarely played the music for which the world reveres him. In 1978, Blake's life and career were celebrated in the Broadway musical *Eubie!* Several thousand people attended concerts at the Shubert Theatre and St. Peters Lutheran Church celebrating Blake's 100th birthday on February 8, 1983. Blake also received honorary doctorates from numerous colleges and universities. He died on February 12, 1983.

John Bubbles (1902–1986)

Dancer, Singer

John Bubbles, inventor of rhythm tap dancing, was born John William Sublett on February 19, 1902, in Louisville, Kentucky. At the age of seven, he teamed with a fellow bowling alley pinboy, Ford "Buck" Washington, to form what became one of the top vaudeville acts in show business. Throughout the 1920s and 1930s, Buck and Bubbles played the top theaters in the country at fees of up to $1,750 a week. The two appeared in several films including *Cabin in the Sky* (1943). Bubbles captured additional fame as Sportin' Life in the 1935 version of *Porgy and Bess.* After Buck's death in 1955, Bubbles virtually disappeared from show business until 1964, when he teamed up with Anna Maria Alberghetti in a successful nightclub act.

John W. Bubbles performing at the 1979 Newport Jazz Festival (AP/Wide World Photos, Inc.).

In 1979, at the age of 77 and partially crippled from an earlier stroke, Bubbles recreated his characterization of Sportin' Life for a one-night show entitled *Black Broadway* at New York's Lincoln Center. The show was repeated in 1980 for a limited engagement at the Town Hall in New York. In the fall of 1980, Bubbles received a Lifetime Achievement Award from the American Guild of Variety Artists and a Certificate of Appreciation from the city of New York.

Bubbles died on May 18, 1986, at the age of 84.

Anita Bush (1883–1974)

Actress, Singer

Born in 1883, Anita Bush was involved with the theater from early childhood. Her father was the tailor for the Bijou, a large neighborhood theater in Brooklyn, and Anita would carry the costumes to the theater for him, giving her a backstage view of performers and productions. Her singing/acting career took off in her early twenties, when she was in the chorus of the Williams and Walker Company. With Williams and Walker, she performed in such Broadway hits as *Abyssinia* and *In Dahomey*, which also had a successful European tour. When the group split up in 1909, she went on to form the Anita Bush Stock Company, which included her own show of chorus girls and such greats as Charles Gilpin and Dooley Wilson, with whom she also founded the Lafayette Players.

Bush died on February 16, 1974.

Donald Byrd (1949–)

Choreographer

Donald Byrd, one of the most important choreographers in modern dance, has created his own unique style of dance based on the influences of some great predecessors. From the styles and movements of Alvin Ailey, the classic ballet of George Balanchine, and the creations of Twyla Tharp, Byrd has established his own distinct contributions to dance.

Byrd was born on July 21, 1949, in New London, North Carolina, and raised in Clearwater, Florida. He was trained in classical flute and active in school theatrics and the debate team. When he was 16, two dancers from Balanchine's New York City Ballet, Edward Villella and Patricia McBride, conducted a lecture-demonstration in

Clearwater, which left a lasting impression on him. An excellent student, Byrd received a scholarship for minority students to Yale University. He majored in philosophy but his exposure to the Yale Theater groups led him to consider being an actor. But the racist attitudes of his classmates at Yale discouraged him, and he transferred to Tufts University in Boston.

Through his friend at Tufts, William Hurt, Byrd learned about the Alvin Ailey Dance Theater. At a performance of Alvin Ailey's signature work *Revelations*, Byrd felt the theatrical power of dance. Inspired, he began taking dance classes at Tufts and eventually went to New York in the early 1970s to study with a variety of dance teachers, among them, the Ailey School, Twyla Tharp, and the Gus Solomons, Jr. company in 1976. When Solomons was named dean of the dance program at the California Institute of the Arts, he took Byrd along to teach.

While in California, Byrd began receiving acclaim for his choreography. By 1977, he was producing shows of his own work on the West Coast as well as at the Dance Theater Workshop back in New York. Byrd founded his own company, Donald Byrd/The Group in 1978. His style was now a unique blend of classical ballet, modern dance, and urban street dancing. Despite his company's success, Byrd struggled for several years with alcohol and drug dependency. After a scathing review by a supporter of his work in 1985, Byrd entered treatment and soon returned to his career.

In 1987, Byrd choreographed a new piece for the Ailey Repertory Company. The work *Crumble* was well received and from then on, he continued to contribute works to the Ailey companies. Byrd staged his next piece *Shards* in 1988 with strong influences of Balanchine. In 1991, the Ailey Dance Theater debuted *Dance at the Gym*, a work about teen culture. Byrd's own troupe, Donald Byrd/The Group, presented *Prodigal* in 1990, a dance inspired by Balanchine's *Prodigal Son*. The next year they produced a controversial piece about racial stereotypes called *The Minstrel Show*. This show won a Bessie Award for Donald Byrd/The Group in 1992.

The 1990s were creative years for Donald Byrd. He and his company toured the United States and Europe in 1993 presenting a repertoire of works choreographed by Byrd, among them *Bristle*, a long work exploring tensions between the genders. For Christmas of 1994, Byrd developed *The Harlem Nutcracker*, an African American version of the classic *Nutcracker*, using Duke Ellington-style big band arrangements of Peter Tchaikovsky's original music. Byrd's *The Beast* premiered in 1996 at the Brooklyn Academy of Music; the piece examines various types of domestic violence. By 1998, Byrd and his work were honored in a program of dances created by African American male choreographers called *Young Choreographers Defining Dance*.

Godfrey Cambridge (1933–1976)

Actor, Comedian

Godfrey Cambridge was born in New York on February 26, 1933, to parents who had emigrated from British Guiana. He attended grammar school in Nova Scotia, while living with his grandparents. After finishing his schooling in New York at Flushing High School and Hofstra College, he went on to study acting.

Cambridge made his Broadway debut in *Nature's Way* (1956) and was featured in *Purlie Victorious* both on stage in 1961 and later on screen. He also appeared off-Broadway in *Lost in the Stars* (1958), *Take a Giant Step*, and *The Detective Story* (1960). Cambridge won the Obie Award for the 1960–1961 season's most distinguished off-Broadway performance for his role in *The Blacks*. In 1965, he starred in a stock version of *A Funny Thing Happened on the Way to the Forum*.

As a comedian, Cambridge appeared on "The Tonight Show" and many other variety hours. His material, drawn from the contemporary racial situation, was often presented in the style associated with the contemporary wave of African American comedians. One of Cambridge's most memorable roles was as the star of a seriocomic Hollywood film *The Watermelon Man* (1970) in which the comedian played a white man who changes color overnight. Cambridge has also performed dramatic roles on many television series.

During the mid-1970s, Cambridge remained in semiretirement, making few public appearances. Cambridge died at the age of 43 in California on November 29, 1976. His death occurred on a Warner Brothers set, where he was playing the role of Ugandan dictator Idi Amin for the television film *Victory at Entebbe*.

Hope Clarke (1943–)

Stage Director, Actress, Choreographer

From duets with Alvin Ailey to a complete revisioning of *Porgy and Bess*, Hope Clarke's career continues to expand the influences of African American culture in the American arts.

Hope Clarke was born in Washington, DC, in 1943. She grew up in a segregated, close-knit African American community. However, her talent and determination propelled her into a career in show business. In 1960 she won a part in the original touring company of Leonard Bernstein's *West Side Story*. From there, she became a principal dancer in two African American dance troupes:

the Katherine Dunham Company and the Alvin Ailey American Dance Theater. Her duets with the late Alvin Ailey became legendary. Armed with talent and discipline, she left the company in the 1970s to pursue a new career in acting.

As an actress, Clarke's most notable feature film performance was in the classic film *A Piece of the Action*, starring Bill Cosby and Sidney Poitier. She also appeared in guest roles on numerous television shows including "The Jeffersons," "Hill Street Blues," "Three's Company," and "As the World Turns."

Besides acting, Clarke was called in to choreograph various stage and television shows. Her years as a dancer prepared her well. She worked for the New York City-based Opera Ebony, helping to produce *Porgy and Bess* in such unlikely venues as Brazil and Finland. She won a Tony nomination for Best Choreography for her work in the 1992 Broadway hit *Jelly's Last Jam*.

Clarke continued to stage projects as diverse as Dorothy Rudd Moore's *Freedom* and Wolfgang Amadeus Mozart's *Cosi Fan Tutte*. She choreographed the production of *Frida* for the Houston Grand Opera. In 1995 she became the first African American, and the first African American woman, to direct and choreograph a major staging of the George Gershwin opera-musical *Porgy and Bess*, also for the Houston Grand Opera.

This major production of *Porgy and Bess* was staged in celebration of the work's sixtieth anniversary. Clarke brought to it her African American, feminine, and artistic sensibilities. She based the opera's setting around the Charleston-based Gullahs, an African American group believed to be Angolan in origin. Her characterizations employ the cultural and linguistic integrity of this unique community. In 1995, Clarke received a Tony Award for her work on *Porgy and Bess*. It toured many major American cities including San Diego, Los Angeles, San Francisco, Houston, and Minneapolis. It also played engagements in Japan and at Italy's famed La Scala opera house in Milan.

In 1998, Clarke received a New York Dance and Performance Award, known as a "Bessie," for her outstanding achievements as a performance professional. She continues to direct and choreograph dances and musicals in New York and elsewhere.

Bill Cosby (1937–)
Actor, Comedian

Born on July 12, 1937, Bill Cosby is one of the most successful performers and businessmen in the United States.

A native of suburban Philadelphia, Cosby left high school to become a medic in the U.S. Navy. As a testament to his commitment to education, he obtained his diploma while in the service. After leaving the military, he entered Temple University, where he played football and worked evenings as a bartender.

Bill Cosby holding an Emmy Award in 1992 (AP/Wide World Photos, Inc.).

While doing this work, Cosby began to entertain the customers with his comedy routines and, encouraged by his success, left Temple in 1962 to pursue a career in show business. He began by playing small clubs around Philadelphia and in New York's Greenwich Village. Within two years, he was playing the top nightclubs around the country and making television appearances on shows hosted by Johnny Carson, Jack Paar, and Andy Williams. In fact, he earned the opportunity to serve as guest host of Carson's "Tonight Show." In the 1960s Cosby became the first African American to star in a prime time television series. "I Spy" ran from 1965 to 1968 and won Cosby three Emmy Awards.

In the 1970s, Cosby appeared regularly in nightclubs in Las Vegas, Tahoe, and Reno, and did commercials for such sponsors as Jell-O, Del Monte, and Ford. From 1969 until 1972, he had his own television series "The Bill Cosby Show." During the early 1970s he also developed and contributed vocals to the Saturday morning children's show "Fat Albert and the Cosby Kids." He appeared in such films as *Uptown Saturday Night* (1974), *Let's Do It Again* (1975), *A Piece of the Action* (1977), and the award-winning television movie *To All My Friends on Shore.*

In 1975, Random House published his book *Bill Cosby's Personal Guide to Tennis: or, Don't Lower the Lob, Raise the Net.* For several years, he was involved in educational television with the Children's Television Workshop. He returned to college, spending five years at the University of Massachusetts earning a master's degree and then in 1977, a doctorate in education.

He was star and creator of the consistently top-rated "The Cosby Show" from 1985 to 1992, author of two best-selling books *Fatherhood* (1986) and *Time Flies* (1987), and a performer at the top venues in Las Vegas, where he earned $500,000 a week. He also won top fees as a commercial spokesman for Kodak and Coca Cola. He has recorded more than 27 albums and has received five Grammy Awards. Cosby also hosted a new version of the old Groucho Marx game show "You Bet Your Life." In 1994, Cosby reunited with Robert Culp, his co-star from the "I Spy" show, for a new television movie *I Spy Returns.* He also starred in the short-lived series "The Cosby Mysteries" in 1995. Toward the end of the decade Cosby hosted "Kids Say the Darndest Things," a show originally hosted by Art Linkletter, and starred in another sitcom entitled "Cosby."

Cosby and his wife, Camille, live in rural New England. The Cosbys made headlines when they donated $20 million to Spelman College in Atlanta.

Katherine Dunham (1910–)

Choreographer, Dancer

Katherine Dunham has for many years been one of the leading exponents of primitive dance in the world of modern choreography.

Born in Joliet, Illinois, on June 22, 1910, Dunham attended Joliet Township Junior College and the University of Chicago, where she majored in anthropology. With funding from a Rosenwald Fellowship, she was able to conduct anthropological studies in the Caribbean and Brazil. She later attended Northwestern University, where she earned her Ph.D.; MacMurray College, where she received a L.H.D. in 1972; and Atlanta University, where she received a Ph.D.L. in 1977.

In the 1930s, she founded the Dunham Dance Company whose repertory drew on techniques Dunham learned while studying in the Caribbean. She has used her training in anthropology and her study of primitive rituals from tropical cultures to create unique dance forms that blend primitive qualities with sophisticated Broadway stage settings. In 1940, she appeared in the musical *Cabin in the Sky,* which she had choreographed with George Balanchine. She later toured the United States with her dance group; after the war, she played to enthusiastic audiences in Europe.

Among Dunham's choreographic pieces are: *Le Jazz Hot* (1938); *Bhahiana* (1939); *Plantation Dances* (1940); *Haitian Suite (II)* (1941); *Tropical Revue* (1943); *Havana 1910/1919* (1944); *Carib Song* (1945); *Bal Negre* (1946); *Rhumba Trio* (1947); *Macumba* (1948); *Adeus Terras* (1949); *Spirituals* (1951); *Afrique du Nord* (1953); *Jazz Finale* (1955); *Ti Cocomaque* (1957); and *Anabacoa* (1963). Under the pseudonym Kaye Dunn, Dunham has written several articles and books on primitive dance. She has been referred to as "the mother of Afro-American dance."

On January 15, 1979, at Carnegie Hall in New York, Dunham received the 1979 Albert Schweitzer Music Award, and selections from her dance repertory from 1938 to 1975 were staged.

In 1982, Dunham founded the Katherine Dunham Center for Arts & Humanities in East St. Louis to promote research and training in the arts and humanities. Its mission is to promote "arts-based communication techniques for people of diverse cultures, and [provide] a multi-art training program to humanize and socialize individuals as well as provide them with marketable skills."

Dunham has founded schools of dance in Chicago, New York, Haiti, Stockholm, and Paris. She has also lectured at colleges and universities across the country.

Garth Fagan (1940–)

Choreographer

Garth Fagan was born on May 3, 1940, in Kingston, Jamaica. He discovered dance by way of gymnastics but was discouraged from a dance career by his father, an academic. However, he studied and danced with Ivy Baxter and the Jamaican National Dance Company, touring throughout Latin American while still in high school.

In 1960, Fagan left Jamaica and enrolled at Wayne State University in Detroit to study psychology. After completing his master's program, he commuted to New York to study with Martha Graham, Jose Limon, and Alvin Ailey. Fagan helped launch several Detroit-based dance companies: Detroit's All-City Dance Company, Detroit Contemporary Dance Company and Dance Theatre of Detroit. Eventually, he moved to Rochester, New York, to become a Distinguished Professor at the State University of New York at Brockport. There he taught young, untrained dancers who became his first company, Garth Fagan Dance.

Fagan always sought to transform dance, using the polyrhythms of Afro-Caribbean dance, modern floor techniques, the theatrics of Alvin Ailey, and the agility of ballet to create new movement. Garth Fagan Dance performs regularly at the Joyce Theater, Spoleto USA, Dance/Aspen, and the National Black Arts Festivals. In 1986, Fagan directed and choreographed *Queenie Pie*, the Duke Ellington *street opera* at the Kennedy Center. Since then, he has created pieces for the Dance Theatre of Harlem, *Jukebox for Alvin* for the Alvin Ailey American Dance Theatre, (1993), a solo work for Judith Jamison, and *Never No Lament* for the José Limón Company in 1994.

Fagan's numerous honors include a Guggenheim Fellowship, the three-year Choreography Fellowship from the National Endowment for the Arts, the Dance Magazine Award for "significant contributions to dance during a distinguished career," and the "Bessie" Award (New York Performance Award) for sustained achievement. In 1996 he was named among 25 American scholars, artists, professionals, and public figures to receive the title, Fulbright Fiftieth Anniversary Distinguished Fellow.

In 1998, Fagan received the Tony Award for best choreography for his critically acclaimed work in the Broadway hit *The Lion King*, which also won the Tony for best musical. Fagan himself danced in the show. In 1998, he also received the Drama Desk Award, the Outer Critics Circle Award, and the Astaire Award.

Fagan's latest work is *Nkanyit* which premiered in 1997 at the John F. Kennedy Center in Washington, DC, and opened at the Joyce Theatre in New York again in November of 1998. The title means "an all-encompassing respect for life, elders, and each other instilled early in childhood." This piece juxtaposes African ancestors dancing to American songs, and modern folk moving to Kenyan percussion. The heart of the work is the dynamic relationship between parent and child and the struggle to create "family." With his ability to produce entertaining, dramatic, and insightful movement, Fagan continues to push the limits, inside and out, of postmodern dance.

Redd Foxx (1922–1991)

Actor, Comedian

Redd Foxx's most famous role was Fred Sanford, the junkman on the popular NBC series "Sanford and Son," which began in 1972. It was the second most popular role on television (after Archie Bunker in "All in the Family"). As a result, Foxx became one of the highest paid actors in show business. In 1976, it was reported that he was earning $25,000 per half-hour episode, plus 25 percent of the producer's net profit.

Sanford is actually Foxx's family name. He was born John Elroy Sanford in St. Louis on December 9, 1922, and both his father and his brother were named Fred. As a boy, he concocted a washtub band with two friends and played for tips on street corners, earning as much as $60 a night. At 14, Foxx and the band moved to Chicago; the group broke up during World War II.

Foxx then moved to New York, where he worked as a rack pusher in the garment district as he sought work in night clubs and on the black vaudeville circuit. While in New York, he played pool with a hustler named Malcolm Little, who was to change his name to Malcolm X.

In the early 1950s, Foxx tried to find work in Hollywood. He had a brief stint with "The Dinah Washington Show," but mostly survived by performing a vaudeville act and working as a sign painter. This comedy act contained adult content, which limited his bookings.

Foxx's first real success came in 1955, when he began to record party records. He ultimately made more than 50 records, which sold over 20 million copies. His television career was launched in the 1960s with guest appearances on "The Today Show," "The Tonight Show," and other variety programs. He also began to appear in Las Vegas nightclubs.

Throughout the long run of "Sanford and Son," Foxx disputed with his producers over money. Originally, he was not receiving a percentage of the show's profits, which led him to sit out several episodes; a breach of contract suit filed by the producers resulted. There were racial undertones to these disputes, with Foxx referring to himself as a "tuxedo slave" and pointing to white stars who owned a percentage of their shows. Eventually, Foxx broke with the show and with NBC.

Foxx then signed a multimillion dollar, multiyear contract with ABC, which resulted in a disastrous comedy variety hour that he quit on the air in October of 1977. The ABC situation comedy "My Buddy" which he wrote, starred in, and produced followed. In 1978, however, ABC filed a breach of contract suit. In 1979, Foxx was back at NBC planning a sequel to "Sanford and Son." He also made a deal with CBS, which in 1981 was suing him for a second time, allegedly to recover advances not paid back.

In 1976, Foxx appeared in the MGM movie *Norman, Is That You?* He continued his appearances in nightclubs in Las Vegas and New York. In 1979, the book *Redd Foxx, B.S.* was published, comprised of chapters written by his friends.

In 1973, Foxx received the Entertainer of the Year Award from the NAACP. In 1974, he was named police chief of Taft, Oklahoma, an all-black village of six hundred people. He also ran a Los Angeles nightclub to showcase aspiring young comedians, both black and white. In addition, Foxx did numerous prison shows, probably more than any other famous entertainer, which he paid for out of his own pocket. Foxx died on October 11, 1991.

Al Freeman, Jr. (1934–)
Actor

Al Freeman, Jr. has won recognition for his many roles in the theater and motion pictures. His title role in the television film *My Sweet Charlie* (1970) earned him an Emmy Award nomination.

Albert Cornelius Freeman, Jr. was born in San Antonio, Texas, on March 21, 1934, son of the pianist Al Freeman Sr. and Lottie Coleman Freeman. After attending schools in San Antonio and then Ohio, Freeman moved to the West Coast to study law at Los Angeles City College. Following a tour of duty with the U.S. Army in Germany, Freeman returned to college and decided to change his major to theater arts after being encouraged by fellow students to audition for a campus production.

Freeman did radio shows and appeared in little theater productions in the Los Angeles area before performing in his first Broadway play *The Long Dream* (1960). Other Broadway credits include: *Kicks and Company* (1961); *Tiger, Tiger Burning Bright* (1962); *Blues for Mr. Charley* (1964); *Conversations at Midnight* (1964); *The Dozens* (1969); *Look to the Lilies* (1970); and *Medea* (1973).

Off-Broadway, Freeman worked in *The Living Premise* (1963), *Trumpets of the Lord* (1963), *The Slave* (1964), and *Great MacDaddy* (1974). He also appeared in *Troilus and Cressida* (1965) and *Measure for Measure* (1966) for the New York Shakespeare Festival. He has also done more than a dozen feature films including: *Dutchman* (1967); *Finian's Rainbow* (1968); *The Detective* (1968); *The Lost Man* (1969); *Castle Keep* (1969); *Malcolm X* (1992); and *Once Upon a Time When We Were Colored* (1995). In 1998, Freeman appeared in the poignant film *Down in the Delta* with Alfre Woodard and Wesley Snipes, which was directed by poet Maya Angelou.

Freeman has appeared in such television series as "The Defenders," "The FBI," and "Naked City," and was featured as Lieutenant Ed Hall in ABC's daytime drama "One Life to Live." He also appeared on television in Norman Lear's "Hotel Baltimore" (1975).

Charles Gilpin (1878–1930)
Actor

Charles Gilpin was born in Richmond, Virginia, on November 20, 1878. After a brief period in school, he took up work as a printer's devil. In 1890, he began to travel intermittently with vaudeville troupes, a practice that continued for two decades. He worked as a printer, elevator operator, prizefight trainer, and porter during long interludes of theatrical unemployment.

From 1911 to 1914, Gilpin toured with a group called the Pan-American Octette. In 1914 he had a bit part in a New York production *Old Ann's Boy.* Two years later he founded the Lafayette Theatre Company, one of the earliest black stock companies in New York.

After Eugene O'Neill saw Gilpin in *Abraham Lincoln,* he was chosen to play the lead in *Emperor Jones,* the role in which he starred from 1920 to 1924. In 1921, Gilpin was awarded the NAACP Spingarn Award for his theatrical accomplishment.

Gilpin lost his voice in 1926 and was forced to earn his living once again as an elevator operator. He died on May 6, 1930.

Savion Glover (1974–)
Dancer, Choreographer

Tap dance wizard Savion Glover was born in Newark, New Jersey, in 1974. His mother noticed his keen sense of rhythm early on, and he began learning percussion at four-years-old. Ready to try something new, he began tap lessons at the Broadway Dance Center in New York City three years later. By the time he was ten, Glover was the understudy for the lead in *The Tap Dance Kid* and later starred in the role of the Kid. After two years in that show, he went on to perform in *Black and Blue* which opened first in Paris before moving to New York. His work earned him a Tony Award nomination in 1989.

Glover's talent developed quickly as he learned by imitating the techniques and sounds of tap greats such as Sandman Sims, Harold Nicholas, Jimmy Slyde, and Sammy Davis, Jr. who appeared with him in the film *Taps* in 1988. He excelled in *close work* (taps without jumps or leaps), acrobatic tap, and admits to creating moves inspired by Michael Jackson.

Glover next appeared in *Jelly's Last Jam,* which opened on Broadway in 1992, playing the young Jelly Roll Morton and co-starring with Gregory Hines. From Broadway, Glover went to television to appear, from 1991 to 1995, in "Sesame Street" and in several feature shows such as "Dance in America: Tap!," "Black Filmmakers Hall of Fame" and performing at the Academy Awards ceremony in 1996 and 1999.

Glover's latest stage success is *Bring in 'Da Noise, Bring in 'Da Funk* which opened in 1995 and for which Glover is the choreographer and prime performer. The show combines poetry, tap, and musical styles such as blues, rhythm and blues, jazz, hip hop, and street drumming in dramatic and satiric sketches that tell of the black experience in America. Glover won the Tony Award for best choreography in 1996 for *Bring in 'Da Noise, Bring in 'Da Funk.* That same year he earned a Dance Magazine Award, a National Endowment for the Arts award, and was named Best New Theater Star by *Entertainment Weekly.* Since then, Glover has been teaching tap classes for children and has moved to Hollywood to develop further shows to showcase his extraordinary talents.

Whoopi Goldberg (1955–)

Actress, Comedienne

Born Caryn E. Johnson in Manhattan's Chelsea district on November 13, 1955, Whoopi Goldberg began performing at the age of eight at the children's program at Hudson Guild and Helen Rubeinstein Children's Theatre. After trying her hand at theater, improvisation, and chorus parts on Broadway, she moved to San Diego in 1974 and appeared in repertory productions of *Mother Courage* and *Getting Out.*

Goldberg joined the Black St. Hawkeyes Theatre in Berkeley as a partner with David Schein, and then went solo to create *The Spook Show,* performing in San Francisco and later touring the United States and Europe.

In 1983, Goldberg's work caught the attention of Mike Nichols, who created and directed her Broadway show a year later. She made her film debut in *The Color Purple* (1985), winning an NAACP Image Award as well as a Golden Globe Award.

Goldberg's other film credits include: *Jumpin' Jack Flash; Burglar; Fatal Beauty; The Telephone; Homer and Eddie; Clara's Heart; Beverly Hills Brats; Ghost* (for which she won an Academy Award as best supporting actress); *The Long Walk Home; Soapdish; Sister Act; The Player; Sarafina; Made in America; Sister Act 2: Back in the Habit; Naked in New York; Corrina, Corrina; Star Trek: Generations; Boys on the Side* and *Moonlight and Valentino.*

On television, she starred in "Whoopi Goldberg on Broadway," "Carol, Carl, Whoopi and Robin," "Funny, You Don't Look 200," and hosted "Comedy Tonight." She received an Emmy nomination in 1985 for her guest appearance on "Moonlighting," has had a recurring role on "Star Trek: The Next Generation," and was a founding member of the Comic Relief benefit shows.

In 1993, Goldberg received the Woman of the Year Award from Harvard University's Halting Pudding Theatricals organization. She also won People's Choice Awards in 1993 and 1994.

Goldberg served as host of the Academy Awards in 1994, 1996, and 1999.

Whoopi Goldberg (AP/Wide World Photos, Inc.)

Dick Gregory (1932–)

Comedian, Civil Rights Activist, Writer, Nutritional Advocate

Dick Gregory was born on October 12, 1932, in St. Louis. His father left the family in a state of poverty, and Gregory helped his mother by earning money through doing odd jobs. After high school, he entered Southern Illinois University on an athletic scholarship. In 1954 he was drafted into the U.S. Army. In the military his superiors, who were not fond of Gregory's flippant attitude, challenged him to win a talent show or face court-martial charges. Gregory won the contest and continued his military stint in the Special Service's Entertainment Division.

After his discharge from the army, Gregory went to Chicago and pursued a career as a stand-up comic. He opened a club called the Apex but failed to attract enough business to make the venue successful. The venture was not a total failure: Gregory ended up marrying his financial partner, Lillian Smith. In January of 1961, Gregory received the opportunity to perform at the Playboy Club for a group of Southern executives. Although initially turned away by the club's booking agent, who had assumed that Gregory was white, the comedian insisted on doing his routine. Although the crowd was expectedly resistant at first, Gregory persevered and won them over. The performance resulted in a three-year contract with the club.

During the early 1960s Gregory's popularity grew. His comedy relied upon discussions of himself and included social commentary on such matters as racism and civil rights. Several national commentators acknowledged Gregory as the first black comedian to gain acceptance as a social satirist. In the 1960s, he wrote *Back of the Bus* (1962) and *Nigger: An Autobiography* (1964).

In the 1960s Gregory involved himself in the burgeoning civil rights movement. He committed himself to events that resulted in increases in political fund raising and voter registration. Not one to contribute passively to causes, Gregory was arrested on numerous occasions and risked violence from local police. His views of nonviolent participation, fostered by Martin Luther King, Jr., were challenged by his paying witness to a sheriff kicking his wife during a protest in Missouri.

As the 1960s progressed, Gregory withdrew from the entertainment arena and participated more actively in politics. He ran for mayor of Chicago in 1967 and earned nearly 200,000 votes for president as the candidate for the Freedom and Peace Party in the 1968 national election.

Nutritional issues have been a focus for Gregory since he became a vegetarian during the 1960s. At one point in his career, he refused to perform in clubs that allowed smoking and drinking. In the 1970s he co-wrote *Dick Gregory's Natural Diet for Folks Who Eat: Cooking with Mother Nature* (1974) with Alvenia Fulton. In 1984 he founded Health Enterprises, a business focused on marketing a powdered diet drink. Gregory also participated in marathons.

In the 1990s Gregory returned to the stage in Brooklyn to bring his comedy and social views to a new generation. His opinions on such issues as world hunger, "gangsta" rap music, drug use, and warfare come through during his performances.

Gregory received the *Ebony*-Topaz Heritage and Freedom Award, along with numerous honorary degrees from major universities.

Moses Gunn (1929–1993)
Actor

Born on October 2, 1929, in St. Louis, Moses Gunn showed dramatic promise at a young age—reading monologues aloud when he was nine. Six scholarships from other schools were offered to Gunn before he chose to earn a degree in speech and drama from Tennessee State University. There he organized a student troupe called Footlights Across Tennessee, a group that toured the South and Midwest, staging shows written by little-known black playwrights. While completing some graduate work at the University of Kansas, Gunn performed in *Othello*.

With his eye on a career on the New York stage, Gunn raised money by teaching drama at Grambling College in the early 1960s. He served as an understudy for an off-Broadway production, later joining the regular cast. Once he had gained more experience, Gunn gained a reputation as a leading Shakespearian actor. He appeared regularly with the New York Shakespeare Festival and won off-Broadway's Obie Award for his portrayal of Aaron the Moor in a 1967 production of *Titus Andronicus*. During the same era, he became a founding member of the Negro Ensemble Company, whose production of *The First Breeze of Summer* led to the actor's second Obie in 1975.

By the 1970s, Gunn had become a favorite on the national and international scenes. As a maturing performer, he did not limit his appearances to stage. Moviegoers enjoyed his supporting performances in films ranging from *Shaft* to *The Great White Hope*. As Booker T. Washington in *Ragtime*, Gunn earned an Image Award from the NAACP in 1981. Gunn was successful on the little screen, too, appearing in the made-for-television epic *Roots;* he earned an Emmy nomination for his portrayal in *Roots* of Kintango, a seventh-century African secret sect leader. He also did sitcoms and cop shows.

From a sensual Othello to a fiery Booker T. Washington, actor Moses Gunn specialized in crafting strong, memorable characters. His career spanned more than three decades. Beyond his own career, Gunn worked tirelessly as an advocate for other African American actors during a time when the theatrical establishment seemed all too willing to limit their presence both onstage and behind the scenes. He died of asthma complications on December 17, 1993, at the age of 64.

Arsenio Hall (1955–)
Actor, Comedian, Talk Show Host

Born on February 12, 1955, in Cleveland, Ohio, Arsenio Hall started his professional career as a standup comic, making the rounds of clubs and honing his presentation. Soon, he was appearing on television specials as well as touring with noted musical performers.

Hall was selected as a guest host of Fox Television's "Joan Rivers Show" when Rivers left, and soon won over both studio and television audiences. When this show concluded, he went on to star with Eddie Murphy in the movie *Coming To America* (1988). Hall also appeared in the movies *Harlem Nights* (1989) and *Bopha!* (1993).

Paramount then hired Arsenio Hall to be the host of his own show. Within weeks after the show's premiere in 1989, Hall had again built a solid audience following, particularly with young viewers, and provided the most substantial competition established evening talk shows had ever faced. In 1994, due to declining ratings and competition from talk show rivals Jay Leno and David Letterman, "The Arsenio Hall Show" went off the air.

Juanita Hall (1902–1968)
Singer

Born on November 6, 1902, in Keyport, New Jersey, Hall studied at the Juilliard School of Music after singing in Catholic Church choirs as a child. Hall devoted her life to music as a singer in stage and movie productions and choirs.

Her first major stage appearance was in Ziegfield's *Showboat* in 1927. Her lengthy stage career culminated in her role as Bloody Mary in Rodgers and Hammerstein's *South Pacific* in 1949. Hall went on to appear in *Flower Drum Song* and the movie versions of both shows. She served as a soloist and assistant director of the Hall Johnson Choir (1931-1936), conducted the Works Progress Administration chorus in New York City (1936–1941), and organized the Juanita Hall Choir in 1942.

Hall performed at the Palladium in London and was a guest on the Ed Sullivan and Perry Como television shows. She was the recipient of the Donaldson, Antoinette Perry, and Bill Bojangles awards. Hall died February 29, 1968, in Bay Shore, New York.

Robin Harris (1953–1990)
Comedian, Actor

Robin Harris was born August 30, 1953, in Chicago, Illinois. He attended Ottawa University in Kansas, where he ran a 4:18 mile on the track team. After college, he pursued a career in comedy rather than athletics, doing stand-up comedy as much as possible while working at Hughes Aircraft and Security Pacific Bank to support himself. Harris's interest in 1970s comedians such as Redd Foxx motivated to create his own act in a similar style. Finally in 1985, after years of hard work, he began to build a name for himself as the master of ceremonies at Comedy Act Theater in Los Angeles. Due primarily to Harris's influence, the Comedy Act Theater became a stopping spot for black celebrities.

Spike Lee was the first in the film industry to recognize Harris's talent and cast him in his 1989 film *Do The Right Thing*, which Harris followed with roles in *I'm Gonna Git You Sucka* and *Harlem Nights*. In 1990, he continued his successfully growing film career playing Pops in *House Party*. His movie career vaulted him into a new level of stardom, and he started playing 2,000-seat auditoriums with his comedy act, though continuing his much smaller and less profitable gigs at the Comedy Act Theater.

In 1990, Harris's life became very hectic between his comedy act gigs, an HBO special, his album and soon-to-be movie *Bebe's Kids*. The schedule proved too much for him, and he died on March 18, 1990, of heart failure in his hometown of Chicago. The animated film version of Harris's comedy album *Bebe's Kids* was released posthumously as was his HBO comedy special.

Richard B. Harrison (1864–1935)
Actor

Richard B. Harrison was one of the few actors to gain national prominence on the basis of one role, his characterization of De Lawd in *Green Pastures*.

Harrison was born in Canada in 1864 and moved to Detroit as a young boy. There he worked as a waiter, porter, and handyman, saving whatever money he could to attend the theatrical offerings playing in town. After studying drama in Detroit, he made his professional debut in Canada in a program of readings and recitations.

For three decades, Harrison entertained black audiences with one-man performances of *Macbeth*, *Julius Caesar*, and *Damon and Pythias*, as well as with poems by William Shakespeare, Edgar Allan Poe, Rudyard Kipling, and Paul Laurence Dunbar. In 1929, while serving on the faculty of North Carolina A & T as drama instructor, he was chosen for the part in *Green Pastures*.

By the time of his death in 1935, Harrison had performed as De Lawd 1,656 times. His work earned him the 1930 Spingarn Medal and numerous honorary degrees.

Gregory Hines (1946–)
Actor, Dancer

After a distinguished career as a tap dancer, Gregory Hines made an unusual transition to dramatic actor.

Born in New York City on Valentine's Day, 1946, Hines began dancing with his brother Maurice under the instruction of tap dancer Henry LeTang. When Gregory was five, the brothers began performing professionally as the Hines Kids. Appearing in nightclubs and theaters around the country, they were able to benefit from contact with dance legends such as "Honi" Coles, Sandman Sims, the Nicholas Brothers, and Teddy Hale.

As teenagers, the two performed as the Hines Brothers. When Gregory reached age 18, the two were joined

Gregory Hines (AP/Wide World Photos, Inc.)

by their father, Maurice Sr., on drums, and the trio became known as Hines, Hines and Dad. They performed internationally and appeared on "The Tonight Show." Eventually, Gregory tired of the touring and settled in California, where he formed the jazz-rock band Severance.

Gregory Hines subsequently moved back to New York and landed a role in *The Minstrel Show* (1978). He would later appear in such Broadway musicals as *Eubie!* (1978), *Sophisticated Ladies* (1981), and *Comin' Uptown* (1990), as well as feature films including *The Cotton Club* (1985), *White Nights* (1985), *Running Scared* (1985), and *Off Limits* (1988). Hines starred in the 1989 Tri-Star film *Tap* with Sammy Davis, Jr., not only acting and dancing, but singing as well. Hines has also appeared in the films *White Man's Burden* (1994), *Renaissance Man* (1995), *Dead Air* (1995), and *Waiting to Exhale* (1995).

On television, Hines appeared in the series "Amazing Stories" and the special "Motown Returns to the Apollo" which earned him an Emmy nomination. His 1997 show "The Gregory Hines Show" was favorably reviewed but short-lived. When not appearing in films or television, he toured internationally with a solo club act. *Gregory Hines*, his first solo album, was released by CBS/Epic in 1988. The album was produced by Luther Vandross, who teamed with Gregory for a single "There's Nothing Better Than Love," which reached number one on the R&B charts in 1987.

Hines has received numerous awards including the Dance Educators Award and the Theater World Award. Hines has been nominated for several Tony Awards, and in 1992 received the award for best actor in a musical for his role in *Jelly's Last Jam*.

Geoffrey Holder (1930–)

Actor, Dancer, Choreographer, Costume Designer, Director

Geoffrey Holder has succeeded as an artist in many areas. Holder was born on August 1, 1930, in Port-of-Spain, Trinidad. At an early age, he left school to become the costume designer for his brother's dance troupe, which he took over in 1948. Holder led the dancers, singers, and steel band musicians through a series of successful small revues to the Caribbean Festival in Puerto Rico, where they represented Trinidad and Tobago. His appearances with his troupe in the mid-1950s were so popular that he is credited with launching the calypso vogue.

Early in his career, Holder appeared in New York as a featured dancer in *House of Flowers* (1954). He later performed with the Metropolitan Opera and as a guest star on many television shows. Film credits include: *Live and Let Die* (1973), the James Bond adventure; and *Dr. Dolittle* (1967), the children's classic starring Rex Harrison.

Holder received two Tony Awards in 1976, as director and costume designer for the Broadway show *The Wiz*, the all-black adaptation of *The Wizard of Oz*. In 1978, he directed and choreographed the successful Broadway musical *Timbuktu*. In 1982, Holder appeared in the film *Annie* based on the hit Broadway musical, playing Punjab, a character from the original comic strip.

Holder received a Guggenheim Fellowship to pursue his painting, and his impressionist paintings have been shown in galleries such as the Corcoran in Washington, DC. In 1995, an exhibition of Holder's paintings was held at the State University of New York in Albany. Holder also has written two books. *Black Gods, Green Islands* is a retelling of West Indian legends; his *Caribbean Cookbook* is a collection of recipes that Holder also illustrated.

In 1998, Holder restaged his 1967 production *The Prodigal Prince* for the fortieth anniversary celebration of the Alvin Ailey Dance Theater.

Holder is married to the ballet dancer Carmen de Lavallade.

Lena Horne (1917–)
Actress, Singer

Lena Horne has been called the most beautiful woman in the world, and her beauty has been no small factor in the continued success of her stage, screen, and nightclub career.

Horne was born on June 30, 1917, in Brooklyn, New York. She joined the chorus line at the Cotton Club in 1933, and then left to tour as a dancer with Noble Sissle's orchestra. She was given a leading role in *Blackbirds of 1939*, but the show folded quickly, whereupon she left to join Charlie Barnett's band as a singer. She made her first records (including the popular "Haunted Town") with Barnett. In the early 1940s she also worked at New York's Cafe Society Downtown.

Horne then went to Hollywood, where she became the first black woman to sign a term contract with a film studio. Her films included *Panama Hattie* (1942), *Cabin in the Sky* (1943), *Stormy Weather* (1943), and *Meet Me in Las Vegas* (1956). In 1957, she took a break from her film and nightclub schedule to star in her first Broadway musical *Jamaica*. Her popular recordings included "Stormy Weather," "Blues in the Night," "The Lady Is a Tramp," and "Mad about the Boy."

Throughout the 1960s and 1970s, Horne appeared in nightclubs and concerts. Her greatest recent success, however, was on Broadway. On May 12, 1981, she opened a one-woman show called *Lena Horne: The Lady and Her Music* to critical and box-office success. Although it opened too late to qualify for the Tony Award nominations, the show was awarded a special Tony at the June ceremonies. The production ran for two years and the soundtrack produced by Quincy Jones won two Grammy Awards. In December of 1981, she received New York City's highest cultural award, the Handel Medallion.

Horne was married for 23 years to Lennie Hayton, a white composer, arranger, and conductor who died April 24, 1971. She had been married previously to Louis Jones. A generous and gracious woman, Horne has quietly devoted much time to humane causes.

In 1994, Horne released her first recording in a decade entitled *We'll Be Together Again*. This album was followed by *An Evening with Lena Horne* (1995) and *Lena Horne at Metro-Goldwyn-Mayer* (1996).

Eddie Hunter (1888–1974)
Comedian

Eddie Hunter got his start when working as an elevator operator in a building frequented by the great tenor Enrico Caruso. Hunter had been writing vaudeville comedy parts on the side, and Caruso encouraged and helped him. In 1923, Hunter's show *How Come?*, a musical revue, reached Broadway.

Hunter performed in his own persona in the majority of the shows he wrote. *Going to the Races*, produced at the Lafayette Theatre in Harlem, had Hunter and his partner live on stage, interacting with a movie of themselves playing on the screen. Hunter considered this show one of his best. As one of the principal performers in *Blackbirds*, he toured Europe during the late 1920s. His show *Good Gracious* also toured Europe.

Depicting himself as "the fighting comedian," Hunter developed a reputation for speaking out against racial discrimination in the performing arts. He frequently told of his experience in Phoenix, Arizona, where the male members of the show were forced to sleep in the theater where they were performing; accommodations for blacks simply did not exist at the time. Hunter characterized his European reception as being relatively free of prejudice and felt that he only received the respect and recognition due to him when abroad.

By 1923, Hunter had a full recording contract with Victor Records. His recordings included "It's Human Nature to Complain," "I Got," and "My Wife Mamie." Shortly thereafter, he suspended his singing career to begin traveling with a new show he had developed. But when "talking" movies came into being, vaudeville fell out of favor. Eddie Hunter thus retired from show business and entered the real estate business in the 1930s.

Earle Hyman (1926–)
Actor

Earle Hyman was born in Rocky Mount, North Carolina, on October 11, 1926. He began his acting career with the American Negro Theatre in New York City.

In 1963, Hyman made his foreign-language acting debut in Eugene O'Neill's *Emperor Jones* in Oslo, Norway, becoming the first American to perform a title role in a Scandinavian language. Hyman had originally become acquainted with Norway during a European trip made in 1957. He had planned to spend only two weeks in the Scandinavian country, but found himself so enchanted with Norway that he all but forgot the rest of Europe. When Hyman returned to New York, he resolved at once to learn Norwegian, and for practice, began to study the role of Othello (which he was performing for the Great Lakes Shakespeare Festival of 1962) in that language. By sheer coincidence, the director of *Den Nationale Scene* of Bergen, Norway, invited

Earle Hyman performing with Frances Sternhagen in the theater production *Driving Miss Daisy* (Courtesy of Carol Rosegg).

him to play Othello there in the spring of the following year, a performance which marked Hyman's first success in the Norwegian theater.

In 1965, Hyman returned to Norway to play *Emperor Jones* for a different theater company and received high critical acclaim for his portrayal. Hyman remained in Norway intermittently for six years and has been the subject of several Norwegian radio broadcasts and television interviews. He still spends six months each year in Scandinavia playing Othello and other classical roles. He played Halvard Solness to Lynn Redgrave's Mrs. Alvine Solness in Henrik Ibsen's *The Master Builder* at the National Actor's Theatre in 1992. A bronze bust of the actor as Othello has been erected in the Norwegian theater where Hyman performed, and he has also been presented with an honorary membership in the Norwegian Society of Artists, the third foreigner and first American to be so honored.

Hyman's many on and off-Broadway credits include: *No Time for Sergeants* (1955); *St. Joan* (with Diana Sands at Lincoln Center) (1956); *Mister Johnson* (1956); *Waiting for Godot* (1957); Lorraine Hansberry's *Les Blancs* (1970); Edward Albee's *Lady from Dubuque;* the black version of Eugene O'Neill's *Long Day's Journey into Night* (at the Public Theatre, 1981); and *East Texas Hot Links* (1994). Among other film and television work, Hyman has appeared on the daytime drama "Love of Life" and "The Cosby Show."

Judith Jamison (1944–)
Dancer, Choreographer

Born in Philadelphia on May 10, 1944, Judith Jamison started to study dance at the age of six. She was discovered in her early twenties by the choreographer Agnes De Mille, who admired her spontaneous style.

From 1965 to 1980, Jamison was a principal dancer for Alvin Ailey's American Dance Theater for fifteen years, performing a wide gamut of black roles, especially choreographed for her by Ailey. She has made guest appearances with many other dance companies, including the American Ballet Theatre, and with such opera companies as the Vienna State Opera and the Munich State Opera. In the 1980s, Jamison scored a great success on Broadway in *Sophisticated Ladies*, a musical featuring the music of Duke Ellington. In 1988, she formed the Jamison Project.

Since 1989, Jamison has served as artistic director of the Alvin Ailey Dance Theater. Among her recent dance

Judith Jamison (center) performing with the Alvin Ailey Dance Theater Troupe (AP/Wide World Photos, Inc.).

works are "Hymn" (1993) and "Riverside" (1995). "Hymn" is featured in the PBS documentary "Hymn: Remembering Alvin Ailey" premiering in 1999. Her 1996 work "Sweet Release" was a collaboration with celebrated trumpeter Wynton Marsalis. Her newest ballet *Echo: Far From Home* opened in New York in December of 1998.

In 1993, Jamison wrote the book *Dancing Spirit: An Autobiography.* She is the youngest recipient ever to receive the Dance USA Award which was presented at the Spoleto Festival, USA, in May of 1998.

Virginia Johnson (1950–)
Dancer

Virginia Johnson was the prima ballerina for the Dance Theater of Harlem from its very beginning in 1969. Her career started very early. She was born in Washington, DC, on January 25, 1950, and began studying ballet when she was three years old at the Washington School of Ballet. She continued to study there under scholarships throughout high school and performed in productions with the American Light Opera Company and in the annual staging of the Washington Ballet's *The Nutcracker Suite.*

Although black ballerinas were rare, Johnson received a scholarship to study dance at New York University's School of the Arts. However, the emphasis on modern dance there dissatisfied her, so she joined a ballet school in Harlem being run out of a church basement by the former New York City Ballet dancer Arthur Mitchell. At 19, she left NYU to become part of the fledgling company. Mitchell created the Dance Theater of Harlem (DTH) as a commitment to the Harlem community after the assassination of Martin Luther King, Jr. His aim was to establish a company of black dancers and add a new style to contemporary classical ballet. DTH and Johnson were a perfect match.

In 1974, Johnson danced her first solo role for the Dance Theatre of Harlem and became its star ballerina. Emotive, romantic, and long-limbed, Johnson was a natural for legendary choreographer George Balanchine's dances, performing them clearly and smoothly. In her tenure at DTH, she danced many traditional roles such the title role in *Giselle.* The DTH then reset the European tale in the bayous of Louisiana to tell the stories of a community of free Creole blacks. Critics praised Johnson's performances as "glorious and subtle touching and authoritative."

Johnson continued to add modern roles to extend her technical facility. She danced Balanchine's *Serenade* and *Allegro Brilliante,* Glen Tetley's *Voluntaries,* Bronoslava Nijinska's *Les Biches,* and portrayed the Accused (Lizzie Borden) in Agnes de Mille's dramatic *Fall River Legend.*

Johnson toured the world with DTH in her capacity as dance diva. During the late 1980s, Johnson was one of the first American ballerinas to visit the Soviet Union where she performed at the Kirov State Theater of Ballet and Opera in Leningrad. In the early 1990s, Johnson traveled to post apartheid South Africa with the DTH where she strove to be an ambassador of change through the beauty of dance.

Among her television presentations, Johnson has danced in Public Broadcasting Service's (PBS) *Dance in America* series and performed *Creole Giselle* for NBC. She also danced in and choreographed the television film *Ancient Voices of Children*.

Johnson continued to received accolades for her roles in the 1990s: as the Accused (Lizzie Borden) in *Fall River Legend* with the Cleveland Ballet in 1991, and as Blanche in *A Streetcar Named Desire* at the Dance Theater of Harlem's 25th anniversary season at Lincoln Center in New York City in 1994.

On September 21, 1997, Virginia Johnson retired from the stage at age 47. For 28 years as the Dance Theater of Harlem's prima ballerina, she brought to her dramatic performances great sensitivity, an intense ferocity, and total generosity to her company and her audiences.

Bill T. Jones (1952–)
Dancer, Choreographer

Jones was born into a family of 12 children in Florida in the early 1950s; eventually his migrant worker parents moved north to New York, where Jones excelled in high school athletics. Jones enrolled in the State University of New York at Binghampton in the early 1970s with the hope of pursuing a career in theater. He was already an accomplished actor, but eventually transferred into the university's dance department. While in college, Jones developed a romantic relationship with fellow dancer Arnie Zane.

Jones and Arnie Zane left Binghampton for the wider pastures of Amsterdam for several years; when they returned to New York City, they founded the American Dance Asylum, whose early mid-1970s performances caused a stir because of the dancers's onstage nudity. Next, Jones and Zane formed a more accessible dance company in 1982. They named the troupe after themselves, and one of their first performances that year earned critical praise at the Brooklyn Academy of Music's innovative Next Wave Festival.

The Bill T. Jones/Arnie Zane dance company continued to thrive until Zane fell ill with AIDS; the principal's inability to tour almost ended the troupe's existence financially, and his death in 1988 added greatly to Jones's burden. However, Jones was able to use the grief to create a dance opus paying homage to his longtime partner, and the 1989 debut of *Absence* received laudatory reviews. The death of another member of the company resulted in another work that addressed issues of loss due to AIDS within the artistic community, *D-Man in the Waters*.

Jones has also addressed issues of the African American cultural experience, especially as experienced by those of alternative sexual orientation, in such productions as *Last Supper at Uncle Tom's Cabin*. He has been candid about his own status as an HIV-positive person. In 1994 he was awarded a MacArthur Foundation fellowship; the following year saw the premier of *Still/Here* at the Brooklyn Academy of Music. Jones co-authored a book, 1995's *Last Night on Earth*, and collaborated with jazz drummer Max Roach and novelist Toni Morrison on a dance piece entitled *Degga* performed at Lincoln Center that same year as well. Later, *Still/Here* became the subject of media sniping between Jones and *New Yorker* writer Arlene Croce, who termed it "victim art" in early 1996. Jones asserted that the New York media is biased in favor of Jewish matters. In 1997, Jones spoke to the American Dance Therapy Association members at their annual conference about the use of such works as *Still/Here* in dance therapy.

Jones has continued to create such works as *Ursonata* whose name comes from a poem by Dada artist Kurt Schwitters. Another work uses poems recorded by Dylan Thomas. Avant-garde musician Laurie Anderson was commissioned to score his *Harriet and Rhonda Ten Rounds*. In January of 1999, Jones staged *We Set Out Early Visibility Was Poor*, a new work exposing a more ecstatic and less political side of his work. It is symbolic and lyric, mixed with a marked desire for peace after the pain of loss. Jones continues to reach into his emotional life to manifest his art.

Martin Lawrence
Comedian, Actor

Martin Lawrence was born in Frankfurt, West Germany, in the mid-1960s. He grew up in Landover, Maryland, and would entertain his mother as a child. Intent on achieving stardom, he appeared on the talent forum "Star Search," but did not immediately meet with success. In New York City's Greenwich Village, he would tell jokes for handouts.

He went to Hollywood and appeared in the sitcom "What's Happening Now!" before being selected for a role in Spike Lee's popular film *Do the Right Thing*. In the early 1990s he appeared in the films *House Party* (1990), *Talkin' Dirty after Dark* (1991), and *Boomerang* (1992).

Lawrence's comedic style earned him a sitcom "Martin" on network television. In the series (which ran from 1992 to 1997), Lawrence played a disc jockey, whose on-air confidence was at odds with his less successful personal life. In addition to playing the title character, Lawrence also played the character's mother and Shenehneh, an outspoken young woman. For his role, Lawrence won an NAACP Image Award in 1996.

Although Lawrence continues to appear in movies including *Life* (1999) with co-star Eddie Murphy, he has earned unfortunate publicity for various scrapes with authority. In 1996, for instance, he was arrested for attempting to bring a handgun on an airplane.

Lawrence was married briefly to Patricia Southall in the mid-1990s.

Jackie "Moms" Mabley (1894–1975)
Comedienne

Mabley was born Loretta Mary Aiken in Brevard, North Carolina, on March 19, 1894, and entered show business as a teenager when the team of Buck and Bubbles gave her a bit part in a vaudeville skit called "Rich Aunt from Utah."

With the help of comedienne Bonnie Bell Drew, Mabley developed a monologue, and was soon being booked on the black vaudeville circuit. Influenced by such acts as Butterbeans and Susie, she developed her own comic character, a world-weary old woman in a funny hat and droopy stockings, delivering her gags with a mixture of sassy folk wisdom and sly insights.

Her first big success came in 1923 at Connie's Inn in New York. Engagements at the Cotton Club in Harlem and Club Harlem in Atlantic City followed.

Moms Mabley was discovered by white audiences in the early 1960s. Her record album *Moms Mabley at the U.N.* became a commercial success and was followed by *Moms Mabley at the Geneva Conference.* In 1962, she made her Carnegie Hall debut on a program with Cannonball Adderley and Nancy Wilson. Her subsequent Broadway, film, television, and record successes made her the favorite of a new generation.

Moms Mabley died on May 23, 1975, at the age of 78 in a White Plains, New York, hospital.

Audra McDonald (1970–)
Singer, Actress

Audra McDonald is one of the American theater's outstanding performers. Within only a few years, she has won three Tony Awards as featured or supporting actress for her work in *Carousel* in 1994, *The Master Class* in 1996, and *Ragtime* in 1998.

McDonald was born in Berlin, Germany, on July 3, 1970, and grew up in Fresno, California, as part of a musical family. Her parents were trained singers and her aunts toured with a gospel singing group. McDonald's professional career began at age nine when she performed in dinner theater for young people. She played roles in *Hello, Dolly!*, *A Chorus Line*, *Grease*, and *The Wiz.* After graduating from the Roosevelt School of the Performing Arts in Fresno, McDonald enrolled at the prestigious Juilliard School of Music in Manhattan. However, since Broadway was always McDonald's first love, she was discontented at the classically oriented Juilliard. She took a break from her studies and landed a role in *The Secret Garden*, both on Broadway and in the touring company. She eventually went back to Juilliard and completed a bachelor's degree in 1993.

McDonald auditioned several times until she landed a role in the extravagant production of *Carousel*, staged at the Lincoln Center in 1994. She won critical praise for her role as Carrie Pipperidge, as well as the Tony, Drama Desk, Outer Critics Circle and Theatre World awards that year. Her next star turn was as Sharon, an aspiring singer in conflict with the great opera diva Maria Callas in *The Master Class.* In the show, Sharon sings a technically demanding aria from Giuseppi Verdi's *Macbeth*, a feat brilliantly carried off by McDonald. She earned her second Tony Award for her performance as best featured actress in a play.

Next, McDonald won a part in one of the most ambitious productions in Toronto and New York in 1997, the musical *Ragtime* based on E. L. Doctorow's best-selling 1975 novel about New York at the turn of the century. Her character, Sarah, a young black washerwoman who abandons her illegitimate child, is a relatively small but pivotal part. McDonald won her third Tony Award for best featured actress in a musical category in 1998.

McDonald continues to expand her scope of musical projects. In the autumn of 1998, McDonald released her debut solo album *Way Back to Paradise*, featuring new songs by some of the promising young musical theater composers writing today. She regularly performs her musical repertoire at the cabaret at the Joseph Papp Public Theater. Her biggest challenge in 1999 is the production of her own musical, a show called *Marie Christine*, based on *Medea* and set in New Orleans and Chicago in the 1880s. The show is being written by Michael John LaChiusa, one of the composers featured on her new CD. *Marie Christine* is scheduled to open sometime in 1999 at Lincoln Center, bringing Audra McDonald's talents before an appreciative audience once again.

Bebe Miller (1950–)
Choreographer, Dancer, Artistic Director

Bebe Miller was born on September 20, 1950, to an elementary school teacher and a ship steward. Although she grew up in the housing projects of South Brooklyn, New York, her arthritic mother took the family to adult dance classes at Manhattan's Henry Street Settlement every Saturday. Soon, Miller was learning creative dance from Murray Louis and Alwin Nikolais who taught children's dance classes there. Miller went on to take traditional ballet classes at the Carnegie Hall school at the age of 13. She soon stopped, unhappy with the formality of classic dance styles.

Miller resumed taking modern dance when she was twenty and studied fine arts at Earlham College in Richmond, Indiana. After graduating from Earlham in 1971, she moved back to New York to resume dance classes with Nikolais. She won a fellowship to study dance at Ohio State University in Columbus and earned a master's degree from there in 1975.

Two years later Miller joined the modern dance company of Nina Wiener, who had studied with Alvin Ailey and Twyla Tharp, and for six years was inspired by Wiener to infuse her technique with fun and intensity. Soon she was creating her own dances, and performing her group and solo pieces at New York City workshops devoted to developing modern dance choreographers. She left Weiner's company in 1982 and formed the Bebe Miller Company two years later.

Miller's dances have always reflected her inner and outer struggles. Her 1984 dance *Trapped in Queens* shows the difficulties of city life. *Two*, her collaborative duet with dancer Ralph Lemon, examines the changing relationships between men and women. Some of the black influences she brings to her dances show up in the accompanying music. She has used reggae (*Jammin'* 1981), gospel (*Heart, Heart* 1986), Duke Ellington (*Spending Time Doing Things* mid-1980s), and Jimmie Hendrix (*The Hendrix Project* 1991) as accompaniment. In addition to music, Miller collaborates with writers, set designers, and visual artists to create her unique performance pieces.

Miller and her company spent much of the mid-1980s touring throughout the United States and earning numerous accolades. She won four National Endowment for the Arts Choreographer's Fellowships, the New York Dance and Performance Award ("Bessie") for choreography for 1986 and 1987, and the American Choreographer Award and John Guggenheim Memorial Fellowship in 1988.

Alvin Ailey commissioned Miller to create new works for his Alvin Ailey Repertory Ensemble in 1987. Miller produced her series of dances called *Habit of Attraction* the next year, another look at the mysteries of relationships. Another work *Allies* was commissioned in 1989 in part by New York's Brooklyn Academy of Music. This was Miller's first appearance at the Academy's Next Wave festival and allowed her to work on a larger scale. *Allies* again studied human interaction and evolving relationships. Alongside *Allies*, Miller danced her signature solo *Rain* which describes in movement some of Miller's own social and spiritual views.

Her 1991 work *The Hendrix Project* tied music by Jimmie Hendrix and Bob Dylan and the vision of the 1960s to the cultural issues of the 1990s. It was danced in Los Angeles and San Francisco in a program titled *Black Choreographers Moving Towards the 21st Century*. Bebe Miller Company then took it to New York and Europe.

In 1993, Bebe Miller conducted a residency class at Walker Art Centre in Minneapolis which performed her work *In Mnemosyne's House, Again and Again* for which she collaborated with environmental sculptor Eve Laramie and the Minneapolis New Dance. The mid-1990s saw the premieres of *Tiny Sisters*, *Yard Dance*, *Heaven and Earth*, and *Blessed*.

In recent years, Miller has been investigating the combination of theatrical narrative and abstract movement to express the human condition through the physical body. Her newest work in progress, *Map of the Body*, is being developed as part of a master's class in September of 1999.

Florence Mills (1896–1927)
Singer, Dancer

Florence Mills was born in Washington, DC, on January 25, 1896. She made her debut there at the age of five in *Sons of Ham*. In 1903, the family moved to Harlem, and in 1910 she joined her sisters in an act called the Mills Trio. She later appeared with a group called the Panama Four, which included Ada "Bricktop" Smith.

In 1921, Mills appeared in *Shuffle Along*, a prototype for African American musicals, and her success led to a long engagement at the Plantation, a New York night spot. After a successful appearance in London, she returned to the United States in 1924 to star in *From Dixie to Broadway*, in which she performed her trademark song "I'm Just a Little Blackbird Lookin' for a Bluebird." Later, her own *Blackbirds* revue was a great success in London and Paris.

Mills returned to the United States in 1927. Exhausted by her work abroad, she entered the hospital on October 25 for a routine appendectomy, and died suddenly on November 1.

Abbie Mitchell (1884–1960)
Singer, Actress

Most celebrated as a concert artist, Abbie Mitchell also performed on the stage and in light musical comedy. At the age of 13, she returned to her native New York City from Baltimore, joining Will Marion Cook's Clorindy Company, and later achieving her first real success with the Williams and Walker Company.

By 1923, having performed in almost every European country, Mitchell returned home to give the first of her many voice concerts in the United States. Mitchell also performed with many opera companies and acted in several plays including *Coquette* (with Helen Hayes; 1927), *Stevedore* (1934) and Langston Hughes's *Mulatto* (1937). She also headed the voice department at Tuskegee Institute for three years.

Arthur Mitchell (1934–)
Dancer, Choreographer

Mitchell was born in Harlem on March 27, 1934, and attended New York's famed High School of the Performing Arts. Mitchell was the first African American male to receive the high school's dance award in 1951.

Upon graduation in 1952, Mitchell enrolled as a scholarship student in the School of American Ballet, run by the eminent choreographer George Balanchine, who also directed the New York City Ballet. In 1955, Mitchell was invited by Balanchine to join the New York City Ballet. Before long, he was a principal dancer in the company, performing in such works as *Agon* and *A Midsummer Night's Dream.*

Mitchell left the New York City Ballet in 1969 to establish the Dance Theater of Harlem, which he founded to give young African Americans an opportunity to get out of the ghetto through the arts. Mitchell and the studio have received numerous awards and citations including the Changers Award given by *Mademoiselle* magazine in 1970 and the Capezio Dance Award in 1971. Surviving a financial crisis in 1990, the school and company are now back on their feet, though treading carefully due to the precarious state of the arts in the United States.

In 1993, New York City Mayor David Dinkins presented Mitchell with the Handel Medallion, the city's highest cultural honor. He was also one of the winners of the Kennedy Center Honors and the National Medal of Arts in 1993. The School of American Ballet presented Mitchell with a lifetime achievement award at its annual dinner on February 6, 1995.

Eddie Murphy (1961–)
Actor, Comedian

Eddie Murphy was born on April 3, 1961, in the Bushwick section of Brooklyn, the son of a New York City policeman and amateur comedian. As a youngster, he did imitations of cartoon characters and, as he grew older, began preparing comic routines with impressions of Elvis Presley, Jackie Wilson, Al Green, and the Beatles.

Murphy attended Roosevelt Junior-Senior High School on Long Island and hosted a talent show at the Roosevelt Youth Center before beginning to call local talent agents to secure bookings at Long Island nightclubs. He was a little known stand-up comedian when he made his first appearance on the late-night television show "Saturday Night Live" in 1980. He made a memorable impression, and within three years was hailed as a major new star based on his work in the hit films *48 Hours* (1982) and *Trading Places* (1983).

Eddie Murphy (Archive Photos, Inc.)

After his success with the first two Paramount films, Murphy starred in *Beverly Hills Cop* (1985) and its sequel *Beverly Hills Cop II* (1987), which were two of the major box-office hits of the decade. The concert film *Raw* followed, as well as an effort at light-hearted fantasy *The Golden Child.*

Murphy's more recent film appearances include: *Coming to America; Harlem Nights; Another 48 Hours; Boomerang; The Distinguished Gentleman; Beverly Hills Cop III; Vampire in Brooklyn;* and *Bowfinger.*

In the 1990s, Murphy has appeared in the comedies *The Nutty Professor, Dr. Dolittle,* and *Life.* He also provides the voice for the main character in television's "The PJs," an animated sitcom that takes a satirical look at life in a housing project. In 1993, Murphy married model Nicole Mitchell.

Fayard (1914–) and Harold (1924–) Nicholas
Dancers

The Nicholas Brothers were one of the great tap dance teams of the first half of the twentieth century. Their acrobatics and precision were admired by the likes of Fred Astaire and George Balanchine, and their appearances in motion pictures provide a record of their astounding abilities.

Fayard Nicholas was born in 1914; Harold in 1924. Their professional debut was, ironically, on the radio program "The Horn and Hardart Kiddie Hour" in 1931. In 1932, they became a featured act at Harlem's Cotton Club. They made their first Broadway appearance in the *Ziegfeld Follies* of 1936; this was followed by *Babes in Arms* in 1937.

The Nicholas Brothers's film debut was in *Pie Pie Blackbird* in 1932, and they appeared in several other movies in the 1930s and 1940s including *The Big Broadcast of 1936* (1936), *The Great American Broadcast* (1941), *Sun Valley Serenade* (1941), *Stormy Weather* (1943), and *The Pirate* (1948). The latter is particularly memorable for the sequence in which they are featured.

Harold Nicholas married actress Dorothy Dandridge in 1942, but the couple later divorced. The two brothers continue to be active in the world of dance: Harold co-starred with Gregory Hines in the movie *Tap* in 1989, and Fayard won a Tony Award for best choreographer for the Broadway musical *Black and Blue* in the same year. In 1992, the Nicholas Brothers were honored by the Kennedy Center. They received awards from *Dance Magazine* in 1995. A gala for the Nicholas Brothers was celebrated at Carnegie Hall in April of 1998 called *From Harlem to Hollywood: A Tribute to the Nicholas Brothers, "Tap Legends."* It starred Gregory Hines, Lena Horne, Savion Glover, Maya Angelou, Maurice Hines, Ben Vereen, and Jimmy Slide, representing the many generations influenced and inspired by these "Tap Legends."

Frederick O'Neal (1905–1992)
Actor

Frederick O'Neal was the first black person to hold the position of president of Actor's Equity, a fitting tribute to his long years of service to the American theater as both actor and teacher.

O'Neal was born on August 27, 1905 in Brookville, Mississippi. After his father's death in 1919, he moved with his family to St. Louis, finishing high school there and appearing in several Urban League dramatic productions.

In 1927, with the help of some friends in St. Louis, O'Neal founded the Ira Aldridge Players, the second African American acting troupe in America. For the next ten years, he played in thirty of its productions. In 1937, he came to New York, and three years later helped found the American Negro Theater. Today, its alumni include such established stars as Sidney Poitier, Earle Hyman, Harry Belafonte, Ruby Dee, Ossie Davis, and Hilda Simms.

O'Neal himself starred in *Anna Lucasta* (1944), for which he won the Clarence Derwent Award and the Drama Critics Award for the best supporting performance by an actor on Broadway. He was later featured in *Take a Giant Step*, *The Winner*, and several other stage productions. His films include *Pinky* (1949) and *The Man with the Golden Arm* (1956). He also appeared on several televised dramatic and comedy shows.

In 1964, O'Neal became the first black president of Actor's Equity. After devoting himself full-time to Actor's Equity, O'Neal was in 1970 elected international president of the Associated Actors and Artists of America, the parent union of all show business performers's unions. He became president and chairman of the board of the Schomburg Center for Research in Black Culture, a position which included such responsibilities as raising money to conserve and preserve materials in the center, soliciting resources for the institution, and lobbying for the construction of a new building. He was a member of the New York State Council on the Arts, President of the Catholic Interracial Council, chairman of the AFL-CIO Civil Rights Committee, and vice president of the A. Philip Randolph Institute. In 1980, he received the National Urban Coalition's Distinguished Trade Unionist Award. In 1990, he received a special tribute from the Black Filmmakers Hall of Fame. O'Neal died on April 27, 1992.

Pearl Primus (1919–1994)
Dancer, Choreographer

Pearl Primus's anthropological approach to dance made her one of the most purposeful figures in that medium: for her, dance was education, not merely entertainment. Her aim was to show audiences and dancers alike the African roots of dance and to bring the African American experience alive.

Primus was born in Trinidad on November 29, 1919. Originally intending to pursue a career in medicine, she received a bachelor of arts degree in pre-medical sciences and biology from Hunter College, with graduate work in medical education and psychology. But 1940s America did not welcome blacks or women in medicine, and after seeking employment in vain, Primus sought assistance from the government's National Youth Administration. She was put into a youth administration dance group, and by 1941 was accepted into New York City's New Dance Group. Her professional debut was at the Young Men's Hebrew Association in New York City on February 14, 1943. In April of that year, she began appearing at Café Society Downtown, the famed New York City nightclub, but left after ten months for an appearance on Broadway at the Belasco Theater. By this time she had her own dance company, Pearl Primus, Percival Borde, and Company. She toured Africa and the southern United States, and incorporated what she learned into her dance style.

Primus is best known for the dances *African Ceremonial* and *Strange Fruit*, which were incorporated into her *Solos for Performance at the Café Society* (ca. 1944) and *Hard Times Blues* (1945).

Primus died on October 29, 1994.

Richard Pryor (1940–)
Comedian, Actor

Comedian Richard Pryor has had great success as a stand-up comedian, writer, actor, and recording star. He has often used elements of his unconventional upbringing and adult life as material in his comedy routines.

Born Richard Franklin Lennox Thomas Pryor III on December 1, 1940, in New York City, he was raised by his grandmother in the Peoria, Illinois, brothel she ran. His mother worked there as a prostitute. His parents married when he was three years old, but the union did not last. His grandmother was a strict disciplinarian and young Richard was often beaten.

In school Pryor was often in trouble with the authorities. Pryor was expelled from high school for striking a teacher. In 1958 he joined the army and spent two years in Germany. He returned to Peoria after his military service and during the early 1960s began his work as a stand-up comic on a local circuit. He moved to New York City's Greenwich Village in 1963 where he honed his stand-up routine. A 1964 appearance on "The Ed Sullivan Show" led to his first movie role in *The Busy Body* (1966), followed by bit parts in *The Green Berets* and *Wild in the Streets*. During this time Pryor continued to play to live audiences.

In 1972, Pryor played Piano Man in *Lady Sings the Blues* and earned an Academy Award nomination for his performance. Throughout the 1970s, Pryor continued his work as a stand-up comic and also contributed his writing talents to television's "The Flip Wilson Show" and "Sanford and Son," Mel Brooks's film *Blazing Saddles*, and Lily Tomlin's television special "Lily" for which he won an Emmy Award. He won two of his five Grammy Awards for his comedy albums *That Nigger's Crazy* (1974) and *Bicentennial Nigger* (1976).

Pryor wrote and starred in *Bingo Long and the Traveling All Stars and Motor Kings* (1976) and received raves for his work in *Silver Streak* (also 1976). In 1979, the comedian's film *Richard Pryor Live in Concert* brought his stand-up act to millions.

In 1978, Pryor suffered a major heart attack, and in 1980, while freebasing cocaine, he set himself ablaze and suffered severe injuries. He addresses these incidents in his second concert movie *Live on Sunset Strip* (1982). In 1985 Pryor co-wrote, directed and starred in *Jo Jo Dancer, Your Life Is Calling*, a semi-autobiographical tale of a comedian who relives his life immediately following a near fatal accident. Pryor's later films include: *The Toy; Some Kind of Hero; Brewster's Millions; Critical Condition; Stir Crazy; Bustin' Loose; Moving;* and *See No Evil, Hear No Evil.* In 1989 Pryor co-starred with Eddie Murphy in *Harlem Nights*. He teamed with Gene Wilder in the 1991 film *Another You* and appeared in *Lost Highway* later in the decade.

Pryor has been in failing health in recent years. He was diagnosed with multiple sclerosis in 1986 and has had triple bypass heart surgery. He is reportedly often wheelchair bound and lives a reclusive life in his Bel Air, California, home. In 1993, Pryor was awarded with a star on the Hollywood Walk of Fame.

In 1995, Pryor's collection of memoirs *Pryor Convictions—and Other Life Sentences* was published, detailing his difficult childhood, failed marriages, and battles with cocaine addiction and multiple sclerosis.

Lloyd Richards (1923?–)
Theatrical Director, Educator

Lloyd Richards, renowned actor, stage director, and educator, was born in Toronto, Ontario, in the early 1920s. He moved to Detroit while still young where he worked to support his family and eventually studied at Wayne State University, first law and then theater, receiving his degree in 1944. After serving in World War II as one of the first black pilots, he returned to Detroit and became active in radio drama and regional theater.

Soon Richards moved to New York to earn a living acting in plays and television dramas and coaching others in his own studio. In 1959, Sidney Poitier convinced him to direct an important Broadway play, Lorraine Hansberry's classic story *A Raisin in the Sun*. This play, the first by a black woman to be produced on Broadway, explores issues of segregation, thwarted ambition, and family tensions. It ran for 530 performances and made its stars and Richards famous. In the wake of that success, Richards began teaching drama at Hunter College and New York University.

In 1966, Richards was named director of the prestigious playwrights's conference at the Eugene O'Neill Theater in Waterford, Connecticut. He continued to nurture and produce new plays for regional theaters by such promising playwrights as August Wilson, Athol Fugard, John Patrick Shanley, Charles Fuller, and David Henry Hwang. In 1979, Richards became dean of the Yale School of Drama and artistic director of the Yale Repertory Theater.

Many famous plays debuted at the Yale Repertory Theater under Richards's direction. These include South African playwright Athol Fugard's *Master Harold . . . and the Boys* and two Pulitzer Prize-winning works by August Wilson, *Fences* and *The Piano Lesson*. He won the Tony Award for best director for *Fences* in 1986.

Richards's most creative partnership was with playwright Wilson for whom he directed, not only *Fences* and *The Piano Lesson*, but also *Ma Rainey's Black Bottom*, *Joe Turner's Come and Gone*, and *Two Trains Running*, for which he was awarded the Helen Hayes Award for best director in 1992.

The Yale Repertory Theater also attracted a number of notable actors while Richards was in residence including James Earl Jones, Glenn Close, Jason Robards, and Colleen Dewhurst. In 1979, Richards directed Jones in a one-man show about the life and career of black actor Paul Robeson.

Lloyd Richards left the Yale Repertory Theater in 1991 after twelve years as dean and artistic director. However, he continued to direct, lecture, and mentor new talent in the theater. In 1995, he directed a Hallmark Hall of Fame production of *The Piano Lesson* for television, starring Charles S. Dutton and Alfre Woodard.

Among his many honors, Richards was inducted into the Theater Hall of Fame in 1990. Other distinctions include the Directors Award from the National Black Theatre Festival, a National Medal of Arts from President Bill Clinton in 1993, the Huntington Award for lifetime achievement in 1995 and a 1996 Outer Critics Award for best director of Wilson's latest play *Seven Guitars*.

Bill "Bojangles" Robinson performing with Shirley Temple in the movie *The Little Colonel* in 1935 (AP/Wide World Photos, Inc.).

Bill "Bojangles" Robinson (1878–1949)

Dancer

Bill Robinson was born in May of 1878, in Richmond, Virginia. Having been orphaned early, he was raised by his grandmother, a former slave. By the time he was eight, he was earning his own way by dancing in the street for pennies and working as a stable boy.

In 1887, Robinson toured the South in a show called *The South Before the War*. The following year, he moved to Washington, DC, where he again worked as a stable boy. By 1896, he had teamed up with George Cooper. This act was successful on the Keith circuit until the slump of 1907 caused it to fold. Robinson returned to Richmond and worked as a waiter until a year later when he was taken up by a theatrical manager and became a cabaret and vaudeville headliner.

In 1927, Robinson starred on Broadway in *Blackbirds*, and in 1932 he had top billing in *Harlem's Heaven*, the first all-black motion picture with sound. Later, he scored a Hollywood success by teaching his famous stair dance to Shirley Temple in *The Little Colonel* (1936). Robinson made 14 movies including *The Littlest Rebel* (1935), *In Old Kentucky* (1936), *Rebecca of Sunnybrook Farm* (1938), *Stormy Weather* (1943), and *One Mile from Heaven* (1938).

Throughout his long career on stage and in movies, Robinson was known as the "King of Tap Dancers." Robinson died on November 15, 1949.

Chris Rock (1967?–)

Comedian, Actor

Chris Rock was born in the late 1960s in Brooklyn, New York. He grew up in the mostly black neighbor-

Chris Rock holding two Emmy Awards in 1997 (AP/Wide World Photos, Inc.).

hood of Bedford-Stuyvesant, but because of a busing policy, he attended school in the predominantly white neighborhood of Bensonhurst. At school Rock had to endure everyday abuse from prejudiced classmates.

Supported by his family, Rock began a stand-up career at a young age. He caught a break when one of his ideals, Eddie Murphy, saw his routine and cast him in *Beverly Hills Cop II.* The role led to another in *I'm Gonna Git You Sucka*, a satire of blaxploitation films of the 1970s. In 1990 Rock auditioned for *Saturday Night Live* and earned a spot on the cast. On the show, Rock became known for his outspoken commentaries during the weekly send-up of the nightly news and for such characters as the talk show host Nat X.

In 1993 Rock left "Saturday Night Live" and became a member of the cast of "In Living Color." He felt more comfortable on the set of the new show, which provided more opportunities to satirize situations involving African American characters. The show only lasted for one season with Rock as a member of the cast, however. After appearing in *CB4*, a movie about the rap industry that he co-wrote, Rock's career entered a dormant period during which his father died. During the off-time, Rock studied the work of other comedians he respected, including Bill Cosby, Eddie Murphy, Richard Pryor, Woody Allen, and Don Rickles.

In the late 1990s Rock found an audience on cable television. He was a popular host of the "MTV Music Video Awards," served as the 1996 presidential election correspondent for Comedy Central's "Politically Incorrect," and earned two Emmy Awards for his comedy special "Bring the Pain." He currently has a series "The Chris Rock Show" on the network.

Rock married public relations executive Malaak Compton in 1996.

Sinbad (1956–)
Comedian, Actor

The 6-foot, 5-inch Sinbad has delighted audiences with his comedy, which combines street parlance—noticeably free of obscenities—with tales of American life. Born David Adkins on November 10, 1956, in Benton Harbor, Michigan, Sinbad aspired to be a basketball star. He earned a basketball scholarship to the University of Denver, but a serious knee injury caused him to give up basketball, and he left college in 1978. Shortly thereafter, he renamed himself Sinbad, after the heroic character in *The Arabian Nights*, to boost his spirits. He spent three and a half years in the U.S. Air Force, hating every minute until his 1983 discharge.

By that time, Sinbad had decided to try his hand at stand-up comedy. A series of low-paying engagements throughout the United States followed, and his break came when he appeared on the television talent contest "Star Search" seven times in the mid-1980s. He later worked as a warm-up comedian for "The Cosby Show," and in 1989 he was cast as dorm director Walter Oakes on "A Different World"—a role that was broadened in 1991 when Oakes became a counselor. In 1993, Sinbad starred in his own situation comedy "The Sinbad Show" about a single foster parent. The show only lasted one season. He appeared in the movie *Houseguest* in 1995.

Noble Sissle (1889–1975)
Lyricist, Singer

Noble Sissle was born in Indianapolis, Indiana, on July 10, 1889. He reaped his early successes teamed up with the great Eubie Blake. Sissle wrote the lyrics and sang them in performance; Blake composed and played the music. Together the two created such songs as "I'm Just Wild about Harry," "It's All Your Fault," "Serenade Blues," and "Love Will Find a Way."

In 1921 *Shuffle Along*, the first black musical with a love theme, made Sissle and Blake famous. Joining forces with the writing and comedy team of Flournoy Miller and Aubrey Lyles, Sissle and Blake wrote the words and music to over a dozen songs for the show. *Shuffle Along* became a huge success in the United States and Europe, where it had a prolonged tour. As with most black performers in the early 1900s, Sissle and his troupe would have to travel as far as twenty or thirty miles out of their way to find a place to eat and sleep, since blacks were not welcome in the white hotels of the towns where they played.

Other Sissle and Blake shows included *Chocolate Dandies* (1924) and *Keep Shufflin'* (1928). Noble Sissle died December 17, 1975, at his home in Tampa, Florida.

Lynne Thigpen (1948?–)
Actress

Lynne Thigpen has spent more than 25 years proving that she could make a living working on stage, screen, and television as a professional actress. She grew up in Joliet, Illinois, "always a singer and always a performer." Her high school English teacher encouraged her theatrical pursuits so, after graduation, she enrolled at the University of Illinois in Champaign-Urbana, where she majored in English and speech. Although pursuing teaching certification, she won an acting fellowship to the University and began a master's degree in theater. After one semester, she left school for New York and Broadway.

Soon after arriving in New York, Thigpen landed a two-year role in the popular musical *Godspell* on Broadway which later led to a role in the 1973 film version. She then worked as a musical performer in various stage productions including *Tintypes*, for which she earned a Tony nomination in 1980. Deciding that singing was not enough, Thigpen switched to acting and won recurring roles on such television shows as "All My Children," "L.A. Law," and "Law and Order." Family shows such as "The Cosby Show," "Dear John," and "Roseanne" showcased her comedic talents. She also appeared in many films, among them, *The Warriors*, *Tootsie*, *The Paper*, *Lean on Me*, and *Bob Roberts*.

Serious drama highlighted Thigpen's versatile talents. In 1988, she won the Los Angeles Drama Critic's Award for her role opposite James Earl Jones in August Wilson's *Fences*. She was also honored with an Obie Award for her portrayal of an itinerant South African woman in Athol Fugard's *Bozeman and Lena* in 1992.

In the 1990s, Thigpen was probably best known for her role as the Chief on the Public Broadcasting Service (PBS) children's show *Where in the World Is Carmen Sandiego?* Over her six years in this series, she was nominated four times for Emmys as outstanding performer in a daytime children's television series. In 1999, she filmed a guest part as the head of WASA (the Worms' Air and Space Agency) for *The Muppet Show*.

Thigpen was named associate artistic director of the Circle Repertory Company in New York City in 1995, along with Austin Pendleton, only to decline it a few months later to continue acting full-time. She played the role of a childless Jewish African American woman in Wendy Wasserstein's *An American Daughter* in 1996, winning the 1997 Tony Award for best featured actress.

Thigpen's voice alone has won her recognition. She has narrated numerous documentaries for PBS. She was heard on radio on *The Garrison Keillor Show*. Listeners of books on tape know her melodic voice from thoughtful narrations of works such as *The Autobiography of Miss Jane Pittman*, *Roll of Thunder, Hear My Cry*, *One Better*, and other audio productions.

Lynne Thigpen continues to prove that stretching one's creative muscles in the performing arts can shape a varied and viable career.

Leslie Uggams (1943–)
Singer, Actress

Born in the Washington Heights section of New York City on May 25, 1943, Leslie Uggams enjoyed a comfortable childhood. She made her singing debut at the age of

Leslie Uggams (AP/Wide World Photos, Inc.)

six, performing with the choir of St. James Presbyterian Church in New York. Shortly thereafter she debuted as an actress in the television series "Beulah." A year later, Uggams began performing regularly at the famed Apollo Theatre in Harlem, opening for such legends as Louis Armstrong, Ella Fitzgerald, and Dinah Washington. Uggams developed her poise and stage presence early in life, attending the Professional Children's School, where she was chosen student body president in her senior year.

Uggams subsequently won $25,000 on the popular television quiz show "Name That Tune," which renewed her interest in a singing career. In 1961, while studying at Juilliard, Uggams became a regular on "The Mitch Miller Show," a variety show featuring old favorites. She was at the time the only black performer appearing regularly on network television.

Throughout the 1960s, Uggams appeared in numerous nightclubs and had several supper club and television engagements. Her big break came when she was signed as a replacement for Lena Horne in *Hallelujah Baby*, a show that presented a musical chronicle of the civil rights movement. Uggams won instant stardom and received a Tony Award for her performance.

In 1977, Uggams appeared as Kizzy in the television adaptation of Alex Haley's novel *Roots*. In May 1982, she performed in a new Broadway show *Blues in the Night* at the Rialto Theater in New York City. She has also appeared on television in "Backstairs at the White House," a miniseries, and "The Book of Lists," in the film *Skyjacked*, and in the musicals *Jerry's Girls*, *The Great Gershwin*, and *Anything Goes*.

After touring during the early 1990s in *Stringbean*, a musical based on the career of Ethel Waters, Uggams joined the cast of the hit daytime soap opera "All My Children" in 1996. In 1995 she released her latest recording *Painted Mem'ries*. More recently, Uggams appeared at Primary Stages in New York in the title role of the well-reviewed play *The Old Settler* by John Henry Redwood in October of 1998.

Ben Augustus Vereen (1946–)
Dancer, Actor

Ben Vereen was born October 10, 1946, in Miami, Florida. After his family moved to the Bedford-Stuyvesant section of Brooklyn, New York, he attended the High School of Performing Arts in Manhattan. His dancing ability had been discovered almost accidentally after he had been sent to dance school by his mother. Vereen has since been called America's premier song and dance man.

Ben Vereen made his stage debut in 1965 in *The Prodigal Son*. He went on to appear in *Sweet Charity* (1966), *Golden Boy* (1968), *Hair* (1968), and *No Place to Be Somebody* (1970). Vereen is best known for his Broadway role in *Pippin* (1972), which won him a Tony Award. He was also nominated for a Tony for his costarring role in *Jesus Christ Superstar* (1971). His film appearances include roles in *Funny Lady* (1975), *All That Jazz* (1979), and *The Zoo Gang*.

Vereen has starred in the ABC comedy series "Tenspeed and Brown Shoe" and is known for his television specials; the highly acclaimed "Ben Vereen—His Roots" (1978) won seven Emmy Awards. He also portrayed Louis "Satchmo" Armstrong and received wide acclaim for his role of Chicken George in television's adaption of Alex Haley's *Roots* (1977) and for his performance in *Jubilee*.

His concert tour in the late 1990s earned Vereen the highest honors awarded by the American Guild of Variety Artists: "Entertainer of the Year," "Rising Star," and "Song and Dance Star." He is the first person to win three of these AGVA awards in one year.

In 1994, Vereen announced plans to start the Ben Vereen School of the Performing Arts in Chicago. The school is designed to help students improve their artistic talents and provide positive alternatives to gangs and drugs.

Fredi Washington (1903–1994)
Actress, Dancer, Civil Rights Activist

Born Fredericka Carolyn Washington in Savannah, Georgia, on December 23, 1903, Washington and her younger sister were sent to a convent after the death of their mother and subsequent remarriage of their father. As a teenager, she left this sheltered world to live with relatives in New York City in order to pursue a career in the performing arts.

One of Washington's first big breaks came in 1919 when she was cast as a member of the Happy Honeysuckles, the back-up troupe for Josephine Baker. Two years later she began earning a good salary in the stage production of an all-black musical called *Shuffle Along.* Washington was next discovered by Broadway impresario Lee Shubert, who urged her to audition for a play called *Black Boy.* In the 1926 production, she starred—under the stage name Edith Warren—opposite Paul Robeson, but unfortunately much media and audience attention at its debut was focused on Washington's light complexion. Indeed, she was often able to pass as white, especially when traveling in the segregated areas of the South with her first husband, a member of Duke Ellington's orchestra.

During the 1920s Washington continued to appear in stage roles and toured Europe for a time; she also appeared in the 1930 production of *Sweet Chariot.* Moving on to film, Washington again teamed with Robeson when she appeared in the 1933 drama *The Emperor Jones*—but Hollywood censors insisted she wear makeup to darken her complexion during her love scenes with him. The following year Washington appeared in her most acclaimed role in the film *Imitation of Life,* portraying a young woman who forsakes her heritage in order to pass as white.

Unfortunately, Washington found her acting career stymied by a lack of roles for African American women in general and especially for ones with light complexions; she fought for many decades to reverse such attitudes in the film industry in Hollywood. In 1937 she founded the Negro Actors Guild of America, and wrote extensively on the subject for the New York City-based paper *The People's Voice* for which she served as theater critic and columnist. During the 1940s and 1950s she worked as a cast consultant on numerous African American-themed films in Hollywood and continued to appear in stage productions. She died on June 28, 1994, in Stamford, Connecticut.

Ethel Waters (1896–1977)
Actress, Singer

The distinguished career of Ethel Waters spanned half a century. She showed her versatility by contributing to virtually every entertainment medium—stage, screen, television, and recordings.

Ethel Waters was born on October 31, 1900, and spent most of her childhood in her hometown of Chester, Pennsylvania. By the age of 17, she was singing professionally at the Lincoln Theatre in Baltimore. During this early phase of her career, she became the first woman to perform W. C. Handy's "St. Louis Blues" on stage.

After several years in nightclubs and vaudeville, Waters made her Broadway debut in the 1927 review *Africana.* In 1930, she appeared in *Blackbirds,* and in 1931 and 1932 she starred in *Rhapsody in Black.* The following year she was featured with Clifton Webb and Marilyn Miller in Irving Berlin's *As Thousands Cheer.* In 1935, she co-starred with Bea Lillie in *At Home Abroad,* and three years later she played the lead in *Mamba's Daughters.*

In 1940, Waters appeared in the stage version of *Cabin in the Sky,* a triumph which she repeated in the 1943 movie version. Her other film appearances include: *Rufus Jones for President* (1931); *Tales of Manhattan* (1941); *Cairo* (1942); *Stage Door Canteen* (1943); and *Pinky* (1949).

Her autobiography *His Eye Is on the Sparrow* was a 1951 Book-of-the-Month Club selection. The title is taken from a song that she sang in her 1950 stage success *Member of the Wedding.*

Waters died on September 1, 1977, in Chatsburg, California.

Damon Wayans (1960–)
Comedian

Damon Wayans was born on September 4, 1960, in New York City. While growing up, Wayans wore leg braces and special shoes to correct problems caused by a foot deformity. As a result, he often found himself teased by fellow classmates. As an adolescent and young adult, he found himself in trouble with the law on a couple of occasions. He blamed the problems of his youth not on his family situation but on being involved with the wrong crowd of people.

In the 1980s Wayans turned to stand-up comedy. His brother Keenan Ivory Wayans was already gaining a following, and Damon quickly became popular on the circuit as well. Headlining appearances in clubs across the country eventually led to his film debut in *Beverly Hills Cop* (1984). In the mid-1980s Wayans was selected as a cast member on "Saturday Night Live." He returned to stand-up after one year and appeared in several films through the remainder of the 1980s including *Hollywood Shuffle* (1987), *Roxanne* (1987), *Punchline* (1988), and

Earth Girls Are Easy (1989), in which he starred as one of three aliens.

In the 1990s Wayans joined the cast of "In Living Color." The show, created by his brother Keenan Ivory Wayans, provided a platform for social commentary. The skits often featured characters that were members of groups that historically faced discrimination. Wayans portrayed a gay movie critic; Homey, a sad-faced, black clown that refused to kowtow to "the [white] man"; and Handyman, a physically challenged superhero.

After three seasons, Wayans left "In Living Color" to pursue film work. He served as the executive producer of *Mo' Money*, a film that he wrote. Wayans also played the main character in the romantic comedy, which tells the story of a man who tries to turn from a life of crime in order to pursue a relationship with a coworker. Wayans appeared in a number of other films in the 1990 including *Major Payne* (1994), *Blankman* (1994), *Celtic Pride* (1996), and *The Great White Hype* (1996). In several of these films, Wayans also served in additional capacities as writer and executive producer.

Wayans returned to television in the 1990s. He created the short-lived drama "413 Hope St." in 1997 before returning to comedy with "Damon," a series that reunited him with "In Living Color" co-star David Alan Grier.

Wayans is married and has four children.

Keenan Ivory Wayans (AP/Wide World Photos, Inc.)

Keenan Ivory Wayans (1958–)
Comedian

Keenan Ivory Wayans was born in New York City on June 8, 1958. He began his career as a stand-up comic at the Improv clubs in New York City and Los Angeles. After appearances on such television series as "Benson," "Cheers," "Chips," and in the movies *Star 80* (1983) and *Hollywood Shuffle* (1987), Wayans struck fame with *I'm Gonna Git You Sucka* (1989)—a hilarious sendup of 1970s "blaxploitation" films—which he wrote and produced. His greatest success was the popular television series "In Living Color," a lively and irreverent show in which celebrities were often outrageously parodied. "In Living Color" won an Emmy Award in 1990.

Wayans is the oldest of a family of ten; three of his siblings—Damon, Shawn, and Kim—were regulars on "In Living Color." In the late 1990s he hosted his own television talk show.

Bert Williams (1874–1922)
Comedian, Dancer

The legendary Bert Williams is considered by many to be the greatest black vaudeville performer in the history of the American stage.

Born on November 12, 1874, on New Providence Island in the Bahamas, Williams moved to New York with his family, and then on to California, where he graduated from high school. After studying civil engineering for a time, he decided to try his hand at show business.

In 1895, Williams teamed with George Walker to form a successful vaudeville team. Five years later, they opened in New York in *The Sons of Ham* and were acclaimed for the characterizations that became their stock-in-trade—Walker as a dandy and Williams in blackface, complete with outlandish costumes and black dialect. The show ran for two years.

In 1902, their show *In Dahomey* was so popular that they took it to England, where it met with equal success. The partners continued to produce such shows as *The Policy Players*, *Bandanna Land*, and *Abyssinia* until Walker's death in 1909.

Thereafter, Williams worked as a featured solo performer in the *Ziegfeld Follies*, touring America for ten years in several versions of the show. His most famous songs were "Woodman, Spare That Tree"; "O, Death, Where is Thy Sting"; and "Nobody," his own composition and trademark.

Williams died of pneumonia on March 4, 1922.

Flip Wilson (1933–1998)

Comedian, Actor

Flip Wilson reached the pinnacle of the entertainment world with a series of original routines and ethnic characters rivaled only by those of Bill Cosby. Wilson's hilarious monologues, seen on a number of network television shows, made him the most visible black comedian of the early 1970s.

Born Clerow Wilson on December 8, 1933, Wilson was the tenth in a family of 24 children, 18 of whom survived. The family was destitute, and Wilson was a troublesome child during his youth in his hometown of Jersey City; he ran away from reform school several times and was ultimately raised in foster homes.

Wilson's comic talents first surfaced while he was serving in the U.S. Air Force. Sent overseas to the Pacific, Wilson entertained his buddies with preposterous routines. Back in civilian life, he worked as a bellhop and part-time showman. Opportunity struck in 1959 when a Miami businessman sponsored him for one year at $50 a week, thus enabling Wilson to concentrate on the evolution of his routine. For the next five years or so, Wilson appeared regularly at the Apollo Theatre in Harlem. In 1965, he began a series of nationwide appearances on "The Tonight Show." Long-term contracts and several hit records followed in quick sequence, and Wilson became firmly established as one of the truly innovative talents in the comedy profession.

With "The Flip Wilson Show" in the early 1970s, Wilson became the first black to have a weekly prime time television show under his own name. He became famous for his original character creations such as "Geraldine." On January 31, 1972, he appeared on the cover of *Time* magazine. In 1976, he made his dramatic debut on television in the ABC series "The Six Million Dollar Man."

During the early 1980s, Wilson appeared in numerous nightclubs and television specials. He starred in the television series "People Are Funny" in 1984 and "Charlie & Co." in 1985. He has also made comedy albums including *The Devil Made Me Buy This Dress*, for which he received a Grammy Award.

Wilson died on December 1, 1998.

George C. Wolfe (1954–)

Playwright, Stage Director, Producer

Wolfe was born September 23, 1954, into a Frankfort, Kentucky, household; his father worked for the state and his mother was an educator and later school principal. Wolfe grew up in an insular African American community that stressed self-sufficiency and achievement, and a visit to New York City as a teenager helped instill a desire for a career in the theater. By 1976 he had earned a degree in theater from Pomona College.

Flip Wilson (AP/Wide World Photos, Inc.)

After working for a few years in the Los Angeles theater scene, Wolfe moved to New York City in 1979. After earning a master's degree in musical theater from New York University, he had his first minor recognition with the 1985 off-off Broadway production of his play *Paradise.* Wolfe's 1986 satire on African American cultural icons, *The Colored Museum*, won rave reviews from critics but also weathered criticism as well; eventually the play was staged at New York's Joseph Papp Public Theater and broadcast on PBS.

Wolfe became affiliated with the esteemed Public Theater, which stages the annual New York Shakespeare Festival, and directed several works for it beginning in 1990 including *Spunk* and *The Caucasian Chalk Circle.* With the 1992 Broadway debut of *Jelly's Last Jam*—a musical about the life of 1920s jazz musician Jelly Roll Morton that Wolfe wrote and directed—he rose in prominence in New York's theater community; in 1993 he directed parts one and two of the Pulitzer Prize-winning trilogy by playwright Tony Kushner, *Angels in America.* For his direction of first segment of the drama *Millennium Approaches*, Wolfe won a Tony Award.

Another honor was accorded Wolfe in 1993 when he was named director of the Joseph Papp Public Theater/ New York Shakespeare Festival; since then he has been praised for giving the venerable institution a more multicultural focus. Recent works under his directorial aegis include a revival of *The Tempest* and the hit Broadway musical *Bring in 'Da Noise, Bring in 'Da Funk*, which won four Tony Awards, one of them for Wolfe's direction.

Since then, Wolfe has been the recipient of the Drama Desk, Outer Critics Circle, Dramalogue and Obie awards. He was named Person of the Year by the National Theater Conference and "a living landmark" by the New York Landmark Conservatory. His alma mater Pomona College gave him an honorary doctorate in 1995.

22

Classical Music

◆ Black Musicians in Early America ◆ Classical Music in the Twentieth Century
◆ Studies in African American Music
◆ Classical Music Composers, Conductors, Instrumentalists, and Singers

by Calvert Bean

When the first Africans arrived in 1619 on the eastern coast of what is now the United States, they brought with them a rich musical heritage. In the culture from which these slaves were torn, music and dance were part of almost every public activity. Each community had expert musicians who transmitted these vital skills, orally and through training, from generation to generation. They brought to the New World not only their songs and dances, but their love of and need for music as an integral part of daily life.

◆ BLACK MUSICIANS IN EARLY AMERICA

As slaves, the Africans absorbed much of the folk and religious music of the white culture—which followed European models—while cherishing their own native practices. The resulting hybrid was a uniquely American style of music adopted by both white and black musicians.

Enslaved Africans sang English psalms and hymns in church as they converted to Christianity. They heard folk and popular tunes in the taverns and homes. Some slaves in the South studied with itinerant music teachers. The most talented musicians gained professional skills that were quickly put to use by whites. Both bonded servants and slave musicians, playing instruments such as the violin, flute, and piano, provided much of the recreational music for their masters. On the self-sufficient plantations of the South, the most musically gifted of the domestic slaves provided evening "entertainments." They accompanied dance balls and played at dancing schools. Once public concerts became possible and popular in the New World, a few talented slaves actually publicly concertized.

Early African American Composers and Conductors

Besides instrumentalists, African Americans were dance and military band leaders, composers and arrangers, singers, church choral directors, and entertainers. Free African Americans in Northern cities, such as Boston, Philadelphia, and New York, established remarkable careers and enjoyed wide esteem before the Civil War. One of the best examples is Frank Johnson (1792–1844), an all-around "music man" who was a virtuoso bugler and flutist, a bandmaster whose organizations were in great demand for military ceremonies and public dances, and an arranger of countless tunes and composer of many others. From his home base in Philadelphia, he toured widely with his band, including travel to England (then unprecedented for an African American ensemble), with as much success on the road as at home. Other leading conductors of both social and military bands included James Hemmenway (1800–1849), Aaron Connor (d. 1850), Isaac Hazzard (1804–1865), and William Appo (1808–1887)—all originally working in Philadelphia—and Peter O'Fake (1820–1884) of Newark, New Jersey, and J.W. Postlewaite (1827–1889) of St. Louis. As styles and customs changed, especially with the appearance of ragtime, musicians such as Will Marion Cook (1869–1944) and James Reese Europe (1881–1919) inherited Johnson's legacy in both public accept-

Sheet music from Francis Johnson's "Boone Infantry Brass Band Quick Step" (The Library of Congress).

Louis Moreau Gottschalk

ance of their music and their anticipation of later musical trends.

African American Pianists

African American pianists found fame in the nineteenth century, beginning with Louis Moreau Gottschalk (1829–1869) of New Orleans, who became an international star as a touring pianist and produced a striking body of piano solos influenced by his African and Cuban backgrounds. "Blind Tom" Bethune (1849–1909) became famous as a virtuoso with a repertoire of thousands of pieces. He was followed by John "Blind" Boone (1864–1927) with similar abilities, who achieved equal if not greater fame as a touring recitalist. Both were child prodigies who produced descriptive showpieces that dazzled audiences. André Watts made a hugely successful debut as a premiere pianist when he was only 16 years of age as soloist with the New York Philharmonic in 1962.

Although other excellent later pianists had varying degrees of success, many of them built their primary careers as teachers in colleges and universities. Hazel Harrison (1883–1969) and Helen Hagan (1891–1964) had long teaching careers after auspicious beginnings as performers, as did Natalie Hinderas (1927–1987).

Finally, African American pianists deserving honorable mention include composer/conductor R. Nathaniel Dett (1882–1943), composer/teacher George Walker (1922–), and Awadagin Pratt (1966–) whom many consider to be the successor to famed performer André: Watts.

African American Women Vocalists

While men dominated instrumental music in the nineteenth century and beyond, women achieved renown with vocal music. Elizabeth Taylor Greenfield (c. 1824–1876) was known as the "Black Swan" for her fluid and graceful phrasing, while M. Sissieretta Jones (1869–1933) was called the "Black Patti," after the famous white diva, Adelina Patti. Contralto Marian Anderson (1902–1993) emerged in the twentieth century as one of its highest-achieving and most durable artists. Mid-century, sopranos Leontyne Price and Jessye Norman were two of dozens of outstanding African American singers who conquered recital and opera stages.

Marian Anderson (Hurok Attractions)

Scott Joplin (Corbis Corporation [Bellevue])

◆ CLASSICAL MUSIC IN THE TWENTIETH CENTURY

Racism in Classical Music

During most of the nineteenth century, African American musicians performed for both black and white audiences. Towards the end of the century, however, white audiences began to favor European performers over any American performer, and white musicians over black. Despite their obvious success in classical music, by the beginning of the twentieth century, African Americans were not considered suitable as classical musicians, and white audiences accepted them only on the vaudeville and minstrel stage.

Whites also considered blacks to be unable to contribute to art music as composers. As as example, in response to composer Scott Joplin's attempt to produce his opera *Treemonisha* in New York, the *The New York Age* stated on March 5, 1908, "Since ragtime has been in vogue, many Negro writers have gained considerable fame as composers of that style of music. From the white man's standpoint of view after writing ragtime, the Negro does not figure."

Flutist D. Antoinette Handy wrote in the preface of *Black Women in American Bands and Orchestras* (1981) that her book originated in the mind of a 14-year-old African American girl who decided that she wanted to be a symphony orchestra flutist. She attended a concerto by the New Orleans Philharmonic and proceeded to go backstage afterwards to see the orchestra's first flutist. After inquiring whether the musician was accepting any pupils, she was stunned when the flutist's response was, "Do you mean that you, a Negro, want to study flute?" This attitude unfortunately prevailed in more subtle ways toward the end of the twentieth century: a 1981 survey by the National Urban League disclosed that of the nearly five thousand musicians playing regularly in 56 leading orchestras, only seventy were African American.

The accomplishments of African Americans are all the more remarkable given the intense racism of the times. The Symphony of the New World (1965–1976) was formed by Elayne Jones and white conductor Benjamin Steinberg as the first racially integrated orchestra in the country. One of its goals was to provide valuable training and experience for instrumentalists striving to be accepted into symphony orchestras. In the 1970s, two national African American opera companies were established. Opera/South was founded in 1970 by Sister Elise, a singer and white member of the Catholic order of the Sisters of the Blessed Sacrament and by members of the Mississippi Inter-Collegiate Opera Guild. The company staged productions of grand opera and of operas by African American composers including *Highway No. 1 USA* and *A Bayou Legend* by William Grant Still and *Jubilee* and *The Juggler of Our Lady* by Ulysses Kay. In 1973, Sister Elise was one of four founders of Opera Ebony, the other three being African American musicians Margaret Harris, Benjamin Matthews, and Wayne Sanders. These companies were effective showcases for African American talent and often provided the first opportunities for individuals to begin careers in opera. Three stage works were also responsible for starting many young artists in successful careers: Virgil Thomson and Gertrude Stein's *Four Saints in Three Acts* premiered in 1934; *Porgy and Bess* by George Gershwin, first produced in 1935; and *Treemonisha* by Scott Joplin, first staged in 1972 in Atlanta.

African American Symphonic Music

African American composers have had increasing numbers of works performed by symphony orchestras from the 1930s and onward. African American symphonic music falls into two categories: black-stream music, synonymous with Gunther Schuller's *Third Stream*, which is serious music influenced by the ethnic background of the composer; and traditional European music created by African American composers. Afro-American Symphony by William Grant Still falls into the former category and was the first symphonic work by an African American composer to be performed by a major symphony orchestra—the Rochester Philharmonic—in 1931. Florence Price was the first African American female composer to have a symphony played by a major orchestra: Symphony in E Minor by the Chicago Symphony Orchestra in 1933. A year later, Price conducted her Concerto in One Movement for piano and orchestra at the Chicago World's Fair, with her student Margaret Bonds as soloist and the Women's Symphony of Chicago. In later years, composers such as George Walker, Howard Swanson, Ulysses Kay, Hale Smith, T.J. Anderson, Olly Wilson, Anthony Davis, and David Baker created a large repertoire of music based on Western European styles and forms that were informed or transformed through their racial heritage. To varying degrees, all of these composers have absorbed and expressed features common to African American music by their use of sacred and secular folk music, including the basic African call-and-response pattern, and of popular or vernacular music, including spirituals, ragtime, blues, and jazz.

◆ STUDIES IN AFRICAN AMERICAN MUSIC

Beginnings of Academic Research

African American literature, music, and art were well-established as subjects of academic study by the end of the twentieth century. In music, Eileen Southern's *The Music of Black Americans: A History* was the first comprehensive presentation of the subject published in 1971. Its subsequent revisions in 1983 and 1997 show its continuing pertinence as both a textbook and reference source. The breadth and depth of information in this volume demonstrate the great variety of African American music and of its myriad creators and practitioners.

Two precursors of this volume were James Monroe Trotter's *Music and Some Highly Musical People* (1878) that presented the accomplishments of African Americans in European styles, and Maud Cuney Hare's *Negro Musicians and Their Music*, (1936), which was more comprehensive in the styles covered. The ever-increasing quality and quantity of research in African American music herald the development of younger scholars who can use wisely the resources available to them at the beginning of their careers and who will increase those resources steadily as they progress. Thus, a much more accurate picture of the history of American music will result.

Recent Research on African American Music

In more recent years, the Center for Black Music Research was founded in 1983 by Samuel A. Floyd Jr. in Chicago. He is the author of *The Power of Black Music* (1995), among several other publications. Located at Columbia College, the center has as its mission "to research and promote the music of people of African descent throughout the world. . . through education, performance, publication, and scholarly discussion." It has actively contributed to the research publications and performances of contemporary and historic compositions that they have sponsored. They also have an ever-growing library and computer database of resources used by scholars all over the country. In addition, the *International Dictionary of Black Composers* (1999) fills a large gap in study materials on African American music and musicians.

At the end of the twentieth century, the trend toward inclusiveness of all kinds of music in formal study—not jazz, blues, classical, or sacred music as distinct and separate artistic worlds—bodes well for a better understanding of African American music. Certainly twentieth-century African American classical composers have worked in a wide variety of styles, from the vernacular to the avant-garde. A large number of these composers are not bound to one style or another, but rather move freely among them to produce unexpected and challenging works.

◆ CLASSICAL MUSIC COMPOSERS, CONDUCTORS, INSTRUMENTALISTS, AND SINGERS

(To locate biographical profiles more readily, please consult the index at the back of the book.)

Adele Addison (1925–)
Singer

Born July 24, 1925 in New York City, soprano Adele Addison completed her musical training at Westminster Choir College in 1946 and studied later at the University of Massachusetts. After making her recital debut at Town Hall in New York City in 1952, she performed recital tours throughout the United States and Canada. In 1963, she toured the Soviet Union under a U.S. State Department cultural exchange program.

While primarily a recitalist, Addison has appeared with the New England, New York City, and Washington opera companies. She gave the premiere performance of John LaMontaine's *Fragments from the Song of Songs* with the New Haven Symphony in 1959 and of Francis Poulenc's *Gloria* with the Boston Symphony in 1961. She was also a soloist during the opening week of concerts at Lincoln Center, New York, in 1962.

Betty Lou Allen (1930–)
Singer, Educator

Born in Campbell, Ohio, Betty Allen studied at Wilberforce University and toured with Leontyne Price in the group the Wilberforce Sisters. She continued her musical studies at the Hartford School of Music and the Berkshire Music Center at Tanglewood and studied voice with Sarah Peck Moore, Paul Ulanowsky, and Zinka Milanov.

Allen made her New York debut in the Virgil Thomson-Gertrude Stein opera *Four Saints in Three Acts* with the New York City Opera in 1953 and made her debut at the Teatro Colón in Buenos Aires in 1964. She has appeared as a soloist with many leading orchestras and conductors including Leonard Bernstein, Antal Dorati, and Lorin Maazel. She has held positions on the faculties of the North Carolina School of the Arts, the Curtis Institute of Music, and the Manhattan School of Music and became the executive director and chair of the voice department at the Harlem School of the Arts in New York City.

Marian Anderson (1902–1993)
Singer

Born in Philadelphia, Pennsylvania, contralto Marian Anderson was brought up in a family of church musicians, and she began singing publicly as a child. Her professional career began in earnest in the 1920s, but her initial New York debuts were unsuccessful. However, her victory in a performance competition with the New York Philharmonic in 1925 led to further engagements, principally in Europe, where she established her reputation as a leading concert artist. On her return to the United States, her 1935 Town Hall performance in New York won her the acclaim that she deserved.

In 1939, Howard University wished to present Anderson in recital at Constitution Hall in Washington, DC. She was barred from performing there, however, by the Daughters of the American Revolution because of her race. Public reaction to this racially-motivated action was immediate and intense and, through the efforts of First Lady Eleanor Roosevelt (who resigned from the organization in protest), Anderson was invited to sing on the steps of the Lincoln Memorial. For this memorable Easter Sunday concert, the audience was an estimated 75,000 strong.

In 1955 Anderson became the first African American artist to perform with the Metropolitan Opera Company when she sang the role of Ulrica in Verdi's *Un Ballo in Maschera* for one season. Two years later she became a goodwill ambassador for the U.S. State Department, and in 1958 she was named to the U.S. delegation to the United Nations.

As a conclusion to her lengthy career, "the world's greatest contralto" toured the nation in a series of farewell concerts that ended on Easter Sunday of 1965 at Carnegie Hall in New York City. Anderson was not only a great singer but also a humanitarian, one who established fellowships for young singers and who toppled racial barriers for succeeding generations.

T(homas) J(efferson) Anderson (1928–)
Composer, Educator

Born on August 17, 1928, in Coatesville, Pennsylvania, to educator parents, T.J. Anderson began to study piano with his mother at the age of five. He began performing with jazz groups in junior high school, which cemented his love of music. He earned a bachelor of music degree in 1950 at West Virginia State College and a master of music education degree at Pennsylvania State University the following year. He was a music instructor for a few years before pursuing his Ph.D. at the University of Iowa, where he studied with Philip Bezanson and Richard Hervig and which he completed in 1958. He also studied with Darius Milhaud in the summer of 1964 at the Aspen (Colorado) School of Music. Following teaching positions at West Virginia State College, Langston and Tennessee State Universities, and Morehouse College, he joined the faculty of Tufts University in Medford, Massachusetts, where he chaired the music department. He retired as professor emeritus in 1990.

Anderson has received over 25 commissions, beginning in 1961, for a large variety of works—instrumental solos and ensembles, chamber and full orchestra, band, dramatic music, and solo vocal and choral music. A few of his notable compositions are: *Spirit Songs* (commissioned by Yo Yo Ma) for cello; *Transitions: A Fantasy for Ten Instruments* (Berkshire Music Center, Tanglewood, and the Fromm Foundation); *Squares: An Essay for Orchestra* (West Virginia State College); *Thomas Jefferson's Orbiting Minstrels and Contraband: A 21st Century Celebration of 19th Century Form* (for string quartet, woodwind quintet, jazz sextet, dancer, soprano, computer, visuals, keyboard synthesizer); *Variations on a Theme by M.B. Tolson* (soprano, instrumental ensemble); *Soldier Boy, Soldier*, a two-act opera (Indiana University and National Endowment for the Arts); and *Walker*, a one-act opera (Boston Atheneum, on a libretto by South African Derek Walcott, Nobel Prize laureate, based on the death of David Walker in 1830 in Boston).

Anderson's deep knowledge and control of twentieth-century musical techniques and developments—including jazz, big band music, blues, and spirituals—formed his compositional style. For the 1972 premiere of Scott Joplin's opera *Treemonisha* Anderson was the orchestrator and helped in its staging. Another notable event was his conducting the first performance of the Black Music Repertory Ensemble in 1988. Among more than thirty awards and honors, he received four MacDowell Colony fellowships, in addition to honorary doctorates and composer residencies.

Martina Arroyo (1936–)

Singer, Educator

Martina Arroyo was born to a Puerto Rican father and an African American mother in Harlem. Although encouraged by her mother in artistic pursuits—piano, ballet, church choir—she was expected to enter a profession that could provide a more secure living than one in the arts. After attending Hunter High School, she continued at Hunter College, where she earned a degree in Romance languages in 1956. During her college years, she met the distinguished voice teacher Marinka Gurewich with whom Arroyo trained almost continuously until Gurewich's death in 1990.

As many other African American artists of her generation, Arroyo did not have an easy time breaking into American operatic performance, but found success in European opera houses. In 1965, while visiting her family in New York on vacation from the Zürich Opera Company, she was called to fill in for Birgit Nilsson as Aida at the Metropolitan Opera. Her performance in this demanding Verdi role led to a contract and made her an international star virtually overnight.

Along with frequent opera appearances in the United States and abroad in the 1970s and 1980s, Arroyo had many engagements with leading orchestras, performing music ranging from Handel to Stockhausen. Arroyo officially retired from performing in 1989. Only two years later, however, she agreed to sing the leading female role, written for her by Leslie Adams in his new opera *Blake* based on a nineteenth-century novel about a slave family. After retirement, Arroyo was in demand as a distinguished visiting professor. Some of the universities where she has taught are the University of California at Los Angeles, Louisiana State University, Wilberforce University, and Indiana University at Bloomington.

David Baker (1931–)

Composer, Instrumentalist, Educator, Author

Born in Indianapolis, Indiana, David Baker was educated in the public schools and Jordan Conservatory of that city. He earned bachelor (1953) and master (1954) degrees in music education at Indiana University at Bloomington and later studied at the Berklee School of Music and the Lenox School of Jazz, from which he received a diploma in 1959. Among his private composition teachers were George Russell, John Lewis, William Russo, and Gunther Schuller. He also studied trombone privately with J.J. Johnson, John Marcellus, and Bobby Brookmeyer, and cello with his Indiana colleague Janos Starker, with Jules Eskin and others.

In the late 1950s and early 1960s, Baker played in the bands of Maynard Ferguson, Quincy Jones, George Russell, Wes Montgomery, and Lionel Hampton. After joining the faculty of Indiana University in 1966 as chairman of the jazz department, Baker continued to perform with various groups, lecture, conduct workshops and clinics, and publish a large number of books and articles in the field of jazz.

Baker's catalog of compositions is very large and includes over sixty commissioned works for solo and ensemble instrumental works, vocal and choral music, pieces for string, chamber, and full orchestra, dramatic music, and well over 150 works for jazz ensembles. Not surprisingly, Baker has issued over sixty books on music improvisation including *Advanced Ear Training for Jazz Musicians; Advanced Improvisation* (two volumes); *Contemporary Techniques for the Trombone* (two volumes); and *Improvisational Patterns: The Bebop Era* (three volumes). In the course of his very active career, he has received over thirty awards and honors. He has participated in many organizations including the National Endowment for the Arts, American Symphony Orchestra League, the National Jazz Foundation, the Afro-American Music Bicentennial, the nominating jury in music for the Pulitzer Prize, and the Smithsonian Institution.

Kathleen Battle (1948–)

Singer

In her high school and early college years, soprano Kathleen Battle, a native of Portsmouth, Ohio, had no ambition to become a professional singer. She studied voice, piano, languages, and dance as she earned her bachelor and master degrees in music education from the University of Cincinnati College-Conservatory. She continued studies during two years of teaching general music in an inner-city school.

An audition with Thomas Schippers, conductor of the Cincinnati Symphony Orchestra and co-founder of the Spoleto (Italy) Festival of Two Worlds, led to her professional debut in Brahms's *German Requiem* in Spoleto. Through Schippers, Battle met James Levine in 1974, who became her friend, mentor, and counselor. She sang with many orchestras as soloist, studied opera and song literature and acting, and, in 1975, was in the Broadway company of Scott Joplin's opera *Treemonisha*. Her New York City opera debut followed in 1976 as Susanna in Mozart's *The Marriage of Figaro*, and her Metropolitan Opera debut took place in 1978 as the shepherd in Wagner's *Tannhäuser*. Since then she has sung a wide range of roles in opera houses throughout the world, notably in operas by Mozart, Rossini, Massenet, and Richard Strauss.

In 1994, Battle was dismissed from the Metropolitan Opera production of Donizetti's *Daughter of the Regiment*, following a much-publicized dispute with management. The rift proved to be no stumbling block to her career, however, as her recordings have been very successful including the "crossover" discs, such as *So Many Stars* and *Honey and Rue*, as well as baroque arias with trumpeter Wynton Marsalis, romantic Lieder, and operatic and symphonic repertoire.

Kathleen Battle (AP/Wide World Photos, Inc.)

Thomas "Blind Tom" Greene Bethune (1849–1908)

Pianist, Composer

"Blind Tom" was the stage name of pianist Thomas Greene, born a slave in Columbus, Georgia. The surname "Bethune" was the name of the family that owned him and his mother. His musical prowess manifested itself when he was four years old, and he received music lessons from Bethune family members. His remarkable skills, especially his ability to memorize pieces practically on first hearing, have caused speculation that he was autistic, an "idiot savant." Tom began performing for money in public before the Civil War. Colonel John Bethune kept control of Tom and his earnings after slavery was abolished and acted, in effect, as his concert manager. His renown grew rapidly after the war, and he toured throughout the United States and in Europe to great acclaim. His immense repertoire included works by standard classical composers, such as Bach, Beethoven, and Chopin; virtuoso display pieces by Gottschalk and Liszt; improvisations on current ballads and other popular tunes; and his own works that combined elements of the virtuosic and improvisational, and often described weather or military events. *The Battle of Manassas* is an example of one of his most effective works of this kind, a potpourri of well-known melodies with special keyboard effects, such as tone clusters and noises made on the piano.

Tom retired in 1898, some ten years before his death.

Margaret Bonds

Margaret Allinson Bonds (1913–1972)

Composer, Pianist

Margaret Bonds, born in Chicago, grew up in an artistic and creative family. Her first piano teacher was her mother, a church organist. Her family's friends consisted of many distinguished musicians and writers including Florence Price and Will Marion Cook who acted as Bonds's mentors. As a youngster she began to compose, and when she was in her teen years she held jobs as accompanist for nightclub acts and as a music copyist.

Bonds was one of very few African American students at Northwestern University in Evanston, Illinois, from which she received both a bachelor and a master of music degree by the time she was 21 years old. In the latter part of the 1930s, she founded and directed the Allied Arts Academy, which closed in 1939 because of financial difficulties. She moved to New York City, where she resumed study at the Juilliard School of Music, and was active as both solo and duo pianist and accompanist, gave lecture demonstrations, and was involved in many professional and community organizations.

Bonds's compositions reflect jazz influence, as well as spirituals and the blues, and she gained a thorough mastery of the techniques of Western music. The greater portion of her music is vocal and choral, but there are many piano solos and dramatic works as well including *The Ballad of the Brown King* (1954) and *Shakespeare in Harlem* (1959), a play by Langston Hughes.

In 1967, Bonds moved again, this time to Los Angeles where she taught piano and worked with the Inner City Cultural Center and Repertory Theater. Written and premiered in 1972, her *Credo*—dedicated to the memories of soprano Abbie Mitchell and Langston Hughes—was performed by the Los Angeles Philharmonic and conducted by Zubin Mehta shortly after her sudden death.

John William "Blind" Boone (1864–1927)

Pianist, Composer

Born fifteen years later than "Blind Tom" Bethune, "Blind" Boone's upbringing and education were considerably different from his predecessor's, although their careers were very similar. Both had tremendous skill at the keyboard and very large repertoires at their fingertips, and they both toured extensively for many years. Boone, however, had more formal training, and received support from the citizens of Warrensburg, Missouri, who raised money for him to study at the Institute for the Education of the Blind (later, St. Louis School for the Blind), in St. Louis. After less than three years of piano lessons at the school, Boone left in order to begin a career in music.

There were several lean years before Boone met John Lange, a Missouri businessman and entrepreneur who set up the Blind Boone Concert Company, a partnership that provided for the pianist and a stipend for his mother. A typical Boone program, following the pattern of Bethune's, included classical works from Bach to Brahms, his own arrangements of popular ballads and dance tunes, descriptive and concert pieces, and, on occasion, improvisations. Boone, unlike Bethune, performed and wrote ragtime pieces as well. His familiarity with this newly-popular music went back to his days as a student in St. Louis.

With Lange's death in 1916, the fortunes of the company declined and, with burgeoning new entertainment media and an apparent increase in racism, so did performing engagements. Nevertheless, Boone continued his partner's practice of benefiting communities and organizations of African Americans with concert revenues. Boone's "farewell concerts" began in the early 1920s, but his final concert was given shortly before his death in 1927.

Gwendolyn Bradley (1952–)

Singer

Soprano Gwendolyn Bradley was born in New York City but grew up in Bishopville, South Carolina. She was a finalist in the 1977 Metropolitan Opera National Council auditions and a graduate of the North Carolina School of the Arts. She also attended the Curtis Institute of Music and the Academy of Vocal Arts in Philadelphia and studied with Margaret Harshaw and Seth McCoy.

Bradley made her professional operatic debut in 1976 with the Lake George (New York) Opera Festival as Nanetta in Verdi's *Falstaff.* Other companies with which she has appeared include Central City Opera (Colorado), Opera/South, and the Opera Company of Philadelphia. Her Metropolitan Opera debut in 1981 was in the Met's first production of Ravel's *L'Enfant et les Sortilèges.* She has been a soloist with several orchestras including the Philadelphia Orchestra, the Kansas City Philharmonic, the Charleston Symphony, the Los Angeles Philharmonic, and the Seattle Symphony.

Grace Ann Bumbry (1937–)
Singer

A native of St. Louis, Missouri, Grace Bumbry was the first African American to perform in Bayreuth, Germany, the shrine of Richard Wagner. She had the role of Venus in *Tannhäuser* in 1961 and sang to great acclaim. She had appeared in the operatic capitals of Europe, so the Bayreuth debut served as a boost to a career that was already flourishing. She made her American operatic debut in this role as well at the Chicago Lyric Opera in 1963.

As a teenager, Bumbry had won a scholarship to the St. Louis Institute in a competition, but the segregationist policy of that school kept her out. Later, however, she attended Boston University, Northwestern University, and the Music Academy of the West in Santa Barbara, California, where her primary teacher was the renowned Lotte Lehmann. She also studied with Pierre Bernac.

Fairly early in her career, Bumbry gradually shifted from mezzo soprano to soprano roles, in which she achieved as much success as in the lower voice range. Among them were Lady Macbeth (*Macbeth*, Verdi), Leonora (in both *Il Trovatore* and *La Forza del Destino*, Verdi), *Salome* (R. Strauss), *Tosca* (Puccini), and *La Gioconda* (Ponchielli). She has sung both Amneris and Aida—mezzo and soprano—in Verdi's *Aida.* Virtuoso soprano roles that became part of her repertoire in the 1970s and 1980s are Abigaille (*Nabucco*, Verdi) and Norma (Bellini).

Henry Thacker "Harry" Burleigh (1866–1949)
Singer, Composer, Arranger, Editor

Born in 1866, baritone Harry Burleigh did not leave his hometown of Erie, Pennsylvania, for formal music study until 1892. He went to New York to study at the National Conservatory of Music from 1892 to 1996, then headed by composer Antonin Dvorak. Dvorak encouraged his students to use folk music and spirituals as the source of their art, which had a decisive influence on Burleigh's musical beliefs and practices. His vocal prowess gained him the position of soloist with a wealthy Episcopal church—where he remained for fifty years—and in the chorus of a synagogue for twenty-five years, both in New York City. Beginning in 1911, he was also an editor for the Ricordi Publishing Company until 1946.

Grace Bumbry performing in Verdi's *Don Carlos* in 1976 (AP/Wide World Photos, Inc.).

Besides his lifelong association with sacred music, Burleigh was involved with Broadway musical shows, and he also toured widely as a recitalist including trips to Europe and England. He was a private teacher of voice, music theory, and composition.

As a composer and arranger, Burleigh was the first to arrange spirituals in the style of art songs with the use of chromatic embellishments and nineteenth-century romantic harmonic practice. Arrangements were also made for chorus which were very popular, as were his original art songs that were widely programmed by leading singers of the day. He did not compose in large forms or dramatic music, and his only instrumental works are suites, one each for piano and for violin and piano. A charter member of the American Society of Composers,

Authors and Publishers, Burleigh was awarded honorary degrees by Atlanta and Howard Universities.

Frances Elaine Cole (1937–1983)
Violinist, Harpsichordist

Frances Cole studied violin at the Cleveland Institute of Music and at Miami University in Ohio, where she was concertmaster of the orchestra. She earned a doctorate at Teachers College of Columbia University, New York, in 1966, and during her years of study played for the National Orchestral Association. As she was finishing her doctorate, she discovered her interest in the harpsichord and began to study the instrument at the Landowska Center in Connecticut. In 1967, she became resident harpsichordist with the Gallery Players in Provincetown, Massachusetts, appeared on national television programs, and began touring throughout the United States and Europe.

Cole was as well known for her humor and innovation as for her elegant musical interpretations. In 1976, for example, she arrived dressed as Anna Magdalena Bach in a horse-drawn carriage for an outdoor concert at Lincoln Center, New York. She played jazz in a trio and was a cabaret singer under the name of Elaine Frances. She also served on the music faculties of Queens College and the Westminster Choir College and presented workshops at many colleges and universities.

Will Marion Cook (1869–1944)
Composer, Violinist, Conductor

Will Cook's earliest musical activities focused on the violin and Western concert music. At the age of fifteen, he left his hometown of Washington, DC, to study at the Oberlin (Ohio) Conservatory and after four years there he travelled to Berlin, Germany, for study with the renowned master violinist Joseph Joachim. A few years after his return to Washington, Cook left for New York, where he studied at the National Conservatory of Music with its director Antonin Dvorak and John White, a virtuoso violinist.

Dissatisfied with the course of his career, which he attributed partly to racial discrimination, Cook took advantage of an opportunity to conduct a newly-formed orchestra in Washington. Soon thereafter, he began to work in the musical theater of New York City with collaborators such as singer Bob Cole, vaudevillians George Walker and Bert Williams, and the writer Paul Laurence Dunbar. Cook was part of some theatrical "firsts": the first all-African American musical comedy on Broadway *Clorindy, or The Origin of the Cakewalk* with Dunbar, a "ragtime operetta" that introduced syncopation to the Broadway musical; and *In Dahomey*, with Williams and Walker, written and performed by African Americans for presentation on Broadway and, subsequently, also the first such show presented in London at Buckingham Palace.

Cook was the composer or co-composer of 17 musical shows in addition to songs that he wrote apart from shows. However, there are only a few piano pieces and no works for violin. Among the several younger musicians to whom he was mentor were Margaret Bonds, Duke Ellington, and Eva Jessye.

Roque Cordero (1917–)
Composer, Educator

Roque Cordero studied clarinet and string instruments as a child growing up in Panama, and he began to write popular songs at an early age before beginning to study composition formally when he was 17. In 1943, he came to the United States to study composition with Ernest Krenek at Hamline University in St. Paul, Minnesota, and conducting with Dmitri Mitropoulos at the University of Minnesota at Minneapolis. He graduated from the latter magna cum laude with a bachelor of arts degree. Back in his native country, he served on the faculty of the National Institute of Music of Panama, serving as director from 1953 to 1964. He returned to the United States to become assistant director of the Latin American Music Center at Indiana University, Bloomington beginning in 1966. From 1972 to 1987, when he retired, he was professor of music at Illinois State University at Normal.

Cordero has written a large number of solo and ensemble instrumental works and several for orchestra including the prize-winning Second Symphony and Violin Concerto. His style blends elements of Panamanian vernacular music with more formal Western European practices including serialism and polytonality. A balance of these two major aesthetic components is the predominant trait of his musical language.

Among many honors and awards that Cordero has received are a Guggenheim Fellowship, an honorary professorship at the University of Chile, an honorary doctorate from Hamline University, and a Koussevitzky International Recording Award. His commissions, numbering over twenty, have come from several countries in South America and prestigious institutions in the United States including the National Endowment for the Arts and the Kennedy Center.

Anthony Curtis Davis (1951–)
Composer, Pianist, Educator

Anthony Davis's father was the first African American professor at Princeton University and was later chair of the Afro-American studies department at Yale University. Born in Paterson, New Jersey, the young Davis grew up in a cultural environment in which he was encouraged to be creative. He earned a bachelor's degree in music from Yale in 1975; later, he returned to teach in the early 1980s and early 1990s. He has also been a visiting professor or lecturer at Harvard, Cornell, and Northwestern Universities and at the University of California at San Diego.

Davis, who had studied piano in his teen years, began to play jazz with different groups while at Yale, and after moving to New York City, he quickly developed a reputation as an advanced player and highly-proficient improviser. Finally, he founded his own group, Episteme, (which means "knowledge") so that he could work out his compositional ideas. Experience with this group caused him to focus on composition as his primary activity, rather than improvisation. He has written in many media including jazz ensembles, opera, instrumental solos and ensembles to orchestra, and voice to chorus.

At the end of the 1990s, Davis had received over twenty commissions from symphonies, opera and dance companies, choral groups, and other organizations. Three of his four operas are based on real characters and events: *Amistad*, 1997, for the Lyric Opera of Chicago (about a slave revolt aboard a ship and its aftermath); *Tania*, 1992, for the American Music Theater Festival (based on the Patty Hearst kidnapping); and *X: The Life and Times of Malcolm X*, 1986, for the Kitchen Center. About *X*, perhaps the work that has made the biggest impact, critic Andrew Porter praised the "constantly impressive" score and believed that " . . . an 'ordinary' opera goer will be able to respond readily to the music." Davis himself stated that "I hope it will open a door for others to create large works and then realize that this separateness in American culture is just a by-product of race, not a by-product of the art. It's important for me that what I do helps the next generation of musicians."

William Levi Dawson (1899–1990)

Composer, Conductor, Educator

Born in Anniston, Alabama, William Dawson became a student at the age of 15 in the Tuskegee Institute, founded by Booker T. Washington. His studies included piano, composition, and trombone. He moved to Kansas City, Kansas, to teach music in high school, and he excelled as a jazz trombonist during his years there. He was also able to earn a bachelor of music degree at the Horner Institute of Fine Arts in 1925.

In 1926, Dawson moved to Chicago, where he continued to play in jazz ensembles (including Jimmy Noone's Apex Orchestra and the Fourteen Doctors of Syncopation) and to study composition at the American Conservatory of Music and the Chicago Musical College. He received a master of music degree in 1927 from the conservatory. By this time he was publishing arrangements of spirituals and conducting a large church choir. Dawson was invited to Tuskegee to head the Institute's School of Music in 1931 and remained there until retirement in 1955. During his tenure, he strengthened the music curriculum and built the Institute Choir into an organization nationally recognized as outstanding. After his retirement, he remained active as a guest conductor in the United States and abroad.

Dawson's most famous work is the Negro Folk Symphony, premiered in 1934 by the Philadelphia Orchestra and conducted by Leopold Stokowski. It was the first symphony by an African American composer to be premiered by a major U.S. symphony orchestra. It was revised in 1952 after Dawson visited West Africa, where he studied African rhythms and their influence on African American music. His arrangements of spirituals have been staples of the choral repertoire, as have some of his original works. A statement about the symphony made by Dawson is a good short description of the goals of "nationalist" composers: his goal was "to write a symphony in the Negro folk idiom, based on authentic folk music but in the same symphonic form used by the composers of the (European) romantic-nationalist school."

James Anderson DePriest (1936–)

Conductor

Born in Philadelphia, James DePriest studied piano and percussion from the age of ten, but he did not decide on a musical career until he reached his early twenties. After finishing high school, he entered the Wharton School of the University of Pennsylvania and received a bachelor of science in 1958 and a master of arts degree in 1961. He also studied music history and theory and orchestration at the Philadelphia Conservatory of Music and composition with Vincent Persichetti.

In 1962, DePriest was engaged as an American specialist in music for a U.S. State Department cultural exchange tour of the Near and Far East. During this tour, he was stricken with polio and paralyzed in both legs. Within six months of intensive therapy, he had fought his way to the point of being able to walk with the aid of crutches and braces. Courage, determination, and talent carried him to the semifinals of the 1963 Dmitri Mitropoulos International Music Competition for Conductors. After another overseas tour, this time as conductor in Thailand, he returned to the United States and conducted several American orchestras including the Philadelphia and the New York Philharmonic. In 1964, he captured first prize in the Mitropoulos Competition. Another career highlight occurred on June 28, 1965,

James DePriest (AP/Wide World Photos, Inc.)

when he conducted his Aunt Marian Anderson's farewell concert in Philadelphia at Robin Hood Dell.

DePriest has been the music director of the Oregon Symphony and has been a guest conductor in most of the capitals of the United States and Europe.

R(obert) Nathaniel Dett (1882–1943)

Composer, Arranger, Conductor, Pianist

Born of musical parents, a Canadian mother and an American father, in Drummondville, Ontario, Dett studied the piano and played in church from an early age. In 1893, his family moved from Canada to Niagara Falls, New York, where he began playing in public in his teen years. After two years of study at a music conservatory in nearby Lockport, he moved to Oberlin, Ohio, in 1903 for baccalaureate studies at the Oberlin Conservatory, where he also began his career as a choral conductor. He received his bachelor of music degree in 1908.

Dett held teaching positions, after graduation, at Lane College (Jackson, Tennessee), Lincoln Institute (Jefferson City, Missouri), and Hampton Institute (Hampton, Virginia) from 1913 to 1932. He raised the standards of the Institute's choir, not only in excellence of performance but also in establishing the spiritual—in arrangements and as the source of original works—as part of the basic choral repertoire. After an unfortunate disagreement with the administration, he moved to Rochester, New York, and earned a master's degree at the Eastman School of Music in 1932. One of his composition teachers there was the school's director, Howard Hanson. After a few more years in Rochester, where he was busy as a choir director and composer, he took a position at Bennett College in North Carolina. In 1943, he directed the Women's Army Corps chorus of the United Services Organization, but his life was cut short in October of that year by a fatal heart attack, nine days before his sixty-first birthday.

Dett's many choral works include collections of Negro spirituals and large-scale dramatic compositions, notably *Chariot Jubilee* (1919) and *The Ordering of Moses: Biblical Folk Scenes*, an oratorio (1932, his master's thesis). There are also several works for piano including: *Cinnamon Grove Suite*, *Enchantment*, *In the Bottoms*, and *Magnolia*.

Dett gave very specific prefaces to several of his scores, many of which were definitely of "that class of music known as 'program music' or 'music with a poetic basis.'" Throughout his life he actively supported African American folk music through his writings, arrangements, conducting, and study. For his essay *Negro Music* (1920), he received the Bowdoin Literary Prize from Harvard University. He was a founder of the National Association of Negro Musicians in 1919 and served as its president from 1924 to 1926. Howard University and the Oberlin Conservatory both awarded him honorary doctorates.

Carl Rossini Diton (1886–1962)

Pianist, Singer, Composer

Carl Diton first learned piano from his father, a professional musician. He studied at the University of Pennsylvania and received his bachelor's degree in 1909. Following graduation, he went on to become the first African American pianist to make a cross-country concert tour. He furthered his piano studies in Munich, Germany, with the aid of an E. Azalia Hackley scholarship. In the 1920s, he began voice study and made his concert debut in Philadelphia in 1926. He continued to study voice at the Juilliard School, New York City, where he was awarded an artist's diploma in 1930.

Teaching began to take up more of his time, although he continued to perform. He also began to compose and received several awards including the Harmon Award. Most of his works are art songs and arrangements of spirituals. He was a founding member of the National Association of Negro Musicians in 1919, which has been a source of much support for young musicians through grants and scholarships and has also honored distinguished musicians of all kinds.

Dean Dixon (1915–1976)

Conductor

Born in Manhattan in 1915, Dean Dixon was exposed to classical music by his parents, who often took him to Carnegie Hall. While he was still in high school, he formed his own amateur orchestra at the Harlem YMCA, which soon grew to seventy members and gave regular concerts. He was admitted to the Juilliard School of Music on the basis of a violin audition, and he was awarded the bachelor's degree in 1936. Three years later, he earned a master's degree from the Teachers College of Columbia University.

Dixon's Symphony Society, founded in 1932, received community support, and in 1941 Eleanor Roosevelt was instrumental in setting up a concert that eventually led to his becoming the music director of NBC radio network's summer symphony. Shortly thereafter, he made his debut with the New York Philharmonic, the first African American to conduct that orchestra.

However, Dixon was unable to find a position as music director with an American orchestra, so he went to Europe, where he worked with several orchestras in

Dean Dixon

Sweden and Germany and to Australia for the Sydney Symphony. After his return to the United States in 1970, he was a frequent guest conductor and left a recorded legacy estimated at twenty discs at the time of his death in 1976.

Lucille Dixon (Robertson)

Double Bassist

Lucille Dixon began playing bass in high school and soon became a pupil of the New York Philharmonic's principal bassist, Fred Zimmerman. After graduating from high school, she joined the Works Progress Administration-sponsored National Youth Administration (NYA) Orchestra, the second of two African American women to play in that orchestra. Its purpose was to serve as a training and hiring mechanism for major United States orchestras, but Dixon realized that she, an African American female, would not be hired by a symphony orchestra. When the NYA orchestra folded, she turned to jazz, playing for two years with Earl Hines's band and, beginning in 1946, in her own band. She continued to work as a classical bass player and was affiliated with, among other orchestras, the National Symphony of Panama, the Westchester Philharmonic (New York), the Scranton Symphony (Pennsylvania), and the Symphony of the New World, which she managed from 1972 to 1976.

Mattiwilda Dobbs (1925–)

Singer

Mattiwilda Dobbs graduated from Spelman College in Atlanta, Georgia, her hometown, as valedictorian of her class in 1946. She majored in voice and studied at Columbia University Teachers College, where she earned a master's degree. She studied voice privately with Lotte Leonard in New York and, in Paris, with Pierre Bernac on a Whitney Fellowship. Soprano Dobbs won the International Music Competition held in Geneva, Switzerland, in 1951 and later was the first African American to sing a principal role at La Scala in Milan, Italy.

In 1955, Dobbs made her American operatic debut in the lead in the San Francisco Opera's *The Golden Cockerel*, becoming the first African American to play a major role in that company. This career achievement was followed by her debut at the Metropolitan Opera in *Rigoletto*—only the third African American to sing on that stage and the first to sing a romantic lead. Her successful showings in American opera companies led to an even greater international fame as she toured all over the world, including the Soviet Union, where she was the first Met artist to appear at the Bolshoi. At the peak of her career, her active repertoire included more than two hundred concert pieces and twenty operatic roles.

In 1974, Dobbs served as artist-in-residence at Spelman College and has likewise taught at Howard University since the 1970s. She was elected to the board of directors of the Metropolitan Opera in 1989.

Robert Todd Duncan (1903–1998)

Singer, Actor, Educator

Baritone Todd Duncan's mother, herself a musician, encouraged him in his ambition to become an opera singer. He was raised in Indianapolis, Indiana, and graduated with a bachelor of music degree from Butler University. He attended Columbia University Teachers College in New York, where he received a master's degree in music. After teaching briefly in a high school, he began college teaching and was on the music faculty of Howard University for some 15 years, where he also served as department head.

Duncan's performance in an all-African American, New York City production of Mascagni's *Cavalleria Rusticana* in 1934 led to his being chosen by George Gershwin to sing the lead role of Porgy in the premiere of his opera *Porgy and Bess*. Duncan also starred in two later revivals. He continued to be active as a concert singer and theatrical performer, and, in the New York City Opera's 1945–1946 season, he became the first African American member of the company with roles in *I Pagliacci*, *Aida*, and *Carmen*. However, he was never invited to sing at the Metropolitan Opera, which would have been the realization of his dream as a singer.

Besides work in films, Duncan appeared in some outstanding Broadway shows including *Cabin in the Sky*, *Show Boat* and Weill's *Lost in the Stars*, in which he created the role of Stephen Kumalo and for which he received both the New York Drama Critics and Tony Awards in 1950. He retired from public performance in 1967 but continued to teach privately in Washington, DC, for many years. Educational institutions with which he was associated during this period are Howard University and the Curtis Institute of Music. Both Valparaiso and Butler Universities awarded him honorary doctorates.

Leslie B. Dunner (1956–)

Conductor, Clarinetist, Composer

A native of New York City, Dunner graduated from Manhattan's High School of Music and Art in 1974. He earned a bachelor's degree in clarinet performance from the Eastman School of Music (1978) and continued study at Queen's College (New York) for a master's

Leslie Dunner (AP/Wide World Photos, Inc.)

degree in music theory and musicology (1979). He received a doctorate in orchestra conducting and clarinet performance from the College-Conservatory of Music of the University of Cincinnati (1982).

Dunner's honors include a 1994 American Symphony Orchestra League Award and, in 1996, becoming the first American prizewinner in the prestigious Arturo Toscanini International Conducting Competition. He was also a semi-finalist in the Herbert von Karajan International Conducting Competition.

Posts held by Dunner include seven seasons with the Detroit Symphony Orchestra as resident conductor and music director of the Annapolis Symphony Orchestra in Maryland as of December, 1998. He has also served as music director of Symphony Nova Scotia in Halifax, guest conductor with the Warsaw Philharmonic for its tour of South Africa, and guest conductor for the New York City Ballet.

In the late 1980s, Dunner began to work with the Dance Theatre of Harlem and had earlier served with the Pacific Northwest Ballet Company as assistant conductor. He has made appearances with many orchestras as guest conductor and has had the opportunity to work with some of the century's greatest conductors.

Dunner performs as a freelance clarinetist, and several of his compositions have been recorded, including his *Short Rhapsody for Clarinet.*

Simon Lamont Estes (1938–)
Singer

Born in Centerville, Iowa, Simon Estes is the grandson of a slave and the son of a coal miner. An athletic scholarship to the University of Iowa provided him with the opportunity to study voice with Charles Kellis. Estes received a full scholarship to the Juilliard School of Music, New York City, where he studied with Sergius Kagen and Christopher West. In 1964, he received grants that allowed him to travel to Germany, where he was soon given a contract with the Deutsche Oper in West Berlin. Bass-baritone Estes recounted the circumstances of his debut as Ramfis in Verdi's *Aida* in April of 1965: "I didn't have any rehearsal. It was the first time, literally, I had ever been on a stage. I didn't meet the conductor until the curtain parted and I saw him on the podium." Other roles followed, and in 1966 he won the silver medal in the Tchaikovsky Competition in Moscow. His European career developed rapidly, appearing with the opera companies of Vienna, Munich, Hamburg, Paris, Milan, and Florence. In 1978, Wolfgang Wagner invited him to appear at Bayreuth in the title role of *The Flying Dutchman*, and Estes became the first African American male singer to sing at the shrine of Richard Wagner.

Estes had been singing with various American opera companies, with performances in San Francisco, Boston, and Chicago, and he had a leading role with the Hamburg State Opera in its production of Gunther Schuller's *The Visitation* that played at the Metropolitan Opera House. His debut with the Met company, however, did not take place until 1982, in the role of the Landgrave in Wagner's *Tannhäuser.* Two seasons later, he played Porgy in the Met's first production of Gershwin's *Porgy and Bess.*

Besides singing in opera houses in Europe and America, Estes has been a busy recitalist from the time of his concert debut in 1980 at Carnegie Hall. Among recordings of major works that he has made are Beethoven's Symphony No. 9, Handel's *Messiah*, Fauré's *Requiem*, and *The Flying Dutchman.* He has also recorded spirituals and highlights from *Porgy and Bess.*

Louis Moreau Gottschalk (1829–1869)
Composer, Pianist

Louis Gottschalk was a native of New Orleans who was a violin prodigy around the age of six. Switching instruments, he soon became an outstanding pianist and studied in Europe with leading teachers when he was in his teen years. In his mid-twenties, he made his New York City debut, having already established a brilliant reputation in Europe. He toured internationally with great success for the rest of his short life.

Gottschalk's compositions for piano reflect the Creole environment of his childhood, and several of them are based in African American- and Cuban-inspired folk music including *Le Bananier* and *Bamboula.* He also wrote characteristic salon pieces. His autobiographical *Notes of a Pianist* provides information about his life, methods of composing, the people he knew, and the places he visited.

Denyce Graves (1965–)
Singer

A native of Washington, DC, mezzo-soprano Denyce Graves was a student at the Duke Ellington School for the Performing Arts in that city. In 1981, she began study with Helen Hodam at the Oberlin College Conservatory (Ohio) and transferred to the New England Conservatory of Music (Boston) in 1984. She received a bachelor of music degree and artist diploma in 1988 and later joined the Houston (Texas) Grand Opera Studio of the University of Houston, where she worked with Elena Nikolaidi.

Some of the prizes Graves won early in her career include awards from the Richard Tucker Music Foundation, Opera Columbus Vocal Competition (the Eleanor Steber Award), the Marian Anderson Award presented by her to Graves in 1991, the Grand Prix Lyrique given once every three years by the Friends of Monte Carlo Opera, and George London and Metropolitan Opera career study grants.

In the 1990s Graves's career as opera and recital singer and orchestra soloist flourished. She has sung the title role in Bizet's *Carmen* in opera houses throughout North and South America and Europe to great acclaim; she and Placido Domingo opened the Metropolitan Opera's 1997–1998 season in that opera. Another signature role for Graves is Dalila in *Samson et Dalila* (Saint-Saens), which she has also sung at the Met. A few of the works in which she has been soloist with leading orchestras worldwide are Verdi's *Requiem*, *La damnation de Faust* by Berlioz, *Shéhérazade* by Ravel, and Mahler's *Kindertotenlieder* and Eighth Symphony.

Reri Grist (1932–)
Singer

Born in New York City, soprano Reri Grist received her bachelor's degree in music from Queens College (New York) in 1954. Performing the role of Consuela in Bernstein's *West Side Story* brought her national attention. She made an equally strong impression in a very different work—Mahler's Symphony No. 4—which she sang with the New York Philharmonic. Since then, she has sung at many of the world's leading opera houses

Denyce Graves (AP/Wide World Photos, Inc.)

Reri Grist (AP/Wide World Photos, Inc.)

including La Scala (Milan), Vienna State, Britain's Royal Opera, and the Metropolitan Opera.

In 1960, the stage director of the Met, Herbert Graf, left that company to become director of the Zürich Opera. Grist was one of several artists to go with him. While she was in Europe, Stravinsky asked Grist to sing in *Le Rossignol* under his direction. Besides performing, Grist has taught at the Hochschule für Musik (Germany) and Indiana University.

Emma Azalia Hackley (1867–1922)
Singer, Choral Director, Educator

E. Azalia Hackley did as much to promote African American musicians as she did their traditional music. Growing up in Detroit, she studied voice and piano and began to perform in public at an early age. She received a degree in music at the University of Denver in 1901 and later traveled to Paris, France, for further voice study.

Hackley traveled extensively as a recitalist in the early years of the century but gradually became more occupied with furthering the careers of young African American artists. She established scholarships, sponsored debut recitals, and also helped many young performers to find college-level teaching positions. Hackley founded the Normal Vocal Institute in Chicago in late 1915 and directed it until its demise in 1917. One of her major activities in the latter part of her life was organizing large community concerts to promote the importance of African American folk music and to raise the level of public interest and pride in the African American musical heritage. The Hackley Collection was established by the National Association of Negro Musicians at the Detroit Public Library some twenty years after her death, in order to preserve her papers, memorabilia, and other materials relating to African American music and musicians.

Helen Eugenia Hagan (1893–1964)
Pianist, Composer, Educator

Helen Hagan was born into a musical family: her mother played piano and her father was a baritone. After receiving her early music training from her mother and in the public school system in New Haven, Connecticut, she became the first African American pianist to earn a bachelor of music degree from Yale University in 1912. She was also the first African American to win Yale's Sanford Fellowship, which permitted her to study in Europe with Vincent d'Indy. She earned a diploma in

1914 from the Schola Cantorum and returned to the United States to earn a master's degree from Columbia University Teachers College in New York City.

Between 1914 and 1918, Hagan toured in the United States, often playing her own compositions. In 1918, she toured Europe, entertaining African American World War I servicemen. When she gave a recital in 1921 at Aeolian Hall, she became the first African American pianist to give a solo performance in a major New York City concert hall. From the 1930s onward, she was a college teacher at Tennessee Agricultural and Industrial State College and Bishop College (Marshall, Texas) and privately in her own New York music studio.

D(orothy) Antoinette Handy (Miller) (1930–)

Flutist, Educator, Author

After studying violin and piano with her mother as a child, Antoinette Handy became determined on a career in music. Flute became her major instrument, and she studied at Spelman College in Atlanta; the New England Conservatory of Music in Boston, where she earned a bachelor of music degree in 1952; and Northwestern University in Evanston, Illinois, where she earned a master of music degree in 1953. Later she studied at the National Conservatory in Paris and received an artist's diploma in 1955.

As was the case with so many African American musicians and vocalists in the mid-twentieth century, Handy could not secure a job as an orchestra musician in the United States because of her race. However, a chance audition during her time in France yielded a position as first-chair flutist with the Orchestre International, an orchestra supported by the French government that toured Germany in the interest of better foreign relations in 1954. This experience served as the beginning of a 25-year career as a symphony musician with such orchestras as the Chicago Civic, Musica Viva Orchestra of Geneva, Switzerland, Symphony of the Air of the NBC radio network, the Symphony of the New World, and the Richmond (Virginia) Symphony.

In addition to performing, Handy devoted much of her life to teaching music history, theory, and arranging at such institutions as Florida A & M University and Tuskegee Institute. She conducted research of her own on the topic of African American music as a Ford Foundation Humanities Fellow in 1971 and has since published numerous articles for professional journals. She is also the author of the books *Black Women in American Bands and Orchestras* (1981), *The International Sweethearts of Rhythm* (1983), and *Black Conductors* (1984).

In 1990, Handy was appointed director of the National Endowment for the Arts' Music Program, after having served as acting director and assistant program director. The Music Program is one of the Endowment's largest operations, and before her retirement in 1993, Handy had administered the distribution of between 11 million and 15 million dollars—money that provided backing for up-and-coming musicians and support for the creation of new music and for musical performances, organizations, and training institutions.

Margaret Rosezarion Harris (1943–)

Pianist, Conductor, Composer

Margaret Harris was a child prodigy; she first performed in public at the age of three, began touring nationally when she was four, and played with the Chicago Symphony when she was ten. She was a student of conducting and piano at the Curtis Institute of Music, Philadelphia, and received bachelor's and master's degrees from the Juilliard School of Music (1964, 1965).

Harris began conducting Broadway shows in 1970, starting with *Hair*. Other shows included *Two Gentlemen of Verona*, *Raisin*, *Guys and Dolls*, and *Amen Corner*. She was a founding member of Opera Ebony and has served as its music director. Among major orchestras that she has conducted are the symphonies of Chicago, Minneapolis, Detroit, San Diego, St. Louis, and Los Angeles. Harris has also taught at the University of West Florida and Bronx Community College of the City University of New York.

Besides having written scores for musical productions and television shows, she has composed choral and instrumental works, the scores for two ballets, and two piano concertos. Harris has been both soloist and conductor for performances of these concertos.

Hazel Harrison (1883–1969)

Pianist, Teacher

Hazel Harrison was born in La Porte, Indiana. She showed prodigious musical gifts from early childhood and may have earned a living as a dance-hall pianist, if it were not for her mother's determination that she pursue a serious music career. Because a European debut was essential for an American concert performer, her major teacher, Victor Heinze, arranged a German tour for her in 1904, during which she was a soloist with the Berlin Philharmonic and attracted favorable notices.

A grant allowed Harrison to return to Germany in 1911, when she became the student of the virtuoso pianist and composer Ferruccio Busoni, who was the biggest influence on her musical life. With the onset of World War I she returned to the United States and stunned critics with her impressive concerts. She debuted in New York City at Town Hall in 1930 to glowing reviews. However, segregation largely confined her talent to concerts played in African American churches, high school gymnasia, and on African American college campuses. This racism caused Harrison to focus on a teaching career, and she joined the faculty of Tuskegee Institute in 1931. Other academic positions followed, at Howard University (1936–1955) and at Alabama State College in Montgomery (1958–1963). She gave her final public concert there in 1959. That Harrison never made commercial recordings is probably the main reason that, in spite of glowing reviews and the devotion of generations of her students, her achievements as a performer are now little known.

Roland Hayes (1887–1977)
Singer

Roland Hayes was born to former slave parents in Curryville, Georgia. His father, a tenant farmer, died when Hayes was 11. His mother, determined that her six children would not share her illiteracy, sent them to Chattanooga, Tennessee, where the brothers would rotate working and attending school. When his turn came for school, Hayes elected to continue working to provide for the family, but he studied at nights including music study. Later, attending Fisk University, he toured with the Jubilee Singers and also traveled to London, England, for further vocal study.

Hayes became an active recitalist beginning around 1915 and was consistently acclaimed as one of the best tenors. In 1917, he became the first African American to give a recital in Boston's Symphony Hall. Three years later, he gave a royal command performance in London and made very successful appearances throughout Europe. His recital programs included Negro spirituals, folk songs, operatic arias, and American art songs. He gave a well-received farewell concert in New York's Carnegie Hall on his seventy-fifth birthday in 1962.

During his long career, Hayes received many awards and citations including eight honorary degrees and the NAACP's Spingarn Medal. His success in the concert field, along with that of Marian Anderson and Paul Robeson, played a large role in broadening the opportunities later available to younger African American singers.

Barbara Hendricks (1948–)
Singer

Soprano Barbara Hendricks, born in Stephens, Arkansas, graduated from the University of Nebraska with a bachelor of science degree in chemistry and mathematics. She then attended the Juilliard School of Music in New York City and received a bachelor of music degree in voice. Hendricks made her debut in 1975 with the San Francisco Spring Opera and has since performed with major opera companies and festivals throughout the United States and Europe. Among them are the Boston Opera, the Metropolitan Opera, St. Paul Opera, Santa Fe Opera, Houston Opera, and the Deutsche Oper in Berlin, and at the Aix-en-Provence and the Glyndebourne Festivals. She has performed frequently as an orchestra soloist as well.

Hendricks has received several awards including a French Grammy for best French performer of classical music in 1986, an honorary doctorate from Nebraska Wesleyan University in 1988, and an honorary membership in the Institute of Humanitarian Law in 1990. She has also served as a human rights activist and, beginning in 1987, as a goodwill ambassador for the United Nations High Commission for Refugees.

Ann Stevens Hobson-Pilot (1943–)
Harpist

Ann Hobson-Pilot, born in Philadelphia, was one of the first African American women to hold a permanent position in a major national symphony orchestra. She began studying piano with her mother at an early age and took up the harp in high school so that she could play an instrument on which her mother could not judge so easily what she might be doing wrong. Her first major teacher in harp was Marilyn Costello, principal harpist of the Philadelphia Orchestra and teacher at the Philadelphia Music Academy. After her second year at the academy, she attended the Maine Harp Colony (her first application for admission had been rejected on racial grounds), where she met Alice Chalifoux, principal of the Cleveland Orchestra and teacher at the Cleveland Institute of Music. Hobson-Pilot decided to transfer to the Institute. Chalifoux was influential in starting Hobson-Pilot on her professional orchestra career at the National Symphony Orchestra in Washington, DC. Three years later, Hobson-Pilot joined the Boston Symphony as the associate principal harpist.

Hobson-Pilot's other activities have included performing with the Boston Symphony Chamber Players and the New England Harp Trio and making solo appearances with orchestras throughout the country. Besides conducting clinics and workshops, she has taught at the Philadelphia Musical Academy and the New England Conservatory in Boston.

Ben Holt (1955–1990)
Singer

Born in Washington, DC, baritone Ben Holt attended the Oberlin College Conservatory of Music and was a scholarship student at the Juilliard School of Music, where he worked with Sixten Ehrling, Tito Gobbi, and Manuel Rosenthal. He also took master classes with Luciano Pavarotti and worked extensively with renowned pianist and coach Martin Isepp. When he was in the

Merola Program of the San Francisco Opera, taking master classes with Elisabeth Schwarzkopf, he was invited to study privately with her at her studio in Zürich, Switzerland.

Holt made his Metropolitan Opera debut in Puccini's *La Bohème* during the 1985–1986 season, and in 1986 he made his debut with the New York City Opera in the title role of *Malcolm X*, by Anthony Davis. Leading roles in Gershwin's *Porgy and Bess* and Mozart's *The Marriage of Figaro* were also in his repertoire. Holt won many competitions, including the Joy of Singing Competition and the D'Angelo Young Artists Competition, and awards from the Oratorio Society of New York and Independent Black Opera Singers.

Isaiah Jackson (1945–)
Conductor

Isaiah Jackson was born in Richmond, Virginia, where he started piano lessons at the age of four, was sent to a private boarding school in Vermont when he was 14-years-old, and traveled with his high school class to the former Soviet Union.

Although Jackson had wanted to be a musician, his parents hoped that he would enter the diplomatic corps. Eventually, he enrolled at Harvard University, from which he graduated cum laude in 1966 with a degree in Russian history and literature. On graduation, he followed his first inclination and went to Stanford University for studies in music. After earning a master's degree there in 1967, he moved to the Juilliard School of Music in New York City, where he earned a master's and a doctor of musical arts degree, finishing in 1973.

Shortly thereafter, Jackson conducted major American orchestras including the New York and Los Angeles Philharmonics and the Vienna Symphony. He was also conductor for the Dance Theatre of Harlem at the Spoleto Festival in Italy. Jackson held concurrent positions with various regional orchestras and, for 14 years, he was associate conductor of the Rochester Philharmonic. In 1985, he was guest conductor with the orchestra of the Royal Ballet, London, and became the first African American to hold a chief position—music director—with the Royal Ballet in 1987. In that year he also became the first African American conductor of the Dayton (Ohio) Philharmonic. Jackson has served as guest conductor in the United States and abroad and has been principal guest conductor of the Queensland Symphony Orchestra.

Eva Jessye (1895–1992)
Choral Conductor, Composer

Ebony magazine cited Eva Jessye as "the first black woman to receive international distinction as a choral director," and she was the first African American woman to succeed as a professional choral conductor. Because of racial discrimination, she could not attend high school in her hometown of Coffeyville, Kansas, so she went to Kansas City to study at the Quindaro State School for the Colored (now Western University). There she met Will Marion Cook, who influenced her to become a musician. She also studied at Langston University in Oklahoma and, on completing her formal education, taught in public schools and at Morgan State (Baltimore) and Claflin (Orangeburg, South Carolina) Colleges.

With her move to New York City in 1922, Jessye began her career as a choral conductor, and a few years later she became successful in radio with her own choir. After that, she was invited to train a choir for the King Vidor film *Hallelujah* and then directed the choirs for two of the operas that would be very important to the careers of so many young African American singers: *Four Saints in Three Acts* (1934) by Virgil Thomson and Gertrude Stein, and Gershwin's *Porgy and Bess*, based on the book by DuBose Heywood (1935). Jessye was involved in many later productions of this opera into the early 1960s. Her choir did not disband until 1970.

Among Jessye's compositions, based largely on spirituals, are the oratorio *Paradise Lost and Regained* (1936) and *The Chronicle of Job*, a folk drama (1936), as well as many arrangements, especially of spirituals. Her very large collection of memorabilia makes up the Eva Jessye Collection of the University of Michigan, Ann Arbor, Afro-American Music Collections. Jessye lived in Ann Arbor for the last ten years of her life.

J(ohn) Rosamond Johnson (1873–1954)
Composer, Performer

J. Rosamond Johnson, born in Jacksonville, Florida, began piano lessons at age four with his mother. At an early age he studied composition and voice with teachers at the New England Conservatory of Music in Boston and, around 1905, privately with Samuel Coleridge-Taylor in London, England, when Johnson was performing there.

Johnson's career as a professional performer began in 1896. In 1899, he went to New York City to work in the musical theater, first in vaudeville. He soon formed a partnership with his brother, writer/poet/political activist James Weldon Johnson (1871–1938) and the established vaudevillian Bob Cole. They were very successful in producing and writing their own works and contributing to many other musicals during the first decade of the century. After Cole's death in 1912, J. Rosamond continued working with his brother and other partners, made several tours in the United States and England, and sang in many stage productions including the original (1935) and subsequent companies of Gershwin's *Porgy and Bess*. Another notable theatrical work in which he performed was *Cabin in the Sky*.

Besides their theatrical collaborations, the brothers Johnson wrote the song "Lift Ev'ry Voice and Sing" premiered in 1900 by a public school chorus in Jacksonville. The song became known as the "Negro National Anthem" and later as the "Black National Anthem." Later, they published two collections of arrangements of spirituals for solo voice and piano (1925, 1926), and J. Rosamond issued two more volumes of arrangements of African American folk music (1936, 1937), the second of which is titled *Rolling Along in Song: A Chronological Survey of American Negro Music*. All of these publications, as well as their works for the musical stage, reflected James Weldon's concern that "a distinct African-American creative voice" be sustained in artistic works and attest to their interest in, knowledge of, and sense of the need for the preservation of the folk music of African Americans.

Elayne Jones (1928–)
Timpanist

Elayne Jones, born in New York City, began to study the piano with her mother when she was six-years-old. She graduated from the High School of Music and Art and then attended the Juilliard School of Music on a scholarship sponsored by Duke Ellington. In 1949, she was hired by the New York City Opera and Ballet Company orchestra at an unusually young age. She worked with many other orchestras in the New York area including the American Symphony Orchestra from 1962, when the orchestra was founded, until 1972. In that year she was invited by the San Francisco Symphony's music director, Seiji Ozawa, to become its timpanist. Accepting, she became the first African American female to hold a principal chair in a major orchestra.

In 1974, Jones was denied tenure with the orchestra, and, on appeal in 1975, was again denied. She lost the fight to retain her position despite her exemplary professional record and the strong support of friends, colleagues, and the San Francisco public. In 1965, she had been one of the movers for founding the Symphony of the New World and was its first president. Additionally, she has worked as a freelance timpanist in the musical theater, films, and television. She has also taught in many institutions in the New York and San Francisco areas and has lectured widely.

In 1993, the National Association of Negro Musicians gave her its Distinguished Service Award.

Scott Joplin (1868–1917)
Composer, Pianist

Scott Joplin was born in Texarkana in 1868 and received an early musical education in guitar and piano. Leaving home in his teens, he became a travelling musician, settling for some periods of time in Sedalia and St. Louis, Missouri. He worked with minstrel companies and other musical groups and began to be recognized as an outstanding ragtime piano player. His enduringly popular "Maple Leaf Rag" was published in 1899, and publication of many more ragtime compositions followed regularly.

Joplin had ambitions for writing more "substantial" works, however, and his first effort was the opera *A Guest of Honor*, which he took on tour in 1903. This was a financial failure (even though it was a "ragtime opera"), and any performance materials were lost. After Joplin's move to New York in 1907, where his compositions continued to be successfully published, he decided to return to the musical theater and, in 1911, completed *Treemonisha*. He himself undertook publication of the vocal score; the storyline was a sort of parable about education being the key to improve the lot of the African American. No performance was mounted during his lifetime. However, there was a premiere of the work given at the Atlanta Memorial Arts Center in January of 1972, for the Afro-American Music Workshop of Morehouse College. T.J. Anderson orchestrated from the vocal score, and Katherine Dunham was responsible for staging and choreography. Two subsequent orchestrations were made, attesting to the work's popularity and attraction to musicians, and the opera reached Broadway for a run in 1975.

The Complete Works of Scott Joplin was issued in 1981 (the piano works), and there have been numerous articles, books, and dissertations written on Joplin's life and works since the resurgence of interest in ragtime in the early 1970s. In 1976, he was awarded the honorary Bicentennial Pulitzer Prize for contributions to American music.

Robert Jordan (1940–)
Pianist, Educator

Robert Jordan was born in Chattanooga, Tennessee in 1940. He earned a bachelor of music degree in 1962 from the Eastman School of Music in Rochester, New York, where his major teacher was Cecile Genhart; and a master of music degree at the Juilliard School of Music, with Rosina Lhevine as his major teacher, in 1965.

Jordan made a successful New York debut as soloist with the Symphony of the New World in 1971 and as recitalist in the next season at Alice Tully Hall in Lincoln Center. He was a Fulbright Scholar for two years, which

Robert Jordan (Courtesy of Robert Jordan)

he spent studying and performing in Germany. He has performed in Africa, South America, Europe, and the United States as recitalist and orchestra soloist. In 1980 he joined the faculty of the State University of New York at Fredonia as professor of piano, and he received the Chancellor's Award for Excellence in Teaching. In 1987, he served as Martin Luther King Visiting Professor at Northern Michigan University in Marquette, and, in 1991, in the same capacity at the University of Michigan, Ann Arbor.

Ulysses Simpson Kay (1917–1995)

Composer, Educator

From the mid-1940s on, Ulysses Kay composed steadily for instrumental solos and ensembles, string, chamber, and full orchestra, band, voice, chorus, opera, and for film and television. A large number of his works—almost sixty—were commissioned. His compositions are strongly based in Western European traditions—he was a student of Howard Hanson and Paul Hindemith—but they are also rooted in African American folk music practices.

Kay was born in Tucson, Arizona, to musical parents, and he benefitted from a number of other musical influences throughout his childhood. His uncle was the legendary cornet player Joseph "King" Oliver, who urged his sister to give the young Ulysses piano lessons before starting him on any other instrument. Besides piano, however, he studied violin and saxophone, sang in the school glee club, and played in the marching band and dance orchestra. He attended the University of Arizona, where he earned a bachelor of music degree in 1938. Two years later, he received a master of music degree from the Eastman School of Music in Rochester, New York.

During service in the Navy from 1942 to 1946, Kay wrote the work that first brought him critical attention, *Of New Horizons*, which was performed by the New York Philharmonic in 1944. Kay's *Suite for Orchestra* in 1945 received a prize from Broadcast Music, Incorporated, a company for which Kay later acted as a consultant from 1953 until 1968. This prize was to be the first of many awards, fellowships, and grants, which would allow the gifted composer to concentrate on his music in both Europe and the United States.

Although he served as a visiting professor at Boston University and the University of California at Los Angeles, he did not receive a permanent teaching position until he joined the faculty of the Lehman College of the City University of New York in 1968. In 1988, he retired from his position as distinguished professor composition and theory.

Some representative works by Kay are the film score *The Quiet One* (1948), *Six Dances for String Orchestra* (1954), *Choral Triptych* (1962), *Markings* (1966), *Southern Harmony: Four Aspects for Orchestra* (1975), and the opera—one of five—*Frederick Douglass* (1991). Kay received over 25 honors and awards, which include a George Gershwin Memorial Award, Fulbright and Guggenheim Fellowships, a National Endowment for the Arts Grant, and election to the American Academy of Arts and Letters, as well as several honorary doctorates.

Tania Justina León (1943–)

Composer, Conductor, Pianist

Tania León is a native of Havana, Cuba, where she earned both a bachelor's and a master's degree in music from the Carlos Alfredo Peyrellado Conservatory. In 1967, she emigrated to the United States and worked for another bachelor's degree in music education and master's in composition from New York University. There she studied with Ursula Mamlok and Laszlo Halasz, and later she studied conducting with Seiji Ozawa and Leonard Bernstein at the Berkshire Music Festival at Tanglewood, Massachusetts.

In New York, León's first professional work in music was as an accompanist and then music director of what became Arthur Mitchell's Dance Theatre of Harlem. She went to the Festival of Two Worlds in Spoleto, Italy, with the company in 1971, and there she made her first appearance as conductor. Additionally, she wrote scores for Mitchell's choreography. With increasing demands on her time for guest conducting, piano performances, and commissions for works, she left the company in 1980. She served as music director for the Alvin Ailey Dance Company for the 1983–84 season, and music director for Broadway musicals from 1978's *The Wiz*, to *The Lion King* in 1996.

León joined the faculty of Brooklyn College in 1985 and became professor in 1994. She was the Revson Composer for the New York Philharmonic from 1993 until 1996, and its new music advisor from 1996 to 1997. She has also served as composer- or conductor/composer-in-residence for many orchestras and educational institutions.

Thoroughly trained in the classical music tradition, León began to incorporate her ethnic backgrounds—encompassing Chinese, African, South American, Cuban, and French—into the creation of unique works with startling juxtapositions, which are informed by her mastery of the contemporary orchestra. Just a few of her colorful works are: *Kabiosile* for piano and orchestra (1988); *Indígena* for chamber orchestra (1991); the chamber opera *Scourge of Hyacinths* for the Fourth Munich Biennale (1994); *Para Viola y Orquesta* (1995); and *Bata* (1995). She has received over thirty commissions and numerous honors and awards including citations from the National Council of the Arts, Havana, the National Endowment for the Arts, Meet the Composer, the Dean Dixon Achievement Award, and a Rockefeller Foundation residency.

Henry Jay Lewis (1932–1996)
Conductor, Double Bassist

Henry Lewis was born in Los Angeles and knew early on that he wanted to be a musician, in spite of his father's disapproval of the profession. He was only 16 years old when he joined the Los Angeles Philharmonic Orchestra in 1948 as a double bassist, becoming the first African American instrumentalist to play with a major American orchestra. In 1954, he was drafted into the U.S. Army. While stationed in Germany, between 1955 and 1957 he conducted the Seventh Army Symphony Orchestra. Following discharge, he returned to the Los Angeles Philharmonic as assistant conductor. Lewis founded the String Society of Los Angeles in 1959 (later known as the Los Angeles Chamber Orchestra) and was engaged as guest conductor with virtually every major American orchestra. From 1965 to 1968 he was also the music director of the Los Angeles Opera Company.

Lewis was selected as conductor and music director of the New Jersey Symphony in 1968 and so became the first African American to serve in that position with a major American orchestra. He conducted the New York Philharmonic in 1972 and became the first African American to conduct the Metropolitan Opera Orchestra. Resigning from the New Jersey Symphony in 1976, Lewis remained active as a guest conductor in the United States and Europe, and made recordings with the Scottish Opera and the Netherlands Radio Symphony Orchestra. In 1991, he was music director of the London production of *Carmen Jones*.

Lewis was founder of the Black Academy of Arts and Letters and a member of the California Arts Commission and the Young Musicians Foundation.

Robert McFerrin (1921–)
Singer, Educator

Baritone Robert McFerrin, born in Marianna, Arkansas, was brought up in St. Louis, Missouri, where he attended public schools and sang in his father's church choir. After a year at Fisk University in Nashville, the young Robert attended the Chicago Musical College, where he earned a bachelor's degree.

McFerrin began his professional singing career in Broadway shows including *Lost in the Stars* and *The Green Pastures*. He also sang with the National Negro Opera Company in William Grant Still's *Troubled Island*, the role of Rigoletto with the New England Opera Company in 1950, and, after winning the 1954 Metropolitan Auditions of the Air, he became a member of the regular roster of the Metropolitan Opera for three seasons, the first African American male singer to do so.

McFerrin has been a guest professor of voice at several institutions in Finland, Canada, and the United States, and has performed widely in North and South America and Europe. Both Stowe Teacher's College in St. Louis and the University of Missouri awarded him honorary doctorates.

Robert "Bobby" McFerrin, Jr. (1950–)
Singer, Conductor, Songwriter

Bobby McFerrin, the son of opera singers Robert and Sara McFerrin, was born in New York City. In 1958, his family moved to Los Angeles, and he attended Sacramento State University and Cerritos College. Dropping out of college, he played piano for several show companies. By 1977 he had decided to concentrate on a singing career, and he was discovered by Jon Hendricks. He performed at jazz festivals and began touring and recording with George Benson and Herbie Hancock, among

Bobby McFerrin (AP/Wide World Photos, Inc.)

other jazz greats. His first of many solo albums was called simply *Bobby McFerrin*, and he went on to win nine Grammy Awards. His song "Don't Worry, Be Happy" topped the popular music charts in 1989.

McFerrin made his conducting debut with the San Francisco Symphony in 1990, and he was appointed conductor and creative chair of the St. Paul Chamber Orchestra. He is in demand as both vocalist and conductor for orchestras around the country and continues to present innovative programming in both capacities.

Lena Johnson McLin (1928–)

Composer, Conductor, Educator

Born in Atlanta, Lena McLin was immersed in music as a child, particularly gospel and classical. Her mother, a choir director, gave her piano lessons and exposed her to various kinds of sacred music. This foundation of religious music became even stronger during the years she lived with the family of her uncle, Thomas A. Dorsey, the "father of gospel music," in Chicago. McLin received a bachelor of music degree from Spelman College in Atlanta in 1951, and she moved to Chicago for graduate study in composition and music theory, first at the American Conservatory of Music and then at Roosevelt University, where she also studied electronic music and voice.

In 1959, McLin began a long teaching career in the Chicago public schools, which was distinguished by her development and implementation of a music curriculum for the school system, and included her writing a textbook on music history. She also conducted a variety of church and community choirs; founded an opera company, the McLin Ensemble, in 1957 and the gospel group, the McLin Singers, in 1968; and has served as guest conductor and in workshops for several national organizations and educational institutions.

The varied list of McLin's compositions includes several piano solos and dozens of choral works, among them the commissioned mass *Eucharist of the Soul*, the dramatic oratorio *Free at Last: A Portrait of Martin Luther King Jr.* and *The Torch Has Been Passed*, based on President John F. Kennedy's inaugural address. Her style shows her love for and mastery of all kinds of music—gospel, rock, popular, and past and current traditions of Western concert music—which can be distinct or interwoven in her scores and always make clear and direct statements.

Dorothy Leigh Maynor (1910–1996)

Singer, Administrator

Born in Norfolk, Virginia, Dorothy Mainor (she changed the spelling of her last name when she became a singer) grew up in an atmosphere of music and singing. She intended originally to become a home economics teacher, and, with this in mind, entered the Hampton Institute College Preparatory School in 1924. However, her development as a singer in the school choir prompted her choir director, R. Nathaniel Dett, to convince her to switch to a voice major. She graduated from the Institute with a bachelor degree in 1933.

Maynor was heard by the director of the Westminster Choir, who made it possible for her to receive a scholarship at the Westminster Choir College in Princeton, New Jersey. She received her bachelor's degree in music in 1935 and went to New York City to continue voice study. At the Berkshire Music Festival in Tanglewood, Massachusetts, in 1939, Boston Symphony Orchestra conductor Serge Koussevitzky immediately took an interest in furthering her career. Maynor was acclaimed by critics on her 1939 Town Hall debut in New York, and thus began her remarkable 25-year career as recitalist, orchestra soloist, and recording artist.

Following her debut, Maynor toured the United States and the rest of the world and performed with the leading orchestras of the day. Additionally, Maynor embarked upon a recording career in which she sang arias, spirituals, and operas. Her interpretations of the latter, however, were limited to the recording studio because no opera company of the time would allow an African American to perform in their productions. Although her singing earned Maynor extremely favorable reviews from critics around the world, she was not allowed to audition for the Metropolitan Opera. In an ironic twist, she would become the first African American member of the Met's board of directors in 1975. In 1952, Maynor became the first African American artist to perform at Constitution Hall in Washington, DC.

Maynor retired from singing after her husband's heart attack in 1963. However, she remained active in the arts through the foundation of what became the Harlem School of the Arts located initially in the St. James Presbyterian Church. By the late 1970s the school boasted more than forty instructors and over one thousand students. With the school rapidly outgrowing the church, Maynor raised $3.5 million to erect a new building, which opened in 1979, the year she retired as its director.

Leona Mitchell (1949–)
Singer

Soprano Leona Mitchell was born in Enid, Oklahoma, and graduated from Oklahoma University in 1971. She made her Metropolitan Opera debut as Micaela in Bizet's *Carmen* in 1975 and also sang the roles of Lauretta in Puccini's *Gianni Schicchi*, Pamina in Mozart's *The Magic Flute*, and Madamoiselle Lidoine in Poulenc's *Dialogues of the Carmelites*. Her outstanding vocal capabilities have caused her to be regarded as the leading American soprano with a career that has taken her to all the major opera houses of the world. She has likewise performed with several orchestras and, in 1980, sang the role of Bess in The Cleveland Orchestra Blossom Festival production of Gershwin's *Porgy and Bess* and in the subsequent recording. In 1983, she was inducted into the Oklahoma Hall of Fame.

Leona Mitchell (Corbis Corporation [Bellevue])

Dorothy Rudd Moore (1940–)
Composer, Teacher, Singer

Born in Wilmington, Delaware, Dorothy Rudd Moore attended the Wilmington School of Music as a teenager and, in 1963, received a bachelor of music degree, magna cum laude, in theory and composition from Howard University, where her major composition teacher was Mark Fax. Later, she studied composition privately with Chou Wen Chung in New York City and with Nadia Boulanger at the American Conservatory in Fontainebleau, France. She also studied voice at Howard University and privately, and she has performed frequently as a singer.

Moore taught piano, voice, sight-singing, and ear-training at the Harlem School of the Arts, New York University, and Bronx Community College. Among her works in various media are: *Dirge and Deliverance*, for piano and cello, commissioned by her husband Kermit Moore; *Flowers of Darkness* for tenor and piano, commissioned by William Brown; *Reflections* for concert band; and the opera *Frederick Douglass*, commissioned and premiered by Opera Ebony in 1985, about which *Opera News* reported that she "displays a rare ability to wed musical and dramatic motion, graceful lyric inventiveness, [and] a full command of the orchestral palette."

Kermit Moore (1929–)
Cellist, Conductor, Composer

Kermit Moore's first musical identity was as a cellist. He studied the instrument at the Cleveland Institute of Music and received a bachelor's degree in 1951. He earned a master of arts degree at New York University in 1952, and, in 1956, he attended the Paris National Conservatory and was awarded an artist's diploma. He gave his New York recital debut at Town Hall in 1949 and has concertized internationally in the major capitals of Europe and Asia. He has also made appearances with many orchestras, particularly in Europe.

In 1964, Moore co-founded the Symphony of the New World in New York. Besides performing as cellist with the group, he also conducted occasionally. He was careful to include a wide variety of works by African American composers on his symphonic programs. One of the most unusual, perhaps, was the Concerto for Violin and Orchestra, premiered in 1867 by its composer, the Afro-Cuban Joseph White, and given its first American performance with Ruggero Ricci as soloist in 1974. He has had many engagements as guest conductor in the United States.

In addition to his work with the Symphony of the New World, Moore served as conductor of the Brooklyn Philharmonic beginning in 1984. He was also one of several founders of the Society of Black Composers. He writes instrumental solos and ensembles including concertos for cello and timpani, and for voice.

Undine Smith Moore (1904–1989)
Composer, Educator

A native of Jarret, Virginia, Undine Smith Moore studied piano in Petersburg and began her college studies at Fisk University in Nashville. In 1926, she was awarded a bachelor of arts degree, cum laude, and a music school diploma, and later attended Columbia University Teachers College, where she earned a master's degree and professional diploma in 1931. She took further graduate studies at several schools including the Juilliard and Eastman Schools of Music.

Moore taught at Virginia State College in Petersburg from 1927 until 1972, when she became professor emerita. Her students included many illustrious contributors to the music world, such as jazz pianist Billy Taylor, opera singer Camilla Williams, conductor Leon Thompson, gospel singer Robert Fryson, music educators Michael V.W. Gordon and James Mumford, and composer Phil Medley. At the university, she co-founded the Black Music Center in 1969 and was co-director until 1972. After retirement, she was a visiting professor at many universities and colleges. Some of her awards include honorary doctorates from Virginia State University and Indiana University, the Seventh Annual Humanitarian Awards from Fisk University, and the National Association of Negro Musicians Award (1975). In 1982, her *Scenes from the Life of a Martyr: To the Memory of Martin Luther King*, an oratorio, was nominated for the Pulitzer Prize.

Moore's style was infused with African American influences and a tonal musical language. Choral music makes up the largest part of her output and there are many works for instrumental solos and ensembles including *Afro-American Suite*, commissioned by Antoinette Handy's Trio Pro Viva. Her 1987 trio *Soweto*, inspired by events in that South African town, was the last work she wrote.

Michael DeVard Morgan (1957–)
Conductor

Born in Washington, DC, Michael Morgan received music training in the public schools he attended, in addition to private piano lessons. He attended the Oberlin College Conservatory of Music from 1975 to 1979. He pursued additional studies in the Vienna master classes of Witold Rowicki and at the Berkshire Music Center at Tanglewood, where he was a conducting fellow and student of Seiji Ozawa and Gunther Schuller. Morgan was selected to work with Leonard Bernstein for one week, which culminated in Morgan's appearance with the New York Philharmonic in September of 1986. From 1980 to 1987, he was Exxon/Arts Endowment assistant conductor of the Chicago Symphony Orchestra and later became affiliate artist conductor; he was also co-resident conductor of the Chicago Civic Orchestra. He became music director of the Oakland East Bay Symphony Orchestra in 1993 and has appeared as a guest conductor with many of the nation's major orchestras and abroad.

The many awards Morgan has earned include first prize in the Hans Swarowsky International Conductors Competition (Vienna, Austria), the first prize in the Gino Marrinuzzi International Conductors Competition (San Remo, Italy), and first prize in the Baltimore Symphony Young Conductors Competition.

Jessye Norman (1945–)
Singer

Soprano Jessye Norman was born into a musical family in Augusta, Georgia. Her mother, a schoolteacher, gave her children piano lessons. The young Jessye's musical talents were evident early, and at the age of 16 she entered the Marian Anderson Scholarship competition. She did not win, but her audition at Howard University led to a four-year scholarship. Receiving her bachelor's degree in 1967, she continued study, first at the Peabody Conservatory with Alice Dushak, and then at the University of Michigan at Ann Arbor with Pierre Bernac and Elizabeth Mannion for a master's degree in 1968. That year, she entered the International Music Competition held in Munich, Germany, and won first place. Her operatic career in Europe was launched, and she made debuts at the Deutsche Oper in Berlin, La

Jessye Norman (AP/Wide World Photos, Inc.)

Scala in Milan, and the Royal Opera House in Covent Garden, London. Her American opera debut took place at the Hollywood Bowl as Aida, and her stage debut with the Opera Company of Philadelphia in the double bill of Purcell's *Dido and Aeneas* and Stravinsky's *Oedipus Rex* (1982). In 1983, she made her Metropolitan Opera debut as Cassandra in *Les Troyens* by Berlioz.

Taking a break from opera performance, Norman was a busy recitalist and orchestra soloist from 1975 to 1980, with a far-ranging repertoire. She continued these activities after resuming operatic appearances as Ariadne in *Ariadne auf Naxos* by Richard Strauss. Her vocal prowess and the breadth of her musicianship are demonstrated by the variety of operas that she sings including Rameau, Mozart, Meyerbeer, Wagner, Verdi, and Bartok. Among her numerous recordings are two compact discs of spirituals (one with Kathleen Battle) and many concert works and operas, and even a "crossover" pop album *Lucky to Be Me*.

Coleridge-Taylor Perkinson (1932–)
Composer, Conductor

A native New Yorker, Coleridge-Taylor Perkinson graduated from the High School for Music and Art in that city and, after two years at New York University, transferred to the Manhattan School of Music, where he studied conducting with Jonel Perlea and composition with Vittorio Giannini. He also studied composing at Princeton University with Earl Kim, and conducting at the Berkshire Music Center at Tanglewood, the Mozarteum in Salzburg, Austria, and the Netherlands Radio Union.

Perkinson worked steadily as a composer and music director. Some of the groups with which he has been associated are the Dessoff Choirs as assistant conductor, the Max Roach Jazz Quartet as pianist, the Symphony of the New World, as founding member and associate conductor from 1965 to 1970, and the Negro Ensemble Company as composer-in-residence. He has received many commissions including three from dance companies: Arthur Mitchell Dance Company, 1971; Dance Theatre of Harlem, 1972 and 1987; and the American Dance Theater Foundation, 1984. He has been guest conductor for several orchestras in the United States and abroad.

Perkinson has written a great deal of incidental and commercial music for film and television programs, and he has written and arranged for many different kinds of artists, such as Harry Belafonte, Max Roach, Marvin Gaye, and Melvin Van Peebles. Instrumental works are predominant in his catalog of works, ranging from solos to mixed ensembles to string, chamber, and full orchestras. His works demonstrate his complete knowledge of twentieth-century compositional techniques and his ease in using them for highly-varied expressive purposes. The folk music of African Americans is a basic part of what and how Perkinson writes.

Julia Perry (1924–1979)
Composer, Conductor

Julia Perry, born in Lexington, Kentucky, was raised in Akron, Ohio. As a child, she studied piano and became interested in composing early on. In 1942, she entered the Westminster Choir College in Princeton, New Jersey, and studied composition and conducting, in addition to violin, piano, and voice. After earning a master's degree in 1948, she studied composition at the Juilliard School of Music, where her music was performed for the first time.

In the 1950s, Perry lived mostly in Europe. Having studied with Luigi Dallapiccola at the Berkshire Music Center at Tanglewood, Massachusetts, she continued studies with him in Italy on two Guggenheim Fellowships in 1954 and 1956. She also studied with Nadia Boulanger in Paris during this time and won a Boulanger Grand Prix for her Viola Sonata in 1952. She continued studying conducting as well, and she had many opportunities to conduct some of her works in Europe. She also was a lecturer on American music through the United States Information Service.

With her return to the United States in 1959, Perry continued to compose and was engaged to teach at several colleges. She concentrated on writing instrumental music in the 1960s, whereas earlier she specialized in vocal music including choral. Among her output of orchestral works were 12 symphonies. Whatever the medium, Perry was almost always availing herself of the rich resources of her African American musical heritage, and she was in command of the Western European tradition including the latest techniques that had been developed in Europe and the United States.

Some of her most-performed works are: *Stabat Mater* (1951) for contralto or mezzo-soprano and string quartet or string orchestra; *A Short Piece for Orchestra* (1952), that was premiered by the Turin Symphony conducted by Dean Dixon; and *Homunculus C.F.* (1960), for eight percussionists, harp, celesta, and piano.

A debilitating stroke in 1973 almost incapacitated Perry, and it was no doubt a major factor in her early death.

Evelyn LaRue Pittman (1910–)

Choral Director, Composer

While a senior at Spelman College in Atlanta studying African American history, Evelyn Pittman committed herself to teaching African American history through music. Her first work, a musical play, was produced at Spelman in 1933, the year she graduated. During the years she taught in the public schools in Oklahoma City from 1935 to 1956, she conducted weekly broadcasts with her own professional vocal group, the Evelyn Pittman Choir, on a local radio station. She also directed a 350-voice choir sponsored by the YWCA and directed orchestras, choirs, and operettas in the schools. She published songs which she composed about African American leaders that she published in the collection *Rich Heritage* in 1944.

In 1948, Pittman went to the Juilliard School of Music in New York City to study composition under Robert Ward. Later, she attended the University of Oklahoma at Norman and studied with Harrison Kerr, receiving a master's degree in 1954. Kerr introduced her to his former teacher, Nadia Boulanger, who became her teacher from 1956 to 1958. During that period, she completed her folk opera *Cousin Esther* written for an African American cast. It was performed many times to favorable reviews in both France and the United States.

Pittman returned to public school teaching in 1958 in New York and continued to compose. After the assassination of Dr. Martin Luther King Jr. in 1968, she wrote the opera *Freedom Child* in his memory. Upon her retirement from teaching, she dedicated herself to directing a touring company of *Freedom Child* and remained committed to improving race relations through music and drama.

Awadagin Pratt (1966–)

Pianist, Conductor, Violinist

Awadagin Pratt was born in 1966 in Pittsburgh, Pennsylvania, and began studying piano at the age of six. In 1975, his family moved to Illinois, and he attended the University of Illinois, Urbana, at the age of 16, majoring in music. In 1986 he enrolled in the Peabody Conservatory of Music in Baltimore, where he earned performer's certificates in piano and violin in 1989 and a graduate performance diploma in conducting in 1992.

In 1992 Pratt's career as a concert pianist began when he became the first African American to win the Naumburg International piano composition. After several major concert successes, he was awarded the Avery Fisher Career Grant in 1994, and his full-time concert career continued at a rapid pace. He has performed with many major American orchestras, and he has given recitals throughout the United States and in Europe, Africa, and Japan.

Pratt has been interested in the education of younger musicians during his career and has given up to ten master classes a year, beginning in 1992, at such colleges as the Eastman School of Music and the Universities of Washington, Missouri, Minnesota, Texas, and many others. He is on the boards of the Pratt Music Foundation and the Next Generation Festival.

An EMI recording artist, Pratt's third recording for that label is entitled *Live from South Africa*, performed from the stage of the Capetown Opera House. Asked by an interviewer for *Piano and Keyboard* magazine about how he chooses music for his repertoire, Pratt responded that his selections "have to be works that express, that evoke something more than themselves. Music and art are about expressing some sort of joy about all states of experience—a celebration, even, of those states."

Florence Beatrice Price (1888–1953)

Composer, Pianist, Educator

As a young child, Florence Price studied piano with her mother in her hometown of Little Rock, Arkansas, and was precocious enough to play in public for the first time at the age of four. When she was only 14 years old, she began study with Frederick Converse and George Chadwick at the New England Conservatory of Music in Boston, where she earned diplomas in organ and piano in 1906. She returned to Arkansas to teach at the high school and college levels and moved to Atlanta in 1910 to become head of the music department of Clark College.

In 1912, Florence married attorney Thomas Price in Little Rock, where they lived until moving in 1927 to Chicago—a move prompted by increasing racial tensions in the South. In Chicago she taught privately and took advanced studies at the Chicago Musical College and the American Conservatory. Price had published her first composition in 1899, and, after her move to Chicago, the number of her publications increased notably, especially of organ, piano, and vocal music.

The best-known of her orchestral works is, perhaps, her Symphony in A Minor, No. 1 that won first prize in the 1930 Wanamaker Music Contest; it was performed by the Chicago Symphony Orchestra at the Chicago World's Fair Century of Progress Exhibition in 1933. Three of her other prizewinning compositions in that competition were Piano Sonata in E Minor (first prize) and Piano Fantasie No. 4 and the orchestral *Ethiopia's Shadow in America* (both honorable mentions). Her Concerto in One Movement for piano had several performances, the solo part often played by her student Margaret Bonds. Price was well-known for her songs and arrangements of spirituals, which were performed by such stellar singers as Marian Anderson, Roland Hayes, Leontyne Price, and Blanche Thebom. Anderson championed her setting of Langston Hughes's "Songs to a Dark Virgin."

Price was thoroughly familiar with and comfortable in using African American folk music, both sacred and secular, and her works in standard concert form usually demonstrate this aspect of her style. Overall, her style is usually described as "neoromantic" and "nationalistic."

Mary Violet Leontyne Price (1927–)
Singer

Soprano Leontyne Price was born in Laurel, Mississippi, where her parents encouraged her in music with piano lessons and participation in their church choir. With the idea of teaching music in school, she attended Central State College in Wilberforce, Ohio. Even before her graduation in 1949 with a bachelor's degree in music education, she received a scholarship at the Juilliard School of Music in New York City. Her work there attracted the attention of critic and composer Virgil Thomson, who cast her in her first professional role as Cecilia in a revival of his and Gertrude Stein's opera *Four Saints in Three Acts*. Soon afterwards, she toured in Europe as Bess in a revival of Gershwin's *Porgy and Bess* (1952–1954). Her marriage to co-star William Warfield ended in divorce in 1973.

After the tour was completed, Price made her New York recital debut at Town Hall and took other operatic roles on both stage and television. She was the first African American to perform opera in television when she played Puccini's *Tosca*. Her performance was so well-received that she was invited back to play Pamina and Donna Anna from Mozart's *The Magic Flute* and *Don Giovanni* respectively, and Madame Lidoine in Poulenc's *Dialogues of the Carmelites*. Her Metropolitan Opera debut was as Leonora in Verdi's *Il Trovatore*. Other Verdi roles in which she was brilliantly successful were in *Aida*, *Un Ballo in Maschera*, *Ernani*, and *La Forza del Destino*. For the opening of the new Metropolitan Opera House in 1966, she was Cleopatra in the specially-commissioned opera by Samuel Barber, *Antony and Cleopatra*. She has sung many roles with other opera companies as well, especially the San Francisco Opera (she was awarded their medal in honor of the twentieth anniversary of her company debut) and the Lyric Opera of Chicago.

Price has received several honorary doctorates, over twenty Grammy Awards, and a Kennedy Center Honor for lifetime achievement in the arts. She ended her operatic career in 1985 in *Aida* at the Metropolitan Opera but has continued performing. Her recordings are numerous and span a wide range of repertory. There are several collections of arias—operatic and concert—art songs, Christmas and patriotic songs, and a collaboration with Andre Previn on 12 pop songs *Right As the Rain*.

Kay George Roberts (1950–)
Conductor, Violinist

Kay Roberts was born in Nashville, Tennessee, and began her professional musical career as a violinist when she joined the Nashville Symphony during her last year in high school. She continued to play with the orchestra until she graduated with a bachelor's degree from Fisk University in 1972. In 1971, she represented the Nashville Symphony in Arthur Fiedler's World Symphony Orchestra. She earned a master of music degree in 1975, a master of musical arts in 1976, and a doctor of musical arts degree in 1986 from Yale University—the first woman and second African American to do so. During her second year of residency at Yale, Roberts's talent as a conductor first came to the attention of her instructor and, thereafter, she focused on conducting rather than the violin.

Roberts has guest conducted many orchestras including the symphonies of Nashville, Chattanooga, Indianapolis, Des Moines, Greater Dallas, and Chicago, in addition to the Cleveland Orchestra, the Mystic Valley Chamber Orchestra, and the Bangkok Symphony in Thailand. She became the music director of the New Hampshire Philharmonic in 1982 and of the Cape Ann Symphony Orchestra in 1986.

Leontyne Price (AP/Wide World Photos, Inc.)

Roberts began teaching at the College of Music at the University of Massachusetts at Lowell in 1978. She has received numerous awards throughout her career including the 1991 Outstanding Achievement in the Performing Arts Award from the League of Black Women and the 1993 National Achievement Award from the National Black Music Caucus.

Paul Robeson (1898–1976)
Singer, Actor

Born in Princeton, New Jersey, Paul Robeson was the son of a runaway slave who worked his way through Lincoln University and became a minister. Paul Robeson entered Rutgers College (now University) on an athletic scholarship and won a total of 12 letters in track, football, baseball, and basketball. His academic ability gained him another prize: Phi Beta Kappa honors in his junior year.

Robeson moved to New York City after graduation and began the study of law at Columbia University in 1920. He also began to act, and this profession eventually took precedence over a law career (he had been admitted to the New York State bar in 1923). He was cast in Eugene O'Neill's *Emperor Jones* in 1923 and, two years later, in *All God's Chillun Got Wings*, gaining excellent reviews for both production. His rich singing voice, coupled with his strong interest in spirituals and international folk songs, led him to concertize in recital, first in New York and later in Europe and England. Besides enjoying great success on the London and Broadway stages, he also acted in several films in the 1930s and early 1940s. He became one of the first African Americans to depart from stereotypical film roles.

Robeson's concern for racial justice came increasingly to the forefront in those years as well, and his travels to the Soviet Union convinced him of the honesty of that country's statements regarding the equal treatment of all people. With the Cold War settling in after World War II, Robeson's freely expressed views brought him into conflict with Congress and federal authorities, and, despite his denials, he was accused of being a communist. His career was effectively ended, and his passport was revoked in 1950—to be restored eight years later by a U.S. Supreme Court decision. He moved to England and traveled widely in Europe and the Soviet Union until 1963, when he returned to the United States. In 1971, his autobiography *Here I Stand* was published. He contin-

Paul Robeson performing the lead role in the Shakespearean play *Othello* in 1943 (AP/Wide World Photos, Inc.).

Philippa Schuyler performs at the piano as an eight year old in 1940 (AP/Wide World Photos, Inc.).

ued to be active in civil and human rights issues until his health began to fail in the 1970s. In 1998, he was posthumously honored with a Grammy Lifetime Achievement Award.

Philippa (Duke) Schuyler (1931–1967)
Pianist, Composer

Born in New York City to an African American father and a white mother, Philippa Schuyler embodied her parents' desire to prove to the world that the intermingling of the black and white races would result in a hybrid which would draw from the strengths of each lineage. She initially fulfilled their expectations: at the age of two and a half she could read and write; by age four she was composing music; and by age five she was performing Mozart. Her IQ, tested by New York University, was 185. She was given piano lessons at the age of three and early in elementary school she began to study harmony, having already written dozens of piano pieces. She gave her first solo recital at the age of six. While Schuyler was studying throughout her childhood and adolescence, she had relatively little formal composition training, and that ended when she was 15. Among her teachers were Dean Dixon and Antonia Brico in conducting, Josef Hoffman, Paul Wittgenstein, and Gaston Dethier in piano, and Clarence Cameron White in violin.

With her parents pushing her career, the child prodigy wowed the critics in both the excellence of her playing and the quality of her compositions. Schuyler began to perform widely as a teenager and appeared as orchestra soloist and recitalist; several of her works were performed by orchestras including the New York Philharmonic, the Chicago Symphony, and the Detroit Symphony. She made three world tours, at first under U.S. State Department auspices, and received numerous awards throughout her career. Among them was a 1939 World's Fair Medal as one of the "Women of Tomorrow," an Award of Merit from the Fair in 1940, a Distinguished Achievement Award from the National Negro Opera Company Foundation, in 1955, gold and silver medals from Haile Selassie, the Emperor of Ethiopia, in 1955, and, after her death, the establishment of a memorial foundation in her name.

However, despite her successes, Schuyler's appeal to white America faded as soon as she entered young adulthood. Stung by the racism she had not encountered as a child, Schuyler left the United States to travel the world and played for numerous foreign dignitaries. But in spite of the acclaim she received outside of the United States, the rejection she experienced in America was a bitter reminder that, regardless of her success abroad, she was still a second-class citizen back home. Her travels became a painful search for identity which she attempted to reconcile through her fiction and non-fiction writing. She even adopted a different identity, claiming to be Felipa Monterro, an Iberian-American, in the hopes of gaining acceptance before white audiences in America. However, initial reviews of her concerts performed in Europe under this new identity were mediocre.

In 1967, Schuyler was killed in a helicopter crash in Da Nang Bay, South Vietnam, where she had gone to help in the rescue of some schoolchildren.

Hale Smith (1925–)

Composer, Educator, Editor

Hale Smith is a native of Cleveland, Ohio, where he attended public schools and earned bachelor (1950) and master (1952) of music degrees from the Cleveland Institute of Music. His only composition teacher, Marcel Dick, was a major influence, as were such jazz figures as Duke Ellington and Art Tatum.

In 1958, on his move to New York City, Smith began arranging for and collaborating with many different kinds of musicians including Chico Hamilton, Dizzy Gillespie, and Oliver Nelson. Active as a music editor and consultant from 1961, he worked for several music publishing companies—Marks Music and C. F. Peters, among them. He joined the faculty of the University of Connecticut at Storrs in 1970 and retired in 1984.

Smith has received over twenty commissions and many prestigious awards in the course of his career and has written frequently on many musical subjects. A few of his outstanding compositions are: *Contours* (1961); *Ritual and Incantations* (1974); *Innerflexions* (1977); *Mirrors: Rondo-Variations for Two Pianos* (1988); and *A Ternion of Seasons* for instrumental ensemble (1996). Among several works for concert band, some with pedagogical aims are: *Somersault: A Twelve Tone Adventure for Band* (1964); *Take a Chance: An Aleatoric Episode for Band* (1964); and *Expansions* (1967).

Smith has used the general term "formal music" as a category for his instrumental, band, orchestra, vocal, and choral scores, and within them can be found, in varying degrees, techniques and idioms of African American music. Highly sensitive to instrumental "color" and with a strong dramatic sense, he has consistently conceived of and found new ways to express a broad spectrum of musical ideas.

William Grant Still (1895–1978)

Composer, Conductor

William Grant Still was born in Woodville, Mississippi, and, because of his father's untimely death, his mother moved to Little Rock, Arkansas, where he attended public schools. His family encouraged his interest in music, and he began to take violin lessons as a teenager. He attended Wilberforce University in Ohio but left before receiving a pre-med degree to study at the Oberlin College Conservatory (Ohio).

Still began playing professionally in several bands, spent some time in the U.S. Navy, and moved to New York City to work for the Pace and Handy Music Company Band. He later became director of the classical division and then musical director for the Pace Recording Company. He had many opportunities to play in theater orchestras and to arrange for shows, radio programs, and the movies.

In the 1920s, Still studied with two very different kinds of composers: first, the traditionalist George Chadwick, who was at the New England Conservatory of Music in Boston, and then Edgard Varèse, a leading member of the avant-garde. This broad experience in Western European music expanded his compositional horizons and complemented his African American musical heritage. He was a student of and apologist for black vernacular music in both his musical and academic writings.

Still believed that folk music was the richest source for sounds needed to make American music stand apart from the European models that had dominated composed music. In his attempt to be instrumental in defining an "American sound," Still spent his life collecting, studying, and analyzing the many melodies and rhythms of the ethnic groups that make up the Western hemisphere. Although he arranged folk songs, especially African American spirituals, for various instrumental and choral combinations, he used the scales and rhythms derived from them as his primary source of inspiration in his larger forms. Still chose to compose his own melodies and to harmonize them using the richly stacked chords of jazz and blues. He wanted to elevate the blues by using its characteristic structures in symphonies, ballets, and operas.

Still's Afro-American Symphony, 1930 (revised 1969), was the first of five symphonies that he wrote. In 1931 it was the first large orchestral work to be performed by a major orchestra, the Rochester Philharmonic under the direction of Howard Hanson. One of his eight operas, *Troubled Island*, was the first by an African American

William Grant Still (Archive Photos, Inc)

composer to be staged by a major U.S. company, the New York City Center's Opera Company, in 1949. Another opera *Bayou Legend* was the first by an African American composer to be telecast nationally, over the Public Broadcasting Service in 1981. He was one of the most prolific composers of his generation and was active as a composer into the early 1960s.

Still was among the accomplished artists whose work will always be associated with the Harlem Renaissance in the 1920s and 1930s, and he and Duke Ellington are the leading composers of that movement. A term by which he was often characterized is "the dean of Afro-American composers," and his achievements as a composer testify to the validity of that title.

Howard Swanson (1907–1978)

Composer

Howard Swanson was born in Atlanta to a family in which there were several educators, including his mother. He and his siblings were given music lessons and sang in church, however, it was only with the family's move to Cleveland, Ohio, in 1918, that he studied the piano formally. Although Swanson began to work for the U.S. Postal Service after high school in order to help support his family, he entered the Cleveland Institute of Music, where he studied composition with Herbert Elwell and earned a bachelor of music degree in 1937.

Through a Rosenwald Fellowship that he received in 1938, Swanson was able to go to Paris to study with Nadia Boulanger at the American Academy in Fontainebleau. His study was interrupted by World War II, and he returned to the United States in 1941. After the war, he returned to Europe until 1966, when he made his permanent home in New York City. By this time he had been receiving commissions and his works were being performed. In 1950, for example, Marian Anderson sang his setting of Langston Hughes's *The Negro Speaks of Rivers* (1942) at Carnegie Hall, and his Short Symphony (1948) was premiered by the New York Philharmonic. This symphony won the New York Music Critics' Circle Award in 1952. He wrote steadily into the 1970s, and his works continued to be performed by a wide variety of ensembles and soloists. Swanson's work is most often characterized as "neoclassic," yet his heritage of African American music and traditions is the basis of his musical language. The largest percentage of his compositional output is vocal music; he never wrote an opera or music for the theater.

Shirley Verrett (1933–)

Singer, Actress, Educator

Born in New Orleans, Shirley Verrett moved to California at the age of 11. Her father was her first voice teacher, and her earliest musical experiences were in the Seventh Day Adventist Church. She briefly attended Oakwood College and Ventura College, where she majored in business administration.

By the mid-1950s, she began taking voice lessons in Los Angeles and train her sights on the concert stage. After winning a television talent show in 1955, she enrolled at the Juilliard School on a scholarship and earned her bachelor's of music degree in 1961. She made her New York City opera debut in 1957 in a production of *Lost In the Stars*, and she returned to the city in 1964 to sing the title role in Bizet's *Carmen* at the Metropolitan Opera. By then, she had performed the role in Spoleto, Italy, Moscow, and had appeared in several concert versions of the opera. The *New York Herald Tribune*'s critic claimed her Carmen as one of the finest "seen or heard" in New York for the past generation.

Verrett's yearly recital tours took her to major music centers throughout the country. Between 1983 and 1986, Verrett lived in Paris and had a series of operas staged especially for her by the Paris Opera including, Rossini's *Mose*, Cherubini's *Medee*, and Gluck's *Iphigenie en Tauride* and *Alceste*. She made a triumphant return to the Metropolitan Opera in 1986 as Eboli in *Don Carlo* and also starred that year in a new production of

Shirley Verrett performing in the opera *Carmen* in 1970 (AP/Wide World Photos, Inc.).

Macbeth with the San Francisco Opera. In the 1987–1988 season, Verrett made her long-awaited Chicago Lyric Opera debut as Azucena in *Il Trovatore.*

In the mid-1990s, Verrett turned her career to dramatic acting. She was featured in a major Broadway revival of Rodgers and Hammerstein's *Carousel.* She is now a distinguished professor of voice at the University of Michigan in Ann Arbor.

George Walker (1992–)
Pianist, Educator

George Walker, born into a musical family in Washington, DC, began piano study at the age of five, attended public schools in Washington—during which time he was also a student in the junior division of the Howard University School of Music—and earned a bachelor of music degree at the Oberlin Conservatory of Music (Ohio) in 1941. His graduate education included two artist diplomas—one in piano and one in composition—from the Curtis Institute of Music, where he was a student of Rudolph Serkin and Rosario Scalero in 1945; a diploma from the American Academy at Fontainebleau, France, in piano in 1947 (he also studied there in the 1950s with Nadia Boulanger); and a doctor of musical arts degree and artist diploma from the Eastman School of Music in 1957. He made his debut with the Philadelphia Orchestra conducted by Eugene Ormandy in 1941 in Rachmaninoff's Piano Concerto No. 3, and his New York recital debut at Town Hall in 1945.

Walker's very promising career as a concert artist began to shift toward teaching and composition in the mid-1950s. After brief tenures at Dillard University, the Dalcroze School of Music, the New School for Social Research, Smith College, and the University of Colorado, he joined the faculty of Rutgers University in 1969, where he remained until his retirement in 1992. Besides many works for piano, including four sonatas, he has written for several other instruments, chamber and full orchestra, solo voice, and chorus. Among his numerous honors and awards are several honorary doctorates and two Guggenheim Fellowships, along with a large number of commissions. In 1996, he won the Pulitzer Prize in Music for *Lilacs for Soprano or Tenor and Orchestra,* based on a text by Walt Whitman—the first for a living African American composer.

A master of twentieth-century musical techniques, Walker shows a deep connection in his works with his African American musical heritage, especially spirituals and jazz. He once stated that "I believe that music is above race. I am steeped in the universal cultural tradition of my art. It is important to stress one's individuality beyond race, but I must do it as a black person who is aspiring to be a product of a civilized society."

William C. Warfield (1920–)
Singer

Baritone William Warfield was born in West Helena, Arkansas, and later moved with his family to Rochester, New York. The son of a Baptist minister, he received early training in voice, organ, and piano and, in 1938, while a student at Washington Junior High School, won the vocal competition at the National Music Educators League Convention in St. Louis, Missouri.

Warfield studied at the Eastman School of Music and received his bachelor's degree in 1942. He made his recital debut at New York's Town Hall in 1950 and, afterwards, made an unprecedented tour of Australia under the auspices of the Australian Broadcasting Commission. A year later he made his film debut in the movie version of Jerome Kern's *Showboat* and also performed the role of Joe on the stage in several productions. He also has appeared on several major television shows and starred in the NBC television version of *Green Pastures.* He became identified with the role of Porgy in Gershwin's *Porgy and Bess* in the 1950s and later. He married his co-star Leontyne Price during the 1952–1954 touring revival of the opera; they were divorced in 1973.

William Warfield

Andre Watts performing at the piano in 1967 (Courtesy of Alix B. Williamson).

In 1974 Warfield accepted a position as professor of music at the University of Illinois School of Music in Urbana. He retired in 1990 as chairman of the voice faculty and has since been a visiting professor at Eastern Illinois University and an adjunct professor of music at Northwestern University.

Warfield has been active in the National Association of Negro Musicians, serving as its president in 1984. He has served also as a board member of the Lyric Opera of Chicago and the New York College of Music; a trustee of the Berkshire Boys Choir; a member of the music panel of the National Association for the Arts, and a judge for the Whittaker Vocal Competition of the Music Educator's National Conference.

Among honors that Warfield has received are honorary doctorates from the University of Arkansas, Boston University, and Milliken University. He has appeared frequently with orchestras as soloist and narrator and has been teacher and mentor to many younger singers.

André Watts (1946–)
Pianist

One of America's most gifted pianists, André Watts was the first African American concert pianist to achieve international stardom. Born in Nuremberg, Germany, of a Hungarian mother and an African American soldier, he spent the first eight years of his life on U.S. Army posts in Europe before moving to Philadelphia. By the time he was nine years old, he was already performing with the Philadelphia Orchestra. After graduating from Lincoln Preparatory School in Philadelphia and attending the Philadelphia Academy of Music, he enrolled at Baltimore's Peabody Conservatory of Music.

In 1962, when Glenn Gould was unable to appear as soloist with the New York Philharmonic, Leonard Bernstein chose Watts as a last-minute replacement. At the conclusion of his performance of Liszt's E-flat Major Piano Concerto, the 16-year-old Watts received a standing ovation, not only from the audience but also from the orchestra.

From the mid-1960s on, Watts has toured the world as a recitalist and has appeared with leading orchestras in the United States and abroad. He has also been a frequent performer of chamber music. His recordings continue to be popular and his performances of works by Liszt and other romantic composers have been especially notable.

Watts was awarded the Lincoln Center Medallion (1971), honorary doctorates from Yale University (1973) and Albright College (1975), and the National Society of Arts and Letters Gold Medal (1982). He performed a concert in 1988 telecast nationally in honor of the twenty-fifth anniversary of his New York Philharmonic debut.

Clarence Cameron White (1880–1960)
Violinist, Composer, Conductor, Teacher

Clarence Cameron White, born in Clarksville, Tennessee, moved with his widowed mother to his grandparent's house in Oberlin, Ohio. They were musically inclined and encouraged their grandson in his musical interests. With his mother's remarriage, the family moved to Washington, DC, where he studied violin with Will Marion Cook and Joseph Douglass. A period at the Oberlin College Conservatory (Ohio) ended without a degree, and he began working in the Washington public schools and the Washington Conservatory of Music.

White became acquainted through correspondence with the British composer Samuel Coleridge-Taylor and performed with him in concert during one of Coleridge-Taylor's American tours. White later studied with him in London, through the aid of an E. Azalia Hackley scholarship.

After his return from London in 1911, White had a heavy schedule of touring, composing, and teaching. He was a founding member of the National Association of Negro Musicians in 1919. In 1924, he settled at West Virginia State College as head of the music department but left in 1930 to study composition with Raoul LaParra in Paris on a Rosenwald Fellowship. On his return to the United States in 1932, he chaired the music department of Hampton Institute (which was discontinued in 1935).

In 1937 White was named a music specialist for the National Recreation Association, established by President Roosevelt under the aegis of the Works Progress Administration. The association's responsibility was to offer aid in organizing community arts programs.

Through these moves and teaching positions, White's catalog of compositions was growing. He wrote, not surprisingly, many works for violin, some of which are teaching pieces. His most performed works have been *Bandanna Sketches* (1918) and *From the Cotton Fields* (1920). The most ambitious of White's compositions is the opera *Ouanga*, a three act opera with a plot revolving around the historical figure Dessalines who ruled Haiti and attempted to eliminate the practice of voodoo. White used the country's folk music, especially rhythmic dance patterns, with which he had become familiar through a visit to Haiti, while casting its structure in a Western European, late nineteenth-century framework. Completed in 1932, the premiere was staged in 1949 by the Burleigh Musical Association in South Bend, Indiana. White became the first African American to receive the Bispham Medal after a performance in 1932.

Olly Woodrow Wilson (1937–)
Composer, Educator

Olly Wilson, born in St. Louis, Missouri, was educated in the city's public schools. He studied the piano and clarinet at an early age and played in his church choir and in the high school band. He graduated from Washington University, in his hometown, with a bachelor's degree and took graduate studies at the University of Illinois at Urbana, and the University of Iowa in Iowa City. He earned the Ph.D. there in 1964.

The diversity of Wilson's interests and breadth of his vision are indicated by his study of electronic music in 1967 at the University of Illinois—he won the Dartmouth Arts Council Prize in the International Competition for Electronic Compositions with *Cetus* in 1968—and his trips to Ghana in 1971 and 1978, for study of African music.

In 1970, Wilson joined the faculty of the University of California at Berkeley, where he has held several positions including associate dean of the graduate division and department chair. Not only has he been a prolific composer, but he has also written many articles on various aspects of contemporary music in general and African American music in particular.

Beginning in the 1970s, Wilson has written mostly in the orchestral medium and has received over twenty commissions. Some of them include: *Akwan* for piano/electric piano and orchestra (1972); *Lumina* for orchestra (1981); *Of Visions and Truth* for vocal soloists and chamber orchestra (1990–1991); *Hold On* for orchestra (1997–1998); and *Spirit Song* for soprano, double chorus, and orchestra, which the composer described as "about the evolution and development of the black spiritual." His musical style is all—encompassing. He has mastered the Western European, twentieth-century tradition, African American vernacular music, and African rhythmic and pitch practices.

Sacred Music Traditions

◆ Early Influences of African American Sacred Music
◆ The Emergence of Spirituals in the Nineteenth Century
◆ The Rise of Gospel Music in the Twentieth Century
◆ Sacred Music Composers, Musicians, and Singers

by Christopher A. Brooks

African American sacred music—slave songs, early religious songs, spirituals, and gospel music—is an expression of African American culture no less significant than blues and jazz. Originally rooted in the enslavement experience of early Africans, African American sacred music was later influenced by evangelical Protestant Christianity and performed at African American churches and camp meeting revivals. As time passed, it took on different forms and gained larger acceptance among European and white American concert audiences. Today through both live performances and commercial recordings, it encompasses a wide range of styles and ensembles, reaches an audience of millions worldwide, and is recognized as a vitally important element in America's cultural heritage.

◆ EARLY INFLUENCES OF AFRICAN AMERICAN SACRED MUSIC

Syncretized Religions of the African Diaspora

Of the 15 million Africans who were brought to the New World, the vast majority of them were enslaved from the sixteenth through the middle of the nineteenth century. Despite the enslavement experience, many Africans maintained and practiced some variation of their traditional beliefs, culture, and musical heritage. An area that combined these customs with some European influences were their religious practices. Many Africans in the New World—especially those in Catholic-colonized areas—became nominal Christians, but continued to practice their traditional African belief systems that they adapted to Western religions. These syncretized religions were fertile ground for maintaining many ritualized African chanting practices and sung styles, while the worshipping practices were nominally Christians. Examples of such New World syncretized religions are *candomble* in Brazil, *santeria* in Cuba and Puerto Rico, *vodun* in Haiti, and to a lesser extent, *kumina* in Jamaica. There is still a rich musical tradition associated with many of these religious beliefs, although local musical influences have had an effect as well. Many of these sacred music practices survived in one form or another well into the twentieth century.

American Colonial and Antebellum Periods

Most musical activity in American colonial society was vocal, although there are late eigteenth century paintings that depict enslaved Africans playing string instruments and dancing. Since much of American colonial society—both black and white—was preliterate, the method of collective song teaching (as in a church service, for example) was done by a technique called "lining out." This process involved a leader who sang a line or two of a song or hymn, sometimes over-enunciating the words. The congregation followed by singing the same line after the leader. This method can still be found in some African American churches.

Other indications of African American musical activity during the eighteenth century can be gleaned from chronicle accounts in news journals in Massachusetts, New York, and Virginia. When papers in these areas reported missing or fugitive African Americans, they frequently commented on their musical ability (on a particular instrument, for example), along with some physical description.

The period after the American Revolutionary War saw the emergence of two important African American institutions: the self-help benevolent societies and the African independent church movement. The benevolent societies, such as the African Union Society (Rhode Island), Free African Society (Philadelphia), Brown Fellowship (Charleston), the Society of Free Africans (Washington, DC), and the African Society of Boston, were among several pseudo-religious moral aid groups that were formed to help recently freed African Americans. By the late eighteenth and early nineteenth century, several independent African churches began emerging in both southern and northern states. Many churches in the South, however, were either very closely scrutinized or shut down because of uprisings that were planned or carried out by insurrectionists, such as Gabriel Prosser in Richmond, Virginia (1800), Denmark Vesey in Charleston, South Carolina (1822), and Nat Turner outside South Hampton, Virginia (1831).

By the late eighteenth century, Methodism had claimed large numbers of African Americans because of its official anti-slavery stance. The celebrated religious leader and Free African Society founding member Richard Allen established the African Methodist Episcopal (AME) Church in 1794, after a break with the mostly white St. Georges Methodist Church in Philadelphia. (In 1816, the AME Church formally separated from the mother Methodist Church.) In 1801, Allen published a collection of religious songs entitled *A Collection of Spiritual Songs and Hymns from Various Authors*. It eventually became the most widely-used religious songbook in African American Protestant churches around the United States and, by the end of the nineteenth century, the eleventh edition was published with notated music.

Another African American religious phenomenon of the early nineteenth century involved the camp meeting. These continuous, outdoor religious services were inspired by the Second Great Awakening movement that spread across the United States in that century. Many African American participants were known to perform dances, such as the "ring shout" and "shuffle step." Such religious behavior was criticized by some purists, such as Richard Allen, but was clearly acceptable among a growing sector of African American worshippers.

◆ THE EMERGENCE OF SPIRITUALS IN THE NINETEENTH CENTURY

Spirituals were perhaps the most significant musical contribution of the enslaved African population of the nineteenth century. They have certainly gained most of the attention of collectors, scholars, and those with a casual interest in the musical genre. Spirituals are an outgrowth of the African American enslavement experience and Protestant Christianity. A similar tradition apparently did not develop on the African continent nor anywhere else within nations of the African Diaspora. So to that degree, the spirituals are, from all existing evidence, uniquely American.

There are few absolute features that can be pointed to when trying to distinguish one spiritual from another. Up-tempo songs such as "A Great Camp Meetin'" might have been called a "jubilee," while an equally spirited "I'm Gonna Lift Up A Standard for My King" might have been regarded as a "shout." The terms "plantation songs" and "slave songs" were also used to describe spirituals. An apparent standard feature of the spiritual, however, was its employment of African American dialect. One of the earliest collections of spirituals was *Slave Songs of the United States* (1867). It was a collaborative work of William Allen, Charles Ware, and Lucy McKim Garrison, all of whom had abolitionist backgrounds. In the preface of the work, they commented on the uniqueness of African American vocal styles and the inability of conventional Western musical notation to accurately transcribe the unique vocal effects such as screams, yodels, falsetto, and glissandi, which they heard when the songs were performed.

It was the apparent disregard of these performance practices, among other things, that would lead some scholars such as George Pullen Jackson, Neuman White, and Donald Wilgus to promote a "white" spiritual theory. They argued that because it was the Europeans who gave Christianity to the enslaved Africans, they also gave them the music with which to worship. This argument has been soundly refuted, however, because Jackson was comparing printed versions of spirituals (i.e., arranged spirituals in Western musical notation) to those of Western European folk songs and saw similarities in melodies and time signatures. This school of thought also neglected the fact that the majority of spirituals employ a call-and-response performance technique, and that was not a traditional feature of Western European folk songs.

Alert and Map Songs

Although they functioned in an entirely different capacity, a tradition related to spirituals was the "alert songs" and "map songs." While the text of these songs was ostensibly religious, the alert songs encoded messages or signals about escape attempts or planned secret meetings of enslaved African Americans. Examples of such songs included "Steal Away to Jesus," "Good News the Chariots Comin," "Wade in The Water," and "I'm Packin' Up." In fact, "Wade in The Water"

Sheet music from the African American spiritual "Down in the Lonesome Valley" (The Library of Congress).

was known to be a frequently used alert song of the celebrated conductor Harriet Tubman. In addition to the religious meaning of the song, there was a very practical use for "wading in the water." It could also mask any body scent, which made it more difficult for the search dogs to follow those who were escaping. Map songs were designed to give directions to fugitive African American slaves. In the song "Sheep, Sheep, Don't You Know the Road?," the use of the word "road" could have encoded some message about a specific escape route. "Follow the Drinking Gourd" was another map song that was a metaphoric allusion to the Big Dipper, and the escapees were to follow it north to freedom.

It was clear that by the 1870s, the genre known alternately as spirituals, plantation songs, and jubilees was inextricably linked to the African American enslavement experience, and it was viewed by much of the American public as an acceptable form of religious expression. Evidence of this can be seen in the large numbers of spiritual collections that appear throughout the balance of the nineteenth century and well into the twentieth century. Volumes and collections such as *Hampton and Its Students* (1874), *The Story of the Jubilee Singers* (1877), *The Jubilee Singers* (1883), *Jubilee and Plantation Songs* (1884), *Old Plantation Melodies* (1899), *Songs of the Confederacy and Plantation Songs* (1901), *Nine Negro Spirituals* (1918), *Sit Down, Negro Spirituals Arranged by Roland Hayes* (1923), and *Book of Negro Spirituals* (1938), among many others, illustrate this point.

Spiritual Concerts

Attention was being drawn to spirituals not only through the collections, essays, books, and articles, but through live performances as well. By the 1870s, concerts of spirituals had become a fund-raising vehicle for several struggling African American colleges, most notably Calhoun College, Fisk University, Hampton Institute, and to a lesser extent Tuskegee Institute. Several of these groups made highly successful overseas tours in what Paul Fritz Laubenstein referred to as the *ausbreitung* (spreading) around the European continent.

With the frequency and popularity of these overseas tours by the 1890s, Europeans audiences and Americans were exposed to a different kind of African Americans musical talent, other than what had been featured in minstrel shows. When the celebrated Bohemian composer Antonin Dvorak recognized the uniqueness of this genre and encouraged his students, such as Harry T. Burleigh and Will Marion Cook, to compose and arrange more spirituals, it was given a new level of acceptance and recognition.

Other arranged spirituals came from other composers and arrangers, such as R. Nathaniel Dett. Dett was best known at Hampton Institute for organizing a choir composed of students and community members and transforming the group into an internationally-renowned touring organization that specialized in African American sacred music. Many of the songs that the choir performed were Dett's own compositions or arrangements of spirituals. Among his choristers was the celebrated soprano Dorothy Maynor who became a distinguished concert singer and recitalist.

On several occasions, Dett was compelled to defend his performance of "arranged" spirituals, which were not viewed as authentic as the "folk" versions of the genre that were accompanied by claps, body swaying, and shouts. Several white observers and benefactors such as George Peabody saw the Dett arrangements as imitations of white classical composers and, as such, not as genuine. However, the Hampton group had a highly successful tour of Europe in 1930.

The production of arranged spirituals would continue in the skillful hands of other musical luminaries, such as Hall Johnson, John W. Work, Florence Price, J. Rosamund Johnson, and W. C. Handy, among many others. The live performances and recorded legacy of African American concert singers featuring spirituals in their recitals is a practice that continued throughout the twentieth century in the artistry of singers, such as Marian Anderson, Roland Hayes, Dorothy Maynor, Paul Robeson, Robert McFerrin, Leontyne Price, Shirley Verrett, Jessye Norman, and many others.

Holy Dancing, Church Song Concerts, and Shout Preaching

Although much scholarly and casual interest was directed to the spiritual, other African American sacred music traditions emerged by the end of the nineteenth century as the African American church movement itself gained momentum. By the 1890s, the Holiness and Sanctified Church movement had crystallized. The largest denomination within this tradition, the Church of God and Christ, was founded by the Memphis-based religious leader, Charles Henry Mason, formerly of Lexington, Mississippi. Collectively, the Holiness/Sanctified churches believed in spirit possession, speaking in tongues (i.e., a form of glossolalia), improvisatory singing. "Holy dancing" was also seen an acceptable form of religious behavior. Certain instruments such as drums, tambourines, triangles, guitars, and cymbals were frequently used to accompany the singing.

A figure at the turn of the century who played role in what would come to be called "gospel" music was Rev. Charles Albert Tindley. Tindley was a Maryland-born Methodist camp meeting preacher and singer who, in the 1870s, settled in Philadelphia. There he founded the East Calvary Methodist Episcopal Church in 1902. It was later renamed the Tindley Temple. Tindley established a practice of sponsoring periodic concerts of church songs and, consequently, had many of his compositions published in a 1916 collection entitled *The New Songs of Paradise*. Included in this collection were such songs as "Leave It There," "What are They Doing in Heaven Tonight," "We'll Understand it Better By and By," and "I'll Overcome Someday," which was the melodic basis of the 1960s Civil Rights anthem "We Shall Overcome." The collection was so popular that several subsequent editions would appear by the 1940s.

Although Tindley had the support of his congregation, other religious songwriters received support from such organizations as the National Baptist Convention, which was founded in the 1880s. It became a vehicle for groups to perform and for exposing congregations and individuals to religious music. In 1921, the National Baptist Convention produced a collection of 165 religious songs entitled *Gospel Pearls*. This work was enormously popular in many African American congregations without regard for denomination.

By the 1920s, singing ministers or so-called "shout" preachers began recording brief three to five minute sermons and song performances. These recorded sermons might include a congregation or a small choir. Celebrated names in this tradition were Revs. F.W. McGee of Memphis, J.C. Burnett of Kansas City, Theodore Frye from Mississippi, E. H. Hall of Chicago, and A.W. Nix and J.M. Gates of Atlanta. Gates's style was captured in several recordings that are still extant, such as "The Need of Prayer" (1926), "Down Here Lord, Waiting on You" (1929), and numerous other examples.

◆ THE RISE OF GOSPEL MUSIC IN THE TWENTIETH CENTURY

Although the term "gospel" music did not become a standard phrase in reference to a specific African American sacred musical genre before the 1930s, its predecessors were in place long before that time. Many scholars regard Chicago as the birthplace of gospel music because many of its churches produced pioneering singers and composers. The figure most closely associated with the rise of the so-called blues-based gospel was Thomas A. Dorsey, commonly known as the "Father of Gospel Music."

Thomas Dorsey: Father of Gospel Music

Born in rural Georgia, Dorsey was the eldest child of a Baptist minister whom he frequently accompanied on the keyboard during his father's evangelizing trips. Dorsey eventually moved to Atlanta when he was a teenager and played keyboard in brothels and saloons. In 1916, Dorsey made a stop in Chicago en route to Philadelphia, and it became his home base for the rest of his life. He initially pursued his career as a blues musician and was known at varying points in his career as "Georgia Tom," "Barrelhouse Tommy," and by a few other names. Several of his blues compositions were recorded by jazz greats such as Joseph "King" Oliver, among others. Between 1923–1926, he was the official accompanist for the great blues singer, Gertrude "Ma" Rainey. He toured with Rainey and was featured in several of her recordings for the Paramount label. When he married Nettie Harper in 1925, Rainey made her a wardrobe mistress so she could travel with the group.

Although Dorsey had strong credentials as a bluesman, he continued to foster his religious music beginnings from his childhood. He attended the National Baptist Convention in 1920 and had one of his songs "Some Day, Somewhere" published in the Convention's 1921 collection *Gospel Pearls*. Around 1927, he began "peddling" (i.e., Dorsey accompanying a singer at the keyboard) his religious songs in Chicago areas churches, but they were rejected by many ministers because of their stylistic affinity to the blues. In 1931, Dorsey

Thomas Dorsey performing with the Wandering Syncopators in 1923 (AP/Wide World Photos, Inc.).

experienced a double personal tragedy when his daughter and first wife, Nettie, died in childbirth. Afterwards, he composed "Take My Hand, Precious Lord," which has remained his most celebrated and frequently performed work.

By the 1930s, Dorsey was more devoted to composing and promoting religious music. In 1931, he formed the world's first gospel choir at Ebenezer Baptist Church in Chicago and opened the first publishing company devoted to the sale of gospel music. With his colleague, Sallie Martin, he founded the National Convention of Gospel Choirs and Choruses as a vehicle for training gospel choirs and soloists. More than any single individual, Dorsey was responsible for elevating gospel music to its current professional status.

Willie Mae Ford Smith Influences Future Singers

In addition to Sallie Martin, who also acted as his business manager and was a celebrated name in gospel music in her own right, Dorsey discovered a talented singer, Willie Mae Ford Smith who, in 1936, Dorsey appointed as the director of the Soloists Bureau of the National Convention of Gospel Choirs and Choruses. In this role, she demonstrated the proper style and delivery of gospel songs to a new generation of younger singers. Also influenced by the blues in her childhood, Smith later abandoned what would have been a prominent career as a gospel singer to become an ordained evangelist in the Holiness Church of God Apostolic. As an evangelist, Smith frequently interspersed songs with a brief sermon, a practice that became known as "sermonette and song." Smith and Dorsey were featured in the 1982 gospel music documentary *Say Amen, Somebody.*

Mahalia Jackson Becomes Gospel's International Star

Among Dorsey's other celebrated discoveries was Mahalia Jackson who became gospel music's first international star. Born in New Orleans, Jackson moved to Chicago in the 1920s to pursue a career as a beautician. Dorsey first met her in 1929 and became her official accompanist between the years 1937–1946. Jackson began a recording career in the 1930s, but did not achieve national fame until she recorded the song of the celebrated Memphis minister and composer, Rev. W. Herbert Brewster, "Move On Up A Little Higher," which sold over one million copies. She toured extensively in

Mahalia Jackson singing in a studio.

Europe, gaining a wide following in several countries. Jackson gave a highly successful concert at New York's Carnegie Hall in early 1950s and was invited to sing at the White House in 1961 by the recently inaugurated President John F. Kennedy.

While the Civil Rights movement was in full swing in the 1960s, gospel music became an unofficial vehicle for the movement because many of its songs became the basis of freedom songs of the era. Mahalia Jackson was a major follower of the Rev. Dr. Martin Luther King, Jr. and reached an international audience when she sang at the 1963 March on Washington.

Gospel Quartets and Choirs

By the end of 1930s, gospel music had established at least two generic performing groups. The first was the all-male "gospel quartet," which was made up of four or five singers dressed in business suits and sang in a cappella barber shop-style harmonies. The second was the "gospel chorus," which could be women and men (or all women) dressed in choir robes and were accompanied by piano or organ. Prominent gospel quartets included such groups as the Golden Gate Jubilee Quartet, the Famous Blue Jay Singers, the Jubilaires, the Mighty Clouds of Joys, the Fairfield Four, the Soul Stirrers, the Five Blind Boys of Mississippi, among many others. Notable gospel choirs included such groups as the Ford Family Quartet, the Roberta Martin Singers, the Clara Ward Singers—another group that Thomas Dorsey would discover and help to promote—and later the Barrett Sisters.

The Golden Age of Gospel

Gospel music experienced a "golden age" from the mid-1940s and 1950s when, in addition to the numerous recordings that were made, such women as Lucie Campbell, Roberta Martin, Queen C. Anderson, Ruth Davis, Dorothy Loves Coates, Edna Gallmon Looke, and Bessie Griffin were among the most celebrated names in the gospel business. Their male counterparts were Julius Cheek, Archie Brownlee, Brother Joe May, Alex Bradford, James Cleveland, Claude Jeter, and Ira Tucker, among others. By the end of this period, gospel music had shaken itself free of its Pentecostal/Holiness roots to reach widespread acceptance in many African American Protestant churches around the United States. Instrumentally, the organ, at this time, also became the standard accompanying instrument for most church-based gospel ensembles.

By the 1960s, gospel was experiencing other changes. As far back as the late 1930s, such religious singers as Sister Rosetta Tharpe had performed gospel music outside of the church by performing in New York's Apollo Theater. However, when such groups as the Clara Ward Singers performed at the Newport Jazz Festival in 1957 and, subsequently, in nightclubs in the early 1960s, gospel music was blended with other popular musical genres and reached a crossover audience. Such gospel groups as the Staple Singers and the Edwin Hawkins Singers scored individual successes. Edwin Hawkins's 1969 recording of "O Happy Day" sold over a million copies on both religious and popular music charts. Large community-based gospel choirs, such as the Mississippi Mass Choir, the Abyssinian Choir led by Alex

An African American gospel choir performs before the congregation (AP/Wide World Photos, Inc.).

Bradford, the Greater Metropolitan Church of Christ Choir led by Isaac Whittmon, the Harold Smith Majestics, the Donal Vail Choraleers, the Charles Ford Singers, the Triboro Mass Choir led by Albert Jamison, the Chicago Community Choir led by Jessy Dixon, the Voices of Tabernacle led by James Cleveland, and the Michigan State Community Choir led by Mattie Moss Clark made successful recordings and/or tours around the United States. Soloists and small groups that emerged in their own right during this era were Shirley Caesar, Marion Williams, who had been a member of the Clara Ward Singers, Albertina Walker, Delois Barrett Campbell and the Barrett Sisters, and the O'Neal Twins.

Contemporary Gospel Sounds

Since the 1970s, gospel music has reached a mainstream audience and become a commercially viable tradition. In vocal harmony music, Sweet Honey in the Rock and Take 6 have continued the tradition of gospel quartets and small choral groups. An a cappella group of female vocalists that performs an eclectic mix of political music, folk songs, spirituals, and gospel, Sweet Honey in the Rock's album *Feel Something Drawing Me On* (1989) focused on sacred music. Take 6, a male ensemble of Seventh Day Adventists, won several Grammy awards for its original song "Spread Love" (1988) and for *Take 6* (1988) and *So Much 2 Say* (1991).

The tradition has also produced several popular musicians, such as Sam Cooke, Lou Rawls, Aretha Franklin, Ray Charles, Al Green, Stevie Wonder, Bobby Womack, and Johnnie Taylor, among others. In fact, Sam Cooke, who had been a lead singer with the Soul Stirrers, was among the first gospel singers to have a successful crossover career and achieve equal success as a popular music performer. Other contemporary musicians who have remained more or less within the tradition, while reaching large crossover audiences include Andrae Couch, Tramaine Hawkins, Walter Hawkins, Lynette Hawkins, Jessy Dixon, the celebrated Winans Family, and Kirk Franklin.

During the 1990s, gospel began to be influenced by rap music, although gospel musicians referred to their performances as "street poetry" rather than rap. Large ensembles such as Sounds of Blackness have used rap music to reinvent sacred songs, while gospel quartets, such as the Williams Brothers, have incorporated synthesizers and percussion overdubs into their modern version of gospel. These innovations have created sizeable controversy among performers and listeners devoted to more traditional styles of gospel music.

Though most gospel music continues to be performed at religious services and African American community events across the United States, it is recognized as a truly significant aspect of America's cultural heritage, as witnessed in such Smithsonian Institution projects as *We'll Understand It Better By and By: Pioneering African American Gospel Composers* (1992) and Smithsonian's gospel music collection *Wade in the Water* (1994).

◆ SACRED MUSIC COMPOSERS, MUSICIANS, AND SINGERS

(To locate biographical profiles more readily, please consult the index at the back of the book.)

Yolanda Adams (1961–)
Singer

A native of Houston, Yolanda Adams was born on August 27, 1961. She is the oldest of six siblings. Her family offered her a solidly religious upbringing, and as a small child she created for herself an imaginary friend she called "Hallelujah" and sang a solo in church at age three. She grew up with the classic gospel sounds of James Cleveland and the Edwin Hawkins Singers, but hers was also a musically eclectic household. Adams's mother, a pianist who majored in music in college, introduced her daughter to jazz, classical music, and rhythm and blues. Adams joined a gospel choir, the Southeast Inspirational Choir, shortly after her father's death when she was 13 years of age.

Adams hoped to become a fashion model even as she embarked on a career as an elementary school teacher. However, her powerful voice propelled her to the forefront of the Southeast Inspirational Choir's performances; she took a solo on the choir's 1980 hit "My Liberty." In 1986 well-known gospel producer, composer, and pianist Thomas Whitfield heard the choir and wasted no time in approaching Adams. The result was the album *Just as I Am* released in 1987 on Sound of Gospel Records.

Adams signed with the Tribute label in 1990, and between 1990 and 1997 released four successful albums, all of which won Stellar awards, a prestigious gospel music industry honor. Albums *Through the Storm* and *Save the World* produced pieces that Adams still sings in concert, such as "The Battle Is the Lord's," but it was 1995's *More Than a Melody* that really moved her style sharply in the direction of secular urban contemporary music. The album was honored with a Soul Train Lady of Soul award and a Grammy award nomination, and 1996's *Yolanda . . . Live in Washington* also earned the singer a Grammy nomination.

In the years following the release of *More Than a Melody*, honors and opportunities have flowed Adams's way with increasing regularity. She performed on the 1996 Soul Train Music Awards, the 1997 Essence Awards, BET's Teen Summit, and the *Tonight Show*. A special thrill was a performance during the Christmas festivities at the White House in 1995. Adams was also named a national spokesperson for the FILA Corporation's *Operation Rebound* youth outreach program, a post that often takes her on the road to speak with students in inner-city schools.

During the late 1990s, Adams's reputation seemed certain to continue to rise. In 1997 she was featured in the fifty-city Tour of Life organized and headed by contemporary gospel sensation Kirk Franklin. That same year, she married stockbroker and former New York Jets football player Tim Crawford at Houston's First Presbyterian Church, and she enrolled in the prestigious divinity program at Howard University in Washington, DC.

Shirley Caesar (1938–)
Singer

The leading gospel music singer of her generation, Shirley Caesar was born in Durham, North Carolina, in 1938. One of twelve children born to gospel great "Big Jim" Caesar, Shirley sang in church choirs as a child. By age 14, Caesar went on the road as a professional gospel singer, touring the church circuit on weekends and during school vacations. Known as "Baby Shirley," Caesar joined the Caravans in 1958. Featured as an opening act in the show, Caesar worked the audience to a near fever pitch. When Inez Andrews left the Caravans in 1961, Caesar became the featured artist who provided crowds with powerful performances of such songs as "Comfort Me," "Running For Jesus," and "Sweeping Through the City."

After leaving the Caravans in 1966, Caesar formed her own group, the Shirley Caesar Singers. Her sheer energy and determined spirit made her one of the reigning queens of modern gospel. Her first album *I'll Go* remains one of her most critically acclaimed. In 1969, she released a ten-minute sermonette with the St. Louis Choir that earned her a gold record. A nine-time Grammy winner, Caesar conducts weekly sermons at the Mount Calvary Holy Church between performances and recording dates.

Reverend James Cleveland holding two Grammy Awards in 1978 (AP/Wide World Photos, Inc.).

Rev. James Cleveland (1932–1991)
Singer, Pianist, Composer

Known by such titles as "King James" and the "Crown Prince," the Rev. James Cleveland emerged as a giant of the postwar gospel music scene. Likened to the vocal style of Louis Armstrong, Cleveland's raw bluesy growls and shouts appeared on more recordings than any other gospel singer of his generation.

Born on December 5, 1932, in Chicago, Illinois, James Cleveland first sang gospel under the direction of Thomas Dorsey at the Pilgrim Baptist Church. Inspired by the keyboard talents of gospel singer Roberta Martin, Cleveland later began to study piano. In 1951 Cleveland joined the Gospelaires, a trio that cut several sides for the Apollo label. With the Caravans, Cleveland arranged and performed on two hits "The Solid Rock" and an uptempo reworking of the song "Old Time Religion."

By the mid-1950s, Cleveland's original compositions had found their way into the repertoires of numerous gospel groups, and he was performing with such artists as the Thorn Gospel Singers, Roberta Martin Singers, Mahalia Jackson, the Gospel Allstars, and the Meditation Singers. In 1960 Cleveland formed the Cleveland Singers featuring organist and accompanist Billy Preston. The smash hit "Love of God" recorded with the Detroit-based Voices of Tabernacle, won Cleveland nationwide fame within the gospel community. Signing with the Savoy label, Cleveland, along with keyboardist Billy Preston, released a long list of classic albums including *Christ is the Answer*, and *Peace Be Still*. As a founder of the Gospel Workshop of America in 1968, Cleveland organized annual conventions that brought together thousands of gospel singers and songwriters. A year later, he helped found the Southern California Community Choir.

In 1972, James was reunited with his former piano understudy Aretha Franklin, who featured him as a guest artist on the album *Amazing Grace*. Recipient of the NAACP Image Award, Cleveland also acquired an honorary doctorate from Temple Baptist College. Although the commercial gospel trends of the 1980s had caused a downturn in Cleveland's career, he continued to perform the gutsy blues-based sound that brought him recognition from listeners throughout the world. Cleveland died February 9, 1991, in Los Angeles, California.

Andrae Crouch (1942–)
Singer, Pianist

An exponent of a modern pop-based gospel style, Andrae Crouch became one of the leading gospel singers of the 1960s and 1970s. Born on July 1, 1942, in Los Angeles, Andrae Crouch grew up singing in his father's church. Along with his brother and sister, Crouch formed the Crouch Trio, which performed at their father's services as well as on live Sunday-night radio broadcasts. In the mid-1960s Crouch was "discovered" by white Pentecostal evangelists and subsequently signed a contract with Light, a white religious record label. Over the last four decades, Crouch has written numerous songs, many of which have become standards in the repertoire of modern gospel groups. Among his most famous songs are "I Don't Know Why Jesus Loved Me," "Through it All," and "The Blood Will Never Lose Its Power." In recognition for this work, Crouch received an ASCAP Special Songwriter Award.

During the late 1960s Crouch, inspired by the modern charismatic revival movement, began adopting street smart language and informal wardrobe. After forming the Disciples in 1968, Crouch recorded extensively and toured throughout the United States and Europe. His California style of gospel music combines rock, country music, and soul with traditional gospel forms. The

Disciples won Grammys in 1975, for *Take Me Back* and in 1979, for *Live in London*, which also received a Dove Award. *This Is Another Day* garnered a Dove Award in 1976, as did Crouch's 1984 solo recording *No Time to Lose*.

Since the 1970s, Crouch's back-up groups have incorporated both electronic and acoustic instruments including synthesizers. The new approach earned Grammys in 1980 and 1981. As the decade ensued, Crouch recorded as a solo artist and was bestowed the Gospel Music Excellence Award for best male vocalist in 1982, for *More of the Best*. During this period, Crouch was also instrumental in helping the Winans Family produce their first recordings.

On September 23, 1995, Crouch assumed the pastorship of the Christ Memorial Church of God in Christ in Pacoima, California, the same pulpit once manned by his father. Nearly one year earlier, Crouch—a two-time NAACP Image Award recipient and one-time Golden Halo awardee—released *Mercy!*, his first album since 1984; others were reissued. His return was well-received.

Thomas A. Dorsey (1899–1993)

Composer, Arranger, Music Promoter

Popularly known as the "Father of Gospel Music," Dorsey was born on July 1, 1899, in Villa Rica, Georgia. He sang in church choirs and occasionally traveled with his father, accompanying him on the keyboard during evangelizing trips. When he dropped out of school at around age thirteen, he began playing in a local saloon and adopted the stage name "Barrelhouse Tommy," which was one of many that he used. In 1916 Dorsey went to Chicago, and it became his home base for the rest of his life. Between 1919 and 1921, he studied at the Chicago School of Composition and Arranging. He worked with the jazz group Will Walker's Whispering Syncopators in local Chicago clubs and scored a triumph when his work "Riverside Blues" was recorded by the great cornettist Joseph "King" Oliver in December 1923.

Although Thomas A. Dorsey was a well-known blues musician as a result of his arrangements, compositions, performances and recordings throughout much of the 1920s, his lasting contribution to the history of American music, if not the world, laid in his talent as a sacred music composer. As early as 1920, he experienced a religious rebirth at the National Baptist Convention, and one of his religious songs "If I Don't Get There" appeared in a later edition of the convention's landmark collection *Gospel Pearls* produced in 1921. As early as 1927, he had begun promoting his religious songs in area churches, but was rejected by many ministers because of the arrangements's stylistic affinity to the blues.

In 1930 Dorsey's song "If You See My Savior" was performed at the National Baptist Convention to a tumultuous response. From that point on, he became more committed to composing, arranging, promoting and recording gospel songs. In 1931, along with Theodore Frye, he organized what is generally recognized as the world's first gospel chorus at Chicago's Ebenezer Baptist Church. During this period, Dorsey formed his own publishing company dedicated to selling gospel music and co-founded the National Convention of Gospel Choirs and Chorus, Inc., with his colleague Sallie Martin. The organization became a vehicle for training gospel choirs and coaching soloist. This booming period in Dorsey's career was not without its personal tragedy, however. In 1932, his first wife, Nettie, died in childbirth. After this traumatic event, he composed his most celebrated work "Take My Hand, Precious Lord."

Among Dorsey's most celebrated discoveries was Mahalia Jackson who became gospel music's first international star. He also served as her official accompanist between the years 1937–1946. Dorsey also promoted Clara Ward, along with many other singers and groups. Dorsey toured extensively in the 1930s and 1940s throughout the United States, Europe, Mexico and North Africa and served as director of the National Convention Gospel Choirs into the 1970s.

By the late 1970s, failing health forced him into semi-retirement. Dorsey reemerged in a 1982 documentary *Say Amen, Somebody*, in which he appeared with Mother Willie Mae Ford Smith; the documentary also featured footage of some Dorsey's historical performances with Ford Smith and several of his protégéges including Mahalia Jackson, the O'Neal twins, Delois Barrett Campbell, and the Barrett Sisters. By the late 1980s he was suffering from the effects of Alzheimer's disease. He died in Chicago, Illinois, in January 1993.

Kirk Franklin (1970–)

Singer, Composer

Born in Fort Worth, Texas, in 1970, Kirk Franklin was reportedly abandoned by his teenage mother when he was an infant; he was adopted by his Aunt Gertrude, who was a strict Baptist. Being raised in a very religious environment, he was teased by his friends who called him "church boy." He began taking keyboard lessons at the age of four and, by the time he was eleven years old,

Kirk Franklin holding the Soul Train Music Award (Archive Photos, Inc.).

led the Mt. Rose Baptist Church near Dallas. After a troubled adolescence, Franklin eventually returned to his religious roots.

By the mid-1980s, Franklin was attracting the attention of religious music producers with his songs and choral works. In 1991 his compositions appeared on a recording by the Dallas-Fort Worth Mass Choir entitled "I Will Let Nothing Separate Me." By 1993, he had put together a 17-piece vocal group, the Family, and released his debut album *Kirk Franklin and the Family.* Selections from this release caused crossover appeal—Franklin's songs, while religious in text, were being played on rhythm and blues charts. While this caused his reputation to spread in many pop music markets, it disturbed many gospel music purists who felt that release was too pop-oriented. Franklin fueled these suspicions further by signing a record deal with B-Rite Records, which also had an association with the rap label, Death Row Records.

In 1995 Franklin and the Family released a Christmas recording, but his next major album *Whatcha Lookin 4* in 1996 took Franklin's combination of rhythm and blues and gospel one further step—the album hit the pop charts running and scored on both the gospel and rhythm and blues charts. As with his first release, it won accolades among pop music followers, much to the disappointment of gospel music's conservative rank. In 1997 he was chosen as *Billboard Magazine's* number one gospel artist and number one contemporary Christian artist and signed a multi-year recording contract with the B-Rite label. In 1998, Franklin released *Nu Nation Project*, which contained biblical references and stylistically was a combination of rap music and gospel. In that same year, his autobiography *Church Boy* was released. Franklin is married to former rhythm and blues singer, Tammy Renee Collins, and they have three children.

Tramaine Hawkins (1951–)
Singer

Tramaine Hawkins began singing when only four years old in the Ephesian Church of God in Christ in Berkeley, California where her grandfather was pastor. Though Hawkins developed her passion for gospel music during childhood, her career accelerated in 1969 when the Northern California State Choir—which she had joined—recorded "Oh Happy Day." Her first performance with the choir after the song's success was at Madison Square Garden.

As a child, Hawkins sang with the Sunshine Band and later with the Heavenly Tones. After eleven years together, the Heavenly Tones began to get offers to sing at secular jobs, but Hawkins felt her calling was still gospel music. When the Northern California State Choir's name was changed to the Edwin Hawkins Singers and the choir started to do a lot of club dates for entertainers, such as the Jackson Five and Diana Ross, Hawkins chose to leave the group.

For eleven months, she sang with Andraé Crouch's Disciples. Yet Hawkins missed her old group and rejoined it. In 1970, after touring Europe with the Edwin Hawkins Singers, Walter Hawkins—who played the piano even when Tramaine sang with the Heavenly Tones and the brother of Edwin—proposed and she accepted. During their many years of marriage, she worked side by side with Walter, also a singer, recording artist, composer, arranger, producer, and the pastor of the Love Center Church in Oakland, California. Eventually they divorced, and Tramaine married Tommy Richardson. On occasion, Walter and Tramaine still work together.

Hawkins has a controversial, contemporary style that has been criticized over the years. She raised suspicion in 1985 within the gospel community when her techno-funk hit "Fall Down" from the *Spirit of Love* album, topped the dance charts despite the religious content of its lyrics. In a 1990 concert, still daring, Hawkins brought in musicians and singers from outside the gospel field to participate in a live-recording project including rock guitarist Carlos Santana, jazz organist Jimmy McGriff, and jazz tenor saxophonist Stanley Turrentine. Her success with her mixing of traditional gospel, blues, jazz, and other singing styles helped create what is called contemporary gospel.

Altogether, Hawkins has recorded at least nine solo albums and won numerous awards including two Grammys, two Dove Awards, and two Communications Excellence to Black Audiences (CEBA) Awards.

Mahalia Jackson (1912–1972)
Singer

Hailed as the world's greatest gospel singer, Mahalia Jackson's rich contralto voice became a national institution. Through her many live engagements, recordings, and television appearances, Jackson elevated gospel music to a level of popularity unprecedented in the history of African American religious music.

The third of six children, Jackson was born on October 26, 1912, in New Orleans, Louisiana. Growing up in New Orleans, Jackson absorbed the sounds of parade music and brass bands. She later discovered the blues, a music labeled the "devil's music" by regular churchgoers, and listened secretly to recordings of singers such as Mamie and Bessie Smith.

In 1927, at the age of fifteen, Jackson moved to Chicago where she joined the Greater Salem Baptist Church. Two years later, Jackson met the gospel musician and songwriter Thomas A. Dorsey who invited her to sing at the Pilgrim Baptist Church. In 1937 Jackson recorded four sides for the Decca label including the song "God's Gonna Separate the Wheat From the Tares."

Jackson's big break arrived in 1947 when she released gospel music's first million-selling record "Move on Up a Little." In 1949 her song "Let the Holy Ghost Fall on Me" won the French Academy's Grand Prix du Disque. Soon afterward, she toured Europe and recorded the gospel hit "In the Upper Room." During the 1960s, Jackson became a musical ambassador—not only did she perform at the White House and at London's Albert Hall, but she sang at the historic 1963 March on Washington. She was asked by the Rev. Martin Luther King Jr. to sing at his funeral should she survive him. She sadly fulfilled this engagement after his assassination in 1968.

On January 27, 1972, Jackson died of a heart condition in Chicago, Illinois. At her funeral at Great Salem Baptist, some 45,000 mourners gathered to pay their respects to a woman who brought gospel music into the hearts and homes of millions of listeners.

Bobby Jones (1939–)
Singer, Televison Host

Bobby Jones, born in Paris, Tennessee, was a schoolteacher in Nashville for a time after earning his master's degree from Tennessee State University. He left his teaching job to become a textbook consultant specializing in elementary education, then began teaching reading skills at Tennessee State University in the early 1970s. Around this same time, he also began a second career as a singer on the gospel circuit and continued his activism in the local civil rights movement and his church. In 1976 he helped create the city's first Black Expo which featured numerous serious workshops, but had also attracted some of its 50,000 attendees with a host of concerts.

Black Expo also attracted the attention of local media executives and inspired Jones to suggest a local gospel show. The *Nashville Gospel Show* was a hit in the area, but Jones jumped ship in 1980 when he was invited by Robert Johnson, founder of the fledgling Black Entertainment Television (BET) network, to bring an hour of gospel television to the new cable network. Similar to its counterparts in pop and soul, the show offers gospel fans live performances by well-known names in the industry along with interview clips and album reviews. The *Bobby Jones Gospel Hour* is also broadcast on the American Christian Network and the Armed Forces radio and television stations, giving Jones an audience of gospel fans around the world.

Jones later expanded his presence on BET with the half-hour show *Video Gospel*, which he also hosts. Jones himself has also performed internationally, including stops in Israel and Africa, and sang at the White House for President Jimmy Carter; he was also invited to appear before Ronald Reagan in a performance at the Kennedy Center for the Performing Arts.

Jones kept his teaching job at Tennessee State as late as the mid-1980s, and by then had also earned a doctorate in curriculum leadership from Vanderbilt University. He has a record label, GospoCentric, and in addition to his television responsibilities has brought an increased awareness for the music form since 1989 with his live tours known as the "Bobby Jones Gospel Explosions." His "Mini-Explosions" bring gospel music to audiences in smaller cities across the United States as well as in Europe and the Caribbean.

Roberta Martin (1907–1969)
Singer, Pianist

Born in Helena, Arkansas, on February 12, 1907, Martin's was a gifted keyboardist with early ambitions of being a concert pianist. After moving to Chicago as a young adult, she became the accompanist for Thomas A.

Dorsey and Theodore Frye's historic gospel choir at Ebenezer Baptist Church in the 1930s. From this group she co-founded, along with Frye, the all-male Martin-Frye Quartet in 1933. The group subsequently became known as the Roberta Martin Singers. In the 1940s, she added women to the group, including a young lead soprano named Delois Barrett, and toured extensively. Martin also established a music publishing company and produced several of her many compositions including "Try Jesus, He Satisfies" (1943), "Yield Not to Temptation" (1944), and "God Is Still on the Throne" (1959). Martin was also influential as an accompanist and promoted the careers of several other groups including the Barrett Sisters. She died in Chicago, Illinois, on January 18, 1969, after brief illness.

Sallie Martin (1896–1988)
Singer

Born in Pittfield, Georgia, on November 20, 1896, Martin traveled to Chicago, Illinois, in 1919. Her church singing took on greater significance after she began a professional relationship with Thomas A. Dorsey. Martin auditioned for his choir at Ebenezer Baptist Church in the early 1930s, and they maintained an association for the next forty years. She became a song demonstrator for Dorsey, and they co-founded the National Convention of Gospel Choirs and Choruses, Inc. in 1932. Later in 1940, Martin co-founded the Martin-Morris Music Company with musician Kenneth Morris. That same year, she also began touring with her own group, the Roberta Martin Singers, throughout the United States and Europe.

As the Civil Rights movement gained momentum in the late 1950s and early 1960s, gospel music would be heavily identified with the movement. Sallie Martin was an active supporter of both the movement and its figurehead, Rev. Martin Luther King, Jr. On several occasions, she represented him in his absence, such as at Nigeria's independence celebration in 1960. After retiring from live performances in the 1970s, she appeared in the French production *Gospel Caravan* in 1979. In 1986, she was honored by the city of Chicago for her achievements as a singer, composer, and promoter of gospel music. She died two years later at the age of ninety-two.

Willie Mae Ford Smith (1906–1994)
Singer

The Ford family moved from Rolling Forks, Mississippi, to Memphis, Tennessee, when Willie Mae, born on April 21, 1906, was a young girl. In the early 1920s, she sang the lead in the Ford family quartet (made up of Ford's sisters), and they appeared at the National Baptist Convention in 1922 singing "Ezekiel Saw the Wheel" and "I'm in His Care." In 1932, she met Thomas A. Dorsey who in 1936 appointed her the director of the Soloists Bureau of the National Convention of Gospel Choirs and Choruses. In this role she demonstrated the proper style and delivery of gospel songs to younger singers.

Because the Baptist Church did not allow women to preach, Smith left in 1939 and joined the Holiness Church of God Apostolic. She became an ordained evangelist and limited her singing to religious services and revivals. As an evangelist, Smith frequently combined a brief sermon with a song. This practice became known as "sermonette and song." In 1982, she was the subject of a gospel documentary *Say Amen, Somebody* which featured footage of the historic performances of many of her protégés, including Mahalia Jackson, the O'Neal twins, and Delois Barrett Campbell, as well as her own performances. In 1988, "Mother Smith" was honored with a National Heritage Fellowship from the National Endowment for the Arts. Her last years were spent in a retirement community in Kansas City, Missouri, which is where she died in 1994.

Sister Rosetta Tharpe (1915–1973)
Singer, Pianist, Guitarist

Born Rosetta Nubin on March 20, 1915, in Cotton Plant, Arkansas, Sister Rosetta Singer Tharpe came from a background of religious music—her mother, Katie Bell Nubin, was a singer in the Holiness Church. At a young age, Rosetta learned to sing and play the piano and guitar. By the 1930s, Tharpe began recording and making appearances in nightclubs. For example, she appeared at New York's Cotton Club with Cab Calloway accompanying herself on guitar.

In 1938, Tharpe performed gospel music at John Hammond's concert at Carnegie Hall entitled *From Sprirituals to Swing at Carnegie Hall.* Tharpe subsequently performed with other well-known popular musicians, including Lucky Millinder, Benny Goodman, and eventually such blues musicians as Muddy Waters. However, she was principally known within religious circles for strong gospel singing and guitar playing. Tharpe later performed with the Dixie Hummingbirds and recorded with her mother, Katie Bell Nubin. Their recorded performance of "Daniel in the Lion's Den" became a gospel music classic. For a time, she also had a backup group known as the "Rosettes." As a result of her many bus tours, Tharpe was particularly well known in rural areas of the South. Tharpe eventually settled in Philadelphia, Pennsylvania, where she died on October 9, 1973.

Charles Albert Tindley (1851?–1933)
Composer

Believed to have been born on July 7, 1851, in Berlin, Maryland, Tindley began preaching at outdoor religious gatherings, also known as camp meetings, in Maryland when he was a teenager. In the 1870s, he relocated to Philadelphia to continue his education. He furthered his religious studies by correspondence through Boston Theological Seminary and became an ordained minister in the mid-1880s. After preaching in surrounding states on the East coast, Tindley returned to Philadelphia to pastor the East Calvary Methodist Episcopal Church, later renamed the Tindley Temple in his honor. He held periodic religious music concerts at his church, which frequently featured songs that he had composed. His compositions include such standards as "We'll Understand It Better By and By," "What Are They Doing in Heaven Tonight," "Stand By Me," and "I'll Overcome Someday," which were published in his 1916 collection *New Songs of Paradise.* This hymnal was quickly adopted by several African American churches around the United States.

Frequently cited as a major influence on gospel music great Thomas A. Dorsey, Tindley unequivocally helped to set the stage for modern gospel music's emergence. He died on July 26, 1933, in Philadelphia, Pennsylvania.

Albertina Walker (1929–)
Singer

Affectionately known as the "Queen of Gospel," Albertina Walker was born and raised on the South side of Chicago, one of nine children in a hardworking Baptist family. Her mother was a member of the West Point Baptist Church, and Albertina and her sister Rose Marie both sang in the choir there. When Walker was still a little girl, the church's choir director formed a small children's gospel group called the Williams Singers. With this group, and occasionally as a duo, the Walker sisters performed in churches throughout Chicago and the Midwest.

The West Point Baptist Church was the site of many rousing gospel concerts during Walker's youth. She was inspired by the performances of such great gospel singers as Sally and Roberta Martin, Mahalia Jackson, and Tommy E. Dorsey. When Walker entered her teen years, she began to sing at various Baptist and Pentecostal churches; the performances were broadcast on radio, giving Walker an entry into the show business side of gospel music.

Along with remaining members of Robert Anderson's ensemble and keyboardist James Cleveland, Walker created the Caravans. From the group's founding in 1952 until virtually the end of the 1960s, the Caravans dominated traditional gospel, performing all over the United States and Europe and in such celebrated theaters as New York's Apollo, Carnegie Hall, and Madison Square Garden. After the Caravans disbanded in 1967, Walker began to perform as a soloist.

Walker was featured in the 1992 film *Leap of Faith* as a member of a spirited gospel choir. In 1993 she received a Grammy Award nomination for *Albertina Walker Live*, and that same year she performed a concert for Nelson Mandela during his visit to the United States. From her base in Chicago she has been active in politics, working with the Reverend Jesse Jackson and organizing the Operation PUSH People's Choir. She is also the founder of and one of the chief contributors to the Albertina Walker Scholarship Foundation, a source of funds for aspiring young gospel singers.

The Winans
Gospel Singing Group

Comprised of Benjamin "BeBe," Cecelia "CeCe," Marvin, Carvin, Michael, and Ronald, this Detroit-based gospel singing group has become one of gospel music's first families. The older Winans brothers, Marvin and Carvin, sang at their great-grandfather's Congregational Church of Christ on Detroit's east side. The younger Winans children's musical talents, especially BeBe and CeCe, were further encouraged by their father, David Winans, Sr. who was also a minister. He was the first to organize the family into a quartet called the "Testimonials." Under this name the family quartet produced two recordings "Love Covers" (1977) and "Thy Will Be Done" (1978).

The Winans eventually came to the attention of the celebrated gospel musician, Andrae Crouch, who was instrumental in helping to produce their first national release *Introducing the Winans* (1981). The album was subsequently nominated for a Grammy award. Two years later another release *Long Time Coming* also received a Grammy nomination.

In 1987, BeBe and CeCe launched a duo career with the release *BeBe & CeCe Winans*, singing mostly jazz, rhythm and blues, and a few religious works. Their next release *Heaven* (1988) included the recordings "Heaven," "Lost Without You," and "Celebrate New Life." It reached gold record status, rated highly on national rhythm and blues charts, and earned them four Grammy nominations. Their third album *Different Lifestyles* (1991) reached number one on the national rhythm and blues charts. Since then, BeBe and CeCe have worked together and individually with other celebrated popular artists including Whitney Houston, Bobby Brown, Gladys Knight, Luther Vandross, Aretha Franklin, among others. The brother-sister duo has also performed at Carnegie Hall, Culturefest in West Africa, and the 1993 inaugu-

The Winans Family (Warner Bros. Records Inc.)

ral celebration of President Bill Clinton. They have also released two additional albums *Relationships* (1994) and *The Greatest Hits* (1996). In a 1997 solo effort, BeBe recorded "Before the Rain" on the Eternal label. In recent times, the Winans's younger sisters, Angie and Debbie, have recorded with the family singing group which has garnished several Dove, Stellar, and Soul Train Awards.

Appendix

◆African American Recipients of Selected Awards
◆African American Federal Judges
◆African American Olympic Medalists

◆ AFRICAN AMERICAN RECIPIENTS OF SELECTED AWARDS

ACADEMY AWARD OF MERIT (OSCAR)—ACADEMY OF MOTION PICTURE ARTS AND SCIENCES

Best Performance by an Actor in a Leading Role

1963 Sidney Poitier, in *Lilies of the Field*

Best Performance by an Actor in a Supporting Role

1982 Louis Gossett, Jr., in *An Officer and a Gentleman*

1989 Denzel Washington, in *Glory*

1996 Cuba Gooding, Jr., in *Jerry Maquire*

Best Performance by an Actress in a Supporting Role

1939 Hattie McDaniel, in *Gone with the Wind*

1990 Whoopi Goldberg, in *Ghost*

Best Original Score

1984 Prince, for *Purple Rain*

1986 Herbie Hancock, for *'Round Midnight*

AMERICAN ACADEMY AND INSTITUTE OF ARTS AND LETTERS AWARD

Art

1946 Richmond Barthé

1966 Romare Bearden

1971 Norman Lewis

Literature

1946 Gwendolyn Brooks; Langston Hughes

1956 James Baldwin

1961 John A. Williams

1970 James A. McPherson

1971 Charles Gordone

1972 Michael S. Harper

1974 Henry Van Dyke

1978 Lerone Bennett, Jr.; Toni Morrison

1985 John Williams

1987 Ernest J. Gaines

1992 August Wilson

Music

1974 Olly Wilson

1981 George Walker

1988 Hale Smith

1991 Tania J. Leon

AUSTRALIAN OPEN

Men's Singles

1970 Arthur Ashe

Men's Doubles

1977 Arthur Ashe

Women's Doubles

1957 Althea Gibson, with Darlene Hard

CONGRESSIONAL GOLD MEDAL

1978 Marian Anderson

1990 Jesse Owens

1994 Colin L. Powell, Jr.

1998 Little Rock Nine: Jean Brown Trickey, Carlotta Walls LaNier, Melba Patillo Beals, Terrence Roberts, Gloria Ray Karlmark, Thelma Mothershed Wair, Ernest Green, Elizabeth Eckford, and Jefferson Thomas

1999 Rosa Louise McCauley Parks

EMMY AWARD—ACADEMY OF TELEVISION ARTS AND SCIENCES

Primetime Awards

Outstanding Lead Actor in a Drama Series

1966 Bill Cosby, in "I Spy" (NBC)

1967 Bill Cosby, in "I Spy" (NBC)

1968 Bill Cosby, in "I Spy" (NBC)

1991 James Earl Jones, in "Gabriel's Fire" (ABC)

1998 Andre Braugher, in "Homicide: Life on the Street" (NBC)

Outstanding Lead Actor in a Comedy, Variety, or Music Series

1959 Harry Belafonte, in "Tonight with Belafonte"

1985 Robert Guillaume, in "Benson" (ABC)

Outstanding Lead Actress in a Comedy, Variety, or Music Series

1981 Isabel Sanford, in "The Jeffersons" (CBS)

Outstanding Lead Actress in a Comedy or Drama Special

1974 Cicely Tyson, in "The Autobiography of Miss Jane Pittman" (CBS)

Outstanding Lead Actress in a Miniseries or Special

1991 Lynn Whitfield, in "The Josephine Baker Story" (HBO)

1997 Alfre Woodard, in "Miss Evers' Boys" (HBO)

Outstanding Supporting Actor in a Comedy, Variety, or Music Series

1979 Robert Guillaume, in "Soap" (ABC)

Outstanding Supporting Actor in a Miniseries or Special

1991 James Earl Jones, in "Heatwave" (TNT)

Outstanding Supporting Actress in a Drama Series

1984 Alfre Woodard, in "Doris in Wonderland" episode of "Hill Street Blues" (NBC)

1991 Madge Sinclair, in "Gabriel's Fire" (ABC)

1992 Mary Alice, in "I'll Fly Away" (NBC)

Outstanding Supporting Actress in a Comedy, Variety, or Music Series

1987 Jackee Harry, in "227"

Outstanding Supporting Actress in a Miniseries or Special

1991 Ruby Dee, in "Decoration Day," *Hallmark Hall of Fame* (NBC)

Outstanding Directing in a Drama Series

1986 Georg Stanford Brown, in "Parting Shots" episode of "Cagney & Lacey" (ABC)

1990 Thomas Carter, in "Promises to Keep" episode of "Equal Justice" (ABC)

1991 Thomas Carter, in "In Confidence" episode of "Equal Justice" (ABC)

1992 Eric Laneuville, in "All God's Children" episode of "I'll Fly Away" (NBC)

Outstanding Producing in a Miniseries or Special

1989 Suzanne de Passe, in "Lonesome Dove"

Outstanding Producing in a Variety, Music, or Comedy Special

1984 Suzanne de Passe, in "Motown 25: Yesterday, Today and Forever"

1985 Suzanne de Passe, in "Motown at the Apollo"

Outstanding Variety, Music, or Comedy Special

1997 "Chris Rock: Bring on the Pain" (HBO)

Outstanding Achievement in Music Composition

1971 Ray Charles, in "The First Nine Months Are the Hardest" (NBC)

1972 Ray Charles, in "The Funny Side of Marriage" (NBC)

Outstanding Achievement in Music Composition for a Series

1977 Quincy Jones and Gerald Fried, in "Roots" (ABC)

Outstanding Choreography

1981 Debbie Allen, for "Come One, Come All" episode of "Fame"

1982 Debbie Allen, for "Class Act" episode of "Fame"

1989 Debbie Allen, for "Motown 30: What's Goin' On!"

Daytime Awards

Outstanding Talk Show

1987 "The Oprah Winfrey Show"

1988 "The Oprah Winfrey Show"

1989 "The Oprah Winfrey Show"

1991 "The Oprah Winfrey Show"

1992 "The Oprah Winfrey Show"

1994 "The Oprah Winfrey Show"

1995 "The Oprah Winfrey Show"

1996 "The Oprah Winfrey Show"

1997 "The Oprah Winfrey Show"

Outstanding Talk Show Host

1987 Oprah Winfrey, "The Oprah Winfrey Show"

1991 Oprah Winfrey, "The Oprah Winfrey Show"

1992 Oprah Winfrey, "The Oprah Winfrey Show"

1993 Oprah Winfrey, "The Oprah Winfrey Show"

1994 Oprah Winfrey, "The Oprah Winfrey Show"

1995 Oprah Winfrey, "The Oprah Winfrey Show"

1996 Montel Williams, "The Montel Williams Show"

Sports Awards

Outstanding Sports Personality/Studio Host

1998 James Brown (Fox Sports Network)

Outstanding Sports Event Analyst

1997 Joe Morgan (ESPN/NBC)

Outstanding Sports Journalism

1995 "Broken Promises" and "Pros and Cons" episodes of "Real Sports with Bryant Gumbel"

1998 "Diamond Buck$" and "Winning at All Costs" episodes of "Real Sports with Bryant Gumbel"

Hall of Fame Award

1992 Bill Cosby

1994 Oprah Winfrey

FRENCH OPEN

Men's Doubles

1971 Arthur Ashe

Women's Singles

1956 Althea Gibson

Women's Doubles

1956 Althea Gibson

1999 Venus and Serena Williams

GRAMMY AWARDS—NATIONAL ACADEMY OF RECORDING ARTS AND SCIENCES

Record of the Year

1963 *I Can't Stop Loving You*, by Count Basie

1967 *Up, Up and Away*, by 5th Dimension

1969 *Aquarius/Let the Sun Shine In*, by 5th Dimension

1972 *The First Time Ever I Saw Your Face*, by Roberta Flack

1973 *Killing Me Softly with His Song*, by Roberta Flack

1976 *This Masquerade*, by George Benson

1983 *Beat It*, by Michael Jackson

1984 *What's Love Got To Do with It?*, by Tina Turner

1985 *We Are the World*, by USA For Africa; produced by Quincy Jones

1988 *Don't Worry, Be Happy*, by Bobby McFerrin

1991 *Unforgettable*, by Natalie Cole with Nat "King" Cole

1993 *I Will Always Love You*, by Whitney Houston

1995 *Kiss From a Rose* by Seal

Album of the Year

1973 *Innervisions*, by Stevie Wonder; produced by Stevie Wonder

1974 *Fulfillingness' First Finale*, by Stevie Wonder; produced by Stevie Wonder

1976 *Songs in the Key of Life*, by Stevie Wonder; produced by Stevie Wonder

1983 *Thriller*, by Michael Jackson; produced by Quincy Jones

1984 *Can't Slow Down*, by Lionel Richie; produced by Lionel Richie and James Anthony Carmichael

1990 *Back on the Block*, by Quincy Jones; produced by Quincy Jones

1991 *Unforgettable*, by Natalie Cole

1999 *The Miseducation of Lauryn Hill*, by Lauryn Hill; produced by Lauryn Hill

HEISMAN MEMORIAL TROPHY—DOWNTOWN ATHLETIC CLUB OF NEW YORK CITY, INC.

1961 Ernie Davis, Syracuse University, TB

1965 Michael Garrett, University of Southern California, TB

1968 O. J. Simpson, University of Southern California, TB

1972 Johnny Rodgers, University of Nebraska, FL

1974 Archie Griffin, University of Ohio State, HB

1975 Archie Griffin, University of Ohio State, HB

1976 Anthony (Tony) Dorsett, University of Pittsburgh, HB

1977 Earl Campbell, University of Texas, FB

1978 Billy Sims, University of Oklahoma, HB

1979 Charles White, University of Southern California, TB

1980 George Rogers, University of South Carolina, HB

1981 Marcus Allen, University of Southern California, TB

1982 Herschel Walker, University of Georgia, HB

1983 Mike Rozier, University of Nebraska, TB

1985 Bo Jackson, Auburn University, TB

1987 Tim Brown, University of Notre Dame, FL

1988 Barry Sanders, Oklahoma State University, HB

1989 Andre Ware, University of Houston, QB

1991 Desmond Howard, University of Michigan, WR

1993 Charlie Ward, Florida State University, QB

1994 Rashaan Salaam, Colorado, RB

1995 Eddie George, Ohio State, RB

1997 Charles Woodson, University of Michigan, DB/R

1998 Ricky Williams, University of Texas at Austin, TB

CLARENCE L. HOLTE LITERARY PRIZE (BIANNUAL)—CO-SPONSORED BY THE PHELPS-STOKES FUND AND THE SCHOMBURG CENTER FOR RESEARCH IN BLACK CULTURE OF THE NEW YORK PUBLIC LIBRARY

1979 Chancellor Williams, for *The Destruction of Black Civilization: Great Issues of a Race from 4500 B.C. to 2000 A.D.*

1981 Ivan Van Sertima, for *They Came Before Columbus*

1983 Vincent Harding, for *There Is a River: The Black Struggle for Freedom in America*

1985 No award

1986 John Hope Franklin, for *George Washington Williams: A Biography*

1988 Arnold Rampersad, for *The Life of Langston Hughes, Volume 1 (1902-1941): I, Too, Sing America*

KENNEDY CENTER HONORS—JOHN F. KENNEDY CENTER FOR THE PERFORMING ARTS

1978 Marian Anderson

1979 Ella Fitzgerald
1980 Leontyne Price
1981 William "Count" Basie
1983 Katherine Dunham
1984 Lena Horne
1986 Ray Charles
1987 Sammy Davis, Jr.
1988 Alvin Ailey
1989 Harry Belafonte
1990 Dizzy Gillespie
1991 Fayard and Harold Nicholas
1992 Lionel Hampton
1993 Arthur Mitchell; Marion Williams
1994 Aretha Franklin
1995 B. B. King; Sidney Poitier
1996 Benny Carter
1997 Jessye Norman
1998 Bill Cosby

MARTIN LUTHER KING, JR. NONVIOLENT PEACE PRIZE—MARTIN LUTHER KING, JR. CENTER FOR NONVIOLENT SOCIAL CHANGE, INC.

1973 Andrew Young
1974 Cesar Chavez
1975 John Lewis
1976 Randolph Blackwell
1977 Benjamin E. Mays
1978 Kenneth D. Kaunda; Stanley Levison
1979 Jimmy Carter
1980 Rosa Parks
1981 Ivan Allen, Jr.
1982 Harry Belafonte
1983 Sir Richard Attenborough; Martin Luther King, Sr.
1984 No award
1985 No award
1986 Bishop Desmond Tutu
1987 Corazon Aquino
1988 No award
1989 No award
1990 Mikhail Gorbachev
1991 No award
1992 No award
1993 Jesse Jackson

MISS AMERICA—MISS AMERICA ORGANIZATION

1984 Vanessa Williams (New York); Suzette Charles (New Jersey)
1990 Debbye Turner (Missouri)

MISS BLACK AMERICA—J. MORRIS ANDERSON PRODUCTION COMPANY

1968 Sandy Willliams (Pennsylvania)
1969 G. O. Smith (New York)
1970 Stephanie Clark (District of Columbia)
1971 Joyce Warner (Florida)
1972 Linda Barney (New Jersey)
1973 Arnice Russell (New York)
1974 Von Gretchen Sheppard (California)
1975 Helen Ford (Mississippi)
1976 Twanna Kilgore (District of Columbia)
1977 Claire Ford (Tennessee)
1978 Lydia Jackson (New Jersey)
1979 Veretta Shankle (Mississippi)
1980 Sharon Wright (Illinois)
1981 Pamela Jenks (Massachusetts)
1982 Phyllis Tucker (Florida)
1983 Sonia Robinson (Wisconsin)
1984 Lydia Garrett (South Carolina)
1985 Amina Fakir (Michigan)
1986 Rachel Oliver (Massachusetts)
1987 Leila McBride (Colorado)
1989 Paula Swynn (District of Columbia)
1990 Rosie Jones (Connecticut)
1991 Sharmelle Sullivan (Indiana)
1992 Marilyn DeShields
1993 Pilar Ginger Fort
1994 Karen Wallace
1995 Asheera Ahmad

MISS USA—MADISON SQUARE GARDEN TELEVISION PRODUCTIONS

1990 Carole Gist (Michigan)

1992 Shannon Marketic

1993 Kenya Moore (Michigan)

1994 Frances Louise "Lu" Parker

1995 Chelsi Smith (Texas)

1996 Ali Landry

MS. OLYMPIA WINNERS—INTERNATIONAL FEDERATION OF BODYBUILDERS, WOMEN'S BODYBUILDING CHAMPIONS

1983 Carla Dunlap

1990 Lenda Murray

1991 Lenda Murray

1992 Lenda Murray

1993 Lenda Murray

1994 Lenda Murray

1995 Lenda Murray

MR. OLYMPIA WINNERS—INTERNATIONAL FEDERATION OF BODYBUILDERS, MEN'S BODYBUILDING CHAMPIONS

1967 Sergio Oliva

1968 Sergio Oliva

1982 Chris Dickerson

1984 Lee Haney

1985 Lee Haney

1986 Lee Haney

1987 Lee Haney

1988 Lee Haney

1989 Lee Haney

1990 Lee Haney

1991 Lee Haney

1998 Ronnie Coleman

NATIONAL BASEBALL HALL OF FAME

1962 Jackie Robinson

1969 Roy Campanella

1971 Leroy R. "Satchel" Paige

1972 Josh Gibson; Walter "Buck" Leonard

1973 Roberto W. Clemente; Monte Irvin

1974 James T. "Cool Papa" Bell

1975 William "Judy" Johnson

1976 Oscar M. Charleston

1977 Ernest Banks; Martin Dihigo; John H. Lloyd

1979 Willie Mays

1981 Andrew "Rube" Foster; Robert T. Gibson

1982 Hank Aaron; Frank Robinson

1983 Juan A. Marichal

1985 Lou Brock

1986 Willie L. "Stretch" McCovey

1987 Ray Dandridge; Billy Williams

1988 Willie Stargell

1990 Joe Morgan

1991 Rod Carew; Ferguson Jenkins

1993 Reggie Jackson

1995 Leon Day

1996 Bill Foster

1997 Willie Wells

1998 Larry Doby

1999 Orlando Cepeda; Joe Williams

NATIONAL BASKETBALL HALL OF FAME

1972 Robert Douglass

1974 Bill Russell

1976 Elgin "The Big E" Baylor; Charles Cooper

1978 Wilt Chamberlain

1979 Oscar Robertson

1981 Clarence Gaines; Willis Reed

1983 Sam Jones

1984 Nate Thurmond

1986 Walt "Clyde" Frazier

1987 Wes Unseld

1988 William "Pop" Gates; K.C. Jones; Lenny Wilkins (player)

1989 Dave Bing; Elvin Hayes; Earl "The Pearl" Monroe

1990 Nate "Tiny" Archibald

1991 Lusia Harris-Stewart; Connie Hawkins; Bob Lanier

1992 Walt Bellamy; Julius "Dr. J" Erving; Calvin Murphy

1994 Kareem Abdul-Jabbar; Cheryl Miller

1995 George Gervin; David Thompson

1996 Alex English

1998 Marques Haynes, Lenny Wilkins (coach)

1999 Wayne Embry, John Thompson

NATIONAL BOOK AWARD—NATIONAL BOOK FOUNDATION

1953 Ralph Ellison, for *Invisible Man*, Fiction

1969 Winthrop D. Jordan, for *White over Black: American Attitudes toward the Negro, 1550-1812*, History and Biography

1983 Gloria Naylor, for *The Women of Brewster Place*, First Novel; Joyce Carol Thomas, for *Marked By Fire*, Children's Literature; Alice Walker, for *The Color Purple*, Fiction

1990 Charles Johnson, for *Middle Passage*, Fiction

1991 Melissa Fay Green, for *Praying for Sheetrock*, Nonfiction

1992 Edward P. Jones, for *Lost in the City*, Fiction

NATIONAL MEDAL OF ARTS—NATIONAL ENDOWMENT FOR THE ARTS

1985 Ralph Ellison (writer); Leontyne Price (singer)

1986 Marian Anderson (singer)

1987 Romare Bearden (artist); Ella Fitzgerald (singer)

1988 Gordon Parks (photographer and film director)

1989 Katherine Dunham (choreographer); Dizzy Gillespie (musician)

1990 Riley "B. B." King (musician)

1991 James Earl Jones (actor); Billy Taylor (musician)

1994 Harry Belafonte (singer)

1995 Gwendolyn Brooks (poet); Ossie Davis (actor); Ruby Dee (actress)

1996 The Harlem Boys Choir (chorale); Lionel Hampton (musician)

1997 Betty Carter (singer)

1998 Fats Domino (singer)

NATIONAL SOCIETY OF ARTS AND LETTERS GOLD MEDAL OF MERIT AWARD

1982 Andre Watts (music)

NATIONAL TRACK AND FIELD HALL OF FAME—THE ATHLETICS CONGRESS OF THE USA

1974 Ralph Boston; Lee Calhoun; Harrison Dillard; Rafer Johnson; Jesse Owens; Wilma Rudolph; Malvin Whitfield

1975 Ralph Metcalfe

1976 Robert Hayes; Hayes Jones

1977 Robert Beamon; Andrew W. Stanfield

1978 Tommie Smith; John Woodruff

1979 Jim Hines; William DeHart Hubbard

1980 Wyomia Tyus

1981 Willye White

1982 Willie Davenport; Eddie Tolan

1983 Lee Evans

1984 Madeline Manning Mims

1986 Henry Barney Ewell

1988 Gregory Bell

1989 Milt Campbell; Edward Temple

1990 Charles Dumas

1994 Cornelius Johnson; Edwin Moses

1995 Valerie Brisco; Florence Griffith Joyner

1997 Evelyn Ashford; Henry Carr; Renaldo Nehemiah

NEW YORK DRAMA CRITICS' CIRCLE AWARD

Best American Play

1959 *A Raisin in the Sun*, by Lorraine Hansberry

1975 *The Taking of Miss Janie*, by Ed Bullins

1982 *A Soldier's Play*, by Charles Fuller

1996 *Seven Guitars*, by August Wilson

Best New Play

1985 *Ma Rainey's Black Bottom*, by August Wilson

1987 *Fences*, by August Wilson

1988 *Joe Turner's Come and Gone*, by August Wilson

1990 *The Piano Lesson*, by August Wilson

NOBEL PEACE PRIZE—NOBEL FOUNDATION

1950 Ralph J. Bunche

1964 Martin Luther King, Jr.

NOBEL PRIZE IN LITERATURE—NOBEL FOUNDATION

1993 Toni Morrison

PRESIDENTIAL MEDAL OF FREEDOM—UNITED STATES EXECUTIVE OFFICE OF THE PRESIDENT

1963 Marian Anderson; Ralph J. Bunche

1964 John L. Lewis; Leontyne Price; A. Philip Randolph

1969 Edward Kennedy "Duke" Ellington; Ralph Ellison; Roy Wilkins; Whitney M. Young, Jr.

1976 Jesse Owens

1977 Martin Luther King, Jr. (posthumously)

1980 Clarence Mitchell

1981 James H. "Eubie" Blake; Andrew Young

1983 James Cheek; Mabel Mercer

1984 Jack Roosevelt "Jackie" Robinson (posthumously)

1985 William "Count" Basie (posthumously); Jerome "Brud" Holland (posthumously)

1987 Frederick Douglass Patterson

1988 Pearl Bailey

1991 Colin L. Powell

1992 Ella Fitzgerald

1993 Arthur Ashe, Jr. (posthumously); Thurgood Marshall (posthumously); Colin L. Powell

1994 Dorothy Height; Barbara Jordan

1995 William Thaddeus Coleman, Jr.; John Hope Franklin; A. Leon Higginbotham, Jr.

1996 John H. Johnson; Rosa Parks

1998 James Farmer

PROFESSIONAL FOOTBALL HALL OF FAME

1967 Emlen Tunnell

1968 Marion Motley

1969 Fletcher "Joe" Perry

1971 Jim Brown

1972 Ollie Matson

1973 Jim Parker

1974 Richard "Night Train" Lane

1975 Roosevelt Brown; Leonard "Lenny" Moore

1976 Leonard "Len" Ford

1977 Gale Sayers; Bill Willis

1980 Herb Adderley; David "Deacon" Jones

1981 Willie Davis

1983 Bobby Bell; Bobby Mitchell; Paul Warfield

1984 Willie Brown; Charley Taylor

1985 O. J. Simpson

1986 Ken Houston; Willie Lanier

1987 Joe Greene; John Henry Johnson; Gene Upshaw

1988 Alan Page

1989 Mel Blount; Art Shell; Willie Wood

1990 Junious "Buck" Buchanan; Franco Harris

1991 Earl Campbell

1992 Lem Barney; John Mackey

1993 Larry Little; Walter Payton

1994 Tony Dorsett; Leroy Kelly

1995 Lee Roy Selmon

1996 Charlie Joiner; Mel Renfro

1997 Mike Haynes

1998 Mike Singletary; Dwight Stephenson

1999 Eric Dickerson; Lawrence Taylor

PULITZER PRIZE—COLUMBIA UNIVERSITY GRADUATE SCHOOL OF JOURNALISM

Biography or Autobiography

1994 *W. E. B. Du Bois: Biography of a Race, 1968–1919*, by David Levering Lewis

Journalism: Commentary

1996 E. R. Shipp

Journalism: Feature Writing

1999 Angelo B. Henderson

Letters: Drama

1970 *No Place To Be Somebody*, by Charles Gordone

1982 *A Soldier's Play*, by Charles Fuller

1987 *Fences*, by August Wilson

1990 *The Piano Lesson*, by August Wilson

Letters: Fiction

1978 *Elbow Room*, by James Alan McPherson

1983 *The Color Purple*, by Alice Walker

1988 *Beloved*, by Toni Morrison

Letters: Poetry

1950 *Annie Allen*, by Gwendolyn Brooks

1987 *Thomas and Beulah*, by Rita Dove

Letters: Special Awards and Citations

1977 Alexander Palmer Haley, for *Roots*

Music: Special Awards and Citations

1976 Scott Joplin

1996 George Walker

1997 Wynton Marsalis

1999 Edward Kennedy "Duke" Ellington (posthmously)

ROCK AND ROLL HALL OF FAME

1986 Chuck Berry; James Brown; Ray Charles; Sam Cooks; Fats Domino; Little Richard; Robert Johnson; Jimmy Yancey

1987 The Coasters; Bo Diddley; Aretha Franklin; Marvin Gaye; Louis Jordan; B.B. King; Clyde McPhalter; Smokey Robinson; Big Joe Turner; T-Bone Walker; Muddy Waters; Jackie Wilson

1988 The Drifters; Barry Gordy, Jr.; The Supremes

1989 The Ink Spots; Otis Redding; Bessie Smith; The Soul Stirrers; The Temptations; Stevie Wonder

1990 Louis Armstrong; Hank Ballard; Charlie Christian; The Four Tops; Holland, Dozier, and Holland; The Platters; Ma Rainey

1991 La Vern Baker; John Lee Hooker; Howlin' Wolf; The Impressions; Wilson Pickett; Jimmy Reed; Ike and Tina Turner

1992 Blue Brand, Booker T. and the M.G.'s; Jimi Hendrix; Isley Brothers; Elmore James; Doc Pomus; Professor Longhair; Sam and Dave

1993 Ruth Brown; Etta James; Frankie Lymon and the Teenagers; Sly and the Family Stone; Dinah Washington

1994 Willie Dixon; Bob Marley; Johnny Otis

1995 Al Green; Martha and the Vandellas; The Orioles

1996 Little Willie John; Gladys Knight and the Pips; The Shirelles

1997 Mahalia Jackson; The Jackson Five; Parliament

1998 Jelly Roll Morton; Lloyd Price

1999 Charles Brown; Curtis Mayfield; The Staple Singers

SPRINGARN MEDAL—NATIONAL ASSOCIATION FOR THE ADVANCEMENT OF COLORED PEOPLE

1915 Ernest E. Just—head of the department of physiology at Howard University Medical School.

1916 Charles Young—major in the United States Army.

1917 Harry T. Burleigh—composer, pianist, singer.

1918 William Stanley Braithwaite—poet, literary critic, editor.

1919 Archibald H. Grimké—former U.S. Consul in Santo Domingo, president of the American Negro Academy, author, president of the District of Columbia branch of the NAACP.

1920 William Edward Burghardt DuBois—author, editor, organizer of the first Pan-African Congress.

1921 Charles S. Gilpin—actor.

1922 Mary B. Talbert—former president of the National Association of Colored Women.

1923 George Washington Carver—head of research and director of the experiment station at Tuskegee Institute.

1924 Roland Hayes—singer.

1925 James Weldon Johnson—former United States Consul in Venezuela and Nicaragua, author, editor, poet; secretary of the NAACP.

1926 Carter G. Woodson—editor, historian; founder of the Association for the Study of Negro Life and History.

1927 Anthony Overton—businessman; president of the Victory Life Insurance Company (the first African American organization permitted to do business under the rigid requirements of the State of New York).

1928 Charles W. Chesnutt—author.

1929 Mordecai Wyatt Johnson—the first African American president of Howard University.

1930 Henry A. Hunt—principal of Fort Valley High and Industrial School, Fort Valley, Georgia.

1931 Richard Berry Harrison—actor.

1932 Robert Russa Moton—principal of Tuskegee Institute.

1933 Max Yergan—secretary of the YMCA in South Africa.

1934 William Taylor Burwell Williams—dean of Tuskegee Institute.

1935 Mary McLeod Bethune—founder and president of Bethune Cookman College.

1936 John Hope—president of Atlanta University.

1937 Walter White—executive secretary of the NAACP.

1939 Marian Anderson—singer.

1940 Louis T. Wright—surgeon.

1941 Richard Wright—author.

1942 A. Philip Randolph—labor leader, international president of the Brotherhood of Sleeping Car Porters.

1943 William H. Hastie—jurist, educator.

1944 Charles Drew—scientist.

1945 Paul Robeson—singer, actor.

1946 Thurgood Marshall—special counsel of the NAACP

1947 Percy Julian—research chemist.

1948 Channing H. Tobias—minister, educator.

1949 Ralph J. Bunche—international civil servant, acting United Nations mediator in Palestine.

1950 Charles Hamilton Houston—chairman of the NAACP Legal Committee.

1951 Mabel Keaton Staupers—leader of the National Association of Colored Graduate Nurses.

1952 Harry T. Moore—state leader of the Florida NAACP.

1953 Paul R. Williams—architect.

1954 Theodore K. Lawless—physician, educator, philanthropist.

1955 Carl Murphy—editor, publisher, civic leader.

1956 Jack Roosevelt Robinson—athlete.

1957 Martin Luther King, Jr.—minister, civil rights leader.

1958 Daisy Bates and the Little Rock Nine—for their pioneer role in upholding the basic ideals of American democracy in the face of continuing harassment and constant threats of bodily injury.

1959 Edward Kennedy "Duke" Ellington—composer, musician, orchestra leader.

1960 Langston Hughes—poet, author, playwright.

1961 Kenneth B. Clark—professor of psychology at the City College of the City University of New York, founder and director of the Northside Center for Child Development, prime mobilizer of the resources of modern psychology in the attack upon racial segregation.

1962 Robert C. Weaver—administrator of the Housing and Home Finance Agency.

1963 Medgar Wiley Evers—NAACP field secretary for Mississippi, World War II veteran.

1964 Roy Wilkins—executive director of the NAACP.

1965 Leontyne Price—singer.

1966 John H. Johnson—founder and president of the Johnson Publishing Company.

1967 Edward W. Brooke III—the first African American to win popular election to the United States Senate.

1968 Sammy Davis, Jr.—performer, civil rights activist.

1969 Clarence M. Mitchell, Jr.—director of the Washington Bureau of the NAACP, civil rights activist.

1970 Jacob Lawrence—artist, teacher, humanitarian.

1971 Leon H. Sullivan—minister.

1972 Gordon Alexander Buchanan Parks—writer, photographer, filmmaker.

1973 Wilson C. Riles—educator.

1974 Damon Keith—jurist.

1975 Hank Aaron—athlete.

1976 Alvin Ailey—dancer, choreographer, artistic director.

1977 Alexander Palmer Haley—author, biographer, lecturer.

1978 Andrew Young—United States Ambassador to the United Nations, diplomat, cabinet member, civil rights activist, minister.

1979 Rosa Parks—community activist.

1980 Rayford W. Logan—educator, historian, author.

1981 Coleman A. Young—mayor of the City of Detroit, public servant, labor leader, civil rights activist.

1982 Benjamin E. Mays—educator, theologian, humanitarian).

1983 Lena Horne—performer, humanitarian.

1984 Tom Bradley—government executive, public servant, humanitarian.

1985 William H. "Bill" Cosby—comedian, actor, educator, humanitarian.

1986 Benjamin Lawson Hooks—executive director of the NAACP.

1987 Percy Ellis Sutton—public servant, businessman, community leader.

1988 Frederick Douglass Patterson—doctor of veterinary medicine, educator, humanitarian, founder of the United Negro College Fund.

1989 Jesse Jackson—minister, political leader, civil rights activist.

1990 L. Douglas Wilder—governor of Virginia.

1991 Colin L. Powell—general in the United States Army, chairman of the Joint Chiefs of Staff.

1992 Barbara C. Jordan—educator, former congresswoman.

1993 Dorothy L. Height—president of the National Council of Negro Women.

1994 Maya Angelou—poet, author, performing artist.

1995 John Hope Franklin—historian.

1996 A. Leon Higginbotham, Jr.—jurist, judge

1997 Carl T. Rowan—journalist.

1998 Myrlie Evers-Williams—former chair, board of directors, NAACP

1999 Earl G. Graves, publisher and media executive

SULLIVAN AWARD—AMATEUR ATHLETIC UNION

1961 Wilma Rudolph

1981 Carl Lewis

1983 Edwin Moses

1986 Jackie Joyner-Kersee

1988 Florence Griffith-Joyner

1991 Mike Powell

1993 Charlie Ward

1996 Michael Johnson

1998 Chamique Holdsclaw

TONY (ANTOINETTE PERRY) AWARD—LEAGUE OF AMERICAN THEATERS AND PRODUCERS

Actor (Dramatic)

1969 James Earl Jones, for *The Great White Hope*

1975 John Kani, for *Sizwe Banzi*; Winston Ntshona, for *The Island*

1987 James Earl Jones, for *Fences*

Supporting or Featured Actor (Dramatic)

1982 Zakes Mokae, for *Master Harold. . . and the Boys*

1992 Larry Fishburne, for *Two Trains Running*

1994 Jeffrey Wright, for *Angels in America*

1996 Ruben Santiago-Hudson, for *Seven Guitars*

Actor (Musical)

1970 Cleavon Little, for *Purlie*

1973 Ben Vereen, for *Pippin*

1982 Ben Harvey, for *Dreamgirls*

1992 Gregory Hines, for *Jelly's Last Jam*

Supporting or Featured Actor (Musical)

1954 Harry Belafonte, for *John Murray Anderson's Almanac*

1975 Ted Rose, for *The Wiz*

1981 Hinton Battle, for *Sophisticated Ladies*

1982 Cleavant Derricks, for *Dreamgirls*

1983 Charles "Honi" Coles, for *My One and Only*

1984 Hinton Battle, for *The Tap Dance Kid*

1991 Hinton Battle, for *Miss Saigon*

1997 Chuck Cooper, for *The Life*

Supporting or Featured Actress (Dramatic)

1977 Trazana Beverley, for *For Colored Girls Who Have Considered Suicide/When the Rainbow Is Enuf*

1987 Mary Alice, for *Fences*

1988 L. Scott Caldwell, for *Joe Turner's Come and Gone*

1997 Lynne Thigpen, for *An American Daughter*

Actress (Musical)

1962 Diahann Carroll, for *No Strings*

1968 Leslie Uggams, for *Hallelujah, Baby*

1974 Virginia Capers, for *Raisin*

1982 Jennifer Holliday, for *Dreamgirls*

1989 Ruth Brown, for *Black and Blue*

1996 Audra McDonald, for *Master Class*

Supporting or Featured Actress (Musical)

1950 Juanita Hall, for *South Pacific*

1968 Lillian Hayman, for *Halleluja, Baby*

1970 Melba Moore, for *Purlie*

1975 Dee Dee Bridgewater, for *The Wiz*

1977 Delores Hall, for *Your Arms's Too Short To Box with God*

1978 Nell Carter, for *Ain't Misbehavin*

1992 Tonya Pinkins, for *Jelly's Last Jam*

1994 Audra McDonald, for *Carousel*

1996 Ann Duquesnay, for *Bring in 'Da Noise, Bring in 'Da Funk*

1997 Lillias White, for *The Life*

Play

1974 *The River Niger*, by Joseph A. Walker

1987 *Fences*, by August Wilson

UNITED STATES MEDAL OF HONOR

Civil War

Army

William H. Barnes, Private, Company C, 38th United States Colored Troops.

Powhatan Beaty, First Sergeant, Company G, 5th United States Colored Troops.

James H. Bronson, First Sergeant, Company D, 5th United States Colored Troops.

William H. Carney, Sergeant, Company C, 54th Massachusetts Infantry, United States Colored Troops.

Decatur Dorsey, Sergeant, Company B, 39th United States Colored Troops.

Christian A. Fleetwood, Sergeant Major, 4th United States Colored Troops.

James Gardiner, Private, Company 1, 36th United States Colored Troops.

James H. Harris, Sergeant, Company B, 38th United States Colored Troops.

Thomas R. Hawkins, Sergeant Major, 6th United States Colored Troops.

Alfred B. Hilton, Sergeant, Company H, 4th United States Colored Troops.

Milton M. Holland, Sergeant, 5th United States Colored Troops.

Alexander Kelly, First Sergeant, Company F, 6th United States Colored Troops.

Robert Pinn, First Sergeant, Company I, 5th United States Colored Troops.

Edward Radcliff, First Sergeant, Company C, 38th United States Colored Troops.

Charles Veal, Private, Company D, 4th United States Colored Troops.

Navy

Aaron Anderson, Landsman, *USS Wyandank.*

Robert Blake, Powder Boy, *USS Marblehead.*

William H. Brown, Landsman, *USS Brooklyn.*

Wilson Brown, *USS Hartford.*

John Lawson, Landsman, *USS Hartford.*

James Mifflin, Engineer's Cook, *USS Brooklyn.*

Joachim Pease, Seaman, *USS Kearsarge.*

Interim Period

Navy

Daniel Atkins, Ship's Cook, First Class, *USS Cushing.*

John Davis, Seaman, *USS Trenton.*

Alphonse Girandy, Seaman, *USS Tetrel.*

John Johnson, Seaman, *USS Kansas.*

William Johnson, Cooper, *USS Adams.*

Joseph B. Noil, Seaman, *USS Powhatan.*

John Smith, Seaman, *USS Shenandoah.*

Robert Sweeney, Seaman, *USS Kearsage, USS Jamestown.*

Western Campaigns

Army

Thomas Boyne, Sergeant, Troop C, 9th United States Cavalry.

Benjamin Brown, Sergeant, Company C, 24th United States Infantry.

John Denny, Sergeant, Troop C, 9th United States Cavalry.

Pompey Factor, Seminole Negro Indian Scouts.

Clinton Greaves, Corporal, Troop C, 9th United States Cavalry.

Henry Johnson, Sergeant, Troop D, 9th United States Cavalry.

George Jordan, Sergeant, Troop K, 9th United States Cavalry.

William McBreyar, Sergeant, Troop K, 10th United States Cavalry.

Isaiah Mays, Corporal, Company B, 24th United States Infantry.

Issac Payne, Private (Trumpeteer) Seminole Negro Indian Scouts.

Thomas Shaw, Sergeant, Troop K, 9th United States Cavalry.

Emanuel Stance, Sergeant, Troop F, 9th United States Cavalry.

Augustus Walley, Private, Troop 1, 9th United States Cavalry.

John Ward, Sergeant, Seminole Negro Indian Scouts.

Moses Williams, First Sergeant, Troop 1, 9th United States Cavalry.

William O. Wilson, Corporal, Troop 1, 9th United States Cavalry.

Brent Woods, Sergeant, Troop B, 9th United States Cavalry.

Spanish-American War

Army

Edward L. Baker, Jr., Sergeant Major, 10th United States Cavalry.

Dennis Bell, Private, Troop H, 10th United States Cavalry.

Fitz Lee, Private, Troop M, 10th United States Cavalry.

William H. Thompkins, Private, Troop G, 10th United States Cavalry.

George H. Wanton, Sergeant, Troop M, 10th United States Cavalry.

Navy

Joseph B. Noil, Non-combatant Service, *USS Powhatan.*

Robert Penn, Fireman, First Class, *USS Iowa.*

World War I

Army

Freddie Stowers, Corporal, Company C, 371st Infantry Regiment, 93rd Infantry Division.

World War II

Army

Vernon Baker, First Lieutenant.

Edward A. Carter, Jr., Staff Sergeant.

John R. Fox, First Lieutenant.

Willy F. James, Jr., Private First Class.

Ruben Rivers, Staff Sergeant.

Charles L. Thomas, First Lieutenant.

George Watson, Private.

Korean War

Army

Cornelius H. Charlton, Sergeant, 24th Infantry Regiment, 25th Division.

William Thompson, Private, 24th Infantry Regiment, 25th Division.

Vietnam War

Army

Webster Anderson, Sergeant, Battery A, 2nd Battalion, 320th Artillery, 101st Airborne Division.

Eugene Ashley, Jr., Sergeant, Company C, 5th Special Forces Group (Airborne), 1st Special Forces.

William M. Bryant, Sergeant First Class, Company A, 5th Special Forces Group, 1st Special Forces.

Lawrence Joel, Specialist Sixth Class, Headquarters and Headquarters Company, 1st Battalion, 173d Airborne Brigade.

Dwight H. Johnson, Specialist Fifth Class, Company B, 1st Battalion, 69th Armor, 4th Infantry Division.

Garfield M. Langhorn, Private First Class, Troop C, 7th Squadron, 17th Cavalry, 1st Aviation Brigade.

Matthew Leonard, Platoon Sergeant, Company B, 1st Battalion, 16th Infantry, 1st Infantry Division.

Donald R. Long, Sergeant, Troop C, 1st Squadron, 4th Cavalry, 1st Infantry Division.

Milton L. Olive III, Private First Class, Company B, 2nd Battalion 503d Infantry, 173d Airborne Brigade.

Riley L. Pitts, Captain, Company C, 2nd Battalion, 27th Infantry, 25th Infantry Division.

Charles C. Rogers, Lieutenant Colonel, 1st Battalion, 5th Infantry, 1st Infantry Division.

Rupert L. Sargent, First Lieutenant, Company B, 4th Battalion, 9th Infantry, 25th Infantry Division.

Clarence E. Sasser, Specialist 5th Class, Headquarters Company, 3rd Battalion, 60th Infantry, 90th Infantry Division.

Clifford C. Sims, Staff Sergeant, Company D, 2nd Battalion, 501st Infantry, 101st Airborne Division.

John E. Warren, Jr., First Lieutenant, Company C, 2nd Battalion, 22d Infantry, 25th Infantry Division.

Marines

James A. Anderson, Jr. Private First Class, 2nd Platoon, Company F, 2nd Battalion, 3rd Marine Division.

Oscar P. Austin, Private First Class, Company E, 7th Marines, 1st Marine Division.

Rodney M. Davis, Company B, First Battalion, 5th Marines, 1st Marine Division.

Robert H. Jenkins, Jr., Private First Class, 3rd Reconnaissance Battalion, 3rd Marine Division.

Ralph H. Johnson, Private First Class, Company A, 1st Reconnaissance Battalion, 1st Marine Division.

UNITED STATES OPEN

Men's Singles

1968 Arthur Ashe

Women's Singles

1957 Althea Gibson

1958 Althea Gibson

Mixed Doubles

1957 Althea Gibson

UNITED STATES POET LAUREATE

1993 Rita Dove (served until 1995)

UNITED STATES POSTAL SERVICE STAMPS ON AFRICAN AMERICAN HISTORY

Louis Armstrong

Benjamin Banneker

William "Count" Basie

James Pierson Beckwourth

Mary McLeod Bethune

James Hubert "Eubie" Blake

Ralph Johnson Bunche

George Washington Carver

Nat "King" Cole

Bessie Coleman

John Coltrane

Allison Davis

Benjamin O. Davis, Sr.

Frederick Douglass

Charles Richard Drew

(W)illiam (E)dward (B)urghardt Du Bois

Jean Baptiste Pointe Du Sable

Paul Laurence Dunbar

Edward Kennedy "Duke" Ellington

Erroll Garner

(W)illiam (C)hristopher Handy

Coleman Hawkins

Matthew Alexander Henson

Billie Holiday

Mahalia Jackson

James Price Johnson

James Weldon Johnson

Robert Johnson

Scott Joplin

Percy Lavon Julian

Ernest Everett Just

Martin Luther King, Jr.

Joe Louis

Hudson William Ledbetter, "Leadbelly"

Roberta Martin

Jan E. Matzeliger

Clyde McPhatter

Charles Mingus

Thelonious Sphere Monk

Ferdinand "Jelly Roll" Morton

James Cleveland "Jesse" Owens

Charlie "Bird" Parker

Bill Pickett

Salem Poor

Gertrude "Ma" Rainey

(A)sa Philip Randolph

Otis Redding

John Roosevelt "Jackie" Robinson

James Andrew "Jimmy" Rushing

Bessie Smith

Henry Ossawa Tanner

Sonny Terry
Sister Rosetta Tharpe
Sojourner Truth
Harriet Tubman
Madame C. J. Walker
Clara Ward
Booker Taliaferro Washington
Dinah Washington
Ethel Waters
Muddy Waters
Ida Bell Wells-Barnett
Josh White
Howlin' Wolf
Carter Godwin Woodson
Whitney Moore Young

WIMBLEDON—ALL ENGLAND LAWN TENNIS AND CROQUET CLUB

Men's Singles

1975 Arthur Ashe

Ladies' Singles

1957 Althea Gibson

1958 Althea Gibson

Ladies' Doubles

1957 Althea Gibson, with Darlene Hard

1958 Althea Gibson, with Maria Bueno

◆ AFRICAN AMERICAN FEDERAL JUDGES

PRESIDENT FRANKLIN D. ROOSEVELT

1937	William H. Hastie*	District Court, Virgin Islands
1939	Harnian E. Moore*	District Court, Virgin Islands

PRESIDENT HARRY S TRUMAN

1945	Irvin C. Mollison*	United States Customs Court
1949	William H. Hastie*	Court of Appeals, Third Circuit
1949	Harnian E. Moore (a)*	District Court, Virgin Islands

PRESIDENT DWIGHT D. EISENHOWER

1957	Scovel Richardson*	United States Customs Court
1958	Walter Gordon*	District Court, Virgin Islands

PRESIDENT JOHN F. KENNEDY

1961	James B. Parsons**	Senior Judge, District Court, Illinois
1961	Wade M. McCree**	District Court, Michigan
1961	Thurgood Marshall**	Court of Appeals, Second Circuit

PRESIDENT LYNDON B. JOHNSON

1964	Spottswood Robinson**	District Court, District of Columbia
1964	A. Leon Higginbotham**	District Court, Pennsylvania
1965	William B. Bryant	Senior Judge, District Court, District of Columbia
1966	Wade H. McCree*	Court of Appeals, Sixth Court
1966	James L. Watson	United States Customs Court
1966	Constance B. Motley	Senior Judge, District Court, New York
1966	Spottswood Robinson	Senior Judge, Court of Appeals for the Federal Circuit
1966	Aubrey E. Robinson	Chief Judge, District Court, District of Columbia
1967	Damon Keith**	District Court, Michigan
1967	Thurgood Marshall*	Associate Justice, Supreme Court
1967	Joseph C. Waddy**	District Court, District of Columbia

PRESIDENT RICHARD M. NIXON

1969	Almeric Christian**	District Court, Virgin Islands
1969	David W. Williams	Senior Judge, District Court, California
1969	Barrington D. Parker	Senior Judge, District Court, District of Columbia
1971	Lawrence W. Pierce**	District Court, New York
1971	Clifford Scott Green	District Court, Pennsylvania
1972	Robert L. Carter	Senior Judge, District Court, New York
1972	Robert M. Duncan**	Military Court of Appeals
1974	Robert M. Duncan**	District Court, Ohio

PRESIDENT GERALD R. FORD

1974	Henry Bramwell**	Senior Judge, District Court, New York
1976	George N. Leighton**	Senior Judge, District Court, Illinois
1976	Matthew Perry**	Military Court of Appeals
1976	Cecil F. Poole**	District Court, California

PRESIDENT JIMMY CARTER

1978	Almeric Christian (a)**	Chief Judge, District Court, Virgin Islands
1978	U.W. Clemon	District Court, Alabama
1978	Robert F. Collins**	District Court, Louisiana

1978	Julian A. Cook, Jr.	District Court, Michigan
1978	Damon J. Keith	Court of Appeals, Sixth Circuit
1978	A. Leon Higginbotham*	Court of Appeals, Third Circuit
1978	Mary Johnson Lowe	District Court, New York
1978	Theodore McMillian	Court of Appeals, Eighth Circuit
1978	David S. Nelson	District Court, Massachusetts
1978	Paul A. Simmons**	District Court, Pennsylvania
1978	Jack E. Tanner	District Court, Washington
1979	Harry T. Edwards	Court of Appeals for the Federal Circuit
1979	J. Jerome Farris	Court of Appeals, Ninth Circuit
1979	Joseph W. Hatchett	Court of Appeals, Eleventh Circuit
1979	Terry J. Hatter	District Court, California
1979	Joseph C. Howard	District Court, Maryland
1979	Benjamin T. Gibson	District Court, Michigan
1979	James T. Giles	District Court, Pennsylvania
1979	Nathaniel R. Jones	Court of Appeals, Sixth Circuit
1979	Amalya L. Kearse	Court of Appeals, Second Circuit
1979	Gabrielle Kirk McDonald**	District Court, Texas
1979	John Garrett Penn**	District Court, District of Columbia
1979	Cecil F. Poole	Court of Appeals, Ninth Circuit
1979	Matthew J. Perry	District Court, South Carolina
1979	Myron H. Thompson	District Court, Alabama
1979	Anne E. Thompson	District Court, New Jersey
1979	Odell Horton	District Court, Tennessee
1979	Anna Diggs Taylor	District Court, Michigan
1979	Horace T. Ward	District Court, Georgia
1979	Alcee L. Hastings***	District Court, Florida
1980	Clyde S. Cahill, Jr.**	District Court, Missouri
1980	Richard C. Erwin	District Court, North Carolina
1980	Thelton E. Henderson	District Court, California
1980	George Howard, Jr.	District Court, Arkansas
1980	Earl B. Gilliam	District Court, California
1980	Norma Holloway Johnson	District Court, District of Columbia
1980	Consuela B. Marshall	District Court, California
1980	George White	District Court, Ohio

PRESIDENT RONALD REAGAN

1981	Lawrence W. Pierce	Court of Appeals, Second Circuit
1982	Reginald Gibson	United States Court of Claims
1984	John R. Hargrove	District Court, Maryland
1984	Henry Wingate	District Court, Mississippi
1985	Ann Williams	District Court, Illinois
1986	James Spencer	District Court, Virginia
1987	Kenneth Hoyt	District Court, Texas
1988	Herbert Hutton	District Court, Pennsylvania

PRESIDENT GEORGE BUSH

1990	Clarence Thomas**	Court of Appeals for the Federal Circuit
1990	James Ware	District Court, California
1991	Saundra Brown Armstrong	District Court, California
1991	Fernando J. Giatan	District Court, Missouri
1991	Donald L. Graham	District Court, Florida
1991	Sterling Johnson	District Court, New York
1991	J. Curtis Joyner	District Court, Pennsylvania
1991	Timothy K. Lewis	District Court, Pennsylvania

1991	Joe B. McDade	District Court, Illinois
1991	Clarence Thomas	Associate Justice, Supreme Court
1992	Garland E. Burrell, Jr.	District Court, California
1992	Carol Jackson	District Court, Missouri
1992	Timothy K. Lewis	Court of Appeals, Third Circuit

PRESIDENT BILL CLINTON

1993	Henry Lee Adams	District Court, Florida
1993	Wilkie Ferguson	District Court, Florida
1993	Raymond Jackson	District Court, Virginia
1993	Gary Lancaster	District Court, Pennsylvania
1993	Reginald Lindsay	District Court, Massachusetts
1993	Charles Shaw	District Court, Missouri
1994	Deborah Batts	District Court, New York
1994	Franklin Burgess	District Court, Washington
1994	James Beaty, Jr.	District Court, North Carolina
1994	David Coar	District Court, Illinois
1994	Audrey Collins	District Court, California
1994	Clarence Cooper	District Court, Georgia
1994	Michael Davis	District Court, Minnesota
1994	Raymond Finch	District Court, Virgin Islands
1994	Vanessa Gilmore	District Court, Texas
1994	A. Haggerty	District Court, Oregon
1994	Denise Page Hood	District Court, Michigan
1994	Napoleon Jones	District Court, California
1994	Blance Manning	District Court, Illinois
1994	Theodore McKee	Circuit Court, Third Circuit
1994	Vicki Miles‐LaGrange	District Court, Oklahoma
1994	Solomon Oliver, Jr.	District Court, Ohio
1994	Barrington Parker, Jr.	District Court, New York
1994	Judith Rogers	Circuit Court, District of Columbia
1994	W. Louis Sands	District Court, Georgia
1994	Carl Stewart	Circuit Court, Fifth Circuit
1994	Emmet Sullivan	Circuit Court, District of Columbia
1994	William Walls	District Court, New Jersey
1994	Alexander Williams	District Court, Maryland
1995	R. Guy Cole	Circuit Court, Sixth Circuit
1995	Curtis Collier	District Court, Tennessee
1995	Wiley Daniel	District Court, Colorado
1995	Andre Davis	District Court, Maryland
1995	Bernice B. Donald	District Court, Tennessee
1996	Charles N. Clevert, Jr.	District Court, Wisconsin
1996	Joseph A. Greenaway, Jr.	District Court, New Jersey
1997	Eric L. Clay	Circuit Court, Sixth Circuit
1997	Algenon L. Marbley	District Court, Ohio
1997	Martin J. Jenkins	District Court, California
1997	Henry H. Kennedy, Jr.	District Court, District of Columbia
1998	Gregory Sleet	District Court, Delaware
1998	Ivan L.R. Lemelle	District Court, Louisiana
1998	Sam A. Lindsay	District Court, Texas
1998	Johnnie B. Rawlinson	District Court, Nevada
1998	Margaret Seymour	District Court, South Carolina
1998	Richard Roberts	District Court, District of Columbia
1998	Gerald Bruce Lee	District Court, Virginia
1998	Lynn Bush	Court of Federal Claims

1998	Stephan P. Mickle	District Court, Florida
1998	Victoria Roberts	District Court, Michigan
1998	Raner Collins	District Court, Arizona
1998	Ralph Tyson	District Court, Louisiana
1999	William Hibbler	District Court, Illinois

(a) Reappointment

* Deceased

** No longer serving

*** Impeached and removed from the court

◆ AFRICAN AMERICAN OLYMPIC MEDALISTS

Place/Year	Athlete	Event	Place	Time/Distance
St. Louis, 1904	George C. Poag	200 M Hurdles	3rd	
	George C. Poag	400 M Hurdles	3rd	
London, 1908	J.B. Taylor	1600 M Relay	1st	3:29.4
Paris, 1924	Dehart Hubbard	Long Jump	1st	24′ 5.125″
	Edward Gourdin	Long Jump	2nd	23′ 10″
Los Angeles, 1932	Eddie Tolan	100 M Dash	1st	10.3
	Ralph Metcalfe	100 M Dash	2nd	10.3
	Eddie Tolan	200 M Dash	1st	21.2
	Ralph Metcalfe	200 M Dash	3rd	21.5
	Edward Gordon	Long Jump	1st	25′ .75″
Berlin, 1936	Jesse Owens	100 M Dash	1st	10.3
	Ralph Metcalfe	100 M Dash	2nd	10.4
	Jesse Owens	200 M Dash	1st	20.7
	Matthew Robinson	200 M Dash	2nd	21.1
	Archie Williams	400 M Run	1st	46.5
	James DuValle	400 M Run	2nd	46.8
	John Woodruff	800 M Run	1st	1:52.9
	Fritz Pollard, Jr.	110 M Hurdles	3rd	14.4
	Cornelius Johnson	High Jump	1st	6′8″
	Jesse Owens	Long Jump	1st	26′ 5.75″
	Jesse Owens	400 M Relay	1st	39.8
	Ralph Metcalfe	400 M Relay	1st	39.8
London, 1948	Harrison Dillard	100 M Dash	1st	10.3
	Norwood Ewell	100 M Dash	2nd	10.4
	Norwood Ewell	200 M Dash	1st	21.1
	Mal Whitfield	400 M Run	3rd	46.9
	Willie Steele	Long Jump	1st	25′ 8″
	Herbert Douglass	Long Jump	3rd	25′ 3″
	Lorenzo Wright	400 M Relay	1st	40.6
	Harrison Dillard	1600 M Relay	1st	3:10.4
	Norwood Ewell	1600 M Relay	1st	3:10.4
	Mal Whitfield	1600 M Relay	1st	3:10.4
	Audrey Patterson	200 M Dash	3rd	25.2
	Alice Coachman	High Jump	1st	5′ 6.125″
Helsinki, 1952	Andrew Stanfield	200 M Dash	1st	20.7
	Ollie Matson	400 M Run	3rd	46.8
	Mal Whitfield	800 M Run	1st	1:49.2
	Harrison Dillard	110 M Hurdles	1st	13.7
	Jerome Biffle	Long Jump	1st	24′ 10″
	Meredith Gourdine	Long Jump	2nd	24′ 8.125″
	Harrison Dillard	400 M Relay	1st	40.1
	Andrew Stanfield	400 M Relay	1st	40.1
	Ollie Matson	400 M Relay	1st	40.1
	Bill Miller	Javelin	2nd	237
	Milton Campbell	Decathlon	2nd	6,975 pts.
	Floyd Patterson	Boxing: Middleweight	1st	
	Norvel Lee	Boxing: Light Heavyweight	1st	
	Nathan Brooks	Boxing: Flyweight	1st	
	Charles Adkins	Boxing: Light Welterweight	1st	
	Barbara Jones	400 M Relay	1st	45.9
Melbourne, 1956	Andrew Stanfield	200 M Dash	2nd	20.7
	Charles Jenkins	400 M Run	1st	46.7
	Lee Calhoun	110 M Hurdles	1st	13.5
	Charles Dumas	High Jump	1st	6′ 11.25″
	Gregory Bell	Long Jump	1st	25′ 8.25″
	Willye White	Long Jump	2nd	19′ 11.75″
	Ira Murchison	400 M Relay	1st	39.5
	Leamon King	400 M Relay	1st	39.5
	Charles Jenkins	400 M Relay	1st	39.5
	Lou Jones	1600 M Relay	1st	3:04.8

Place/Year	Athlete	Event	Place	Time/Distance
	Milton Campbell	Decathlon	1st	7,937 pts.
	Rafer Johnson	Decathlon	2nd	7,587 pts.
	K.C. Jones	Men's Basketball	1st	
	Bill Russell	Men's Basketball	1st	
	James Boyd	Boxing: Light Heavyweight	1st	
	Mildred McDaniel	High Jump	1st	5′ 9.25″
	Margaret Matthews	400 M Relay	3rd	44.9
	Isabelle Daniels	400 M Relay	3rd	44.9
	Mae Faggs	400 M Relay	3rd	44.9
	Wilma Rudolph	400 M Relay	3rd	44.9
Rome, 1960	Les Carney	200 M Dash	2nd	20.6
	Lee Calhoun	110 M Hurdles	1st	13.8
	Willie May	110 M Hurdles	2nd	13.8
	Hayes Jones	110 M Hurdles	3rd	14
	Otis Davis	400 M Run	1st	44.9
	John Thomas	High Jump	3rd	7′ .25″
	Ralph Boston	Long Jump	1st	26′ 7.75″
	Irvin Robertson	Long Jump	2nd	26′ 7.25″
	Otis Davis	1600 M Relay	1st	3:02.2
	Rafer Johnson	Decathlon	1st	8,392 pts.
	Oscar Robertson	Men's Basketball	1st	
	Walt Bellamy	Men's Basketball	1st	
	Bob Boozer	Men's Basketball	1st	
	Wilbert McClure	Boxing: Light Middleweight	1st	
	Cassius Clay	Boxing: Light Heavyweight	1st	
	Edward Crook	Boxing: Middleweight	1st	
	Quincelon Daniels	Boxing: Light Welterweight	3rd	
	Earlene Brown	Shot Put	3rd	53′ 10.25″
	Wilma Rudolph	100 M Dash	1st	11
	Wilma Rudolph	200 M Dash	1st	24
	Martha Judson	400 M Relay	3rd	44.5
	Lucinda Williams	400 M Relay	3rd	44.5
	Barbara Jones	400 M Relay	3rd	44.5
	Wilma Rudolph	400 M Relay	3rd	44.5
Tokyo, 1964	Robert Hayes	100 M Dash	1st	9.9
	Henry Carr	200 M Dash	1st	20.3
	Paul Drayton	200 M Dash	2nd	20.5
	Hayes Jones	110 M Hurdles	1st	13.6
	Robert Hayes	400 M Relay	1st	39
	Paul Drayton	400 M Relay	1st	39
	Richard Stebbins	400 M Relay	1st	39
	John Thomas	High Jump	2nd	7′ 1.75″
	John Rambo	High Jump	3rd	7′ 1″
	Ralph Boston	Long Jump	2nd	26′ 4″
	Walt Hazzard	Men's Basketball	1st	
	Lucius Jackson	Men's Basketball	1st	
	Charles Brown	Boxing: Featherweight	3rd	
	Ronald Harris	Boxing: Lightweight	3rd	
	Joe Frazier	Boxing: Heavyweight	1st	
	Robert Carmody	Boxing: Flyweight	3rd	
	Wyomia Tyus	100 M Dash	1st	11.4
	Edith McGuire	100 M Dash	2nd	11.6
	Edith McGuire	200 M Dash	1st	23
	Wyomia Tyus	400 M Relay	2nd	43.9
	Edith McGuire	400 M Relay	2nd	43.9
	Willye White	400 M Relay	2nd	43.9
	Marilyn White	400 M Relay	2nd	43.9
Mexico City, 1968	Jim Hines	100 M Dash	1st	9.9
	Charles Greene	100 M Dash	3rd	10
	Tommie Smith	200 M Dash	1st	19.8
	John Carlos	200 M Dash	3rd	20
	Lee Evans	400 M Run	1st	43.8

Place/Year	Athlete	Event	Place	Time/Distance
	Larry James	400 M Run	2nd	43.9
	Ron Freeman	400 M Run	3rd	44.4
	Willie Davenport	110 M Hurdles	1st	13.3
	Ervin Hall	110 M Hurdles	2nd	13.4
	Jim Hines	400 M Relay	1st	38.2
	Charles Greene	400 M Relay	1st	38.2
	Mel Pender	400 M Relay	1st	38.2
	Ronnie Ray Smith	400 M Relay	1st	38.2
	Wyomia Tyus	400 M Relay	1st	42.8
	Barbara Ferrell	400 M Relay	1st	42.8
	Margaret Bailes	400 M Relay	1st	42.8
	Mildrette Netter	400 M Relay	1st	42.8
	Lee Evans	1600 M Relay	1st	2:56.1
	Vince Matthews	1600 M Relay	1st	2:56.1
	Ron Freeman	1600 M Relay	1st	2:56.1
	Larry James	1600 M Relay	1st	2:56.1
	Edward Caruthers	High Jump	2nd	7′ 3.5″
	Bob Beamon	Long Jump	1st	29′ 2.5″
	Ralph Boston	Long Jump	3rd	26′ 9.25″
	Spencer Haywood	Men's Basketball	1st	
	Charlie Scott	Men's Basketball	1st	
	Michael Barrett	Men's Basketball	1st	
	James King	Men's Basketball	1st	
	Calvin Fowler	Men's Basketball	1st	
	John Baldwin	Boxing: Light Middleweight	3rd	
	Alfred Jones	Boxing: Middleweight	3rd	
	Albert Robinson	Boxing: Featherweight	2nd	
	Ronald Harris	Boxing: Lightweight	1st	
	James Wallington	Boxing: Light Welterweight	3rd	
	George Foreman	Boxing: Heavyweight	1st	
	Wyomia Tyus	100 M Dash	1st	11
	Barbara Ferrell	100 M Dash	2nd	11.1
	Madeline Manning	800 M Run	1st	2:00.9
Munich, 1972	Robert Taylor	100 M Dash	2nd	10.24
	Larry Black	200 M Dash	2nd	20.19
	Vince Matthews	400 M Run	1st	44.66
	Wayne Collett	400 M Run	2nd	44.80
	Rod Milburn	110 M Hurdles	1st	13.24
	Eddie Hart	400 M Relay	1st	38.19
	Robert Taylor	400 M Relay	1st	38.19
	Larry Black	400 M Relay	1st	38.19
	Gerald Tinker	400 M Relay	1st	38.19
	Randy Williams	Long Jump	1st	27′ .25″
	Arnie Robinson	Long Jump	3rd	26′ 4″
	Jeff Bennet	Decathlon	3rd	7,974 pts.
	Wayne Collett	400 M Dash	2nd	44.80
	Marvin Johnson	Boxing: Middleweight	3rd	
	Ray Seales	Boxing: Light Welterweight	1st	
	Cheryl Toussain	1600 M Relay	2nd	3:25.2
	Mable Fergerson	1600 M Relay	2nd	3:25.2
	Madeline Manning	1600 M Relay	2nd	3:25.2
Montreal, 1976	Millard Hampton	200 M Dash	2nd	20.29
	Dwayne Evans	200 M Dash	3rd	20.43
	Fred Newhouse	400 M Run	2nd	44.40
	Herman Frazier	400 M Run	3rd	44.95
	Willie Davenport	110 M Hurdles	3rd	13.38
	Edwin Moses	400 M Hurdles	1st	47.64
	Millard Hampton	400 M Relay	1st	38.83
	Steve Riddick	400 M Relay	1st	38.83
	Harvey Glance	400 M Relay	1st	38.83
	John Jones	400 M Relay	1st	38.83
	Herman Frazier	1600 M Relay	1st	2:58.7

Place/Year	Athlete	Event	Place	Time/Distance
	Benny Brown	1600 M Relay	1st	2:58.7
	Maxie Parks	1600 M Relay	1st	2:58.7
	Fred Newhouse	1600 M Relay	1st	2:58.7
	Arnie Robinson	Long Jump	1st	27′ 4.75″
	Randy Williams	Long Jump	2nd	26′ 7.25″
	James Butts	Triple Jump	2nd	56 8.5″
	Phil Ford	Men's Basketball	1st	
	Adrian Dantley	Men's Basketball	1st	
	Walter Davis	Men's Basketball	1st	
	Quinn Buckner	Men's Basketball	1st	
	Kenneth Carr	Men's Basketball	1st	
	Scott May	Men's Basketball	1st	
	Philip Hubbard	Men's Basketball	1st	
	Johnny Tate	Boxing: Heavyweight	3rd	
	Leo Randolph	Boxing: Flyweight	1st	
	Howard David	Boxing: Lightweight	1st	
	Sugar Ray Leonard	Boxing: Light Welterweight	1st	
	Michael Spinks	Boxing: Middleweight	1st	
	Leon Spinks	Boxing: Light Heavyweight	1st	
	Rosalyn Bryant	1600 M Relay	2nd	3:22.8
	Shelia Ingram	1600 M Relay	2nd	3:22.8
	Pamela Jiles	1600 M Relay	2nd	3:22.8
	Debra Sapenter	1600 M Relay	2nd	3:22.8
	Lusia Harris	Women's Basketball	2nd	
	Charlotte Lewis	Women's Basketball	2nd	
Los Angeles, 1984	Carl Lewis	100 M Dash	1st	9.9
	Sam Graddy	100 M Dash	2nd	10.19
	Carl Lewis	200 M Dash	1st	19.80
	Kirk Baptiste	200 M Dash	2nd	19.96
	Alonzo Babers	400 M Run	1st	44.27
	Antonio McKay	400 M Run	3rd	44.71
	Earl Jones	800 M Run	3rd	1:43.83
	Roger Kingdom	110 M Hurdles	1st	13.20
	Greg Foster	110 M Hurdles	2nd	13.23
	Edwin Moses	400 M Hurdles	1st	47.75
	Danny Harris	400 M Hurdles	2nd	48.13
	Sam Graddy	400 M Relay	1st	37.83
	Ron Brown	400 M Relay	1st	37.83
	Calvin Smith	400 M Relay	1st	37.83
	Carl Lewis	400 M Relay	1st	37.83
	Sunder Nix	1600 M Relay	1st	2:57.91
	Roy Armstead	1600 M Relay	1st	2:57.91
	Alonzo Babers	1600 M Relay	1st	2:57.91
	Antonio McKay	1600 M Relay	1st	2:57.91
	Michael Carter	Shot Put	1st	21.09 m
	Carl Lewis	Long Jump	1st	8.54 m
	Al Joyner	Triple Jump	1st	17.26 m
	Mike Conley	Triple Jump	2nd	17.18 m
	Evelyn Ashford	100 M Dash	1st	10.97
	Alice Brown	100 M Dash	2nd	11.13
	Valerie Brisco-Hooks	200 M Dash	1st	21.81
	Florence Griffith	200 M Dash	2nd	22.04
	Valerie Brisco-Hooks	400 M Run	1st	48.83
	Chandra Cheeseborough	400 M Run	2nd	49.05
	Kim Gallagher	800 M Run	2nd	1:58.63
	Benita Fitzgerald-Brown	100 M Hurdles	1st	12.84
	Kim Turner	100 M Hurdles	2nd	12.88
	Judi Brown	400 M Hurdles	2nd	55.20
	Valerie Brisco-Hooks	1600 M Relay	1st	3:18.29
	Chandra Cheeseborough	1600 M Relay	1st	3:18.29
	Lillie Leatherwood	1600 M Relay	1st	3:18.29
	Sherri Howard	1600 M Relay	1st	3:18.29

Place/Year	Athlete	Event	Place	Time/Distance
	Jackie Joyner	Heptathlon	2nd	6,386 pts.
	Tyrell Biggs	Boxing: Super Heavyweight	1st	
	Henry Tillman	Boxing: Heavyweight	1st	
	Frank Tate	Boxing: Light Middleweight	1st	
	Virgil Hill	Boxing: Middleweight	2nd	
	Evander Holyfield	Boxing: Light Heavyweight	3rd	
	Steven McCrory	Boxing: Flyweight	1st	
	Meldrick Taylor	Boxing: Featherweight	1st	
	Pernell Whitaker	Boxing: Lightweight	1st	
	Jerry Page	Boxing: Light Welterweight	1st	
	Mark Breland	Boxing: Welterweight	1st	
	Patrick Ewing	Men's Basketball	1st	
	Vern Fleming	Men's Basketball	1st	
	Michael Jordan	Men's Basketball	1st	
	Sam Perkins	Men's Basketball	1st	
	Alvin Robertson	Men's Basketball	1st	
	Wayman Tisdale	Men's Basketball	1st	
	Leon Wood	Men's Basketball	1st	
	Cathy Boswell	Women's Basketball	1st	
	Teresa Edwards	Women's Basketball	1st	
	Janice Lawrence	Women's Basketball	1st	
	Pamela McGee	Women's Basketball	1st	
	Cheryl Miller	Women's Basketball	1st	
	Lynette Woodard	Women's Basketball	1st	
Seoul, 1988	Carl Lewis	100 M Dash	1st	9.92
	Calvin Smith	100 M Dash	2nd	9.99
	Joe DeLoach	200 M Dash	1st	19.75
	Carl Lewis	200 M Dash	2nd	19.79
	Steve Lewis	400 M Run	1st	43.87
	Butch Reynolds	400 M Run	2nd	43.93
	Danny Everett	400 M Run	3rd	44.09
	Roger Kingdom	110 M Hurdles	1st	12.98
	Tonie Campbell	110 M Hurdles	3rd	13.38
	Andre Phillips	400 M Hurdles	1st	47.19
	Edwin Moses	400 M Hurdles	3rd	47.56
	Butch Reynolds	1600 M Relay	1st	2:56.16
	Steve Lewis	1600 M Relay	1st	2:56.16
	Antonio McKay	1600 M Relay	1st	2:56.16
	Danny Everett	1600 M Relay	1st	2:56.16
	Carl Lewis	Long Jump	1st	8.72 m
	Mike Powell	Long Jump	2nd	8.49 m
	Larry Myricks	Long Jump	3rd	8.27 m
	Florence Griffith-Joyner	100 M Dash	1st	10.54
	Evelyn Ashford	100 M Dash	2nd	10.83
	Florence Griffith-Joyner	200 M Dash	1st	21.34
	Shelia Echols	400 M Relay	1st	41.98
	Florence Griffith-Joyner	400 M Relay	1st	41.98
	Evelyn Ashford	400 M Relay	1st	41.98
	Alice Brown	400 M Relay	1st	41.98
	Jackie Joyner-Kersee	Long Jump	1st	24′ 3.5″
	Jackie Joyner-Kersee	Heptathlon	1st	7,291 pts.
	Denean Howard-Hill	1600 M Relay	2nd	3:15.51
	Valerie Brisco	1600 M Relay	2nd	3:15.51
	Diane Dixon	1600 M Relay	2nd	3:15.51
	Florence Griffith-Joyner	1600 M Relay	2nd	3:15.51
	Kim Gallagher	800 M Run	3rd	1:56.91
	Andrew Maynard	Boxing: Light Heavyweight	1st	
	Ray Mercer	Boxing: Heavyweight	1st	
	Kennedy McKinney	Boxing: Bantamweight	1st	
	Riddick Bowe	Boxing: Super Heavyweight	2nd	
	Roy Jones	Boxing: Middleweight	2nd	
	Kenny Monday	Wrestling: Freestyle	1st	

Place/Year	Athlete	Event	Place	Time/Distance
	Nate Carr	Wrestling: Freestyle	3rd	
	Zina Garrison	Tennis: Doubles	1st	
	Zina Garrison	Tennis: Singles	3rd	
	Tom Goodwin	Baseball	1st	
	Ty Griffin	Baseball	1st	
	Cindy Brown	Women's Basketball	1st	
	Vicky Bullett	Women's Basketball	1st	
	Cynthia Cooper	Women's Basketball	1st	
	Teresa Edwards	Women's Basketball	1st	
	Jennifer Gillom	Women's Basketball	1st	
	Bridgette Gordon	Women's Basketball	1st	
	Katrina McClain	Women's Basketball	1st	
	Teresa Weatherspoon	Women's Basketball	1st	
	Willie Anderson	Men's Basketball	3rd	
	Stacey Augmon	Men's Basketball	3rd	
	Bimbo Coles	Men's Basketball	3rd	
	Jeff Grayer	Men's Basketball	3rd	
	Hersey Hawkins	Men's Basketball	3rd	
	Danny Manning	Men's Basketball	3rd	
	J.R. Reid	Men's Basketball	3rd	
	Mitch Richmond	Men's Basketball	3rd	
	David Robinson	Men's Basketball	3rd	
	Charles D. Smith	Men's Basketball	3rd	
	Charles E. Smith	Men's Basketball	3rd	
Barcelona, 1992	Dennis Mitchell	100 M Dash	3rd	10.04
	Gail Devers	100 M Dash	1st	10.82
	Mike Marsh	200 M Dash	1st	20.01
	Michael Bates	200 M Dash	3rd	20.38
	Gwen Torrence	200 M Dash	1st	21.81
	Quincy Watts	400 M Run	1st	43.50
	Steve Lewis	400 M Run	2nd	44.21
	Johnny Gray	800 M Run	3rd	1:43.97
	Mike Marsh	400 M Relay	1st	37.40
	Leroy Burrell	400 M Relay	1st	37.40
	Dennis Mitchell	400 M Relay	1st	37.40
	Carl Lewis	400 M Relay	1st	37.40
	Evelyn Ashford	400 M Relay	1st	42.11
	Esther Jones	400 M Relay	1st	42.11
	Carlette Guidry-White	400 M Relay	1st	42.11
	Gwen Torrence	400 M Relay	1st	42.11
	Tony Dees	110 M Hurdles	2nd	13.24
	Kevin Young	400 M Hurdles	1st	46.78
	Sandra Farmer	400 M Hurdles	2nd	53.69
	Janeene Vickers	400 M Hurdles	3rd	54.31
	Andrew Valmon	800 M Relay	1st	2:55.74
	Quincy Watts	800 M Relay	1st	2:55.74
	Michael Johnson	800 M Relay	1st	2:55.74
	Steve Lewis	800 M Relay	1st	2:55.74
	Natasha Kaiser	800 M Relay	2nd	3:20.92
	Gwen Torrence	800 M Relay	2nd	3:20.92
	Jearl Miles	800 M Relay	2nd	3:20.92
	Rochelle Stevens	800 M Relay	2nd	3:20.92
	Hollis Conway	High Jump	3rd	7′ 8″
	Carl Lewis	Long Jump	1st	28′ 5.5″
	Mike Powell	Long Jump	2nd	28′ 4.25″
	Joe Greene	Long Jump	3rd	27′ 4.5″
	Jackie Joyner-Kersee	Long Jump	3rd	23′ 2.5″
	Mike Conley	Triple Jump	1st	59′ 7.5″
	Charlie Simpkins	Triple Jump	2nd	57′ 9″
	Jackie Joyner-Kersee	Heptathlon	1st	7,044 pts.
	Tim Austin	Boxing: Flyweight	3rd	
	Chris Byrd	Boxing: Middleweight	2nd	

Place/Year	Athlete	Event	Place	Time/Distance
	Kevin Jackson	Wrestling: Middleweight	1st	
	Charles Barkley	Men's Basketball	1st	
	Clyde Drexler	Men's Basketball	1st	
	Patrick Ewing	Men's Basketball	1st	
	Magic Johnson	Men's Basketball	1st	
	Michael Jordan	Men's Basketball	1st	
	Karl Malone	Men's Basketball	1st	
	Scottie Pippen	Men's Basketball	1st	
	David Robinson	Men's Basketball	1st	
	Vicky Bullett	Women's Basketball	3rd	
	Daedra Charles	Women's Basketball	3rd	
	Cynthia Cooper	Women's Basketball	3rd	
	Teresa Edwards	Women's Basketball	3rd	
	Carolyn Jones	Women's Basketball	3rd	
	Katrina McClain	Women's Basketball	3rd	
	Vickie Orr	Women's Basketball	3rd	
	Teresa Weatherspoon	Women's Basketball	3rd	
Atlanta, 1996	Dominique Dawes	Gymnastics: Floor Exercise	3rd	
	Dominique Dawes	Gymnastics: Team	1st	
	Michael Johnson	200 M Dash	1st	19.32
	Michael Johnson	400 M Run	1st	43.49
	Allen Johnson	110 M Hurdles	1st	12.95
	Mark Crear	110 M Hurdles	2nd	13.09
	Derrick Adkins	400 M Hurdles	1st	47.54
	Calvin Davis	400 M Hurdles	3rd	47.96
	Tim Harden	400 M Relay	2nd	38.05
	Jon Drummond	400 M Relay	2nd	38.05
	Michael Marsh	400 M Relay	2nd	38.05
	Dennis Mitchell	400 M Relay	2nd	38.05
	LaMont Smith	1600 M Relay	1st	2:55.99
	Alvin Harrison	1600 M Relay	1st	2:55.99
	Derek Mills	1600 M Relay	1st	2:55.99
	Anthuan Maybank	1600 M Relay	1st	2:55.99
	Dan O'Brien	Decathlon	1st	8,824 pts.
	Charles Austin	High Jump	1st	7′ 10″
	Carl Lewis	Long Jump	1st	27′ 10.75″
	Joe Greene	Long Jump	3rd	27′ .50″
	Kenny Harrison	Triple Jump	1st	59′ 4″
	Gail Devers	100 M Dash	1st	10.94
	Gwen Torrence	100 M Dash	3rd	10.96
	Kim Batten	400 M Hurdles	2nd	53.08
	Tonja Buford-Bailey	400 M Hurdles	3rd	53.22
	Gail Devers	400 M Relay	1st	41.95
	Chryste Gaines	400 M Relay	1st	41.95
	Gwen Torrence	400 M Relay	1st	41.95
	Inger Miller	400 M Relay	1st	41.95
	Rochelle Stevens	1600 M Relay	1st	3:20.91
	Maicel Malone	1600 M Relay	1st	3:20.91
	Kim Graham	1600 M Relay	1st	3:20.91
	Jearl Miles	1600 M Relay	1st	3:20.91
	Jackie Joyner-Kersee	Long Jump	3rd	22′ 11″
	Floyd Mayweather	Boxing: Featherweight	3rd	
	Terrance Cauthen	Boxing: Lightweight	3rd	
	Rhoshii Wells	Boxing: Middleweight	3rd	
	Antonio Tarver	Boxing: Light Heavyweight	3rd	
	Nate Jones	Boxing: Heavyweight	3rd	
	David Reid	Boxing: Light Middleweight	1st	
	Teresa Edwards	Women's Basketball	1st	
	Ruth Bolton	Women's Basketball	1st	
	Lisa Leslie	Women's Basketball	1st	
	Katrina McClain	Women's Basketball	1st	
	Sheryl Swoopes	Women's Basketball	1st	

Place/Year	Athlete	Event	Place	Time/Distance
	Nikki McCray	Women's Basketball	1st	
	Dawn Staley	Women's Basketball	1st	
	Venus Lacey	Women's Basketball	1st	
	Carla McGhee	Women's Basketball	1st	
	Mitch Richmond	Men's Basketball	1st	
	Scottie Pippin	Men's Basketball	1st	
	Gary Payton	Men's Basketball	1st	
	Charles Barkley	Men's Basketball	1st	
	Hakeem Olajuwon	Men's Basketball	1st	
	David Robinson	Men's Basketball	1st	
	Penny Hardaway	Men's Basketball	1st	
	Grant Hill	Men's Basketball	1st	
	Karl Malone	Men's Basketball	1st	
	Reggie Miller	Men's Basketball	1st	
	Jacque Jones	Baseball	3rd	

Index

Personal names, place names, events, organizations, and various subject areas or keywords contained in the *Reference Library of Black America* are listed in this index with corresponding volume and page numbers indicating text references. Page numbers appearing in boldface indicate major treatments of topics, such as biographical profiles and organizational entries. Page numbers appearing in italics refer to photographs, illustrations, and maps found throughout the reference work.

A

B

C

D

E

H

I

J

K

M

N

P

Q

R

T

U

W

X

Y

Z